Daring to Be BAD

Radical Feminism in America 1967–1975

AMERICAN CULTURE

Edited by Stanley Aronowitz, Sandra M. Gilbert, and George Lipsitz

Alice Echols, *"Daring to Be Bad": Radical Feminism in America, 1967–75*

Henry Giroux, *Schooling and the Struggle for Public Life*

George Lipsitz, *Time Passages: Collective Memory and American Popular Culture*

Nancy Walker, *"A Very Serious Thing": Women's Humor and American Culture*

Daring to Be BAD

Radical Feminism in America 1967–1975

Alice Echols

Foreword by Ellen Willis

American Culture 3

University of Minnesota Press
Minneapolis • Oxford

Published by the University of Minnesota Press
2037 University Avenue Southeast, Minneapolis, MN 55414.
Printed in the United States of America on acid-free paper
1st edition, 2nd printing, 1991

Library of Congress Cataloging-in-Publication Data

Echols, Alice.
"Daring to be bad": radical feminism in America, 1967–75 / Alice Echols.
p. cm. — (American culture)
Bibliography: p.
Includes index.
ISBN 0-8166-1786-4 — ISBN 0-8166-1787-2 (pbk.)
1. Feminism—United States—History—20th century. 2. Women's rights—United States—History—20th century. I. Title. II. Series: American culture (Minneapolis, Minn.)
HQ1421.E25 1989
305.4'2'097309047—dc20 89-5058
CIP

A CIP catalog record for this book is available from the British Library

Contents

Foreword

Ellen Willis

For those of us who are the subjects of Alice Echols's *Daring to Be Bad: Radical Feminism in America*, her vivid account of our political history is (among other things) a rare confirmation of our concrete existence as a movement. Radical feminism, along with civil rights the most influential social struggle of the '60s, transformed the cultural and political landscape; its imprint is everywhere in American life. Yet the radical feminist *movement* has largely disappeared from history. As Echols demonstrates, the movement took shape in 1968 and ended, for all practical purposes, five years later. Since then, its achievements have been by turns denied and credited to the liberal mainstream of the women's movement, its original political meaning has been obscured by the female counterculturalism that today goes under its name, and its mistakes and failures are typically used not to learn from its flaws but to dismiss its whole project. In this book, Echols brings the movement out of the half-light of myth into political and historical visibility: in detailing the trajectory of radical feminism, its explosive rise, wrenching schisms, and abrupt decline, she provides a foundation for understanding its legacy.

It is particularly fitting that Echols's history should appear as the tumultuous battle over abortion rights goes into a new phase. Radical feminists' first major public effort was a militant campaign for abortion law repeal; more than any other issue, abortion embodied and symbolized our fundamental demand—not merely formal equality for women but genuine self-determination. Our target was not only those who opposed abortion altogether but the growing ranks of (mostly male) reformers, who proposed to allow the (overwhelmingly male) medical profession the right to grant abortions to "deserving" women in limited circumstances—rape, substantial threat to health, likelihood of fetal deformity, and so on. The issue, we insisted, was not how cruelly or compassionately a male-dominated society should treat women with unwanted pregnancies, but women's moral right to control their fertility and therefore the direction of their lives. Though we didn't get what we wanted—the repeal of all abortion restrictions—we did change the terms of the debate and as a result won qualified constitutional protection for the right to end a pregnancy without giving a reason.

With the eclipse of radical feminism, the debate shifted again, its focus no longer the pregnant woman but the fetus. While the shift itself reflected the anti-abortionists' view of women as vessels rather than people in their own right, the charge of baby-killing was also potent code for a male-supremacist culture's worst nightmares: women cut loose from their anatomical destiny; women putting their needs and desires before their age-old obligation to create and nurture new life; women having sex on their own terms and without fear; women becoming players on the world stage instead of providing the backdrop—and the safety net—for men. On the deepest level, the right-to-life movement spoke to primal fears that if women stop subordinating themselves to their role as caretakers of men and children, civilization and morality as we know them will give way to destruction and chaos. To which a women's movement deprived of a radical language could only respond, with ludicrous weakness, that it was for "choice."

In the aftermath of the Supreme Court's *Webster* decision narrowing the scope of women's constitutional right to abortion and inviting a state-by-state struggle over abortion laws, commentators have repeatedly declared that "abortion is our new Vietnam." But in fact it is less the act of abortion that so deeply divides us than what that act represents: it is women's freedom that's our new Vietnam. And once again, women's freedom is under attack not only by abortion prohibitionists but by today's equivalent of the old abortion reformers. Indeed, while only a small minority favors criminalizing all abortion, there is considerable sentiment for rational-sounding "compromises" that would allow women to have abortions for "good reasons" but not for "convenience," i.e., the simple desire to determine for oneself whether, when, and under what circumstances one bears children. And if the resistance to this agenda is passionate enough to compare to Vietnam, it is because however muted the language of radical feminism, the sense of entitlement that language expressed remains widespread among women—both those who went through the feminist upheaval and those who have grown up taking legal abortion and the illegitimacy of sexism for granted. To put the abortion conflict and its prospects in perspective, to avoid continually reinventing the wheel, we need to understand a complex piece of history—how the issue was defined and the battle lines drawn, why and how feminists won legal abortion, the limitations of that victory, and why we couldn't transcend them. We need, in short, to understand radical feminism.

If this is most clearly true of abortion, it also holds for a whole complex of issues having to do with sex, gender, and the family: gay rights, teen-age sex and pregnancy, sex education, pornography, sexual and domestic violence, the high rate of divorce and single motherhood, the dilemma of who will care for children and home in place of the vanishing housewife, the demand for recognition of "domestic partnerships," surrogate motherhood and reproductive technology, the future of the sexual revolution in the age of AIDS. While it would be too simple to say that radical feminism created these issues, the movement's far-reaching impact on public consciousness has been instrumental in defining them and bringing them to the forefront of American politics.

Radical feminists coined the terms "sexism" and "sexual politics" to express the idea—novel and even shocking in the contemporary American context, though in fact it had ample historical precedent—that sexuality, family life, and the relations between men and women were not simply matters of individual choice, or even of social custom, but involved the exercise of personal and institutional power and raised vital questions of public policy. Sexism, the movement contended, was neither the natural expression of sexual differences nor a set of bad attitudes or outmoded habits but a social system—embedded in law, tradition, economics, education, organized religion, science, language, the mass media, sexual morality, child rearing, the domestic division of labor, and everyday social interaction—whose intent and effect was to give men power over women. A sexist society enforced women's prescribed behavior with a wide range of sanctions that included social condemnation, ridicule, ostracism, sexual rejection and harassment, the withholding of birth control and abortion, economic deprivation, and male violence condoned by the state. It followed that there was no area of social life, public or private, that was exempt from a feminist critique.

These ideas quickly spawned another radical sexual political movement, gay liberation. Ever since, the challenge posed by both movements to established sexual institutions and values, and the virulent backlash against it, have been central to the ongoing debate over what kind of society we are and aspire to be, a debate that has been taking place everywhere from courts, legislatures, and political campaigns to street corners, kitchens, and bedrooms. Because it focused on the immediate facts of daily life, radical feminism captured women's imagination and permeated popular culture in a way liberal feminist reformers had not been able to do. And though the radical feminist surge helped liberals win support for economic and legal reforms (the ERA, which had been languishing for decades, passed Congress easily in 1970) its distinctive accomplishment was the destruction of the prevailing common sense about male-female relations. A whole set of lies about women and men and their lives together could never be told again, at least not with a straight face; and increasingly, women were refusing to live by those lies.

Changes of this sort are hard to quantify. Nor is it easy to distinguish the effects of a specific political movement from those of other cultural and economic influences. For instance, can the obsolescence of the traditional patriarchal family be attributed to feminism? Or—as the conventional economistic wisdom would have it—is feminism itself the result of economic changes that forced women out of the home? Is it feminism that has generated women's recent massive influx into the labor force—or the decline of the industries that once paid male breadwinners a decent "family wage"?

Ironically, the most reliable measure of the impact of radical feminism may be the intensity and power of the countermovements it inspired. Mobilizing on the premise that feminism was undermining the family and with it society's moral underpinnings, the "pro-family" Christian right succeeded in electing a national administration that embraced its ideology and in scuttling the ERA, giving the anti-abortion movement its militant cutting edge, transforming the federal judiciary and ultimately the Supreme Court; beyond these considerable concrete achievements, its propaganda has been so effective at tapping people's guilt about wanting freedom and pleasure, along with their fear of sexual anarchy, that it has moved the entire political spectrum in a socially conservative direction (even mainstream feminists now feel constrained to justify their political goals as "strengthening the family"). At the same time, neoconservatives (who come from the putative left as well as the frankly right) have not only centered their campaign to reverse the cultural changes of the '60s on moral condemnation of the feminist and gay movements as selfish, narcissistic, and frivolous, but have attacked the core of the radical feminist argument by insisting that the personal relations between women and men are not a legitimate political issue, and that feminists' radical critiques of marriage, sex, and family life amount to a totalitarian colonization of the private sphere. (Alice Echols's account of debates within the movement makes clear that while some early radical feminists saw the concept of "the personal is political" less as a tool for understanding women's lives than as an invitation to prescribe "correct" feminist behavior, this view began to predominate only after radical feminism had devolved into an essentially countercultural movement. Still, the caricature of the Stalinist feminist has routinely been invoked to discredit the movement's radical ideas.)

In my view, radical feminism did exactly what its opponents accuse it of: it played a key role in subverting traditional values and destabilizing the family. (I am speaking primarily of the white majority, since the classic male breadwinner-female dependent family has never been economically feasible for most black people.) Women, including mothers, go to work not only out of sheer economic necessity (though this is certainly an important reason) but because feminism has made it socially acceptable for women to want a life outside the home, expanded women's opportunities for interesting work, and encouraged women's aspirations for the increased independence and mobility that come of earning even a modest living. Women also realize, of course, that even in the white middle class, marriage can no longer be counted on as a permanent means of support—and the growing instability of marriage in itself reflects the influence of feminism. Women need marriage less than they once did: while it's still a struggle for most women to support children on their own earnings, it's more feasible than ever before; social pressure to get married and stay married has waned; nonmarital sex is the norm and contraception readily accessible (at least for adults); having children out of wedlock is no longer a social scandal or an automatic economic disaster. Men, for their part, enjoy fewer privileges in marriage and more sexual choices outside it, and open antagonism between the sexes has escalated as women's demands for equal relationships meet male resistance.

On the surface, the impact of radical feminism on sexuality has been ambiguous. Radical feminists attacked both traditional morality and the sexism that had distorted a so-called sexual revolution that envisioned women's sexual freedom mainly as women's right-cum-obligation to have sex on men's often exploitative terms. Most of us wanted the sexual revolution extended to women: we demanded an end to the double standard of morality that still lingered despite men's lip service to women's emancipation; equal consideration for women's sexual pleasure and emotional needs; the right to actively pursue sexual relationships as men have always done—and without forfeiting our right to refuse sex; the social acceptance of lesbianism; and, of course, reproductive freedom. But as Echols shows, the movement also gave voice to a strong strain of sexual conservatism that viewed sexual freedom—or even sex itself—entirely in terms of male irresponsibility, misogyny, and violence.

In recent years, it is this conservatism that has been most conspicuous. Feminist anti-sexual rhetoric, particularly that of the anti-pornography movement, has been used by the right to legitimize its opposition to sexual freedom; anti-abortionists have even argued that "abortion is violence against women." Yet while feminist sexual conservatives abet the backlash, they also undercut it, for they are hardly out to resurrect the sexual ideology of the '50s. Rather, they espouse either unprecedented demands for emotional commitment and fidelity from men, or sexual separatism and/or celibacy. In the long run, the crucial and irreversible effect of radical feminism has been to demystify and discredit the old morality of good girls and bad girls, conquest and surrender, man the virtuoso and woman the violin.

Twenty years after the first stirrings of radical feminism, we are living with the disappointments, problems, and confusions of an unfinished revolution. A once coherent, if oppressive, set of sexual and domestic arrangements is in an advanced state of disintegration, but the egalitarian future has not yet arrived; women's consciousness and expectations have changed far more than men's behavior or society's institutional structures. While women have taken on paying jobs, men have not assumed their share of responsibility at home; the result is an exhausting double burden for employed women, especially mothers. At the same time, business and government still operate as if all workers have, or ought to have, someone at home caring for the children, the sick, and the elderly: women with primary responsibility for their households are expected to function in the work world on the same terms as men who have wives to run domestic interference, and social policy on child care and related issues is in such a primitive state that unpaid parental leave is controversial. The high divorce rate is also harder on women, who typically must struggle to support and bring up their children alone, while men, who have more economic resources to begin with, tend to keep a disproportionate share for themselves and abdicate both the financial and the social responsibilities of fatherhood. Single heterosexual women experience the "consciousness gap" as difficulty in establishing or maintaining intimate relationships with men. And gay or straight, alone or coupled, women feel more vulnerable to sexual victimization—in part because its ubiquity is publicly acknowledged, no longer a secret shame; in part because the demise of the "good girl" has also meant an end to the paternalism that offered her some degree of protection.

Since present discontents are always more vivid than past ones, conservatives have had a good deal of success purveying an idealized image of the past while blaming feminism—rather than men's resistance to feminism—for the disruptions of the present. Yet paradoxically, the vacuum created by historical amnesia about radical feminism has also been filled by the stereotype of a women's movement consisting, on the one hand, of elitist ladies solely concerned with giving women a leg up the corporate ladder, and on the other an irrelevant fringe of man-hating, separatist cranks.

I think, for instance, of Sylvia Ann Hewlett's *A Lesser Life: The Myth of Women's Liberation in America*, which angrily dismisses American feminism as "irrelevant to women's lives" because it demanded "formal equality" instead of special supports and protections for mothers. Hewlett, whose polemic was inspired by her own frustrating struggle to reconcile career and motherhood, clearly has no concept of the *substantive* equality radical feminists demanded; the idea that men could share housework and child rearing equally is not real to her, and so special treatment seems to her the only alternative to the present untenable situation. She does not recognize that before feminism, her career-family conflict would probably have been resolved before it started—by job discrimination and social pressure on mothers to stay home. Nor does she see that her indignant, unquestioned sense of her right to combine child rearing and other work without unreasonable sacrifice is the product of the anti-sexist values the movement fought for. Nor does she know that many of her arguments against this culture's pervasive anti-mother bias were first made by radical feminists, who pointed out the hypocrisy of a society that sentimentalizes motherhood while devaluing the work mothers do; who called attention to the double burden of "working" mothers (and coined the slogan "Every mother is a working mother"); who decried the double bind faced by women who want children, but also want, as men do, to be out in the public world.

Any woman who says that radical feminism has made no difference in women's lives either is too young to have lived through the pre-feminist years, or has thoroughly repressed them. I lived through them, and remember them all too well. I remember a kind of blatant, taken for granted, un-self-conscious sexism that no one could get away with today pervading every aspect of life. I remember, as a Barnard student, wanting to take a course at Columbia and being told to my face that the professor didn't want "girls" in his class because they weren't serious enough. I remember, as a young journalist, being asked by an editor to use only my first initial in my byline because the magazine had too many women writers. I remember having to wear uncomfortable clothes, girdles and stiff bras and high heels. I remember being afraid to have sex because I might get pregnant, and too tense to enjoy it because I might get pregnant. I remember the panic of a late period. I remember when a friend of a friend came to New York for an illegal abortion, remember us trying to decide whether her pain and fever were bad enough to warrant going to the hospital and then worrying that we'd waited too long, remember her fear of admitting what was wrong, and the doctor yelling at her for "going to a quack" and refusing to reassure her that she would live. I remember that I was supposed to feel flattered when men hassled me on the street, and be polite and tactful when my dates wouldn't take no for an answer, and have a "good reason" for refusing. I remember, too, feeling pleased to be different from other women—better—because I was ambitious and contemptuous of domesticity and "thought like a man," while at the same time, in my personal and sexual relationships with men, I was constantly being reminded that I was after all "only a woman"; I remember the peculiar alienation that comes of having one's self-respect be contingent on self-hatred.

But such particulars only begin to describe the profound difference between a society in which sexism is the natural order, whether one likes it or not, and one in which sexism is a problem, the subject of debate, *something that can be changed*. It is a difference made largely by minutiae. Given the horrendous inequalities women still face, it's easy to dismiss as trivial the small everyday gains—that it's now commonplace for married women to keep their names; that "people working" signs are no longer unusual; that a politician who couldn't care less about feminism nonetheless feels constrained to speak of "his or her" something-or-other. Yet it's the constant accretion of such "trivia" that creates the texture of our lives, increases our impatience with its contradictions, and promotes our expectation of larger changes. The history of radical feminism is, above all, about a dramatic launching of this process; and in that sense, the movement still lives.

Acknowledgments

Since I embarked on this project in 1983 I have accumulated many debts. This study originated as a dissertation in the history department at the University of Michigan. The members of my dissertation committee—Louise Tilly, Barbara Fields, Nora Faires, and June Howard—were precisely the exacting critics one wants (in the end, if not always at the moment) as readers. I feel very lucky to have had the benefit of their support and their searching criticism.

I am especially grateful to the following individuals who offered both encouragment and trenchant criticism of the dissertation (and in some cases of the manuscript as well): Stanley Aronowitz, Carol Karlsen, Elizabeth Pleck, Ann Snitow, Martha Vicinus, and Ellen Willis. Ros Baxandall read a final draft of the manuscript and shared parts of it with Kathie Sarachild and Carol Hanisch. Their comments proved extremely helpful in making the final revisions. I also received very useful criticisms from Robert Currie, Deborah Evering, Cynthia Gair, Margaret Lourie, Annette Wilson, and Patricia Yeghessian. The staff at the University of Minnesota Press was everything a writer could hope for—intelligent, responsive, and enthusiastic. I want to thank Terry Cochran and Beverly Kaemmer, in particular, for their work on the manuscript.

This study is not the product of isolated scholarship; rather, it is very much embedded in the community I was a part of while a graduate student at Michigan. I owe an enormous intellectual debt to the individuals who made up that community, the

Women's Studies Program. In particular, I would like to thank Marti Bombyk, Ruth Bradley, Susan Contratto, Elizabeth Douvan, Jacqueline Eccles, Jo Goodwin, Melanie Hawthorne, Janis Holm, June Howard, Laura Kipnis, Margaret Lourie, Ilene O'Malley, Charlotte Nekola, Paula Rabinowitz, Catharine Raissiguer, Gayle Rubin, Bette Skandalis, Barbara Scott-Winkler, Sandra Silberstein, Victoria Sork, Domna Stanton, Kathleen Stewart, Betsy Taylor, Louise Tilly, Martha Vicinus, Pat Yeghessian, and Marilyn Young. Of course, none of these individuals should be held responsible for any of the opinions expressed in this book.

This book could not have been written without the cooperation of those people who agreed to be interviewed. (See Appendix D.) My debt to them is enormous. The following people were especially helpful, either giving me material from their files or putting me in touch with other activists: Jane Alpert, Ros Baxandall, Minda Bikman, Susan Brownmiller, Cindy Cisler, Corinne Coleman, Charlotte Bunch, Anne Forer, Jo Freeman, Carol Hanisch, Helaine Harris, Pam Kearon, Amy Kesselman, Tobey Klass, Jesse Lemisch, Beverly Manick, Barbara Mehrhof, Irene Peslikis, Kathie Sarachild, Alix Kates Shulman, Ann Snitow, Meredith Tax, and Ellen Willis. I also want to thank Lucia Valeska, who very generously let me photocopy transcripts of interviews she had conducted with former Furies members for her own dissertation research.

To undertake the extensive interviewing I believed necessary to complete this study I had to live in New York City for much of the summer of 1984. Had it not been for the generosity of Ann Snitow and Daniel Goode, who let me stay in their apartment while they were in Europe, I would have been able to interview only a handful of people under very harried, and probably, very trying, circumstances. I cannot thank them enough for their generosity.

I conducted much of my research for this book at the Labadie Collection in the Rare Book Room in the Harlan Hatcher Library at the University of Michigan. The staff of the Rare Book Room—Jennifer Barlow, Kathryn Beam, Helen Butz, Kristi Kiesling, Anne Okey, Mary Ann Sellers, Robert Starring, David Whitesell, and Edward Weber—was knowledgeable, interested, and always very helpful. The staff at the Women's History Archive at Northwestern University was also helpful during my brief visit there.

Grants from the University of Michigan's Center for Gender Research and Horace H. Rackham Graduate School helped to fund the research for my dissertation. I would also like to thank the University of Michigan Society of Fellows, which awarded my dissertation the Horace H. Rackham Distinguished Dissertation Award in 1987.

Inspiration can come from a variety of places. In my case, it sometimes came from the Washtenaw Dairy's donuts, Pastabilities' blueberry muffins, Aretha Franklin, Prince, Joni Mitchell, the Detroit Tigers & Pistons, and my two cats. It can, of course, also come from students. I have presented some of the material in this book in courses on the history of American feminism. I would like to thank the following students from the University of Michigan and SUNY-Buffalo for posing new and challenging questions: Elizabeth Armstrong, Mary Messer, Adrienne Neff, Donna Santman, Julie Sherman, and Amy Simon.

My parents, Dorothy and Edward Echols, have been supportive of this project from the very beginning, for which I am very grateful. My friend, Robert Currie, with his highly developed sense of the absurd, helped me retain a sense of perspective when this book threatened to consume all of my energies. Finally, Connie Samaras read more drafts of the dissertation and book than I'm sure she cares to remember. Her enthusiasm about the subject, her faith in my ability, and her incisive criticism of all the various drafts proved crucial to its completion. I feel very lucky to have had her love, wit, and support during these years.

Daring to Be BAD

Radical Feminism in America 1967–1975

Introduction

In the fall of 1967 small groups of radical women began meeting in the United States to discuss the problem of male supremacy. At that time the majority were committed to organizing a women's liberation movement within the larger radical Movement.[1] Indeed, most early women's liberation groups were dominated by "politicos" who attributed women's oppression to capitalism, whose primary loyalty was to the left, and who longed for the imprimatur of the "invisible audience" of male leftists.[2] "Feminists," or radical feminists, who opposed the subordination of women's liberation to the left and for whom male supremacy was not a mere epiphenomenon of capitalism, were an embattled minority in the movement's infancy.

However, within two years radical feminism had established itself as the most vital and imaginative force within the women's liberation movement. Radical feminism rejected both the politico position that socialist revolution would bring about women's liberation and the liberal feminist solution of integrating women into the public sphere. Radical feminists argued that women constituted a sex-class, that relations between women and men needed to be recast in political terms, and that gender rather than class was the primary contradiction. They criticized liberal feminists for pursuing "formal equality within a racist, class-stratified system," and for refusing to acknowledge that women's inequality in the public domain was related to their subordination in the family.[3] Radical feminists articulated the earliest and most provocative critiques of the family, marriage, love, normative heterosexuality, and rape. They fought for safe, effective, accessible contraception; the repeal of all abortion laws; the creation of high-quality, community-controlled child-care centers; and an end to the media's objectification of women. They also developed consciousness-raising—the movement's most effective organizing tool.[4] And in defying the cultural injunction against female self-assertion and subjectivity, radical feminists "dared to be bad."[5] By 1970, there was such enormous interest in radical feminism that some have even argued it was on the verge of becoming a mass movement.[6]

Radical feminists succeeded in pushing liberal feminists to the left and politicos toward feminism. By September 1969 Betty Friedan, founder of the liberal National Organization for Women (NOW), declared that "those people who think NOW is too activist may be less important in the future than the youth." While she criticized the younger women for failing to see that "the gut issues of this revolution involve employment and education and new social institutions and not sexual fantasy," she nonetheless urged NOW to "form a power bloc or alliance" with women's liberation groups "whose style, origins, structure and general ambience may be quite different from ours."[7] NOW did move in this direction. On August 26, 1970, NOW joined with women's liberation groups to stage a national women's strike, the Women's Strike for Equality, and demanded twenty-four-hour child-care centers, abortion on demand, and equal employment and educational opportunities for women.[8]

Similarly, many socialist-feminists, who in their earlier incarnation as "politicos" had repudiated radical feminism, began incorporating elements of radical feminism into their analysis. For instance, in May 1970, in the wake of the American invasion of Cambodia, a ten-woman delegation from Bread and Roses, a Boston-based "socialist women's liberation organization," delivered a speech at a National Student Strike rally at Harvard Stadium. Although the women from Bread and Roses did not entirely jettison the politico analysis, they did speak of male dominance as "the original and basic form of domination from which all others flow," and they did identify themselves as part of an "independent women's movement to destroy male supremacy."[9]

But by the early '70s radical feminism began to flounder, and after 1975 it was eclipsed by cultural feminism—a tendency that grew out of radical feminism, but contravened much that was fundamental to it.[10] With the rise of cultural feminism the movement turned its attention away from opposing male supremacy to creating a female counterculture—what Mary Daly termed "new space"—where "male" values would be exorcized and "female" values nurtured.[11] Although this woman-only space was envisioned as a kind of culture of active resistance, it often became instead, as Adrienne Rich has recently pointed out, "a place of emigration, an end in itself" where patriarchy was evaded rather than engaged.[12] Concomitantly, the focus became one of personal rather than social transformation. Feminist activist and writer Meredith Tax recalls that as early as 1971 some feminists seemed to be defining their politics completely in terms of their lifestyle. Tax remembers women boasting, "we worked on our car all weekend," as though it were an act of great political significance. She "worried about what else was going to happen. This wasn't going to be the whole thing, was it?"[13] But as the '70s wore on this was, if not the whole thing, then a large part of it. And by 1975 radical feminism virtually ceased to exist as a movement. Once radical feminism was superseded by cultural feminism, activism became largely the province of liberal feminists. According to Washington, D.C. women's liberationist Frances Chapman, radical feminism was "like a generator that got things going, cut out and left it to the larger reform engine which made a lot of mistakes."[14]

****

It has been over twenty years since the emergence of the women's liberation movement and yet, with the exception of Sara Evans's ground-breaking monograph *Personal Politics*, there has been no book-length scholarly study of the movement.[15] Moreover, Evans ends her narrative in 1968 as the first women's liberation groups were just beginning to form. It is my hope that this study will begin to fill the lacuna in the literature. This book analyzes the trajectory of the radical feminist movement from its beleaguered beginnings in 1967, through its ascendance as the dominant tendency within the movement, to its decline and supplanting by cultural feminism in the mid-'70s. This is not a comprehensive history of the contemporary women's movement. (For example, the principal focus of recent feminist activism, the Equal Rights Amendment, is barely mentioned in these pages.) Rather, this is a thorough history of one wing of the women's movement.

A study of this sort seems to me especially important because radical feminism is so poorly understood and so frequently conflated with cultural feminism.[16] This conceptual confusion arises in part because radical feminism was not monolithic and aspects of radical feminism did indeed anticipate cultural feminism. As this book demonstrates, radical feminists disagreed on a number of critical questions. Was women's behavior the result of conditioning or material necessity? Was heterosexuality a crucial bargaining chip in women's struggle for liberation (as in "a revolutionary in every bedroom cannot fail to shake up the status quo") or a source of women's oppression?[17] Should women's sexual pleasure be enhanced or men's sexuality curbed? If the personal was political, was the political personal? Did men oppress women because of the material benefits they reaped or because they found it intrinsically pleasurable to do so? There was even some disagreement on the question of whether radical feminism implied the minimization or maximization of gender differences.

But while cultural feminism did evolve from radical feminism, it nonetheless deviated from it in some crucial respects. Most fundamentally, radical feminism was a political movement dedicated to eliminating the sex-class system, whereas cultural feminism was a countercultural movement aimed at reversing the cultural valuation of the male and the devaluation of the female. In the terminology of today, radical feminists were typically social constructionists who wanted to render gender irrelevant, while cultural feminists were generally essentialists who sought to celebrate femaleness. Thus, we find radical feminists mobilizing women on the basis of their similarity to men and cultural feminists organizing women around the principle of female difference. Moreover, in contrast to radical feminists who believed that feminism entailed an expansion of the left analysis, cultural feminists conceived of feminism as an antidote to the left. And whereas radical feminists were anti-capitalist—if often only implicitly—cultural feminists dismissed economic class struggle as "male" and, therefore, irrelevant to women.

The conflation of radical and cultural feminism has other sources as well. Most leftists and socialist-feminists mistakenly characterized radical feminism as apolitical. To them radical feminism involved changing the "cultural superstructure" and developing alternative lifestyles, rather than effecting serious economic and political change.[18] In fact, it was socialist-feminist Elizabeth Diggs who in 1972 labeled radical feminism "cultural feminism."[19] So when radical feminism began to give way to cultural feminism, socialist-feminists simply did not notice. For example, in their influential 1972 manifesto, "Socialist Feminism: A Strategy for the Women's Movement," the Hyde Park chapter of the Chicago Women's Liberation Union argued that there were "two ideological poles representing the prevailing tendencies within the movement":

> One is the direction toward new lifestyles within a women's culture, emphasizing personal liberation and growth, and the relationship of women to women. . . . The other direction is one which emphasizes a structural analysis of our society and its economic base.[20]

Nowhere in the manifesto did they suggest that the preoccupation with women's culture represented a shift away from earlier radical feminism. To add to the conceptual confusion, cultural feminists almost always identified themselves as radical feminists and insisted that they were deepening rather than jettisoning radical feminism. Indeed, some writers prefer to label this strand "contemporary radical feminism" rather than cultural feminism. However, I have chosen to use the term cultural feminism to underscore its disjuncture from radical feminism.[21]

How did radical feminism come to be eclipsed by cultural feminism? First, it should be noted that the women's liberation movement was not the only radical movement of the '60s that succumbed to counterculturalism. With the rise of black nationalism, the black freedom movement became more involved in promoting black culture than in confronting the racist policies of the state. In fact, black social critic Harold Cruse chided black radicals for proposing "to change, not the white world outside, but the black world inside, by reforming it into something else politically and economically."[22] And, of course, quite a few new leftists abandoned confrontational politics to build alternative communities or to take up the task of self-transformation. When faced with the intransigence of the system, some '60s radicals either retreated from political activism or were drawn to vanguardism and violence.[23]

Of course, the government had a hand in the disintegration of these radical movements. The government's draconian campaign of repression debilitated the black movement and the new left. Agents provocateurs promoted violence, which was in turn used to justify greater state repression.[24] And government agents tried to subvert the Movement by exacerbating factionalism. We now know that the FBI tried to undermine the fragile 1968 alliance between the Student Nonviolent Coordinating Committee (SNCC) and the Black Panther Party, and played a large role in the lethal conflicts between the Panthers and Ron Karenga's nationalistic organization, US.[25] The women's liberation movement initially escaped the FBI's scrutiny, but by 1969 the FBI began to spy upon and infiltrate it as well.[26] In fact, one civil liberties lawyer familiar with the FBI's subversion of dissident groups has argued that "in terms of the amount of time, effort, and agents deployed," the FBI's surveillance and infiltration of the women's liberation movement "was comparable to its campaign against the Socialist Workers Party, the Communist Party, and anti-war groups."[27] Although I am not convinced that the evidence supports such a broad conclusion, I do think it is reasonable to assume that agents aggravated the conflicts around class, elitism, and sexual preference that convulsed the women's liberation movement in the early '70s.[28]

At the same time that the system was suppressing political dissent, it was busy making concessions in an effort to quell the protests. During this period the government enacted civil rights legislation, established anti-poverty programs, and lowered the voting age from twenty-one to eighteen. Colleges and universities instituted black studies programs, funded black student unions, and eliminated most of the restrictive regulations governing campus life in an attempt to mollify students. Radicals understood that these reforms failed to eliminate the deep structural inequalities in the system, but they found it more difficult to mobilize great numbers of people once the most obvious targets of discontent had been eradicated. President Nixon's policy of Vietnamization represented the most successful attempt to defuse dissent, for it lulled many Americans into believing that peace was at hand. By intensifying the bombing and shifting the burden of ground fighting to the Vietnamese, Nixon reduced American casualties and, as a consequence, opposition to the war itself.

Radical movements of the '60s were also victims of the political retrenchment and the economic and cultural constriction of the '70s. The spectre of economic marginality persuaded some radicals to resume their careers or to acquire a marketable skill, and it dissuaded many people from becoming politically active. But these movements were not brought down solely by the economic recession. Radicals also found it difficult to maintain an oppositional stance, to resist the conservatism of the period. For instance, in some respects cultural feminism represented a capitulation to dominant cultural values and assumptions. Unlike radical feminists who typically rejected as sexist "the whole idea of opposing male and female natures and values," cultural feminists treated gender differences as though they reflected deep truths about the intractability of maleness and femaleness.[29] By arguing that women are more nurturant, less belligerent, and less sexually driven than men, cultural feminists have simply revalued dominant cultural assumptions about women. Like its French counterpart *néo-féminité*, cultural feminism is "an ideal bound up through symmetrical opposition in the very ideological system feminists want to destroy."[30] Moreover, cultural feminism's excoriation of '60s radicalism as irredeemably "male" provided feminists with a rationale for retreating from the tumultuous activism and the marginality that many had embraced in the '60s. This anti-left feminism was, in Charlotte Bunch's words, "a way back into the establishment on limited terms."[31] In her autobiography *Growing Up Underground*, Jane Alpert, a radical who renounced the left and wrote a major cultural feminist text, "Mother Right," noted that this version of feminism led her "back to my family, to the friendships I'd formed in college, and to the world of middle-class values I had violently rejected in 1969."[32]

But one cannot attribute cultural feminism's supplanting of radical feminism simply to the conservatism of the '70s or to government subversion. The theoretical shortcomings, contradictions, and fuzziness of radical feminism also contributed to the emergence of cultural feminism. Some of radical feminism's theoretical deficiencies can be traced to its reactive stance toward the new left. For instance, politicos' insistence that socialism was sufficient to liberate women led radical feminists to make the counterclaim that women's liberation would automatically undermine capitalism. Their failure to confront capitalism more directly led their friends and enemies to conclude that they believed "the overthrow of capitalism [was] irrelevant to the equality of women."[33] Moreover, radical feminists failed to clarify their position toward the left. To many, their angry denunciations of the left seemed to imply a wholesale repudiation of it. Nor did it help that radical feminists sometimes failed to make it clear that they were criticizing the left for its sexism, not its radicalism. In her enormously influential book, *The Dialectic of Sex*, Shulamith Firestone derided politicos who ominously declared that feminism would "go off the deep end" and become counterrevolutionary if divorced from the organized left.[34] She contended that radical feminism was intrinsically revolutionary, and for Firestone, who conceived of radical feminism as "enlarging" rather than repudiating a socialist analysis, it was.[35] However, those women who joined the radical feminist movement did not always share Firestone's commitment to eradicating all forms of social domination. The radical feminists' declaration, "organize around your own oppression," soon degenerated into the narrower position, "organize around your own interests."[36] In fact, the history of both the first and second waves of feminism demonstrates that Firestone was far too sanguine when she proclaimed feminism inherently revolutionary.[37]

Finally, radical feminists' tendency to subordinate class and race to gender and to speak hyperbolically about a universal sisterhood was in large measure a reaction to the left's penchant for privileging class and race over gender. Radical feminists organized the movement in such a way as to persuade women that gender united them more than class or race divided them. For instance, according to the major architect of consciousness-raising, Kathie Sarachild, the assumption behind consciousness-raising was "that most women were like ourselves—not different."[38] But radical feminists' emphasis upon women's commonality masked a fear of difference, one which had serious consequences for the movement. Differences—either those rooted in class, race, and sexual preference, or those of skill and expertise—were seen as undermining the movement. When lesbians and working-class women finally pierced the myth of women's commonality, the movement was temporarily paralyzed, thus proving to some that differences were inevitably crippling. Indeed, cultural feminism's ascendance within the movement is in part attributable to the turmoil created by the issues of lesbianism and class. Cultural feminism's vision of a global sisterhood, however atavistic and chimerical in 1973, seemed to offer an escape from the debilitating discourse of difference.

Not surprisingly, liberal feminism benefited from the dissipation of radical feminism. As countercultural activity replaced radical political activism, liberal feminism became the uncontested voice of feminism, thus allowing it to define the political agenda of the women's movement for the public-at-large. Certainly one of the reasons for liberal feminism's success in the '70s was that it moved closer to radical feminism as it embraced the idea that the personal is political and the practice of consciousness-raising—both of which it had earlier rejected. But radical feminism it was not, and this was equally important to its success. To many women, liberal feminism's considerably more modest goal of bringing women into the mainstream seemed more palatable, not to mention more realistic, than the radical feminist project of fundamentally restructuring private and public life.

****

In order to understand radical feminism it is helpful to relate it to both prior feminist struggles and other radical movements of the '60s. Recent scholarship has emphasized the "continuity" between social-change movements of the '60s and earlier attempts at activism. According to this view, the movements that flourished in the '60s did not "spring fullblown out of nowhere"; rather, they had their origins in the activism of the previous decade.[39] This perspective is a useful corrective to the depiction of the '50s as devoid of dissent, a kind of American "Dark Ages."[40] But while leftist, civil rights, feminist, and homosexual activists of the '50s certainly helped to create a climate where injustice could be challenged, they did not always have a great deal in common politically with the radical activists who followed them.[41] In its rejection of liberalism, its embrace of participatory democracy, and its fusion of the personal and the political, '60s radicalism represented a break with politics as usual.[42]

The chasm that separated '60s radicals from those who immediately preceded them is nicely illustrated by radical feminist Barbara Mehrhof's account of a disputatious encounter between first- and second-wave feminists.[43] Mehrhof was part of a women's liberation group that organized a feminist action as part of the leftist Counter-Inaugural demonstration in January 1969. The purpose of their protest was to declare that suffragism, which they claimed had vitiated the earlier wave of feminism, was dead and that a new movement for genuine liberation was underway.[44] In a display of remarkable chutzpah, they decided to contact the famous suffragist and founder of the National Women's Party, Alice Paul, to see if she would join them in "giving back the vote." As one might expect of someone who had endured jail for the suffrage cause, Paul was not interested in repudiating suffrage as "a sop for women."[45] Indeed, when Shulamith Firestone asked her to join them on stage in burning their voter registration cards, Paul reportedly "hit the ceiling."[46] To Paul, woman suffrage constituted a significant breakthrough in women's struggle for equality. But to women's liberationists who had acquired their political education in the civil rights movement and the new left, voting was a "mockery of democracy," and equality in a fundamentally unequal society an obscenity.[47] Liberation, not equality, was their goal.

Radical feminism was especially distant from the narrow and conservative version of feminism articulated by Alice Paul and her National Women's Party in the postsuffrage era. In this period, the party refused to speak out against labor conditions and black disenfranchisement (although in both cases women were involved) on the grounds that these were not "purely feminist" issues.[48] Nor did radical feminists bear much resemblance to nineteenth-century feminists whose embrace of motherhood and domesticity was antithetical to radical feminism.[49] Of course, there were individual exceptions, most notably Elizabeth Cady Stanton, whose increasingly outspoken views on marriage cost her considerable support among suffragists. The almost sacrosanct position accorded the family in much early feminist literature is understandable, given women's economic dependence upon men, the absence of reliable contraception, and the centrality of motherhood to women's lives. Likewise, the historical conditions that prevailed by the mid-twentieth century—improved possibilities for female economic independence, and accessible and reliable (if not always safe) contraception—made the radical feminist assault on the family possible.[50]

The radical feminists of the '60s differed from earlier feminists in other respects as well. For example, while radical feminists generally repudiated the idea that men and women are essentially different and advocated the degendering of society, nineteenth-century feminists deployed arguments of both "sameness" and "difference" in an effort to justify equal rights for women. Thus first-wave feminists sometimes argued that women deserved equal access to the public sphere because they were men's equals intellectually and morally; on other occasions they argued that sexual equality would benefit society because women's more pacific, nurturant, and moral nature would counterbalance men's aggressiveness, belligerence, and competitiveness.[51]

Finally, the vast majority of first-wave feminists believed that women's lives would be ameliorated if a female sexual standard of purity replaced the male-defined double standard. This was true in England as well where suffragette Christabel Pankhurst popularized the slogan, "Votes for Women and Chastity for Men."[52] In their struggle to constrain male lust, women's rights advocates often assumed a protectionist stance toward younger and working-class women. Thus they typically condemned divorce because they believed it would leave women and children unprotected, and they opposed artificial contraception because they feared it would render all women prostitutes by irrevocably separating reproduction and sexuality.[53] Nineteenth-century feminists were often sexually conservative, but it is important to keep in mind that their assertion of women's right to say "no" was, for that time, a significant demand.[54] As Nancy Cott points out, the ideology of women's sexual passionlessness was a way for women to "assert control in the sexual arena." However, even

Cott admits that it was a control which was, unfortunately, rooted in denial.[55] But while nineteenth-century women's rights activists equated sex with danger, radical feminists believed that sexuality is simultaneously a realm of danger and of pleasure for women. Radical feminists shamelessly asserted women's right to sexual pleasure while resisting male-defined ideas of sexual liberation. Interestingly, in its emphasis on female difference and sexual danger cultural feminism bears a closer resemblance to nineteenth-century feminism than does radical feminism.

However, as Nancy Cott's recent book, *The Grounding of Modern Feminism*, demonstrates, by the 1910s there were feminists (or rather Feminists, as they called themselves) whose feminism in many respects prefigured radical feminism.[56] In their promotion of female self-assertion—especially women's right to sexual pleasure—their challenges to culturally received notions of femininity and masculinity, their commitment to radical politics, and, not least, their own risk-taking, these Greenwich Village Feminists were the foremothers of radical feminists. While these Feminists constituted but a minority of women's rights activists, they were a significant and influential minority that included Charlotte Perkins Gilman, Crystal Eastman, Rheta Childe Dorr, and Elizabeth Gurley Flynn. Of course, there are important differences between these early twentieth-century Feminists and contemporary radical feminists who are the focus of this study. While radical feminists almost always de-emphasized gender differences, Feminists simultaneously affirmed "women's human rights and women's unique needs and differences."[57] And in contrast to radical feminists, Feminists ignored the material impediments to female sexual expression, and their faith in the liberatory potential of passionate heterosexual relationships blinded them to the possibility that heterosexuality could reinforce rather than subvert female subordination.[58]

Students familiar with the history of the first women's movement may experience a strong sense of déjà vu when reading this study of the contemporary movement. Indeed, one can discern recurrent tensions in both waves of feminist activism. The question of whether women should be mobilized on the basis of their sameness to or their difference from men—at the center of the disagreement between radical and cultural feminists—occurred in the '20s as well. The relationship between the feminist movement and other social movements—should feminists organize within or outside other social movements—surfaces again and again as a point of contention. One finds this issue dividing feminists in the '60s, the postsuffrage era, and in the aftermath of the Civil War when radical Republicans refused to include women in the Fifteenth Amendment. Sexuality appears to be an especially problematic area for feminists past and present, as some emphasize sexuality as a domain of sexual pleasure, others as one of danger and exploitation, while still others strive for a stereographic view. Last, the evidence suggests that the heterogeneity of women's lives vexed feminists immediately following passage of the suffrage amendment and in the contemporary period. In both periods we find that some feminists acknowledged women's differences from one another while others ignored them in an effort to nurture women's consciousness of themselves as a class.

Although it is instructive to locate radical feminism within the feminist tradition, one cannot really comprehend radical feminism unless one situates it within the '60s movements from which it emerged. For while radical feminism was fiercely critical of the Movement's trivialization of women, it was in many respects intellectually and ideologically indebted to it.

One of the most striking characteristics of '60s radicalism was its aversion to liberalism. Radicals' repudiation of liberalism was not immediate; rather, it developed in response to liberalism's defaults—specifically, its timidity regarding black civil rights and its escalation of the Vietnam war. By 1967 radicals were no longer making distinctions between "humanist" and "corporate" liberals. Radicals not only disagreed with the liberal solution of repairing the system, they also quite understandably feared, liberalism's ability to co-opt and contain dissent. Radical feminists shared new leftists' and black radicals' hostility toward liberalism. As a result, their relations with the liberal feminists of NOW were often strained. Whereas liberal feminism sought to include women in the mainstream, radical feminism embodied a rejection of the mainstream itself. And while liberal feminists defined the problem as women's exclusion from the public sphere, radical feminists focused on the sexual politics of personal life. Indeed, radical feminists' politicization of personal life infuriated Betty Friedan, who frequently attacked them for waging a "bedroom war" which diverted women from the real struggle of integrating the public sphere.[59]

The radicalism of the '60s was less concerned with reforming society than with developing forms that would prefigure the utopian community of the future.[60] Thus there was little enthusiasm for electoral politics and enormous interest in creating political processes that would maximize individual participation and equalize power. Anxious to avoid the "manipulated consent" that they felt typified American politics, '60s radicals struggled to develop alternatives to hierarchy and centralized decision-making.[61] Their attempts to create a "democracy of individual participation" baffled many outsiders who marveled that the Movement managed to accomplish anything.[62] But to those radicals who craved political engagement, "freedom" was, as one radical group enthused, "an endless meeting."[63] As we shall see, women's liberationists, who had discovered first-hand that the Movement's commitment to egalitarianism did not apply to women, often took extraordinary measures to try to ensure egalitarianism. Fundamental to this "prefigurative politics," as sociologist Wini Breines terms it, was the commitment to build counter-institutions that would foreshadow the desired society.[64] Radicals believed that alternative institutions would not only satisfy needs unmet by the current system, but could, by dramatizing the failures of the system, radicalize those not served by the system. Rather than working within the system, new leftists and black radicals developed alternative political parties, media, schools, universities, and assemblies of oppressed and unrepresented people. Women's liberationists created an amazing panoply of counter-institutions, including health clinics, abortion referral services, rape crisis centers, and credit unions.[65]

While the women's liberation movement popularized the slogan "the personal is political," the idea that there is a political dimension to personal life originated with the new left.[66] Rebelling against a social order whose public and private spheres were highly differentiated, new leftists called for a reintegration of the personal with the political. New leftists reconceptualized apparently personal problems, specifically the alienation and powerlessness which they so acutely felt, as political problems. The idea that the personal is political also suggested its converse—that the political is personal. It was not enough to sign leaflets or participate in marches; the point was to change one's life, to transform oneself through radical action. The challenge was to find one's authentic self rather than to seek meaning through materialism and slavishly bow to social conventions. In a sense the individual became the site of political activity in the '60s. In the black movement the task was to discover the black inside the negro, and in the women's movement this took the form of challenging the taboo against female self-assertion.[67]

The prefigurative and personal politics of the Movement made '60s radicalism distinctive, setting it apart from politics as it has typically been practiced. But as this study makes abundantly clear, '60s radicalism was not without flaws. The obsession with process did not always translate into egalitarianism because the very structurelessness of the Movement often allowed the most articulate and charismatic people to dominate.[68] Moreover, the opposition to centralized organizations and hierarchy impeded organizational efficacy and efficiency. The radical black movement, the new left, and the women's liberation movement were all unable to reconcile egalitarianism with organizational effectiveness.[69] And too often the global rejection of all reform—the failure to distinguish between reform and reformism—led to immobilization.[70] Finally, "the personal is political" was one of those ideas whose rhetorical power seemed to work against or undermine its explication. It could, as we shall see, encourage a solipsistic preoccupation with self-transformation. As new leftist Richard Flacks presciently noted in 1965, this kind of politics could lead to "a search for personally satisfying modes of life while abandoning the possibility of helping others to change theirs."[71] Thus the idea that "politics is how you live your life, not who you vote for," as Yippie leader Jerry Rubin put it, could lead to a subordination of politics to lifestyle.[72] But if the idea led some to confuse personal liberation with political struggle, it led others to embrace an asceticism that sacrificed personal needs and desires to political imperatives. This was certainly true of the women's movement, where the idea that the personal is political was often prescriptively recast by radical feminists to mean that one's personal life should conform to some abstract standard of political correctness. At first this tendency was mitigated by the founders' insistence that there were no personal solutions, only collective solutions, to women's oppression. However, over time one's hair length, marital status, and sexual preference came to determine whether one would be deemed radical or not. At the same time, what was personally satisfying was sometimes upheld as politically correct. In the end, both the women's movement and the larger Movement suffered as the idea that the personal is political was often interpreted in a way that made questions of lifestyle absolutely central.

****

Against the current backdrop of political and cultural conservatism and "fiscal responsibility," the radicalism of the '60s seems remote, and perhaps futile and foolish, even to some who participated in the political upheaval. For instance, in the middle of her interview one former activist abruptly asked me, "Don't you sometimes feel as though you're writing a book about crazy people?" Because I had come of age politically in the '60s, the thought had never crossed my mind. Quite the contrary—these were the women I admired, the women who had "dared to be bad." But some people will undoubtedly react in this way. Much of the current belittling of the '60s stems from conservatives' hugely successful disinformation campaign against '60s radicalism. Now when people speak of the violence of the '60s they often mean the violence of white and black radicals, not the incomparably greater violence of the police, the FBI, the CIA, the national guard, and the military. Of course, every time another well-known '60s radical joins the Republican Party or converts to Christian fundamentalism it seems to further demonstrate that the activism of the era was silly and infantile.

Of course, '60s radicalism could be impetuous and reactive—the romanticization of poverty, the valorization of third-world liberation movements, the faith in heroic action, the almost willful ignorance of history, and the arrogance of youth. But I suspect that what people find most incomprehensible, objectionable, or embarrassing about the '60s is its utopianism. It is certainly true that the '60s sensibility of limitless possibilities appears at the very least anachronistic in an era such as ours where visible limits and constraints abound. However, if one is to understand the '60s, one must recognize that at that point in time it really did seem that economic and social justice could be achieved, the family reorganized, and all hierarchies based on gender, race, or class erased. The inability of the most technologically advanced country to defeat an army of poorly equipped Vietnamese peasants or to contain dissent at home seemed proof to radicals and conservatives alike of the system's fragility and vulnerability. Although it appears naïve in retrospect, at the time it did not seem unreasonable to think that America was on the threshold of revolutionary change.

My task is to make the '60s, or at least the women's rebellion of that era, more comprehensible. It is also my hope that by excavating the history of radical feminism I can demonstrate that early radical feminism was far more varied and fluid, not to mention more radical, than what is generally thought of as radical feminism today. Although I write as a partisan of radical feminism, I do not mean to suggest that the radical feminism which existed for a few brief years in the late '60s and early '70s is adequate for today's movement. Rather, it is my hope that by illuminating the reasons for the movement's decline, this study will help to stimulate discussion on how the movement might be revitalized.

****

Finally, a word about the book's method, sources, and organization. This is not simply an intellectual history, a social history, or a collective biography; rather, it combines elements of all three. I believe that to understand the evolution of radical feminism one must study not merely the major texts, but the minor texts, as well as the influential groups and personalities. For instance, one could never grasp the heterogeneity of early radical feminism solely by reading Shulamith Firestone's *Dialectic of Sex* or Kate Millett's *Sexual Politics*.[73] Equally problematic is the more inclusive approach that considers both obscure and well-known writers, but treats them as disembodied voices unconnected to the movement and the groups from which they emerged.[74] And while Ti-Grace Atkinson's Republican roots and Kathie Sarachild's background in the civil rights movement might help to illuminate their very different articulations of radical feminism, the movement is ultimately not reducible to personalities.

As British historian Gareth Stedman Jones has observed, history is not coterminous with the past, but consists, rather, of the "residues of the past."[75] In studying the early years of the radical feminist movement, I sometimes found few residues of that past. While most of the movement's early theoretical writings are available, there is surprisingly little written information on the first protests and conferences, and almost no material on early conflicts within the movement. The written record of the movement's first years is full of elisions, in large part because feminist newspapers did not begin publishing until early 1970.[76] To construct a history of the movement's early years I interviewed forty-one women who were involved in the women's liberation movement in New York, Washington, D.C., Boston, and Chicago.[77] I concentrated on interviewing women who had become active in the movement before 1970. Although I focused on interviewing radical feminists, I also interviewed several women who were on the politico side of the politico-feminist divide. Of course, oral history is not without pitfalls. Many years separated my interviewees from the events I was inquiring about, and their recollections were, of course, filtered through the present. Sometimes, as with several members of one New York group, their stories assumed a canonical quality, as though they had been recited many times before. Therefore, in my text I have assumed a critical stance toward the interview material. And whenever possible I have attempted to corroborate the oral evidence with references to written sources—feminist and leftist publications, underground newspapers, and personal papers.[78]

Some might object that this is, in fact, a history of East Coast radical feminism. I have focused on East Coast groups not out of regional chauvinism, but because with few exceptions these were the groups that made significant theoretical contributions.[79] And while these groups were often quite small, they had an influence far beyond their numbers. Of course, New York groups in particular benefited enormously from the presence of eager media. Their easy access to the media not only helped them to get their ideas out, but also gave them a special consciousness about themselves. The very title of New York Radical Women's 1968 publication, *Notes from the First Year* (a name suggested by Firestone), reflected a certain awareness of their place in history.[80] Although I concentrated on East Coast groups, I read feminist periodicals from across the country. While some of the conflicts I recount here were peculiar to New York, the major debates over the left, class, race, elitism, and lesbianism occurred everywhere, if somewhat later and with somewhat less ferocity. Although the details of my analysis might vary from region to region, I believe the essence of the argument would remain unchanged. For instance, the politico-feminist schism that convulsed New York between 1967 and 1969 occurred in Bay Area women's liberation in 1970.[81] And the "gay-straight split" continued to rage in some parts of the country long after a cease-fire had been reached in other areas.

The book is organized into six chapters. The first briefly discusses the process whereby women—or more typically white women—in the new left and the civil rights movement came to see the disjuncture between the Movement's rhetoric of equality and their own subordination within it. The second chapter explores the development of the women's liberation movement from late 1967 to early 1969. This section analyzes the movement's earliest groups and its first fissures, especially the aforementioned politico-feminist fracture which so debilitated the nascent movement. The third chapter examines the deteriorating relationship between the women's liberation movement and the larger Movement, and its culmination in radical feminists' decision to organize women outside the confines of the left. The fourth chapter analyzes the different strands of radical feminism, especially as they were articulated in the four most influential early radical feminist groups—Redstockings, Cell 16, The Feminists, and New York Radical Feminists. The fifth chapter concerns the intra-movement struggles around the issues of class, elitism, and lesbianism that rocked the movement between 1970 and 1972, and suggests the ways in which these struggles contributed to the rise of cultural feminism. The final chapter deals with the period from 1973 to 1975 when cultural feminism superseded radical feminism as the foremost tendency within the movement. This section explores the articulation of cultural feminism, the development of a feminist counterculture, and the radical feminist resistance to cultural feminism. The epilogue analyzes the ways in which feminism has developed since 1975. This section will pay particular attention to the anti-pornography movement and the sex debate it has sparked, and to the important theoretical contributions that women of color have made to feminism in this period.

1

Prologue: The Re-emergence of the "Woman Question"

> Thinking we were involved in the struggle to build a new society, it was a slowly dawning and depressing realization that we were doing the same work *in* the Movement as out of it: typing the speeches men delivered, making coffee but not policy, being accessories to the men whose politics would supposedly replace the Old Order.[1]

This is how Robin Morgan characterized women's situation in the Movement in the introduction to her best-selling anthology of women's liberation writings, *Sisterhood is Powerful.* Morgan's view that the Movement was as resolutely sexist as the "Old Order" it sought to overturn was shared by many of her contemporaries who had participated in the new left and the civil rights movement. But, as Sara Evans demonstrates in *Personal Politics,* women's experiences in the Movement were considerably more complicated than Morgan's account suggests.[2] Before we explore the ways in which the civil rights movement and the new left helped to generate the second wave of feminism, we must first acquaint those readers who are strangers to the world of '60s radicalism with the Student Nonviolent Coordinating Committee (SNCC) and Students for a Democratic Society (SDS)—two groups that are virtually synonomous with what is commonly referred to as the "Movement."

SNCC was founded in 1960 by black students who had participated in the lunch-counter sit-ins that swept across the South in early 1960. SNCC established voter registration projects throughout the South and initiated Freedom Summer, the 1964 voter registration campaign that brought 800 northern white students to Mississippi to help with the registration effort. SNCC also organized the Mississippi Freedom Democratic Party, an alternative political party for disenfranchised blacks, whose delegates unsuccessfully challenged the all-white regular delegation from Mississippi at the 1964 Democratic Convention. Like the civil rights activists in the Congress for Racial Equality (CORE) and the Southern Christian Leadership Conference (SCLC), the college students who founded SNCC were committed to nonviolent direct action. However, in many other respects SNCC had more in common with the newly established SDS than with other civil rights organizations. Like SDS, its membership was young, valued action, and its politics were typically more expressive than strategic. SNCC deliberately provoked confrontations with the Southern power structure and ventured into areas of the deep South considered untouchable by other groups. Through their dedication to the cause and their willingness to "put their bodies on the line," SNCC workers quickly gained a reputation as the "shock troops" of the civil rights movement.[3] In contrast to other civil rights groups, SNCC struggled to develop local leadership—an idea embodied in the slogan "let the people decide"—and, especially in its early years, was committed to participatory democracy. SNCC disintegrated by the end of the decade, but throughout much of the '60s it was the cutting edge of the black freedom movement, becoming the first civil rights group to oppose the Vietnam war and advocate black power.

SDS was founded in 1960 as the youth group of the League for Industrial Democracy (LID), an old left group whose politics were social-democratic and staunchly anti-Communist. Its manifesto, "The Port Huron Statement," drafted by Tom Hayden in 1962, lamented the evisceration of American democratic traditions and called for their revitalization through "participatory democracy." Stifling bureaucratic structures would be replaced by new institutions that would allow "the individual [to] share in those social decisions determining the quality and direction of his life."[4] Despite (or perhaps because of) its affiliation with LID, SDS evolved in a manner that put it light years away from the old left, both philosophically and organizationally.[5] While the old left focused on "class-based economic oppression," SDS stressed "how late capitalist society creates mechanisms of psychological and cultural domination over everyone."[6] While old left groups like LID strove for ideological clarity and organizational coherence, SDS believed that "what counts is that which creates a movement."[7] Nothing confused political pundits more than SDS's indifference toward traditional political activity, especially electoral politics. SDS'ers were less interested in repairing society than in developing new forms that would prefigure the desired society.[8] Indeed, SDS saw itself "creating space—breathing space, living space, freedom space."[9] And, most heretical of all, at least from the standpoint of the old left, was SDS's anti-anti-communism.[10]

From 1964 to 1965 SDS tried to ignite an "interracial movement of the poor" by organizing community unions in northern ghettoes. Its architects hoped that the Economic Research and Action Project (ERAP) would "bring poor whites into an alliance with the Negro freedom movement on economic issues," thereby averting a backlash against the civil rights movement.[11] ERAP organizers failed to organize a poor people's movement, but they did gain valuable organizing experience and their work did lay the basis for a revitalized welfare rights movement. In 1965 SDS began to turn its attention to the war, and in April of that year it organized the first national demonstration against the Vietnam war. Frustrated by liberals' unwillingness to move decisively to end civil-rights abuses in the South and their apparent eagerness to expand the war in Vietnam, many SDS'ers were coming to feel by 1965 that liberalism was the problem.[12] But, as we shall see, it proved easier to identify the deficiencies of liberalism than to build a genuinely American radicalism. SDS grew tremendously during the decade, from 2,500 in 1964 to between 80,000 and 100,000 in 1968.[13] Until its dissolution in 1969 SDS was "a wedge into American society," as it struggled to "build a democratic and humane society in which Vietnams are unthinkable, in which human life and initiative are precious."[14]

The relationship of women's liberation to social change movements of the '60s is complicated and paradoxical. Both the new left and the civil rights movement were dominated by men who were, at best, uninterested in challenging sexual inequality. Unlike the old left which acknowledged the existence of male chauvinism and gave token support to women's issues, the new left initially lacked any critical consciousness of gender relations. Indeed, this was one of the more unfortunate consequences of the yawning gulf between old and new leftists. Barbara Epstein, who was at one point active in both old and new left groups, recalled:

> SDS members criticized certain aspects of American culture, but the sexism of American culture was for the most part adopted uncritically. . . . "Male chauvinism" was a phrase that one did not utter unless one was ready to be laughed at. I was a member of both SDS and the Communist Party in the early sixties. I found the only way to deal with sexist behavior in SDS, if it was on the part of another [Communist] Party member, was to bring it up in the Party. In SDS I would not be listened to.[15]

Ellen Kay Trimberger, a political scientist studying the American Left, goes so far as to argue that "women in the Old Left had less reason to revolt because the [Communist] party treated them better."[16] Not everyone agrees with Trimberger. Peggy Dennis, who was active in the American Communist Party for fifty years and was married to high-ranking Party official Eugene Dennis, believes that Trimberger's view of the old left "is too generous."[17] The Communist Party did have a rhetoric to describe women's condition and it did incorporate women's issues into its program. However, as Paula Rabinowitz suggests, "there was a rhetoric of inclusion, but, for women, the reality was typically one of exclusion."[18]

Despite the sexism of the new left and the civil rights movement, women's experiences in these movements were not of unrelieved and unmitigated oppression. As Evans demonstrates, these movements also gave white women the opportunity to develop skills and to break out of confining, traditional roles. Both in the civil rights movement and in northern community organizing projects, like SDS's Economic Research and Action Project (ERAP), women began to acquire political skills. The danger of civil rights work and the persistent tradition of chivalry generally confined white women to the office or the freedom school. But even though women in the new left and the civil rights movement were often engaged in "women's work," they nonetheless felt themselves to be involved in socially meaningful work. In fact, it would seem, as sociologist and Movement activist Wini Breines has argued, that the "fantastic amount of personal and political growth experienced by women" blinded them initially to the Movement's sexism.[19] Certainly this was the case for new leftist and early women's liberation activist Naomi Weisstein, who found that the Movement simultaneously silenced and empowered her. Weisstein recalled a 1966 anti-draft sit-in at the University of Chicago where she experienced "that schizophrenia of not being able to talk, of being terrified to talk . . . and yet feeling ecstasy," for she imagined that they were "mak[ing] the new world right there."[20] Of course, as Breines points out, women's activism empowered them and eventually enabled them to discern the disjuncture between the Movement's rhetoric of equality and women's subordination within it.

Furthermore, white female activists began to question culturally received notions of femininity as they met powerful, young black women in SNCC and older women in the black community who were every bit as effective as male organizers and community leaders. Civil rights activist Dorothy Dawson Burlage explained that "[f]or the first time I had role models I could really respect."[21] And, later in the decade, radical women found role models in those Vietnamese and Cuban women who were playing critical roles in their respective national liberation struggles.[22]

In ERAP projects white women not only encountered positive female role models, but became seasoned community organizers. Although the male architects of ERAP had imagined themselves organizing unemployed white and black men in Northern ghettoes, this was not how the projects evolved. The ERAP founders assumed, as did some economists, that unemployment would become epidemic as a result of increased automation. However, as the Vietnam war escalated and heated up the ecomony, the unemployment rate sharply declined. The only men to be organized were the most unstable—the "winos and street youths."[23] Many male ERAP organizers tried, nonetheless, to organize men, especially those who were in youth gangs. But the men often ended up imitating the street swagger and Southern accents of the young men they were trying to organize. Rennie Davis, who worked in the Chicago ERAP project, explained that he had succeeded in getting to know the gang in his neighborhood by staying "virtually drunk" throughout his first week in the project.[24] Vivian

Leburg Rothstein, who had been involved in both SNCC and Chicago ERAP, recalled that the male organizers in her ERAP project competed with strong men from the community, discouraging the emergence of local leadership. "The only people we could attract," she remembers, "were quite incompetent men who were willing to be bossed around. That was a real issue."[25]

But while the men's organizing efforts often led them into pointless competition with neighborhood men, the women made considerable headway in organizing women, especially welfare mothers. SDS leader Steve Max recalls:

> When it actually came to relating to people in the community, particularly because so many of the early ERAP activities were regarding welfare mothers, it was the women who were able to relate to the community people and the ideological men were always kind of hanging back, you know, trying to develop southern accents.[26]

As Evans points out, the interpersonal skills required of good organizers—warmth, empathy, attentiveness, and noncompetitiveness—were precisely those skills that women have traditionally been encouraged to cultivate.[27]

Before long, ERAP projects abandoned all hope of mobilizing unemployed men and began to focus on "nitty-gritty" issues such as improved schools, housing, lighting, and garbage removal. With this shift women assumed greater importance both as organizers and as the organized. As Evans points out, neighborhood women were more organizable than men because they were generally more affected by community issues and more accessible to organizers. But while ERAP women developed skills and self-confidence, their accomplishments were not readily acknowledged by their male co-workers. In fact, Evans claims that "[w]omen were effective, but men were the stars."[28]

The new left contributed to the development of feminist consciousness in another important way. While the new left lacked the old left's awareness of the "woman question," its rejection of the old left's narrow understanding of politics encouraged female activists to define apparently personal concerns as political issues. It was Tom Hayden who in 1962 called for a "re-assertion of the personal."[29] And the 1962 "Port Huron Statement" declared that a new left

> must give form to . . . feelings of helplessness and indifference, so that people may see the political, social, and economic sources of their private troubles and organize to change society.[30]

By expanding political discourse to include the subject of personal relations, new leftists paved the way for feminists to criticize marriage, the family, and sexuality.[31] Moreover, in contrast to the old left, which demanded the subordination of personal needs to "the struggle," the new left encouraged people to seek personal fulfillment through the Movement. Thus, when women felt their needs trivialized, they were somewhat less inclined to push their needs aside for the sake of the Movement.

But at the same time that the Movement was building women's self-confidence and giving them the opportunity to break out of stultifying roles, it was, paradoxically, becoming a less congenial place for white women. In fact, Evans contends that "[f]eminism was born in that contradiction—the threatened loss of new possibility."[32] Within SNCC, white women, even "powerful insiders" like Mary King and Casey Hayden, saw their influence wane in the aftermath of the 1964 Freedom Summer.[33] The organizers of Freedom Summer hoped that the involvement of large numbers of whites would spark the media's interest and thereby force the federal government to intervene in the struggle against segregation. While this strategy proved somewhat successful, it marked the end of the interracial "beloved community" within SNCC as racial antagonisms surfaced. Many black civil rights workers resented the white volunteers whose behavior they often found patronizing and imperious. Moreover, the frequency with which black men and white women became sexually involved with each other infuriated many black women staffers. In 1965 one black woman on the SNCC staff contended:

> Sex is one thing; The Movement is another. And the two shouldn't mix. There's an unhealthy attitude in The Movement towards sex. The Negro girls feel neglected because the white girls get the attention. The white girls are misused. There are some hot discussions at staff meetings.[34]

Some civil rights workers blamed white women for becoming sexually entangled with black men. For instance, SNCC veteran Jimmy Garrett claimed that white female volunteers:

> spent that summer on their backs, most of them, servicing not only the SNCC workers but anybody else who came. . . . Where I was project director, we put white women out of the project within the first three weeks because they tried to screw themselves across the city.[35]

However, Staughton Lynd, a well-known new leftist who served as director of the freedom school program, contended that:

> every black SNCC worker with perhaps a few exceptions counted it a notch on his gun to have slept with a white woman—as many as possible. And I think that was just very traumatic for the women who encountered that who hadn't thought that was what going south was about.[36]

Certainly, the sexual test was a no-win situation for white women. If a white woman accepted a black man's sexual advance, she risked being ridiculed as loose; if she spurned him, she left herself vulnerable to the charge of racism. Of course, the interracial relationships that developed in these projects often grew out of genuine caring and affection. But some black men used white women in an effort to reclaim their manhood and some white women used black men to prove their liberalism or to "expiate their guilt."[37]

Given the heightened sexual and racial tensions, it was hardly surprising that the first serious discussions of sexual inequality within the Movement occurred during Freedom Summer. Having resolved to write a position paper on women for the upcoming SNCC staff meeting, King spent a good deal of time that summer raising the issue of sex roles with Casey Hayden and her other women friends in SNCC—Ruth Howard, Maria Varela, Dona Richards, Muriel Tillinghast, and Emmie Shrader. King drafted the paper with help from Casey Hayden, and it was among the thirty-seven papers discussed at the November 1964 SNCC meeting in Waveland, Mississippi.[38] Hayden and King decided against assuming authorship of the paper because they feared they would be ridiculed.[39] However, other staffers quickly pegged them as the authors. The paper cited instances of sexual discrimination, likened male supremacy to racial supremacy, and took SNCC to task for denying women an equal role in the decision-making process. The authors worried that their paper would meet with "crushing criticism." And, indeed, some staffers did mock their concerns.[40]

It was at this November meeting that Stokely Carmichael uttered his legendary one-liner about women's position in SNCC. After the meeting had ended, King was unwinding with a group that included Carmichael. According to King, Carmichael launched into one of his frequent comic monologues:

> He made fun of everything that crossed his agile mind. Finally, he turned to the meetings under way and the position papers. He came to the no-longer-anonymous paper on women. Looking straight at me, he grinned broadly and shouted, "What is the position of women in SNCC?" Answering himself, he responded, "The position of women in SNCC is prone!" Stokely threw his head back and roared outrageously with laughter. We all collapsed with hilarity. His ribald comment was uproarious and wild. It drew us all closer together, because, even in that moment, he was poking fun at his own attitudes.[41]

Among feminists Carmichael's comment came to symbolize Movement men's hostility toward women's liberation. But while Carmichael's comment betrayed a terrible insensitivity to women's situation, it was not, according to King, intended as a serious declaration on women's position in SNCC. Indeed, King's version of the story suggests that Carmichael's rejoinder was in part a self-parodic joke that referred to the days of Freedom Summer when sexuality seemed irrepressible.

Several years later Cynthia Washington, a black woman who directed one of SNCC's projects, recalled that neither she nor Muriel Tillinghast, another project director, was amused by Carmichael's comment. However, neither did they understand or sympathize with those women who raised the issue of sex discrimination. Washington remembered feeling baffled by a coversation she had with Hayden in 1964 on women's status in SNCC:

> [Casey] complained that all the women got to do was type, that their role was limited to office work no matter where they were. What she said didn't make any particular sense to me because, at the time, I had my own project in Bolivar County, Miss. A number of other black women also directed their own projects. What Casey and other white women seemed to want was an opportunity to prove they could do something other than office work. I assumed that if they could do something else, they'd probably be doing that.[42]

Certainly black women's tendency to dismiss women's liberation as "white women's business" was related to the fact that middle-class, white women were struggling for those things—independence and self-sufficiency—which racial and class oppression had thrust upon black women. For example, Washington explained that "[i]t seemed to many of us . . . that white women were demanding a chance to be independent while we needed help and assistance which was not always forthcoming."[43] Moreover, while white women often found themselves sexually objectified and exploited within the Movement, black women were often treated as though they were somehow sexless. Washington complained that black women were typically treated as "one of the boys":

> We did the same work as men—organizing around voter registration and community issues in rural areas—usually *with* men. But when we finally got back to some town where we could relax and go out, the men went out with other women. Our skills and abilities were recognized and respected, but that seemed to place us in some category other than female.[44]

Of course, it may seem ironic that black women, whose example so inspired white women to fight for sexual equality, were often unresponsive or antagonistic to feminism. Evans maintains that black and white women lacked the trust necessary to make common cause. But, more important, they lacked a common history. The rise of black power in 1966 further disinclined black women from becoming involved in the women's movement. Of course, this situation did change and by the late '70s there had emerged a dynamic black feminist movement. But within SNCC in the mid-'60s sexual inequality was an issue more likely to arouse white women, whose influence was waning, than black women.

Another factor made white women like Hayden and King feel as though they were losing ground in SNCC. Mary King's recent book, *Freedom Song*, suggests that her feelings of powerlessness related to SNCC's shift from the expressive or "personal politics" which had originally drawn her to the group.[45] By the time of the Waveland meeting, two factions were emerging within SNCC. Bob Moses (Parris), Mary King, and Casey Hayden were among those identified with the "freedom high" faction, which wanted

SNCC to remain committed to decentralization and democratization.[46] James Forman and Ruby Doris Smith Robinson were among the growing number of staffers who favored a more strategic, centralized, and hierarchical SNCC. To King, "The questions Casey and I raised ran parallel to the larger debate about SNCC's future course."[47] Indeed, by calling for greater equality between the sexes, King and Hayden were trying to hold SNCC accountable to its humanistic and democratic values and to avert their attenuation.

To James Forman those who opposed a more centralized, hierarchical structure "failed to distinguish between SNCC as an organization fighting for the creation of a better society, and SNCC as that better society itself."[48] But the commitment to building the "new society within the shell of the old," to developing alternative political processes and forms that would prefigure the ideal society, was the essence of prefigurative politics, and indeed the essence of '60s radicalism.[49] Most important from our standpoint, it was the promise of prefigurative politics and its premature foreclosure, or the "threatened loss of new possibility," that nurtured women's rebellion within the Movement. With the decline of expressive politics, first in SNCC and later in SDS, the Movement became a less hospitable place for women whose concerns were dismissed as "personal" or "apolitical."

Evans maintains SDS was also changing in ways that made it less responsive to women's needs. After SDS's hugely successful antiwar march on Washington in April 1965, the organization's ranks swelled. SDS's hypertrophied growth made it markedly more competitive and its leadership more impenetrable for women. The sense of community which SDS veterans so valued dissipated as new members tried to assert themselves and the old guard struggled to defend itself. Although the SDS old guard may not have been anxious to discuss the existence of sex discrimation within the organization, Evans observes that many of the most powerful men within SDS were married to women who were questioning sex roles within the Movement. Evans hypothesizes that the men might have been somewhat less resistant had the issue been raised while SDS was still a cohesive movement of friends.[50]

In fact, some men did respond favorably when the question of sex roles was first raised within SDS at the December 1965 National Council meeting.[51] According to SDS chronicler Kirkpatrick Sale, the December "rethinking conference," as it was optimistically dubbed, was supposed to rekindle the spirit of the 1962 SDS Convention at Port Huron. SDS oldtimers hoped that the conference would help SDS solve its problems and grow into an effective "multigenerational" and "multi-issued," radical organization.[52] Many SDS members came to the meeting dissatisfied with the group's lack of ideological coherence and organizational cohesion, and the absence of working democracy. Many of the veterans were also resentful of the newcomers who they felt were taking control of their organization. Moreover, Evans argues that many relationships and marriages among SDS couples "were reaching a breaking point."[53] Evans speculates that this personal turbulence made the issue of sex roles especially compelling. But it was Casey Hayden and Mary King's, "Sex and Caste"—a "kind of memo" they had circulated among women in the Movement—that finally prompted the National Council to hold a workshop on women's role in SDS. Their paper, an elaboration of the position paper they had written for SNCC a year earlier, was printed with other conference papers. In it, they located the struggle for sexual equality within the new left tradition of dissolving the barrier between the personal and the political:

> all the problems between men and women and all the problems of women functioning in society as equal human beings are among the most basic that people face. We've talked in the movement about trying to build a society which would see basic human problems (which are now seen as private troubles), as public problems and would try to shape institutions to meet human needs rather than shaping people to meet the needs of those with power. To raise questions like those above illustrates very directly that society hasn't dealt with some of its deepest problems and opens discussion of why that is so.[54]

According to Evans, when the women's workshop first convened, it was composed of both men and women. However, a number of men reacted so defensively that some women resolved to meet by themselves, without the obstructionist men. The women who chose to leave were followed by several men who angrily demanded that they be allowed to participate in the women's discussion group. Even some women who had stayed in the mixed group because they wanted to discuss the issue with men became so frustrated by the men's behavior that they too withdrew to meet with other women.[55] Marilyn Webb recalls that the issue

> galvanized enormous numbers of meetings of women endlessly. I don't even remember anything else happening at that convention. We always used to talk about other people's problems. The reason it was so incredibly interesting was that it was the first time we applied politics to ourselves.[56]

The workshop issued a statement, endorsed by the National Council, criticizing SDS for failing to encourage women to participate fully in the organization. It further argued that women's status in SDS "reflects not only the inadequacies within SDS but . . . also greater societal problems, namely the role of women in American society today."[57]

Some people considered the discussion of sex roles the bright light in an otherwise dreary event. Former SDS president Todd Gitlin declared the conference a "disaster" and criticized the "SDS status scale (which is in turn a condensation of American political values)" and the "unbridled ego-involvement" of many who gave speeches and made proposals.[58] But Gitlin, like many women and some men, saw the women's workshop as a positive development. Gitlin suggested that SDS combat the problem of elitism by holding workshops

> as informal and open as the very fruitful December workshops on women in SDS. . . . A determined effort at the December conference forced an honest confrontation with the man-woman issues; if we were able to talk about those elitisms, we can talk about others, though it may be harder.[59]

The SDS newspaper, *New Left Notes*, published a highly favorable summary of the women's workshop which read:

> Movement men unaware of the problem of women should reflect that in most ERAP projects, in many "radical" marriages, and in the National Office, women frequently get relegated to "female" types of work. . . . In an atmosphere where men are competing for prestige, women are easily dismissed, come to believe that their ideas aren't worth taking the time of the confer-

> ence; in short, they accept the definitions men impose on them and go silent.[60]

The issue of "sex roles" remained dormant for the next year and one-half as other issues took precedence. To understand why this was so, we must make a detour of sorts and discuss developments within the Movement that precluded further discussion of the "woman question."

Between December 1965 and June 1967 the American political landscape changed irrevocably. Faced with the inexorability of white racism, a federal government apparently indifferent to Southern white terrorism, and the dissolution of the "beloved community" within SNCC itself, many young black activists were, by 1966, advocating that the civil rights movement abandon its original goal of integration and work instead toward black power. Most simply, black power meant black self-determination, or black control of the political, economic, and cultural life of the black community.[61] But black power signified much more; it represented a fundamental departure from the gradualist, integrationist, and nonviolent approach favored by the civil rights establishment. To proponents of black power, integration, by presuming that blacks needed to become assimilated into white society, fostered the myth of white superiority. Stokely Carmichael argued that integration was nothing more than a "subterfuge for the maintenance of white supremacy."[62] Black power, by contrast, was a way to build racial consciousness, pride, and solidarity. And, to its original proponents, it seemed the way to build an independent, oppositional power base in the black community. Black power theorists echoed influential black nationalist Malcolm X, who had been urging blacks since 1964 to seize control of their own communities, "so you don't have to "picket . . . and beg some cracker downtown for a job."[63] Black power, with its cynicism about the prospects for racial reconciliation, also implied a rejection of Dr. King's program of nonviolence. Writer and SNCC activist Julius Lester conceded that "nonviolence might do something to the moral conscience of the nation," but argued that "a bullet doesn't have morals and it was beginning to occur to more and more organizers that white people had plenty more bullets than they did conscience."[64]

Black power had enormous consequences for the Movement

because it effectively barred whites from organizing in the black community.[65] White organizers were told that they impeded the development of black consciousness and pride, and that their involvement in the civil rights movement smacked of liberal paternalism. Carmichael and others urged whites to acknowledge that they could fight racism more effectively by confronting it where it lived, in the white community.[66] White radicals responded with much talk about organizing an anti-racist movement in the white community. However, very little organizing of this sort occurred because, as even Carmichael admitted, "to go into a poor white community in Mississippi or Alabama and talk about integration is to invite suicide upon oneself."[67]

The expulsion of whites from the civil rights movement and the collapse of ERAP projects forced whites to reconceptualize their role in the Movement. SDS leader Greg Calvert contends that black power, by "throwing us back upon ourselves, our own lives, our own situations . . . offered us the possibility for being sincerely radical, and not the liberal adjunct of the black movement."[68] Influenced by black power, some white radicals declared that organizing on behalf of others was merely liberal, while organizing on behalf of one's own group was truly revolutionary.[69] The idea that revolutionary consciousness emanates from "the perception of oneself as one of the oppressed" would prove central to the emergence of the women's movement, but in 1966 the new left embraced the idea in ways that further marginalized women.[70]

From mid-1966 until late 1967 the new left responded to the challenge of black power by concentrating its efforts upon draft resistance and student organizing. The draft resistance movement was launched by white veterans of the civil rights movement who, in Staughton Lynd's words, "wanted to retain a politics of daring, but wanted to get away from the role of . . . auxiliary to a radicalism [whose] center of gravity was in other people's lives." They were searching for "something white radicals could do which would have the same spirit, ask as much of us, and challenge the system as fundamentally as had our work in Mississippi."[71]

Unfortunately, the draft resistance movement contributed to women's growing peripheralization within the Movement.

Whereas men could engage in heroic action by resisting the draft, women were reduced to helpmates. Mimi Feingold, who had been active in both CORE and the Cleveland ERAP project, became alienated from the Resistance when she realized that:

> here was a movement where women were playing the most unbelievably subservient role, because that was the only role the women could play, because women couldn't burn draft cards and couldn't go to jail so all they could do was to relate through their men and that seemed to me the most really demeaning kind of thing.[72]

In fact, one of the draft resistance movement's most popular slogans was "Girls Say Yes to Guys Who Say No!"[73] Moreover, to counter the public's image of draft resisters as cowardly "draft-dodgers," the movement often portrayed resistance as the quintessential act of courage and manliness. Lynd himself had declared that "the emotional thrust of the resistance movement is not . . . emasculation but manhood."[74]

In late 1966 and early 1967, some women, like Heather Tobis Booth and Francine Silbar, tried to challenge the anti-draft movement's stance toward women. Booth organized a women's workshop at the December 1966 "We Won't Go" conference.[75] However, most of the women who attended the conference avoided the workshop, and many of those who did show up agreed with Alice Lynd that "our duty [is] to support our men."[76] In the March 1967 issue of *New Left Notes*, Francine Silbar pointed out that the resistance movement had placed women in a position similar to that experienced by whites in the civil rights movement as a result of black nationalism.[77] Eventually white women, feeling themselves pushed out of the Movement, would follow the example of others and organize on their own behalf.

In the fall of 1966 SDS also turned its attention toward the campus. From the very early days of SDS some thought that SDS should focus its energies off campus because they believed that students were too privileged to commit themselves to radical social change. However, that view was challenged in early 1967 by several prominent SDS leaders, including Greg Calvert and Carl Davidson, who embraced what was termed "new working-class theory."[78] They argued that people with "technical, clerical, and professional jobs" constituted a new sector of the working class, better educated than the traditional working class, but working class nonetheless. Mistakenly dismissed by leftists, these workers constituted a new working class that "lies at the very hub of production" under advanced industrial capitalism.[79] According to this logic, students were not part of the privileged middle class, but, rather, "trainees" for the new working class and thus could be considered a radical force for social change.

New working-class theory seemed to provide Calvert and Davidson with the ideological justification they needed to organize students. But by the end of 1967 much of the new left had rejected new working-class theory and had reverted to the self-deprecating position that students as an elite, privileged class would have to abandon the university for "the people" to be true revolutionaries. In a September 1967 issue of *New Left Notes*, SDS'er John Veneziale proclaimed:

> I don't think the working class people of this country will ever take the student struggle seriously until students become people again, and come off the campus, and be willing to kill and die for their (i.e. the people's) freedom.[80]

And that same month in a stunning reversal of his earlier stance, SDS leader and former new working-class theorist, Carl Davidson, declared:

> What can students do? Organizing struggles over dormitory rules seems frivolous when compared to ghetto rebellions. And white students are no longer wanted or necessary in the black movement. . . . Students are oppressed. Bullshit. We are being trained to be the oppressors and the underlings of the oppressors.[81]

According to this view, the growing student power movement demonstrated not that students were becoming radicalized, but, rather, that as members of the privileged bourgeoisie they were eager to extend their privileges.[82]

How does one account for such a rapid shift in orientation? Calvert had hoped that by "grafting" the "most intelligent parts of the Marxist tradition . . . onto the libertarian mainstream of the movement," new working-class theorists could "legitimize the New Left in terms of the socialist tradition" and leave behind the orthodox, sectarian left.[83] More specifically, Calvert and others were hoping that new working-class theory would mark the demise of the Progressive Labor Party (PL), a traditional Marxist-Leninist group which was trying to seize control of SDS. But the new left was unable to invoke Marxism without succumbing to the "coherence and neatness of its orthodox line."[84] As Calvert later admitted, by expanding the "labor metaphysic," new working-class theory ended up legitimating the sectarian left rather than student activism:

> new working class theorists like myself developed that particular analysis in order to legitimate the student movement. Unfortunately, by adopting the terms of class analysis, we opened the door to the wholesale adoption of orthodox Marxist rhetoric and, within a year, the New Left was wallowing in a religious orgy of Marxification and Leninization with the vultures of the Old Left sects and cults moving in for the kill or the carcass.[85]

But there were other reasons for the new left's sudden rejection of new working-class theory. First of all, it was becoming clear by 1967 that black power involved not only the right of the oppressed to organize themselves, but their right to lead the larger Movement as well. Increasingly, black militants argued that blacks, by virtue of their most-oppressed status, possessed the moral authority to direct the Movement. The seeds of this thinking were present in the earliest articulations of black power. For instance in an influential 1966 position paper, members of SNCC's Atlanta Project contended:

> Whites are the ones who must try to raise themselves to our humanistic level. We are not, after all, the ones who are responsible for a genocidal war in Vietnam; we are not the ones who are responsible for neocolonialism in Africa and Latin America; we are not the ones who held a people in animalistic bondage over 400 years.[86]

By late 1967 many white radicals agreed that the Movement's leadership belonged in black hands. Their willingness to accept black leadership was not unrelated to that summer's riots in Newark and Detroit. To many radicals the rioting "marked the beginning of the second American Revolution," as SDS leader Carl Davidson put it.[87] Black and white radicals alike exaggerated the political significance of the riots, or "insurrections." Tom Hayden, for one, maintained that "conditions are slowly being created for an American form of guerrilla warfare based in the slums."[88] By contrast to these new urban guerrillas, students seemed irredeemably reformist. Moreover, the escalation of the Vietnam war, despite the efforts of the anti-war movement, only seemed to confirm the impotence of the white left. Radical journalist Andrew Kopkind captured the powerlessness and guilt that began to overwhelm the white left in the summer of 1967:

> To be white and radical in America this summer is to see horror and feel impotence. It is to watch the war grow and know no way to stop it, to understand the black rebellion and find no way to join it, to realize that the politics of a generation has failed and the institutions of reform are bankrupt, and yet to have neither ideology, programs, nor the power to reconstruct them.[89]

How could one talk about the oppression of middle-class students when the American military was slaughtering Vietnamese peasants and the police and National Guard were gunning down black insurrectionists? Greg Calvert and Staughton Lynd were among the few who continued to argue that whites must organize around their own oppression and resist the temptation to cast themselves in the role of "auxiliaries" to the black struggle. In late 1967 Calvert maintained that the

> student movement has to develop . . . an image of its own revolution . . . instead of believing that you're a revolutionary because you're related to Fidel's struggle, Stokely's struggle, always somebody else's struggle.[90]

And Lynd decried the "politics of middle-class flagellation" that seemed to be taking over the Movement.[91] But as the war intensified, the ghettoes burned, and the government embarked upon its campaign against black militants, white radicals found the pull toward fighting "somebody else's struggle" irresistible. By the spring of 1968 SDS abandoned the university and made support of the black liberation struggle its top priority.[92]

By late 1967 SDS was, like SNCC before it, beginning to disassociate itself from the expressive politics which had so distinguished it from the old left. Much of its leadership claimed that SDS would have to become a more strategic organization if it was serious about fighting racism and imperialism and joining forces with the working class. This was not the first time SDS debated the merits of strategic versus expressive politics. Almost from the beginning there were SDS'ers who favored an economistic analysis and a more strategic orientation for the group. Former SDS president Paul Potter recalled that as early as 1965 some people began to dismiss "The Port Huron Statement" as a "kind of simpy, rhetorical exercise that had covered up or masked the hard, crisp, basic economic analysis that was now emerging."[93] But by late 1967 discussion of personal issues, political process, and counter-institutions seemed a middle-class luxury which SDS could hardly afford to indulge. Greg Calvert noted that by the late '60s it had become

> very fashionable in SDS . . . to denounce something called personal liberation. If you talk about what you feel or what's meaningful to you in a political forum, you're suddenly one of those personal liberation people.[94]

Suddenly "the struggle" took precedence over all else, including political process.

These debates may seem arcane and unrelated to women, but one cannot understand the emergence of the women's liberation movement without reference to them. First of all, it is hardly surprising that the issue of women's inequality resurfaced in the summer of 1967. The idea that a revolutionary must look first to her or his own oppression gave women the ideological ammunition they needed to examine their own situation. However, the idea was losing credibility at the very moment women were invoking it. Women who were demanding that their oppression be acknowledged ran up against a left concerned only with supporting the struggles of blacks, the working class, or the Vietnamese. Women who were declaring that the "personal is political" encountered a Movement reverting to the old left's definition of political.

There were other factors contributing to the women's revolt within SDS. Evans contends that women's position in the Movement deteriorated even further as countercultural ideas about free love penetrated the new left. She maintains that men expected women to adopt their "own more promiscuous [sexual] standards."[95] Certainly, some women in the Movement felt sexually exploited rather than liberated by the sexual revolution, which they claimed had created a new compulsory sex ethic. For instance, Francine Silbar complained that women were treated by Movement men like "sexual garbage cans . . . and reservoirs of mechanistic lust to be tapped at the whim of our thoughtless, self-centered 'small master.' "[96] But, as Deirdre English points out, those who dismiss the sexual revolution as exploitive of women ignore the opportunities it could afford them:

> my recollection of it is that it was not an unmitigated disaster. The sexism was there, but women were actually having more sexual experience of different kinds and enjoying it. Women were having more sex that was not procreational, and claiming the right to it as well as paying a lower social and emotional cost.[97]

According to Marge Piercy, Movement women were not getting too much, but, rather, too little sex. Piercy wrote that the "liberated woman . . . can expect to get laid maybe once every two months, after a party or at councils or conferences, or when some visiting fireman comes through and wants to be put up."[98] For Piercy the problem was that Movement men were emotionally distant and exploitive in their relationships with women. According to Barbara Epstein, both Movement men and women were skittish about making commitments, but for different reasons:

> Women often resisted making commitments to particular men, because they were not satisfied with the quality of these relationships; it was men who were more likely to reject, or at least feel ambivalence about, the idea of commitment itself.

Epstein suggests that commitment may have been more problematic for men because it evoked memories of the "trapped quality of their fathers' lives."[99] Men's desire for sexual relationships without emotional commitment certainly created a groundswell of resentment. And, in opening up new sexual vistas, the sexual revolution made it possible for women to demand genuine sexual self-determination.

In the spring of 1966 there were, as Evans points out, signs of incipient feminism. Naomi Weisstein taught a course on women at the University of Chicago and Heather Booth organized the women's workshop at the anti-draft conference. (And Juliet

Mitchell's important article, "Women: The Longest Revolution" was circulated among radical women.[100]) In the winter and spring of 1967, *New Left Notes* published articles by Jane Addams, Heather Booth, and Francine Silbar attacking the Movement's uncritical acceptance of sex roles. But these were isolated and individual protests. This all changed when radical women raised the issue of sexual inequality at SDS's June 1967 National Convention in Ann Arbor. This time the rhetoric and analysis were markedly different, reflecting the enormous changes that had occurred since 1965. And this time the women met with a far chillier reception.

The "Women's Liberation Workshop" thrashed out an analysis and a series of demands to present to the entire convention. The statement was written by Jane Addams (perhaps the most prominent woman in SDS), Elizabeth Sutherland (formerly of SNCC), Susan Cloke, and Jean Peak.[101] They declared:

> As we analyze the position of women in capitalist society and especially in the United States we find that women are in a colonial relationship to men and we recognize ourselves as part of the Third World.

They argued for communal child-care centers, accessible abortion, the dissemination of birth-control information, and the sharing of housework to free women from the confines of domesticity. They maintained that women's continued subordination within SDS would retard the revolutionary struggle, and they recommended that SDS pursue an aggressive educational campaign concerning women's liberation. However, after demanding that the men in SDS confront their "male chauvinism," the authors ended on a conciliatory if not an apologetic note:

> We seek the liberation of all human beings. The struggle for the liberation of women must be part of the larger fight for human freedom. We recognize the difficulty our brothers will have in dealing with male chauvinism and we will assume our full responsibility in helping to resolve the contradiction. freedom now! we love you![102]

But the men's fears were not assuaged. As soon as the statement was read, a man leaped from his seat to suggest that they separate the analysis from the resolutions for purposes of debate and voting. When the chair announced that the workshop's analysis was open neither to debate nor to a vote:

> The meeting hall erupted. Men were yelling, arguing, cursing, objecting all over the floor. But the women were adamant . . . and united. . . . When someone proposed that all discussion on the issue involve only women there was applause. Some men were furious. They thought the analysis was stupid.[103]

Shortly after the convention, SDS veteran Don McKelvey wrote that the

> men were noisy throughout, obtuse on connection to black nationalism and in objection to unamendable women's resolution on grounds that it violated participatory democracy.

For McKelvey, the men's reaction demonstrated "the existence of a really vicious and deep-seated sexual caste system." Although most of the men who spoke reportedly "agreed that women were the victims of a sexual caste system," they found the third-world analogy completely untenable.[104] As Evans points out, in defining themselves as part of the third world, women were trying to establish the legitimacy of their cause. While Evans argues that the analogy was flawed, she suggests that men opposed it because they were not willing to grant that women, like blacks, "had rights to self-determination."[105] The men probably also resented the women's analysis because it seemed to challenge their legitimacy as revolutionary actors. Attacked first by blacks as racist and then by women as male chauvinist, white men must have wondered what role, if any, they could comfortably play in the struggle.

The convention ultimately passed the programmatic section of the women's statement. However, when it was published the following week in *New Left Notes*, it was printed next to a "cartoon of a girl—with earrings, polkadot minidress, and matching . . . panties—holding a sign [which read]: 'We Want Our Rights and We Want Them Now.' "[106] But it took yet another encounter with Movement chauvinism before some women decided to organize on their own behalf.

During Labor Day weekend of 1967 2,000 activists from 200 organizations descended upon Chicago's elite Palmer House for the National Conference for New Politics (NCNP). Organizers of the

NCNP had hoped that the convention would unite the disparate factions of the Movement—"the electoral reformers, radical organizers and Black militants." To NCNP founder Arthur Waskow, "the times seemed to require" the unification and solidification of the Movement:

> the Vietnam War seemed on the verge of a new and finally disastrous escalation—perhaps an invasion of the North; the Black communities had burned down Newark and Detroit. Surely we needed a single movement.[107]

However, the convention not only failed to unite the Movement, but it also shattered the assumption that there was *one* Movement. One of the main objectives of the conference was to launch a presidential ticket headed by Martin Luther King and Benjamin Spock. Although the NCNP leadership favored an electoral strategy, many radicals who were committed to grass-roots organizing opposed such efforts. Shortly after the convention, Rennie Davis and Staughton Lynd berated the NCNP leaders for promoting "electoral politics without first having built a base through non-electoral organizing."[108] However, this was only one of many schisms that undermined the organizers' hopes for unity.

The NCNP convention represented a critical turning point in the new left's relationship to the black freedom movement.[109] By the time of the August convention, black power had been embraced by virtually everyone within the black liberation movement. While the white delegates hoped for an interracial coalition, many black delegates were extremely skeptical about any such undertaking. Some blacks favored a separatist stance, while others proposed working with whites, but on *their* terms, not on whites' terms. In fact, the black caucus refused to participate in the convention unless the delegates accepted their thirteen demands. The black caucus demanded that blacks, who comprised roughly one-sixth of all delegates, be given fifty percent representation on all committees. They further demanded that the convention condemn the "imperialist Zionist war" in the Middle East and encourage whites to humanize the "savage and beastlike character" of white communities. In his speech to the black caucus, James Forman of SNCC declared that black people, as the "most dispossessed," must lead the Movement and proclaimed that those who disagreed could "go to hell."[110] SNCC's chairperson, H. Rap Brown, not only refused to talk to white delegates, but he apparently declared that the leadership of the Movement "should never be shared, it should always remain in the hands of the dispossessed."[111] In the end, the convention voted three to one to accept the caucus' thirteen points. The following day the black caucus demanded fifty percent of the convention vote, and again the white delegates capitulated. Arthur Waskow, who opposed the demands, argued that those whites who voted for the caucus demands were so anxious for validation from the black delegates that they were willing to collude in their own "castration."[112] But capitulation did not bring about the desired coalition, and at the convention's conclusion NCNP was in shambles. To Waskow, the Chicago convention proved "that there was not one movement but two: one Black and one white."[113]

The Movement emerged from the NCNP convention more badly fractured than most participants understood at the time. Although most press accounts focused exclusively upon the racial tension, the convention was also marked by conflicts over women's liberation. Of course, the NCNP convention occurred a mere two months after the SDS Convention where the issue of women's liberation had caused such a fracas. Moreover, there was a good deal of discussion around women's issues that summer in Chicago. Naomi Weisstein and Heather Tobis Booth, both long-time SDS members, taught a course on women that summer at Chicago's Radical Research Center. SDS leader Jane Addams organized a meeting of women at the SDS national office in Chicago.[114] Meanwhile, pacifist Barbara Liken organized a discussion group composed of liberal women to discuss the cultural devaluation of women's roles. Former SCLC worker Jo Freeman began to attend Liken's group and, through it, heard about Weisstein and Booth's course. Freeman went to a session that Jane Addams was leading and apparently suggested to the class that they should raise the issue of women's liberation at the upcoming NCNP convention. Freeman organized a few planning sessions, but it was Liken who apparently spoke with the NCNP organizers and arranged for her friend, Madlyn Murray O'Hair, to facilitate a women's workshop. O'Hair was well known for her role in banning prayer from the public schools, but Freeman claims that "she knew nothing about women and cared less."[115] Roughly fifty to seventy women, including NOW's Ti-Grace Atkinson, attended the women's workshop at the NCNP and drafted a resolution.

But whereas radical white men seemed eager to do penance for their racism, they actively resisted women's attempts to raise the issue of sexual inequality. When representatives from the women's workshop spoke with the resolution chairperson about getting their resolution on the agenda, they were rebuffed. The chairperson explained that Women Strike for Peace (WSP) had already submitted a women's resolution, the gist of which was simply that women should work for peace. He suggested that they meet with women from WSP to draft a compromise resolution. O'Hair met with two representatives from WSP and, according to Freeman, "sold out" the radical women's workshop. Only two of the points of the women's workshop were included in the new resolution. Freeman was outraged by the compromise resolution and stormed out of the meeting with O'Hair. The compromise resolution might well have gone unchallenged had Freeman not encountered Shulamith Firestone on her way out of the hall. Firestone was equally furious about the betrayal, and the two spent the rest of the night writing a new resolution. Freeman doubts that they would have acted separately, "but together we fed on each other's rage."[116]

Following the example of the black caucus, Firestone and Freeman's resolution demanded that women receive fifty-one percent of the convention votes and committee representation because, they argued, women comprise fifty-one per cent of the population. They demanded that the convention condemn the mass media "for perpetuating the stereotype of women as always in an auxiliary position to men [and as] sex objects." They also called upon the convention to endorse "the revamping of marriage, divorce, and property laws." Finally, they demanded "complete control by women of their own bodies, the dissemination of birth control information to all women regardless of their age and marital status, and the removal of all prohibitions against abortion."[117] After typing up the resolution—which differed from the original resolution—they paid a return visit to the resolutions chairperson. When he claimed that the convention lacked the time to debate their resolution, Freeman countered, "You know, there's an awful lot of women in that audience. We can tie up this conference on procedural motions for far longer than it will take you to debate our little resolution." With that, he agreed to make the women's resolution number eleven on the agenda. Freeman and Firestone made about 2,000 copies of the resolution and succeeded in recruiting three or four other women to their cause. However, when the time came to debate resolution number eleven, the chair introduced Madlyn Murray O'Hair's resolution, not theirs. According to Freeman:

> There we were standing at the microphones, hands stretched up. [The chairman] rams [Murray's] resolution through; refuses to call on us; as soon as the whole thing is over this little kid, smaller than I am, rushes in front of me to the microphone, raises his hand, is recognized and the first thing he says is "ladies and gentlemen, I'd like to speak to you today about the most oppressed group in America, the American Indian." Shulie Firestone and about three or four other people, who we didn't know, were ready to pull the place apart. Then [the chair] William Pepper patted Shulie on the head and said, "Move on little girl; we have more important issues to talk about here than women's liberation." That was the genesis. We had a meeting the next week with women in Chicago.[118]

That fall the Chicago group issued a manifesto, "To the Women of the Left," which was subsequently published in *New Left Notes*. In it, they counseled new left women to avoid making "the same mistake the blacks did at first of allowing others (whites in their case, men in ours) to define our issues, methods, goals. Only we can and must define the terms of our struggle." Thus, they contended, "it is incumbent on us, as women, to organize a movement for women's liberation."[119] Like those white radicals who believed that students could be legitimate agents of social change, the radical women who began meeting in Chicago that fall took their inspiration from black power. Black power enabled them to argue that it was valid for women to organize around their own oppression and to define the terms of their struggle.

But black power was double-edged. In privileging the struggles of the "most oppressed," black power contributed to the trivializing of women's issues. While black power made it possible for women to conceive of organizing women, it also provided radical men with a rationale for ignoring or disparaging women's liberation. Likewise, the new left's unreflective appropriation of old left categories and analysis made it more difficult for women's demands to be heard. With the emphasis on supporting the struggles of the "truly" oppressed, students' concerns and women's issues were dismissed as "bourgeois."

Nor were these radical women entirely immune to such criticisms. Indeed, when Chicago women established the first independent women's group, they were not severing their relationship with the Movement. Although the founders of the women's liberation movement were committed to organizing women apart from men, they still envisioned themselves remaining personally involved in the Movement. Moreover, many radical women wanted the new movement to remain closely tied to the new left, both organizationally and ideologically. In fact, the new left continued to have an enormous influence on women's liberationists, even those who favored an autonomous women's movement. For, as we shall see in chapter 2, this question of the relationship between the women's liberation movement and the larger Movement became a wedge that seriously divided women in the early years of the movement and profoundly affected the development of radical feminist theory.

2

The Great Divide: The Politico-Feminist Schism

Radical women agreed that they needed to organize separately from men, but they disagreed over the nature and purpose of the separation. Indeed, was it a separation or was it a divorce that they wanted? Was it correct for women to exclude men from their meetings not simply for the tactical reason that men dominated discussion, but out of the conviction that women needed "to organize out of the earshot of the oppressor"?[1] Should women's groups focus exclusively on women's issues, or should they commit themselves to struggling against the war and racism as well? What groups of women should be organized—all women or only poor and working-class women? And, perhaps most troublesome of all, what or who was the enemy?

From the beginning radical women debated these questions, often hotly. In fact, these debates were often as corrosive as those engulfing the black movement and the new left during the same period. Within the first year of the women's movement there had emerged two distinct theoretical positions, and by early 1969 women were referring derisively to each other as "politicos" and "feminists."[2] Although the feminist tendency would come to prevail within the women's liberation movement, in the years 1967 and 1968 the feminists—or radical feminists as they came to call themselves—were clearly in the minority. Even in New York Radical Women (NYRW) where they constituted an especially vocal faction, radical feminists were nonetheless "the underdogs."[3] This chapter will examine the development of the women's liberation movement between late 1967 and early 1969, and will explore the movement's early fissures, especially the near lethal politico-feminist schism.

Believing that women's oppression derived from capitalism, or "the system," as they often called it, politicos maintained that women's liberation groups should remain connected and committed to the larger Movement. While politicos acknowledged that women needed to meet in separate, all-female groups, they generally thought of women's liberation as an "important 'wing' of the left; as a tool, perhaps, for organizing as-yet apolitical women into . . . the Movement."[4] Although politicos often viewed women's liberation opportunistically as a way to expand and strengthen the Movement's base, they also deserve much of the credit for organizing the movement. According to Jo Freeman, their very embeddedness in the left—"their contacts and their knowledge of how to organize"—was a major factor in the rapid proliferation of women's liberation groups across the country. Freeman contends that

> the Chicago group, more than any other women's liberation group, was responsible for the growth of the early women's liberation movement precisely because the women who were in it were so well-located in left-wing networks.[5]

But, while their connection to the left facilitated the movement's rapid growth, it also ensured that most of the early groups would be dominated by politicos who were often more responsive to what Chicago activist Marlene Dixon called the "invisible audience . . . of [leftist] male heavies," than to other women.[6]

By contrast, their opposition, the so-called feminists, argued against the subordination of women's liberation to the left, and blamed not only capitalism, but male supremacy and, later, men, for women's oppression. These women were not anti-left as their opponents frequently charged, but they were critical of the left's treatment of women's liberation as peripheral at best, or counter-revolutionary, at worst. They saw themselves "criticizing the left *from the left* for refusing to broaden its analysis to account for women's oppression"[7] [emphasis mine]. However, in their frustration at the left's intransigence, they seemed sometimes to condemn the left as a whole rather than its sexism. Feminists, somewhat more often than politicos, were veterans of the civil rights movement, who, if they were involved in the left, were more likely to see themselves as being on its margins.[8] They were very much influenced by Black Power theorists whose ideas they routinely invoked when arguing for an autonomous women's movement. The fact that they were not entrenched in the left enabled them to advocate an independent women's movement without feeling as if they were betraying all around them.

Of course, these political positions were hardly monolithic. Nor were the lines frozen and static. Most often, politicos came to embrace a more feminist position, although some feminists did move toward sectarian left politics. These categories were also relative. For instance, Jo Freeman felt very much the feminist in Chicago's politico-dominated Westside group, but she felt much more like a politico when she encountered the feminists of NYRW.[9]

The "politico-feminist" fracture made it difficult for radical women to even name their movement. Although the term "women's liberation" was used as early as the summer of 1967 by the SDS women who organized a workshop by that title, the term did not achieve immediate acceptance among radical women. According to Kathie Sarachild, there were those in New York Radical Women who "counseled us that using the term women's liberation was too radical."[10] Amy Kesselman of Chicago remembers that Jo Freeman insisted some years later that she had encountered resistance from other women in the Chicago group when she suggested that they use the term, "women's liberation."[11] Indeed, the earliest groups were called organizations of radical women, such as New York Radical Women, rather than organizations *for* women's liberation. However, "women's liberation" became the preferred term following the Sandy Springs gathering of women's liberationists in August 1968. Cindy Cisler of NYRW believes the term was quickly accepted because it was in the leftist vernacular of "liberation movements."[12] No doubt Freeman helped to popularize the term by entitling the first national women's liberation newsletter, *The Voice of the Women's Liberation Movement*.[13]

But the term "women's liberation" was not nearly as controversial as the term, "feminism." As Shulamith Firestone pointed out in June 1968, that word conjured up images of a "granite-faced spinster obssessed with the vote . . . [or] a woman 'against Nature.' "[14] This was often true even for those who helped establish the contemporary women's movement. For instance, Anne Forer of NYRW admits that she initially disliked the term for she thought it sounded "unfeminine."[15] Moreover, as Amy Kesselman points out, feminism was "one of those horribly discredited terms" because radical women associated it with the first wave of feminism which they dismissed as bourgeois and reformist.[16]

Firestone was the first to publicly challenge radical women's belittling of first-wave feminism.[17] She took other women's liberationists to task for denying the "connection with the old feminism, calling it kop-out [sic], reformist, bourgeois, without having bothered to examine the little . . . information there is on the subject."[18] She maintained that the Stanton-Anthony branch of the feminist movement had been radical, but that its history "had been buried for political reasons."[19] Firestone's reclamation of nineteenth-century feminism was an act of considerable daring since radical men and women regularly cited its deficiencies to prove that an autonomous women's movement would inevitably be counterrevolutionary. In fact, most radical women initially took their inspiration from the revolutionary women of Vietnam, Cuba, and China, and not from earlier generations of feminists. For instance, Marilyn Webb of D.C. Women's Liberation proclaimed the "women's movements of the past irrelevant," but praised the "Vietnamese woman [who] has literally won her equality with a weapon in her hand and through the sheer strength of her arms."[20] Of course, the term "feminism" was eventually rehabilitated, but even many "feminists" preferred the term "radical feminism" because it differentiated them from the reformist branch of the women's movement.[21]

The Jeannette Rankin Brigade Protest

Although the politico-feminist fracture was already somewhat in evidence that fall in the Chicago and New York groups, the January 1968 Jeannette Rankin Brigade protest in Washington, D.C. marked the first of many serious disagreements between these factions. The Jeannette Rankin Brigade (named for the first woman elected to Congress, and the only member of Congress who voted against U.S. intervention in both World Wars) was a coalition of women's groups opposed to the Vietnam war. The Brigade wanted to mobilize American women to petition Congress on its opening day for an immediate withdrawal of all U.S. forces from Vietnam.

To add to the disputatiousness between politicos and radical feminists, there were the predictable generational conflicts that afflicted '60s demonstrations aimed at uniting people across the generational fault line. The older, liberal women planning the protest wanted to ensure that theirs would be a peaceful demonstration, while the younger, leftist women whom they approached about participating felt that nonviolent protest had long since outlived its usefulness. The older women were especially wary of those women trying to launch a women's liberation movement, for they feared that the issue of women's liberation would divert attention and energy away from the primary struggle—ending the war. Charlotte Bunch, who had been active in the politically moderate University Christian Movement and in more radical anti-war groups, was, in her words, "chosen [to speak at the protest] as the compromise candidate to represent young women."[22] However, Bunch's inclusion in the program did not alter the perception of most younger women that the protest was hopelessly liberal. Marilyn Webb spoke for most Movement women—inside and outside the women's liberation movement—when she declared the demonstration "moderate, ineffectual and absurd." Why petition Congress, she asked, when Congress had proven itself "impotent" to end the war, when, in fact, Congress had "never even had the chance to vote on this war"?[23] And radical women in Chicago attacked the Brigade for "petitioning the U.S. Congress rather than talking to the people about taking power."[24]

However, women in NYRW and the Chicago group not only criticized the Brigade's liberalism, but the very idea of organizing an all-women's anti-war demonstration in the first place. Soon after the protest, Heather Booth, Sue Munaker, and Evelyn Goldfield of Chicago argued that "[u]ntil women go beyond justifying themselves in terms of their wombs and breasts and housekeeping abilities, they will never be able to exert any political power."[25] And Shulamith Firestone of NYRW accused the Brigade of "playing upon the traditional female role in a classic manner":

> They came as wives, mothers and mourners; that is, tearful and passive reactors to the actions of men rather than organizing as women to change the definition of femininity to something other than a synonym for weakness, political impotence, and tears.[26]

The New York women criticized the Brigade leadership for reinforcing dominant cultural assumptions about women and urged women to unite not as "passive supplicants," but, rather, as a "political force to be reckoned with . . . [because] power only cooperates with power."[27] Despite their objections to the demonstration, radical women came to Washington to meet and develop a program for radical women and to "appeal to women not to appeal to Congress," or to protest the protest.[28] Radical women were not the only ones perturbed by the Brigade's equation of femaleness with pacifism. Betty Friedan allowed the Brigade to list her among the protest's sponsors, but reportedly said, "I don't think the fact that milk once flowed within my breast is the reason I'm against the war."[29]

The Brigade succeeded in turning out 5,000 women for the demonstration at Capitol Hill on January 15, 1968, as the Ninetieth Congress convened its second session. But the Brigade protest was as feeble as the younger women had predicted. The Brigade was prevented from petitioning Congress when Vice-President Hubert Humphrey invoked a long-standing precedent which barred Congress from conducting any business until after the president had delivered his State of the Union address. According to one account, the women were stranded outside in the snow singing "We Shall Overcome" with folk singer Judy Collins until a small delegation, which included the eighty-seven-year-old Rankin and Coretta Scott King, was permitted inside the Capitol to present their petition to the House speaker and the Senate majority leader.[30] The Brigade's "mild-mannered and liberal opposition" to the war so angered 200 of the younger women that they split off from the Brigade to plan a "militant mass action."[31] However, their plans for a militant protest fizzled when they were unable to agree on an appropriate action.

If the protest was a washout for many of the younger, more militant women, it wasn't for the thirty to fifty women (many of whom belonged to New York Radical Women and the Westside group) who met over a two-day period to develop a program and organization for radical women. They met with the as yet unorganized D.C. women, and although the meeting was not completely harmonious, the D.C. women did decide to begin meeting as a result of these discussions. According to Pam Allen, the group agreed to hold regional conferences that spring to develop ideology and strategy, and to "map out plans for radical women's participation in the resistance at the upcoming Chicago Democratic Convention."[32] Moreover, women from NYRW organized their own demonstration against the protest in Washington—a funeral procession and burial of "Traditional Womanhood" in Arlington Cemetery. According to Firestone:

> we staged an actual funeral procession with a larger-than-life dummy on a transported bier, complete with feminine get-up, blank face, blonde curls, and candle. Hanging from the bier were such disposable items as S&H Green Stamps, curlers, garters, and hairspray. Steamers floated off of it and we also carried huge banners such as "DON'T CRY: RESIST!"[33]

In her "Liturgy for the Burial of Traditional Womanhood," Peggy Dobbins of NYRW urged women to stop "acquiesing to an order /that indulges peaceful pleas/And writes them off as female logic /Saying peace is womanly."[34] The protest marked the first time that the slogan "sisterhood is powerful" was used. In a leaflet for the protest, Kathie Sarachild declared, "Sisterhood is Powerful! . . . Humanhood the Ultimate!"[35]

Despite all the talk about sisterhood, it was not always much in evidence that weekend. New York radical feminists clashed with the Brigade leadership and with the politicos, especially the D.C. women. According to Ros Baxandall, several New York women, including Kathie Sarachild, got into an argument with members of Women Strike for Peace—a major force in the Brigade—about the proper relationship between women's liberation and the larger Movement.[36] Charlotte Bunch remembers finding the New York women "very disruptive and disrespectful of the history of the older women and what the church and peace movement women had really done and were really about." However, she also recalls feeling very excited by the New York women because "I liked what they were doing and saying."[37]

Some radical women like Bunch may have been excited by this contingent of New York radical feminists, but few of them were persuaded by their argument that women should be organizing to end their own oppression rather than the war in Vietnam. Moreover, many of the D.C. women objected to the New York protest against traditional womanhood on the grounds that it was apolitical.[38] To Firestone the D.C. experience demonstrated

> where women, even so called [*sic*] women radicals were *really* at. We confirmed our own worst suspicions that the job ahead, of developing even a minimal consciousness among women will be staggering.[39]

Firestone's assessment of her peers may seem gloomy, but it was not entirely unwarranted. Shortly after the Brigade action Pam Allen and Marilyn Webb wrote separate accounts of the protest which seemed to confirm Firestone's worst fears. Allen's piece was published by the leftist newspaper the *Guardian*, and in it she claimed that "most of the women radicals" who met in D.C. had "moved beyond a mere feminist stance to a position of seeing that women's liberation is intimately bound up with the movement for social change in the U.S." (In fact, most radical women could not have moved beyond feminism because they had yet to embrace it!) Moreover, for Allen the most pressing issue facing women seemed to be the Chicago Democratic Convention, not abortion rights or child care.[40]

Webb's account of the protest seemed designed to appease leftist men who were apprehensive about women's liberation and to rebuke the New York faction with which she had disagreed.[41] She maintained that by shunting women into limited and subordinate roles, the Movement prevented women from doing their share to bring "the system" down. Like other radical women, she argued that the anti-draft movement, in particular, had marginalized women. "Men can refuse induction, burn Draft cards, et cetera, but all women can do in opposing the Draft is to aid and abet." Webb suggested that women remedy the situation by analyzing their "complicity" with the system so they could identify "those places where women could say 'NO!' and cause the same disruption as men do in saying 'NO!' to the draft." Webb believed that women could inflict the greatest damage on the system by challenging consumerism. Indeed, she quoted SDS'ers Bernardine Dohrn and Naomi Jaffe who had recently defined "Woman Power" (they avoided the term "women's liberation") as "the power to destroy a destructive system by refusing to accept its definition of us as passive consumers, for example, and by actively subverting the institutions which create and enforce that definition."[42]

In marked contrast to radical feminists like Sarachild and Firestone who argued that women should organize only around issues of special concern to women, Webb envisioned radical women organizing around "corporate power, militarism, poverty, Vietnam and the 1968 election."[43] Webb emphasized that radical women were organizing for "our own equality *within* this broader struggle" [emphasis mine]. To underscore this, she claimed that radical women understood the importance of remaining "active within other, co-ed . . . movement organizations and actions" while they were "building a women's movement."[44] Whereas Firestone argued that separate women's groups were necessary in large part because "power only cooperates with power," Webb suggested that these groups would give radical women an opportunity to "develop ourselves personally, politically, and as a power base" to gain the Movement's respect.[45] Finally, in an attempt to distinguish herself from the radical feminists of New York, Webb stressed that radical women "are not at all anti-men, but see men as much victimized by this social system as we are." So eager was Webb to prove that radical women like herself were not humorless man-haters, that she added:

> We have developed our own kind of feminity [sic] and enjoy being women who love men and do not see them as the enemy. We are not the cold, gray-suited women of the Twenties, nor the "masculinized" ones of the present. Staid suits have been replaced by the colorful dress of a turned-on generation of women who are asserting themselves as females as well as intellectual politicos.[46]

Early Theory Building

Several important articles appeared in 1968 which illuminate the differences between and within these two camps. Jo Freeman's article "What in the Hell Is Women's Liberation Anyway?" was printed under her movement nom de plume, Joreen, in the *The Voice of the Women's Liberation Movement*.[47] Anxious that women's liberation not be confused with liberal feminism, Freeman asserted that "women's liberation does not mean equality with men" for "equality in an unjust society is meaningless." Rather, she argued that radical women wanted "equality in a just society." While Webb treated women's oppression largely as a Movement problem, Freeman argued that "it is a social problem of national significance not at all confined to our struggle for personal liberation within the Movement." Whereas politicos believed that women should organize to fight "the system"—variously defined as capitalism or imperialism—Freeman advocated "organizing ourselves for our own liberation and . . . organizing all women around issues which directly affect their lives." Freeman was interested in organizing a movement *for* women, not merely one *of* women. However, Freeman shared the politico analysis of women's liberation as a strategy for "organizing other women into the Movement" and thus "thoroly [*sic*] integrating" its leadership and expanding its base. Thus, Freeman situated herself in the middle of the politico-feminist divide, arguing that women should organize around their own interests, yet very much within the larger Movement.

While Freeman tried to avoid the question "Which movement takes precedence?" SDS activist Anne Koedt, writing in NYRW's *Notes from the First Year*, asked women to fight the "primary struggle," by which she meant male supremacy.[48] Citing the example of the Soviet Union, which Koedt contended had "simply transferred male supremacy, paternalism and male power onto a new economy," she suggested that radical women demand that the Movement commit itself to fighting male supremacy. In an explicit rejection of the politico program, she argued that radical women should "begin to expose and eliminate the causes of our oppression as women . . . rather than storming the Pentagon as women or protest[ing] the Democratic Convention as women."

Koedt was not advocating that women withdraw from the Movement, but that women's liberation groups concentrate on women's issues. Finally, Koedt argued that radical women must understand that women's oppression was not merely the fault of "the system," but was rooted in the idea that woman "is at all times secondary to man . . . that her life is defined in terms of him." Although Koedt conceded that women were oppressed by "psychological/economic dynamics," what she emphasized both here and in her later work was the psychological dimension of women's oppression.

With Koedt's article, Firestone's summary of the Jeannette Rankin Brigade protest, and Sarachild's D.C. speech, "Funeral Oration for Traditional Womanhood," NYRW's *Notes from the First Year* was an implicit, and sometimes explicit, rejection of the politico analysis. Within two months of its publication, Evelyn Goldfield of Chicago's Westside group issued a rebuttal of sorts in the *The Voice of the Women's Liberation Movement.* Goldfield took women's groups to task for concentrating on consciousness-raising rather than action. And in contrast to those New York women who argued that women needed to organize separately to build a power base from which to attack male supremacy, Goldfield advised that if men were to be excluded initially from women's meetings, it be for the "tactical" reason that women had difficulty expressing themselves around men, and not as a "matter of principle." In fact, Goldfield argued that the very notion of a separate women's movement was divisive. She admitted that the bromide "there can be no liberation for women outside a general movement for liberation, and no such movement can exist without a movement for women's liberation" had failed to silence those who asked which movement came first. But Goldfield proposed shelving any further debate by declaring that radical women should henceforth "not think of the women's movement as separate but as a united force within the radical movement."[49] She chastised the women of *Notes* for envisioning "the women's movement as very separate from other movement struggles," and declared that a "women's movement which confines itself to issues which only affect women can't be radical." To prove her point, she argued:

> A demand for equal pay is not a critique of meaningless work, a demand for more women professors need not include a radical analysis of the university, a demand for legalized abortion need not raise the question of why the bearing of a child is perceived as a personal rather than a social responsibility, the demand for child-care centers is not in itself a criticism of the familial structure. As soon as we broaden our analysis, issues affecting men are included.

Goldfield not only feared that a separate women's movement would become liberal, but, quite properly, worried that women's issues would become ghettoized in women's liberation groups rather than integrated into the Movement. Goldfield argued that those "questions of life-style, sex, community, [and] personal relationships" which "presently only women discuss in an organized, coherent manner" should be raised in the larger Movement.[50] New York radical feminists agreed that these issues needed to be reconceptualized as human rather than women's issues, and they wanted to see the left tackle these questions in a serious manner. But, unlike Goldfield, they believed that women's oppression was central rather than peripheral, and thus argued that it was incumbent upon the left, not women's liberation, to broaden its analysis. As Firestone would later point out:

> contemporary politicos see feminism as only tangent to " 'real" radical politics, instead of central, directly radical in itself; they still see male issues, e.g., the draft, as universal, and female issues, e.g., abortion, as sectarian.[51]

Indeed, Goldfield's analysis suggested that it was not so much men's responsibility to change as it was women's responsibility to help them change.

Politicos who were distressed by the incipient radical feminism of *Notes from the First Year* must have been outraged by the polemical "Toward a Female Liberation Movement," written by Beverly Jones and Judith Brown, two long-time veterans of CORE and the Gainesville (Florida) SDS. Jones and Brown first published their paper (actually the article consisted of two parts, one written by Jones, the other by Brown) in June of 1968, and it soon became known in movement circles as the "Florida Paper."[52] Later that summer, after Jones had moved to Pennsylvania, Brown and

Carol Giardina co-founded the first women's liberation group in the South—Gainesville Women's Liberation.

Jones and Brown presented the article as a "radical" alternative to the "desegregation model" favored by politicos.[53] Indeed, the "Florida Paper" was nothing less than a frontal assault on the politico position. Jones attacked the June 1967 SDS women's liberation workshop statement for its "NAACP logic and . . . its Urban League list of grievances and demands."[54] Brown excoriated Marilyn Webb for "refus[ing] to acknowledge that for a time at least, men are the enemy," and for contending that women's liberation groups should remain wedded to the larger Movement.[55] With *Notes from the First Year*, the "Florida Paper" was the earliest articulation of radical feminism. Despite its renunciation of left feminism, the "Florida Paper," like other early radical feminist statements, did not represent a repudiation of radical politics. Indeed, Brown emphasized that "[a]ny thorough radical analysis would, of course, incorporate a stance vis-a-vis the war, racism, and the Savage Society."[56] And she maintained that women needed to organize a women's movement most crucially so they could "begin to dismantle this system's deadly social and military toys, and stop the mad dogs who rule us every place we're at."[57]

Although many New York radical feminists were deeply affected by it, the "Florida Paper" nonetheless differed in certain respects from the strain of radical feminism developing in New York City. Whereas the New York group had declared male supremacy the enemy in *Notes from the First Year*, Brown went further, pronouncing *all* men the enemy:

> In the life of each woman, the most immediate oppressor, however unwilling he may be in theory to play that role, is "the man." Even if we prefer to view him as merely a pawn in the game, he's still the foreman on the big plantation of maleville.[58]

And while feminists like Firestone argued that women should form their own movement, they did not suggest that as individuals women should withdraw from the left. Jones may have intended to make such a distinction, but she did not. Jones contended that "[w]omen must resist pressure to enter into movement activities other than their own."[59] And while New York feminists had not excluded the possibility of working with other Movement groups, Brown speculated that it might be "a long and dark passage before [our movement] should risk co-educational alliances or actions."[60] Although Brown suggested that this was only provisionally so, she nonetheless argued that "the most serious problem for the moment is not the war, the draft, the presidency, the racial problem, but our own problem."[61]

There were other differences as well. In contrast to the radical feminists of NYRW who envisioned female separatism as a temporary political strategy confined to the political arena, Brown hinted that women might need to temporarily separate from men in their personal lives as well. She argued that marriage, by keeping women isolated from each other and tied to their oppressors, impeded female solidarity. In fact, Brown maintained that marriage was "to women what integration is to blacks."[62] Therefore, Brown recommended that some women remain single and that married women take periodic leaves of absence from their marriages to "revitalize their commitment to their sex and to the liberation movement."[63] Well before the Boston group Cell 16 made this its program, Brown urged radical women to live in all-female communes and to practice karate and "periodic, self-imposed celibacy"—the latter as a strategy for gaining "time and energy [and] getting themselves together."[64] It might seem strange given their indictment of marriage that both Brown and Jones were married in 1968 when they wrote this paper. But Brown suggests that "it was our very close and on-going marital relationships—that we wanted to preserve and wondered if we could—that caused the heat in our writing."[65]

Whereas New York radical feminists were relatively unconcerned with lesbianism, Brown presciently noted that radical women's "continued fear of homosexuality may be the one last strand by which the male order can pull us back into tow," and thus sabotage the movement.[66] She was the first to suggest that women might begin to explore lesbianism as a result of their involvement in the movement and to contend that women could gain "political strength" from this "non-elitist, non-colonial love." But, unlike the lesbian feminists of the early '70s, Brown argued that all-female communes might make women's "coexistence with *men* in the future all the more equal and all the more humane."[67] [emphasis mine] Finally, like other radical feminists, Brown argued that society should embrace the "traditional female approach: attention to personal needs, caring for others, making decisions on the basis of a multitude of human data."[68] Interestingly, both Jones and Brown, in contrast to other radical feminists, raised the possibility that gender differences might be biologically rooted.[69]

Early Women's Liberation Groups

Who were the women who came together to form the women's liberation movement? To their opponents on the left and the right, they were upper- and upper-middle-class women without legitimate grievances. Although generalizations of this sort are treacherous, it is fair to say that most early women's liberationists were college-educated women in their mid-to-late twenties who grew up in middle-class families. Given the pervasiveness of sex discrimination in the labor force, however, most of these women were unable to parlay their college degrees into good-paying jobs. A few were pursuing careers—Naomi Weisstein as an experimental psychologist, Robin Morgan as an editor at Grove Press, Cindy Cisler as an architect, Ros Baxandall as a social worker, and Ellen Willis as a journalist.[70] But many more were either working as secretaries or waitresses or working for the Movement for subsistence pay, or juggling both.[71] While a number were red diaper babies, they were more commonly raised by liberal parents who revealed to their children, if to no one else, their contempt for McCarthyism. With the exception of Helen Kritzler whose mother belonged to the Lucy Stone League, their mothers were not involved in those remnants of the feminist movement that survived into the '50s.

The Westside Group of Chicago

Although many of the women in the Westside group had been involved in the civil rights movement, most of them identified more strongly with the new left, SDS in particular. The Chicago group began meeting immediately after the NCNP fiasco, and it initially consisted of Heather Booth, Naomi Weisstein, Amy Kesselman, Sue Munaker, Shulamith Firestone, Jo Freeman, Frances Rominsky, and Evelyn Goldfield. Vivian Rothstein, Sara Evans Boyte (who would later write *Personal Politics*), Linda Freeman, and Firestone's sister, Laya, soon joined the group. Booth, Rothstein, Goldfield, Munaker, Weisstein, Evans, and Linda Freeman all had roots in SDS. But Booth, Goldfield, and Rothstein, all of whom had been involved in SDS long before it became *de rigeur* on college campuses, were especially committed new leftists. While Kesselman was not an SDS'er, she was nonetheless deeply involved in the Movement. Politically active since high school, Kesselman had been president of the City College Independent Committee to End the War in Vietnam and had later worked as a field organizer for NCNP. Dissatisfied with NCNP, she left it to work for a radical community organizing project, Citizens for Independent Political Action (CIPA)—whose slogan was "if the Machine shortchanges you, kick it." CIPA, which was formed by former SDS national secretary Clark Kissinger, attracted other Chicago radicals, including Fran Rominsky.[72]

By contrast, Jo Freeman received her political education in the Southern Christian Leadership Conference (SCLC). After graduating from Berkeley where she had been active in the Free Speech Movement, Freeman went South to work for Dr. King's organization. To get a field assignment and avoid what Judith Brown termed "the secretarial tour of duty" that awaited most women in the Movement, Freeman quickly "unlearned how to type."[73] She succeeded, and for most of her sixteen months with SCLC she was the only white woman on the field staff. Shulamith Firestone's activism seems to have been limited to her involvement in a socialist Zionist group.[74] It is not clear if her sister had ever been active in the Movement. Thus, the Firestone sisters, both of whom lacked long-term experience in the American left, and Jo Freeman, who had been involved with the more moderate wing of the civil rights movement, were somewhat anomalous in this group of veteran new leftists.

According to Amy Kesselman, the Chicago women had varying degrees of commitment to women's liberation. She recalls that "it took a bit of wrenching for the people in the group to pull away from the male left, and people did that at different paces, and with varying degrees of anger."[75] However, these differences were largely containable because their views were not widely divergent. The situation might have been different had Shulamith Firestone not moved to New York in October 1967 to organize New York Radical Women with Pam Allen. After Firestone left Chicago she became one of the most important architects of radical feminism, both as the author of the provocative bestseller *The Dialectic of Sex* and as the editor of the 1968 and 1970 women's liberation anthologies, *Notes*.[76]

Sometime after Firestone moved to New York, Freeman claims she was "nudged out" of the group for reasons she does not fully understand.[77] Freeman's problems in the group probably stemmed both from her status as an outsider and from her take-charge style which was very much at odds with the collective ethos of the Westside group. For the Chicago women, as for the movement as a whole, individual initiative was suspect. Most of these women wanted the women's liberation movement to avoid repeating the left's pattern of routinely invoking egalitarianism, while often ignoring it in practice. At points, this commitment to egalitarianism was taken to an extreme as when Munaker, Weisstein, and Goldfield published an article on women's liberation and found it necessary to "apologize to our sisters throughout the country for being so presumptuous as to speak for them."[78]

Freeman's experience in the Westside group devastated her because she felt that she "was being attacked, but no one would admit it."[79] Kesselman concedes that the group had difficulty handling conflict:

> We were terribly inept at dealing with conflict and as a result we shoved it under the rug and tried to pretend it wasn't there. But it came out in these covert and damaging ways which ended up hurting people more.[80]

Excluded from the friendship network and treated as though she were largely "invisible," Freeman dropped out of the group in April 1968. Freeman continued to write about the movement and, in fact, three of her most memorable articles about the women's liberation movement—"The Tyranny of Structurelessness." "Trashing," and "The Bitch Manifesto"—were all attempts "to understand my experience" in the Chicago group.[81] Certainly,

Freeman's experience suggests that the group had some difficulty in assimilating women who were outside its political orbit.

While there was a range of opinion in the Westside group, it was nonetheless decidedly politico in orientation. They tried to avoid discussions that focused on the personal because they believed they should be formulating theory. Freeman argues that group members were afraid to talk about themselves because they were "so bound by the leftist mentality" that favored abstract theorizing. But Freeman agrees with Kesselman that "despite our attempts to remain detached and theoretical we did talk about ourselves."[82]

By contrast to NYRW where this was quite controversial, the Westside group saw itself organizing women around non-gender-related issues and events, specifically the Democratic National Convention. And, like other politicos, they were especially interested in exposing the ways in which consumerism exploited women and sustained capitalism. In fact, Rothstein and several other women tried to interest others in a "uniform" for radical women. Rothstein proposed the uniform "primarily . . . [as] a public way to disassociate ourselves from the 'women as consumer and clothes-horse image.' "[83] Besides raising awareness of women's oppression and creating solidarity among radical women who wore it, Rothstein argued that the uniform "is un-co-optable by the fashion industry unlike our previous uniform of sandals, turtlenecks, and long hair. No clothing manufacturer would adopt the idea of a wardrobe consisting of one dress." Apparently, it did not occur to Rothstein that the vast majority of women might be equally unenthusiastic about a one-dress wardrobe. Indeed, Rothstein suggested that those who feared that a uniform would erode individuality were merely dupes of consumerism. (One such women's liberation dress was produced by California feminists. However, it is doubtful that many dresses were sold because the only thing which distinguished this dress from a McDonald's uniform was its hand-embroidered women's symbol.[84])

Like other early women's liberation groups, the Westside group did become more feminist over time. In an early 1969 article, Munaker, Weisstein, and Goldfield argued that "female liberation . . . gets to the essence of all political questions," and they warned male radicals that radical women might withdraw from the movement unless treated with "dignity, respect and justice."[85] However, they continued to cling to certain politico assumptions. For instance, they emphasized that the women's revolution should remain in the "context of a *total* revolution." [emphasis mine] And they discussed male supremacy as though it were part of capitalism's cultural superstructure rather than its own distinct system. Freeman thinks that the women in the Westside group were afraid to jettison the left analysis of women's oppression because they were invested in accommodating the men in their lives. It is true that a number of women in the group—Heather Booth, Vivian Rothstein, and Evelyn Goldfield—were married to new left heavies. And the men were not above pressuring the women to stop meeting. In fact, Kesselman recalls that Richard Rothstein asked her to disband the group because he felt it was "dividing the Movement."[86] Kesselman ignored Rothstein's plea and the group continued to meet. But as her story demonstrates, the Chicago women were under considerable pressure to make women's liberation conform to the left agenda with a minimum of discomfiture to Movement men. However, precisely because of their years in the left they were enormously effective organizers for the women's liberation movement. Within a six-month period the Westside group organized four other Chicago groups—a Hyde Park group for married women and women's caucuses within CIPA, the New University Conference, and the University of Chicago SDS chapter.[87]

D.C. Women's Liberation

The Washington, D.C. group was even less variegated than the Chicago group because all of its members were deeply involved in the Movement and virtually everyone was in some way associated with the local leftist think tank, the Institute for Policy Studies (IPS). Although D.C. women had discussed the possibility of starting a women's group before the Jeannette Rankin Brigade protest, they did so only after the protest. According to Charlotte Bunch, it was Marilyn Webb who persuaded the others that they needed to form a women's group. Bunch was swayed both by Webb and her former college roommate, Sara Evans Boyte, who was by that point involved in the Westside group.[88] Webb held the first meeting at her "Salvation Army-furnished apartment" and Judith Coburn, Charlotte Bunch, Sue Orrin, Linda Carcione, Sue Thrasher, Barbara Haber, and Marcia Kallen attended.[89] Alice Wolfson, Heidi Steffens, and Norma Lesser, whose husband was at IPS, joined shortly thereafter. These women were seasoned radicals who were, for the most part, deeply enmeshed in D.C.'s left community. For example, Marilyn Webb had been active in SDS for years and had recently been involved in Vietnam Summer, a left-liberal project directed by her husband, Lee Webb, one of SDS's early leaders. She also wrote for the *Guardian*, the self-proclaimed "organ of the new left." Judith Coburn was a journalist whose work was (and still is) published in radical publications. Both she and Charlotte Bunch were IPS's first women fellows. Barbara Haber had been active in SDS since 1962 and was married to Alan Haber, the organization's first president. She and her husband had just moved to D.C. from Ann Arbor so that he could accept a position at IPS. The one woman whose roots really were in the civil rights movement, Sue Thrasher, the former executive secretary of the Southern Student Organizing Committee, chose not to remain in the group.

The D.C. group was especially congenial because the women already knew each other from the local left community. According to both Bunch and Webb, the group was not divided along familiar politico-feminist lines. Bunch contends that the group "was determined not to split" along those lines, and instead tried to incorporate elements of both positions into their analysis.[90] Writing about this conflict in 1971, Bunch remarked:

> The usual DC response to these debates was to discuss the issues, to agree we had to combine some of both sides (i.e. we agreed with feminists that women should organize separately and that men were individually oppressive to women and we agreed with "movement" women that the real cause of our oppression was the system, not the men who were agents of it, and that while organizing separately we still had to address ourselves to other than women's ("broader") issues as well), and to breathe a sigh of relief that we in DC were not so factionalized.[91]

But, in fact, the D.C. women avoided factionalism of this sort because they incorporated so little of the feminist analysis into their own. They talked about their "own problems" with marriage, family, and especially their "own experience of alienation in work," but in terms of "how these problems related to *capitalism*." (emphasis mine) In fact, the D.C. group did not encounter "feminism and a strong men-are-the-enemy position" until the August 1968 Sandy Springs Conference.[92]

The first crack in the congeniality appeared after Sue Orrin had her baby, Chevara—named by Bunch for Latin American revolutionary Che Guevara. Orrin was reportedly "aggressive" about asking others to do child care and her assertiveness made some women in the group angry and resentful.[93] Webb remembers that some women felt, "I didn't choose to have a kid, so why should I take care of yours?" But a large part of the problem seems to have been that the D.C. women found it difficult to accept women whose lives were more typical of non-Movement women. In a 1971 article on the D.C. movement, Bunch admitted that the group's exclusivity undermined their efforts to organize women whose lives differed from theirs:

> In trying to reach out to women different than ourselves, we still did not basically change the nature of our group. Instead, we required that they become more like us to participate. Some did, but others found this impossible.[94]

Frances Chapman, who joined DCWL in 1969, was frustrated by the group's old guard who she felt had "this terrible need to control and were afraid of giving any authority or autonomy to these [new] women." She believes that the founders distrusted the new women in part because they feared that they might talk too freely and to the wrong people about the group's activities. Indeed, Chapman remembers some women were anxious that the group find "ways to organize so we could have security." One woman even suspected Chapman of being an agent. Chapman realized at the time that both her suburban address and her lack of experience in the organized left in D.C. made her vulnerable to that charge. However, Chapman was no novice to the Movement, for she had some experience in the civil rights movement and at least an intellectual understanding of anarchism. She remembers thinking that if they "can't connect to me, then what are they doing to other women who have no experience or prior interest in political activism?" Chapman remained involved in

DCWL despite frequently feeling as though she were the "test case" for feminism, or the "archetypal" new woman. But the paranoia about agents prompted her friend and veteran new leftist, Onka Dekkers, to ask, "Did I have to join the women's movement to belong to a sorority?"[95] This was precisely the problem. These groups were composed of women whose backgrounds were very similar and who were denizens of a Movement subculture which was in some respects as exclusionary as a sorority. The desire for solidarity and security were understandable, but the cliquishness of these groups impeded the acculturation of new women outside the left and promoted parochialism within the movement.

New York Radical Women

According to Ros Baxandall, the difference between the Chicago and New York groups is rather like the difference between Heather Booth and Ellen Willis.[96] Booth was a veteran new leftist who had been actively involved in SDS for years. Her husband, Paul, had twice served as that group's vice-president and once as its national secretary. By contrast, Willis, a rock critic at *The New Yorker*, thought of herself as a leftist, but had no organizational ties to the left. In fact, Willis reports having "always felt like the left was sort of this clique that I was left out of."[97] Baxandall's analogy, if used cautiously, is instructive. Although most of the early members of NYRW had some experience in the new left or the civil rights movement, they were more likely than their Chicago counterparts to feel as though they were on the Movement's periphery rather than at its epicenter. For example, Ros Baxandall was a red diaper baby whose great uncle, Meyer London, had been a prominent socialist. She was a paid staff member at the leftist Mobilization for Youth and was married to Lee Baxandall, a well-known leftist writer. Nonetheless, she thought of herself as "on the fringes" of the new left subculture.[98]

Not only did the New York group include a number of women whose relationship to the left was somewhat attenuated; it also contained several key women who acquired their political education in the civil rights movement rather than in the left. For example, Kathie Sarachild grew up in a "left-leaning middle- to lower-middle class family . . . loving Pete Seeger and Paul Robeson renditions of folk songs and freedom songs."[99] In 1962 while an editor of the Harvard *Crimson* she wrote a series of articles criticizing U.S. policy in Vietnam—three years before the first nationwide protest against the war.[100] However, her political understanding, her sense of how to get people "moving," was formed in the black freedom struggle, specifically as an organizer for the 1964 Summer Voter Registration Project in Mississippi. This was true as well for her good friend Carol Hanisch, a native Iowan who in 1965 quit her job as a UPI reporter to join the civil rights struggle in Mississippi. As several early feminist activists have noted, women like Sarachild and Hanisch who came of age politically in the civil rights movement and who had to personally come to terms with the meaning of black power often saw the need for an autonomous women's liberation movement more quickly than women whose background was primarily in the new left.[101] As Willis observes, "they [not only] supported black power [they] transferred that model" to organizing women.[102] Of course, there were exceptions, most notably, Pam Allen, who had been involved in SNCC and was married to black activist and writer Robert Allen. Despite, or perhaps because of, her experience in SNCC, Allen favored Marxism over black nationalism as it was being articulated within SNCC at the time. She also disagreed frequently with the feminists in NYRW, especially over the relationship of women's liberation to the left, and feminists' fondness for likening women's oppression to that of blacks.

Generally speaking, the New York women were more marginally connected to the Movement and to Movement men than women's liberationists in other parts of the country—some of whom, Baxandall contends, were "practically speaking for their husbands' factions."[103] Of course, not everyone who attended NYRW meetings felt that the group was especially feminist. For instance, Minda Bikman, who lacked any Movement experience, felt that the group was considerably more leftist than it was feminist.[104] However, the New York women were far less constrained by new left orthodoxy than radical women in Chicago, and were, consequently, as Jo Freeman observes, much "freer to experiment."[105]

New York Radical Women was formed by Pam Allen and Shulamith Firestone in the fall of 1967. However, Hanisch reports that she and Sarachild had talked about starting a women's group before they met Firestone. Carl Braden, director of the Southern Conference Education Fund (SCEF), where Hanisch worked, encouraged Hanisch and Sarachild to start organizing women in the city. However, before they could initiate a women's group, they were introduced to Firestone through a mutual acquaintance, Bill Price, who wrote for the *Guardian* and knew Firestone from NCNP.

Although NYRW was not a closed group, it required some skill to locate it. For the first few months before the group acquired the SCEF office for its weekly Thursday night meetings, NYRW met in members' apartments. Its changing venue made NYRW, like other early women's liberation groups, difficult to track down. Cindy Cisler recalls that in those days even locating NOW was a "little like trying to find the early Christians."[106] Estimates of group size vary considerably. Hanisch claims that at its largest there were about twenty to thirty regulars, but that between fifty to sixty women crammed into the SCEF office each week.[107] However, others estimate that at its peak in the fall of 1968 NYRW meetings were attended by about one hundred women.[108] The New York group included a number of the movement's most significant thinkers—women like Kathie Sarachild, Shulamith Firestone, Anne Koedt, Kate Millett, Robin Morgan, and Ellen Willis.[109]

The New York group quickly acquired a reputation for factionalism. To Marilyn Webb it seemed as though the New York women fought constantly among themselves and with women from other cities.[110] Much of the disputatiousness in NYRW was related to the politico-feminist split and was in large part attributable to the fact that the group was not formed from a pre-existing leftist friendship network. From the beginning NYRW was divided along politico-feminist lines. Many of the women in NYRW report that Pam Allen was especially troubled by the feminist faction within the group. Baxandall recalls writing Allen after reading her *Guardian* article on women's liberation. In her letter she said she was "fed up with working on the war and everyone else's issues," and requested information about the group's meeting place and time. Although Allen reportedly never answered her letter, Baxandall did manage to locate the group at the Jeannette Rankin Brigade protest. Sometime after she started attending meetings, she claims that Sarachild told her that Allen had avoided contacting her because she believed that Baxandall favored an autonomous women's movement.[111]

However, Allen's problems with the radical feminists of NYRW are not entirely reducible to the familiar politico-feminist feud. According to Baxandall, Allen's conflicts with Sarachild, in particular, were related to earlier disagreements about the black movement.[112] Sarachild and others routinely likened women's oppression to the oppression of blacks. Allen felt that in using "the black analogy," as it was termed, white women were avoiding their own racism. In a May 1968 interview with Julius Lester, Allen astutely observed that the black analogy

> seems to be an attempt to solve the guilt by saying that we're oppressed too and therefore not really responsible. "It's white men who run the show so it's white men who are guilty."

She also maintained that women should avoid making comparisons between the two liberation movements because "there's a strong contradiction to women making any positive remarks about a movement which has a very strong wing saying, 'put women back in the home.' "[113]

Although feminists generally characterized Allen as a politico, she was hardly a conventional politico. In fact, by May of 1968 she too had grown distrustful of the left.[114] Her clashes with radical feminists in NYRW seem to reflect in part her disagreements with the particular strain of feminism being developed in the group. In fact, the many fissures that developed in NYRW's brief existence would be only imperfectly understood if analyzed exclusively through the prism of the politico-feminist fracture. For instance, in the aftermath of the Brigade protest, Judy Duffett and Peggy Dobbins, both of whom were regarded as politicos, formed their own groups. However, Duffett and Dobbins's actions not only reflected the widening rift between radical feminists and politicos, but their frustration with the group's focus on consciousness-raising and the specific form it took in NYRW. Duffett and Dobbins continued to attend NYRW meetings, but Allen's estrangement from the group was reportedly so complete that by the spring of 1968 she attended only Dobbins's group.

The politico-feminist cleavage was aggravated by the fact that key members of each faction also disagreed on questions unrelated to feminism. A number of the politicos in NYRW were drawn to a particular strand of left politics whose strategy and tactics were very much at odds with those of the civil rights movement and other segments of the left. Robin Morgan and Florika were among those politicos who were drawn to the Yippie style of organizing through outrageous acts. Indeed, they took their inspiration from the Yippies when they formed WITCH (Women's International Conspiracy from Hell)—an offshoot of NYRW—in the fall of 1968. The Youth International Party (or Yippie) was formed in December 1967 and functioned primarily as a vehicle for Abbie Hoffman and Jerry Rubin, two Movement activists who delighted in offending middle-class sensibilities. Their guerrilla theater actions were not designed to raise the consciousness of average Americans whose "straightness" put them beyond the pale as much as they were calculated to capture time on network news programs. The Yippie approach to politics seemed elitist and frivolous to women like Sarachild and Hanisch whose experience in the civil rights movement gave them a far more generous view of ordinary, non-Movement people and persuaded them that the oppressed could best be organized through consciousness-raising rather than through zap actions designed to shock and offend.

Despite the politico-feminist split, NYRW functioned for over a year. Over time, tension escalated as politicos with a tenuous commitment to women's liberation and women with no prior Movement experience joined the group. The schism also widened as radical feminists began to develop a distinct politic which challenged left shibboleths. Although the radical feminist faction was outnumbered by the politicos, they possessed some of the group's most original and compelling thinkers. Nor, according to Willis, were they shy about asserting themselves:

> The radical feminists in NYRW who later formed the core of Redstockings were at first in a sort of underdog position which we were asserting very strongly. There was Kathie [Sarachild] who was a complete tank, Irene [Peslikis] who was totally outspoken, Pat [Mainardi], Shulie [Firestone] and me—hardly retiring, feminine women.[115]

The situation was made more volatile as certain radical feminists developed a dogmatic style which rivaled that of their politico adversaries. By the time Willis joined the group in December 1968—on the brink of its dissolution—the fracture was so great that she felt it was an "issue in which [it seemed] I had to take sides almost immediately."[116]

The group dynamic was made more complicated by the fact that political differences were, according to Willis, in some sense "associated with differences in personality." This was perhaps especially true of Robin Morgan whose flamboyant personality matched her Yippie-inspired politics. Willis felt that

> Robin was very much into creating an image of herself as a radical, bohemian, glamour girl in a certain way which Shulie (Firestone) and Kathie (Sarachild) were just not into at all. They were very blunt. They didn't care who liked them. You could call that personality or you could call it politics.[117]

But, of course, substantive issues divided them as well. Politicos indicted capitalism, especially consumerism, advertising, and the media, while they generally avoided implicating men in women's oppression. For instance, Florika, one of the founders of the New York politico group WITCH argued:

> the corporation is the institution which dominates our lives. . . . Woman is directly oppressed and subjugated by the corporation wherever she functions as a consumer. Her mind is saturated with ads, products and gadgets at all times. She is not only projected by the mass media as an object and a commodity for consumption—she has in fact emulated and reinforced that image by becoming a self-conscious, self-acting commodity.[118]

This line of argument infuriated radical feminists in the group who believed it shifted blame from men to women and felt that the focus of their attack should be male supremacy rather than women's purported complicity with the capitalist system. But it was a very common argument among politicos. For example, Marilyn Lowen of The New Women—a NYRW splinter group—seemed to suggest that women in their role as dutiful consumers had financed the war machine:

> Those same companies [Whirlpool, GE, and Bendix] manufacture anti-personnel weaponry for use against our sisters in Southeast

> Asia and Latin America. But remember, they got their start from us ladies. We got them into BIG business by buying those washing machines or paying rent to use them at the laundromat. Just to fulfill our unwanted task of uniforming "our men" and "our children" properly each day to be respectable looking slaves.[119]

Although Lowen admitted that "men as individuals and as a group do profit from [women's] subordination to them," she nonetheless defined the enemy as "the 3-headed monster of racism, capitalism, imperialism."[120]

In 1975, Sarachild asserted that the "founding women's groups [were clearly] anti-capitalist and anti-racist, as well as anti-male supremacist."[121] Indeed, the radical feminists in NYRW generally argued that women were oppressed by *both* male supremacy and capitalism. In early 1969, Willis wrote that "the American system consists of two interdependent but distinct parts—the capitalist state, and the patriarchal family." She contended that it was "primarily in terms of the family system that we are oppressed *as women*." Willis agreed with politicos that capitalism exploited women "as cheap labor and as consumers," but argued that capitalism exploited women "primarily by taking advantage of women's subordinate position in the family and our historical domination by man." She emphasized that this did not mean that women should abandon the struggle against capitalism because "unless the power of the corporate state is broken, there can be no revolution in the family system."[122] However, many politicos depicted radical feminists as "man-haters" who ignored the inequities of capitalism.[123] Radical feminists deeply resented politicos' "caricature" of them as man-haters.[124] An exasperated Hanisch lamented:

> If we don't blame the capitalist system for everything, they think we hate men. They can't seem to get it through their heads that we can blame men *and* capitalism at the same time. They are so concerned that we think men are *the* enemy that they can't hear anything else we say. They call us everything from "reactionaries" to "cultural nationalists."[125]

However, radical feminists sometimes countered politicos' criticism that they were indifferent to capitalism by arguing that women's liberation would automatically undermine both male supremacy and capitalism. For instance, Willis contended that "to attack male supremacy . . . consistently, inevitably means attacking capitalism in vulnerable places."[126] And at a 1968 women's liberation conference one radical feminist declared that her group believed that "when you talk women's liberation you inherently talk anti-capitalism and anti-private property."[127] As Deirdre English points out, radical feminists were fond of arguing that "feminism alone projected such sweeping and utopian changes that it could socialize the economy as well as revolutionize private relations, the family, and . . . the left itself."[128] For instance, Firestone maintained that radical feminism "alone succeeds in pulling into focus the many troubled areas of the leftist analysis, providing for the first time a comprehensive revolutionary solution."[129] The problem was not that radical feminists opposed economic class struggle, but, rather, that they overestimated the extent to which feminism alone would undermine capitalism.

The grandiosity of radical feminists' claims worried politicos who not only doubted that feminism was comprehensively revolutionary but also feared that an independent women's movement unattached to the left would inevitably degenerate into reformism. For instance, Florika of WITCH maintained that capitalism or "the system" "should be attacked directly" because she doubted that women's liberation was "intrinsically revolutionary" and believed that "the existing system with its technological sophistication might be able to absorb and accommodate" women's demands.[130] To prove their point, politicos cited the example of the woman suffrage movement which they claimed did swing to the right when it severed its ties to the black struggle.[131] What was to keep the women's movement, they asked, from replicating its history or from following in the footsteps of the current civil rights establishment which seemed ready to accept tokenism rather than substantive change? Without an explicitly anti-capitalist analysis, they argued, the women's movement would be unable to resist the system's attempts to co-opt it and would merely advance the interests of white, middle-class women.[132] Politicos' apprehensions were not entirely without foundation, for by claiming that feminism was intrinsically anti-capitalist—that "feminism *includes* socialism"—radical feminists seemed to suggest that class analysis was expendable and thus unintentionally paved the way for cultural feminists who would later dismiss the struggle against capitalism as altogether irrelevant to women's liberation.

The radical feminists in NYRW were perceived by some women inside, and many more outside, the movement as anti-left. However, many radical feminists, including Baxandall and Hanisch, remained involved in the larger Movement. And Willis became very much involved in the leftist GI Coffeehouse movement after having joined the women's movement. All three women maintain that they made a distinction between an individual woman's participation in the left—which they believed was valid, at the very least—and the attachment of women's liberation to the left—which, they argued, resulted in its subordination to the left. In the summer of 1969, Hanisch wrote that "where possible women (as individuals, not as WL) should participate with men in the struggle against worker exploitation."[133] And in May 1969, Sarachild argued that because women "are oppressed in other ways besides as women . . . we have to fight for other issues as well." However, she emphasized that "[w]hen we organize on working class issues . . . we will be organizing as workers, not as women."[134] Radical feminists also held open the possibility of alliances with "radical men on matters of common concern," and they emphasized that rapprochment with the left could be achieved as soon as radical men "grasp that we have a grievance and that we are serious."[135] Hanisch contends that from the beginning she believed that the women's movement should be independent from the left. But she insists she also realized that "neither [movement] would ever succeed without the other's success."[136]

Although radical feminists criticized the left for being insufficiently radical rather than too radical, it is understandable that some people believed that they were anti-left. Increasingly, radical feminists began to argue that the larger Movement was irrelevant to women, and to most people as well. Some radical feminists today admit that they failed to emphasize that their critique of the left did not entail a repudiation of economic class struggle. Their failure to make this distinction adequately left them open to attacks from politicos like Kathy McAfee and Myrna Wood, who argued that "anti-left radical feminists [believe that] the overthrow of capitalism is irrelevant to the equality of women."[137] Both Baxandall and Peslikis acknowledge that some of the women who flooded into the women's movement at a later date might not have understood that radical feminists were, in Peslikis's words, "attacking the left from the left."[138] Baxandall reflects:

> It wasn't so much that we meant the left was the enemy, rather we were making ourselves distinct from those left women who really weren't feminists . . . and were only interested in feminism because they could [use it to] recruit women to the left. That was what we opposed, so perhaps we overstated it sometimes.[139]

If they seemed to condemn the left in blanket fashion, Peslikis contends that it was largely because "we were talking to each other," and assumed that everyone shared an anti-capitalist perspective.[140] However, as the movement grew they were no longer talking with women who understood or necessarily shared their commitment to radical politics. As Willis observes, radical feminists' exclusive focus on male dominance, while unavoidable, put them up against an "insoluble contradiction":

> To build a women's liberation movement we had to take male supremacy out of the context of social domination in general. Yet from the very beginning we ran into problems of theory and strategy that could only be resolved within a larger context.[141]

While the radical feminists of NYRW were angry at men, they were hardly the "man-haters" that liberal and left feminists accused them of being. While they claimed that men oppressed women, they were generally careful to qualify that assertion. For example, Willis argued that "men, as a group, are oppressing us (*in so far* as they uphold and exercise their privileged position in the family system)"[142] [emphasis mine]. And while the radical feminists of NYRW believed that women needed to separate from men in the political arena, they did not counsel women to withdraw from men in their personal lives. Rather, they suggested that women engage men in struggle over their chauvinism. Recognizing that women might find it difficult to confront men individually, they sometimes confronted men as a group, in what they termed "truth squad" actions. For instance, if the group felt that a woman's lover, husband, or employer was mistreating or exploiting her, they would occasionally take it upon themselves to collectively confront him.[143] Although they understood that women's intimate relationship with their oppressors was a political liability in the sense that it inhibited "class consciousness" and solidarity among women, they contended that it could be used to women's advantage as well. Indeed, Firestone declared that "a revolutionary in every bedroom cannot fail to shake up the status quo."[144] Some women in NYRW, most notably Kathie Sarachild, even argued that women benefited more from marriage than from "free love."[145]

Not everyone in the group agreed that women's energies were best spent struggling with men or that marriage was the best bargain for women. In what seems an early prefiguring of cultural feminism, some women argued that women should "develop a sense of [their] true identity" as women rather than confront recalcitrant men.[146] For instance, Pam Allen criticized her adversaries in NYRW for "attack[ing] and push[ing] men into allowing us to be part of their society" rather than focusing on "who and what we are in our own terms." Allen further defied the politico tag when she said of her radical feminist opposition:

> many women who say they are for women's liberation still really are looking towards men for sanction for what they are doing. We have women who still talk in terms of the fact that you need marriage and monogamy because it is the only way to keep a man, whereas there are many of us who are inclined to feel that if men can't take us as human beings, then we'll leave the men.[147]

However, it seems that the predominant feeling among women in NYRW was that men should be challenged, not abandoned. And, although women's liberationists were frequently taunted as lesbians at demonstrations, the members of NYRW do not seem to have questioned the "naturalness" of heterosexuality. The group was overwhelmingly heterosexual and, at least on the surface, uninterested in the question of sexual preference. One woman who belonged to NYRW observes, "When we were called lesbians in NYRW who would have thought that the movement would really become predominantly lesbian?"[148] In fact, there was even some discomfort with the suggestion that the group hold an all-women's party at the conclusion of its first year. Firestone spoke for many members when she reportedly asked, "What's a party without men?" Several members even boycotted the party because no men had been asked.[149] Of course, the fact that others kept making connections between feminism and lesbianism made it difficult for radical feminists to avoid the issue of sexual preference for long.

While the politico-feminist fracture was the major conflict in NYRW, the group clashed over other issues as well. These fissures were sometimes related to the politico-feminist split, but they should not be viewed reductively as mere manifestations of the larger fracture. One of these was the debate over the importance of consciousness-raising and the form it should take. Amy Kesselman describes consciousness-raising as "the political reinterpretation of one's personal life."[150] The purpose of consciousness-raising, according to its principal architects in NYRW, was to "awaken the latent consciousness that . . . all women have about our oppression." In talking about their personal experiences, it was argued that women would come to understand that what they had previously believed were personal problems were, in fact, "social problems that must become social issues and fought together rather than with personal solutions."[151] Sarachild maintained that consciousness-raising was crucial in developing a sense of "class consciousness" and class solidarity, or "sisterhood," among women. More controversial was her insistence that the movement's theory and strategy be based upon the insights that emerged from consciousness-raising.[152]

The group began doing consciousness-raising at an early meeting when Anne Forer, having "no idea how women were truly oppressed," suggested that they go around the room so that each woman could describe the ways in which she felt oppressed as a woman. She suggested that this process might "raise her own consciousness" about women's oppression. The discussion that followed proved revelatory, and the women reportedly decided to spend more time raising their consciousness.[153] Sarachild subsequently coined the term "consciousness-raising."[154] While the term may have been coined in NYRW, the technique of consciousness-raising did not originate in this group. As a civil rights worker in Mississippi, Sarachild knew that the sharing of personal problems, grievances, and aspirations could be a radicalizing experience. In a 1973 speech, she explained, "[w]e were applying to women and to ourselves as women's liberation organizers the practice a number of us had learned in the civil rights movement in the South in the early 1960's."[155] The proponents of consciousness-raising took their inspiration from the civil rights movement where the slogan was "tell it like it is," the Chinese revolution when peasants were urged "to speak pains to recall pains," and from the revolutionary struggle in Guatemala where guerrillas used similar techniques.[156]

Sarachild declared that all previous theorizing about women was inadequate and maintained that women were the only genuine experts on women. As Irene Peslikis puts it, "we felt we were the repository of real information about women."[157] In constructing theory from personal experience, Sarachild argued that they "were in effect repeating the 17th century challenge of science to scholasticism: 'study nature, not books,' and put all theories to the test of living practice and action."[158] The technique of going around the room was used "to get the experience of as many people as possible in the common pool of knowledge," apparently not, as was widely believed, as a measure to ensure that everyone participate equally. Sarachild and others argued that consciousness-raising would bring the group "closer to the truth" from which theory could be developed and appropriate action taken.[159]

However, some women's liberationists questioned whether theory should be constructed primarily from personal experience.[160] This was especially true of politicos who felt that left theory could prove instructive in understanding women's oppression. Marlene Dixon of Chicago argued that their eschewal of left theory was "anti-intellectual."[161] But Willis contends that those who lobbied for consciousness-raising were not opposed to "reading per se, but [were] against this reliance on the authoritative written word to the complete exclusion of other kinds of knowledge." Willis does acknowledge that they were ambiguous on this point:

> There were a lot of contradictions. On the one hand Kathie [and others] were saying, "we must look at our own experience and criticize all other previous ideologies." And on the other hand,

> they were saying, "look at history, we have to learn what other people have said."[162]

Both Alix Kates Shulman and Cindy Cisler suggest that in emphasizing consciousness-raising as the foundation of theory, Sarachild and others were trying to counter the recondite rhetoric of the left with "straight talk and simple language."[163] Sarachild was undoubtedly influenced by Mao, who maintained that education did not necessarily bring one closer to the truth and who cautioned revolutionaries against reading too many books, even those with a Marxist orientation.[164] Her thinking also bears the obvious influence of SNCC organizers who, like Mao, developed a great respect, sometimes bordering on reverence, for the wisdom of "the people"—a respect embodied in the SNCC slogan "let the people decide." However, some of "the people" in NYRW—the non-Movement women with little or no college education—thought it elitist of Sarachild, who after all had been schooled at Harvard, to counsel them against reading theory. For example, Irene Peslikis, a working-class Greek woman, shared Sarachild's commitment to consciousness-raising but also wanted to understand Marxist theory, and she resented Sarachild's advice that she avoid reading it. "I didn't want to be ignorant. I wasn't afraid that [reading Marxist theory] was going to destroy my authenticity."[165]

Moreover, women on both sides of the politico-feminist divide were concerned that consciousness-raising was being done to the exclusion of action. Again, politicos were more likely than radical feminists to complain about this, but some radical feminists were also uneasy about the dearth of action. For instance, Baxandall, who was on the feminist side of the split, admits that she was influenced by the "knee-jerk activism of the anti-war movement," but explains that she and others "wanted to oppose the war. We liked direct actions and missed them."[166] It is crucial to remember that by 1968—a pivotal year marked by the assassinations of Martin Luther King and Robert Kennedy, violence in 125 cities in the aftermath of King's assassination, the student strike at Columbia, and the police riot at the Chicago Democratic Convention—people across the political spectrum believed that the country was moving inexorably toward revolution or fascism. Some radicals even argued that "the system" could be defeated if Movement people would just overcome their "middle-class" aversion to violence. For those radical feminists, who, like others, mistook a conflagration for the revolution, it was hard to resist feeling that by engaging in consciousness-raising they were abdicating their responsibility to actively resist the system. Pam Kearon remembers one occasion in particular when Judy Thibeau declared that "we were indulging ourselves" by even holding NYRW meetings.[167]

While radical movements frequently used consciousness-raising as an organizing tool, they also typically demanded that personal needs be subordinated to the needs of the Movement. As we have seen, by late 1967 the new left was certainly moving in this direction. Jean Tepperman, who was involved in ERAP and later in the Boston politico group Bread and Roses, suggests that for women like herself who were accustomed to putting the Movement's needs first and to "fighting self" like Chinese revolutionaries, "the women's movement seemed to offer opportunities to accept one's own needs as legitimate." However, Tepperman also felt that this "had to be kept in perspective, [as it involved] the temptation to go all the way to extreme personalism."[168] Tepperman speaks for many politicos and radical feminists who sometimes wondered if consciousness-raising wasn't a retreat from action into self-indulgent "personalism." However, Sarachild and Hanisch seem not to have been plagued by such doubts. Sarachild cautioned against "mindless activism" and argued that action was only appropriate after it had been thoroughly analyzed in consciousness-raising sessions.[169] Hanisch went even further and defined consciousness-raising as "a political action."[170]

But the desire for activism led some members of NYRW to engage in all-female protests unrelated to women's oppression. Baxandall and others considered carrying out an action against the House of Revlon beauty salon because they thought the company was involved in the manufacture of napalm.[171] On another occasion, at Florika's suggestion, a number of NYRW members participated in an April 1968 anti-war demonstration as a contingent from NYRW. They dressed like Vietnamese women, handed out leaflets about women's liberation to women only, and ran through the crowd ululating like the Algerian women in Gillo

Pontecorvo's 1966 film, "The Battle of Algiers." Sarachild labeled these actions "reactionary" because she believed that women should organize as people rather than as women when the cause was unrelated to gender:

> Only if the *stated* purpose of a women's group is to fight *against* the relegation of women to a separate position and status, in other words, to fight for women's liberation, only then does a separate women's group acquire a revolutionary character. Then separation becomes a base for power rather than a symbol of powerlessness.[172]

However, Baxandall maintains that their participation in anti-war demonstrations was productive because they did establish a women's presence which in turn helped them recruit women to the movement.[173]

Initially politicos and liberal feminists derogated consciousness-raising as "therapy," or as so much "navel-gazing," as Betty Friedan put it.[174] Yet the proponents of consciousness-raising made every effort to distinguish it from therapy. They argued that the purpose of consciousness-raising was to analyze male supremacy in order to dismantle it, while the purpose of therapy was to carve out personal solutions to women's oppression.[175] Years later, Sarachild contended that the purpose of consciousness-raising had always been social transformation as opposed to self-transformation:

> The purpose of hearing people's feelings and experience was not therapy. . . . The importance of listening to a woman's feelings was collectively to analyze the situation of women, not to analyze *her*. The idea was not to change women, not to make "internal" changes except in the sense of knowing more. It was and is the conditions women face, it's male supremacy, we want to change.[176]

Of course, no one denies that consciousness-raising had a salutary effect on those who did it. Peslikis believes that in exposing "the objective reality, consciousness-raising made everybody feel better about themselves because they could see the truth for a change."[177] Cisler maintains that while "c-r isn't therapy, it's certainly therapeutic."[178] And at the time, Hanisch wrote that consciousness-raising was therapeutic in the sense that it eliminated women's "self-blame."[179]

However, Hanisch and others contend there were women in the group who envisioned the consciousness-raising group as an "uncritical support group."[180] In her widely reprinted 1970 article, "Free Space," Pam Allen maintained that consciousness-raising should take place in a "*non-judgmental* space"[181] [her emphasis]. Allen stressed the psychological benefits rather than the theoretical breakthroughs which could be achieved through consciousness-raising. Indeed, Allen believed that consciousness-raising should "free women to affirm their own view of reality and to think independently of male-supremacist values."[182] By contrast, Sarachild felt that the purpose of consciousness-raising was to develop "generalizations" about women's lives from which theory could be made and male power challenged.[183] Allen also wanted the consciousness-raising sessions to be more structured. Yet in the early days of NYRW, these sessions were spirited and unstructured, during which people freely interrupted one another. And while Sarachild carefully avoided passing judgment on others' lives, she did not hesitate to challenge anyone's testimony. Sarachild's style was, in fact, confrontational. She reportedly pushed people, especially if she suspected they were resisting identifying with other women. Although Sarachild eschewed therapy, Baxandall maintains that her style in consciousness-raising sessions was "delving and penetrating. Kathie would question people after they had talked. She'd say, 'what *aren't* you saying?' and [proceed] to ask twenty-five questions." Baxandall thought Sarachild's style was "brilliant," but some women found her more intimidating than illuminating.

Sarachild's approach to consciousness-raising helped to spark the debate about egalitarianism, which in NYRW was dubbed "let the quiet women talk." Variations of this debate occurred in women's liberation groups across the country, but the debate seems to have been especially heated in NYRW where this sort of unstructured, confrontational method of consciousness-raising allowed some women to dominate discussion. The major proponents of egalitarianism were Pam Allen, Judy Thibeau, and Judy Duffett, while those who were most often attacked for dominating discussion were Kathie Sarachild, Shulamith Firestone, Ros Baxandall, and Ann Forer. Baxandall reports having felt that the proverbial "quiet women" should be made to feel comfortable, but also that the anti-leader line was "a put-down of women who didn't fit the feminine stereotype." Baxandall argues that "the quiet women were much more feminine, polite, sweet, and quiet" and were censorious toward those women who were not.[184] While Willis believes that the issue was handled poorly, she maintains "it was a legitimate demand for people to make [because] the people who talked easily wanted to talk all the time."[185] Perhaps because most of the women who favored egalitarianism were politicos, Hanisch argues that the issue was used to silence the radical feminist faction. However, even Hanisch admits that at the time she supported the anti-leader line because she was "particularly bitter about the 'honcho' type of leadership of the left." Although the "quiet women" may have been invoked upon occasion to muzzle radical feminists, the issue reflected women's genuine desire to develop a group process not predicated upon dominance and subordination. Of course, as Firestone observed, the movement's concern with internal democracy presented strong women with something of a conundrum:

> And though it is true that many females have never assumed the dominant . . . role, there are many others who, identifying all their lives with men, find themselves in the peculiar position of having to eradicate, at the same time, not only their submissive natures, but their dominant natures as well, thus burning the candle at both ends.[186]

Cindy Cisler takes a less sanguine view, maintaining that the emphasis on egalitarianism "hobbled people who had escaped certain things that others had been saddled with."[187] Although consciousness-raising was modified by subsequent groups to promote equal participation and support, the issue never died; it reemerged in somewhat different form as the "equality issue," the "leadership issue," and the "class issue."

There was another problem with consciousness-raising which was not voiced at the time, but which had long-term consequences for the movement. Since the purpose of consciousness-raising was the awakening of "class consciousness" and "sisterhood," women's similarities were stressed and their differences largely ignored. Sarachild's consciousness-raising guidelines encouraged women to analyze "whatever privileges we may have—

the white skin privilege, the education and citizen of a big power nation (imperialist) privileges . . . [and to see] how these help to perpetuate our oppression as women, workers, etc.''[188] But Sarachild makes it clear that consciousness-raising organizers like herself

> made the assumption, an assumption basic to consciousness-raising, that most women were like ourselves—not different—so that our self-interest in discussing the problems facing women which most concerned us would also interest other women.[189]

And Hanisch contends that "our theory [of consciousness-raising] was that differences still had a common root.''[190] Ann Snitow, who helped form New York Radical Feminists in 1969, notes:

> The dream was that underneath our differences, our oppression unified us in a very fusing way. Women's experience had an interior coherence—both political and historical. There was a great desire to find in those c-r questions that, different as we all were, we were not. The c-r questions structured the answers.[191]

Although Snitow believes that consciousness-raising can be "quite a strong intellectual tool,'' she admits that its usefulness depended in large part upon the particular group:

> The good c-r groups allowed material that contradicted the fantasy feminist answers. The less successful groups I visited [were those in which] people were hysterically scrambling to get the line down so they could be stamped.[192]

The premise behind consciousness-raising was that women's experience was in some sense universal, and that gender, not race or class, was the primary and defining contradiction. While radical feminists acknowledged that some women enjoyed more privileges than others, they suggested that class and racial conflicts, when properly analyzed in consciousness-raising, could be overcome or transcended by eschewing "equality in an unjust society,'' and identifying with those women who were the most downtrodden. Willis admits:

> we were acting on the unconscious racist assumption that our experience was representative, along with the impulse to gloss

> over racial specificities so as to keep the "complication of racism" from marring our vision of female unity.[193]

Snitow now finds the way in which race was ignored "unbearable. I'm ashamed."[194] Certainly, the new left's insistence that class and race were by far the most serious social divisions and its denigration of women's liberation as a white, middle-class movement, also contributed to radical feminists' tendency to overstate the significance of gender. Radical feminists' claims that women constituted a universally oppressed class also enabled them to feel that they were legitimate agents of revolutionary change. Willis acknowledges that feminism seemed a way to escape the dilemma facing white, middle-class radicals whose privileged position, many argued, disqualified them as revolutionaries:

> we no longer had to see ourselves as privileged people wondering where we fit into the revolutionary struggle; we too were part of an oppressed class with a historic destiny.[195]

Consciousness-raising not only reflected radical feminists' discomfort with difference, it also contributed to the muting of differences. Snitow believes that consciousness-raising would have revealed "enormous hidden tensions and differences" had women been asked to explore their class identification.[196] But even in NYRW, which was overwhelmingly white and middle-class, differences did emerge. While consciousness-raising discouraged women from articulating their differences, it would seem that for some working-class women, it further distanced them from the middle-class women in the group. Pam Kearon argues, as have others, that middle-class women who had been "therapized" tended to be more comfortable with consciousness-raising than were working-class women.[197]

Finally, NYRW was divided over the question of whether women's behavior was determined by material conditions or conditioning. Many radical feminists—most notably Cell 16 of Boston and The Feminists of New York City—argued that women's behavior demonstrated the extent to which they were conditioned to see themselves as men's inferiors. They assumed that women complied with the system largely because they were brainwashed into believing that they must. By contrast, radical feminists who subscribed to what they called the "pro-woman

line" argued that "women as oppressed people act out of necessity . . . not out of choice."[198] They maintained that women's apparent acquiescence to the system reflected their powerlessness, not their diffidence or passivity. Or, as Hanisch put it, "[w]omen are messed over, not messed up!"[199] If women did not rebel, Willis contended in 1969, it was because they understood too well the risks involved in defying the male supremacist order. "If we step out of line too often, the penalties are loneliness, sexual deprivation and in most cases the economic and spiritual dead end of menial jobs."[200]

Patricia Mainardi, NYRW member and author of the widely read article "The Politics of Housework," suggests that many radical feminists in NYRW had an "allergic reaction" to the conditioning thesis which they felt implied that women were damaged and, in some important respects, complicitous in their oppression.[201] According to Willis, radical feminists developed the pro-woman line

> to counter the prevalent *anti*-woman line—put forward by leftist women (all of whom were needless to say, white, middle-class, educated and childless)—that women who rebelled against the traditional female role (i.e. lefties and bohemians) were "liberated," while women who hadn't, who'd gotten married and had children instead of joining SDS (i.e. most women), were "brainwashed."[202]

This is not to suggest that all radical feminists in New York wholeheartedly supported the pro-woman line. In fact, many radical feminists later criticized it, especially when it was amplified in the New York group, the Redstockings. But many radical feminists initially found the pro-woman line a very persuasive model for understanding women's apparent compliance with the system. The fact that the radical feminist faction in New York favored the pro-woman line, while the politicos generally preferred the conditioning thesis, meant that the debate was defined as yet another wrinkle in the politico-feminist struggle.

The Miss America Protest and the Dissolution of NYRW

Tensions between the politicos and the pro-woman feminists of NYRW escalated as a result of the Miss America protest on September 7, 1968. The Atlantic City protest was initiated by NYRW and was its most significant action. It also marked the end of the movement's obscurity because the protest—the movement's first national action—received extensive press coverage. Carol Hanisch came up with the idea for the protest that summer after watching Gunvor Nelson's mid-'60s, experimental, feminist film "Schmearguntz," containing footage of the Miss America Pageant.[203] Approximately one hundred women's liberationists from New York, Boston, D.C., Detroit, Florida, and New Jersey gathered in Atlantic City to protest the pageant's exploitation of women. From early afternoon until midnight, they picketed the pageant and performed guerrilla theater on the boardwalk before what one *New York Times* reporter characterized as "650 generally unsympathetic spectators."[204] They refused to speak with male reporters—an action designed to force newspapers to pull women reporters from the society pages to which women were typically relegated. And for most of the action they reportedly refused to speak to men. When queried about the policy, Marion Davidson said, "Why should we talk with them? It's impossible for men to understand."[205] (Indeed, when Kathie Sarachild discovered that her sixty-five-year old grandmother was talking with one of the male onlookers, she reportedly yelled at her to stop.[206]) Like the Yippies who the previous week had nominated a pig for the presidency at the Chicago Democratic Convention, they crowned a live sheep "Miss America." They paraded the sheep on the boardwalk to "parody the way the contestants (all women) are appraised and judged like animals at a county fair."[207] Some women chained themselves to a life-size Miss America puppet to emphasize women's enslavement to "beauty standards." They tossed "instruments of torture to women"—high-heeled shoes, bras, girdles, typing books, curlers, false eyelashes, and copies of *Playboy, Cosmopolitan*, and *Ladies Home Journal*—into a "Freedom Trash Can."[208] (It is interesting to note that NOW members just a few months earlier "made a ceremony of dumping aprons into a huge trash pile" as part of their Mother's Day protest to demand that the Equal Rights Amendment be brought before Congress for a vote.[209]) Although the protestors had hoped to burn the contents of the "Freedom Trash Can," they were prohibited from doing so by the city which purportedly wanted to prevent another fire from breaking out on its flammable boardwalk.[210]

The women decided to comply with the city order because they envisioned the protest as a "zap action" to raise the public's consciousness about beauty contests rather than as an opportunity to do battle with the police. Alluding to the recent violence at the Democratic Convention, Robin Morgan told a reporter, "We don't want another Chicago."[211] The protestors were also anxious to avoid arrests because the group lacked the resources to cover legal expenses. Although it was widely reported in the mainstream media that the women burned a bra during the protest, there was, in fact, no bra-burning. Most feminist accounts of the protest suggest that the media invented the bra-burning to discredit the movement. But at least one of the organizers of the protest reportedly leaked word of the bra-burning to the press to stimulate media interest in the action.[212] Those feminists who sanctimoniously disavowed the bra-burning as a media fabrication were either misinformed or disingenuous.[213]

But if they failed to burn a bra, they did disrupt the pageant as it was being broadcast into millions of homes. Alix Kates Shulman purchased sixteen tickets to the pageant so they could stage a protest inside the auditorium. The women "tried to disguise themselves with 'straight' clothes and lots of makeup," but the security guards suspected they were demonstrators.[214] As the outgoing Miss America read her farewell speech, four or five women unfurled a large banner which read, "Women's Liberation," and all sixteen women shouted, "Freedom for Women," and "No More Miss America." The television audience knew that something unexpected had happened, for they heard shouting, saw that heads were turning and that suddenly Miss America was trembling and stuttering. But viewers did not know exactly what had transpired because the producer reportedly ordered the camera crew to ignore the protest. The police, anticipating trouble, quickly ushered the protestors out of the hall, and five of the women were arrested. All charges were subsequently dropped. Earlier that evening, in a controversial action which had not been authorized by the group, Peggy Dobbins sprayed Toni home-permanent spray around the mayor's box in the auditorium. She was arrested and charged with disorderly conduct and "emanating a noxious odor."[215] What was wonderful about Dobbins's action was that in declaring Toni, one of the pageant's sponsors, a "noxious odor," the police ended up doing the movement's work for it. But the "do-your-own-thing" attitude implicit in Dobbins's renegade action annoyed a number of other demonstrators who felt the group should have been consulted.[216]

While the protest was collaboratively conceived, Robin Morgan, who had recently joined the group, did the bulk of the organizing. Many NYRW members credit Morgan with the widespread coverage given the protest. According to Baxandall, Morgan had extensive contacts in the media from her days as a child actress on the television program "I Remember Mama," and she used them now.[217] However, some women felt that Morgan took control of the action and resented her for that.[218] Moreover, the pro-woman faction charged that Morgan and her friends distorted the protest's original message, transforming it from an attack on the pageant to an attack on the contestants themselves. In a lengthy critique of the action, Hanisch argued:

> One of the reasons we came off anti-woman was our lack of clarity. We didn't say clearly enough that we women are all *forced* to play the Miss America role—not by beautiful women but by men who we have to act that way for and by a system that has so well institutionalized male supremacy for its own ends.[219]

Politico Judith Duffett contended that their "purpose was *not* to put down Miss America but to attack the male chauvinism, commercialization of beauty, racism and oppression of women symbolized by the Pageant."[220] But the demonstration's "Ten Points," which Morgan wrote and were distributed as NYRW's explanation of the protest, confirms Hanisch's contention. The first point read:

> Pageant *contestants* epitomize the roles we are all forced to play as women. The parade down the runway blares the metaphor of the 4-H county fair, where nervous animals are judged for teeth, fleece, etc. . . . So are women in our society forced to compete for male approval, enslaved by ludicrous "beauty standards" we ourselves are conditioned to take seriously.[221] [emphasis mine]

And Hanisch pointed out that many of the posters and aspects of the guerrilla theater were "anti-woman":

> Posters which read "Up Against the Wall, Miss America," "Miss America Sells It," and "Miss America Is a Big Falsie" hardly raised any woman's consciousness and really harmed the cause of sisterhood. Miss America and all beautiful women came off as our enemy instead of as our sisters who suffer with us. . . . Also, crowning a live sheep Miss America sort of said that beautiful women *are* sheep.[222]

Certainly, chants such as "Ain't she sweet/making profit off her meat" did seem to indict the contestants. Finally Hanisch criticized the "hippie/yippy" lingo that the protestors used and called upon women's liberationists to "abandon the 'in-talk' of the New Left/Hippie movements" in an effort to reach "the masses of women."[223]

However, everyone involved with the protest felt that they had succeeded in jeopardizing the pageant's future. In the aftermath of the protest it was revealed that Pepsi-Cola had withdrawn its sponsorship and that pageant officials were considering taping the show without a studio audience to avoid the embarrassment of another such disruption.[224] This was enough to make Judith Duffett speculate that with continued pressure from the movement the pageant might be forced to fold for lack of contestants and judges.[225]

While the protest in Atlantic City put the women's liberation movement on the map, it also further destabilized NYRW. The demonstration aggravated tensions between pro-woman radical feminists who felt that the protest conclusively proved the need for continued consciousness-raising and politicos who felt that the movement had finally shown what it was capable of in Atlantic City. Finally, a group of politicos decided to form an action-based group, WITCH. Robin Morgan, Florika, Peggy Dobbins, Judy Duffett, Cynthia Funk, and Naomi Jaffe were among the "approximately 13 heretical women" who comprised WITCH. WITCH was reportedly inspired by HUAC's decision to hold hearings to investigate Communist involvement in the demonstrations during the August 1968 Democratic Convention. In late September, HUAC subpoenaed a number of prominent male radicals—including Dave Dellinger, Abbie Hoffman, Jerry Rubin, and Tom Hayden—to appear before the Committee. Baxandall reports that the mood among New York women's liberationists was, "How come we, the real subversives, the real witches, aren't being indicted?"[226] WITCH undertook its first action, appropriately enough, on Halloween when they dressed up as witches and descended upon Wall Street to "hex" the financial district. Carol Hanisch felt that the action was little more than an "attempt to keep up with Abbie Hoffman [who had earlier] thrown money at the stock market."[227] Several years later, Morgan conceded that the action "emphasized the class struggle between the rich and the poor with little mention about the class struggle between the class of *men* and the class of *women*."[228] Indeed, in one of their earliest pronouncements, WITCH targeted corporate America, not men, as the enemy:

> WITCH is a total concept, a new dimension of women. It means breaking the bond of woman as a biologically and sexually defined creature. It implies the destruction of passivity, consumerism and commodity fetishism. . . . Who is the enemy? WITCHes must name names, or rather we must name trademarks and brand names.[229]

And in a later statement, WITCH pledged itself to "freeing our brothers from oppression and stereotyped sexual roles."[230] Morgan later dismissed their Yippie style as "clownish proto-anarchism," and admitted that the women of WITCH had not "raised our own consciousness very far out of our own combat boots."[231] Although the general wisdom among radical feminists in NYRW was that WITCH's feminism was rather "mealy-mouthed," a number of them did occasionally participate in WITCH actions because they too longed for activism.[232]

In their subsequent actions, the women of WITCH at least tried to address women's issues. However, they often did so in a way that betrayed their contempt toward non-Movement women. The most egregious example of this was their February 1969 protest of the Bridal Fair at Madison Square Garden. To publicize their Bridal Fair action, WITCH glued stickers across the city which proclaimed, "Confront the Whore-makers"—a clever play on the leftist battle cry, "Confront the Warmakers." Incredibly, though, they had not considered the possibility that the women attending the fair might resent WITCH's characterization of them as prostitutes in the making. To make matters worse, WITCH members appeared at the fair wearing black veils and sang, "Here come the slaves/off to their graves." They topped off their protest by releasing live white mice into Madison Square Garden.[233] Radical feminists excoriated WITCH for reinforcing sexist stereotypes and noted with pleasure that the women attending the fair did not respond by scrambling desperately to stand on their chairs but, rather, tried to save the mice.[234] Radical feminists contended that actions such as these whose sole point seemed to be "we're liberated, and you're not" only served to distance the movement from its natural constituency. They argued that actions should be done in a manner that promoted dialogue and developed consciousness. In fact, Hanisch remembers talking with Sarachild after the action and agreeing that it would have been more productive had feminists run a sex education workshop at the fair.[235] What made WITCH especially galling to radical feminists was that it was immediately embraced by the left as embodying the right kind of feminism, one that attacked "the system" and eschewed consciousness-raising. WITCH women continued to participate in NYRW, although by the end tensions ran fairly high. Interestingly, sometime after the disastrous Bridal Fair protest, WITCH abandoned action for consciousness-raising.[236]

At roughly the same time that WITCH was formed, Marilyn Lowen and Joan Lester (who was married to radical black writer Julius Lester) established another group called "The New Women." Unlike the women of WITCH who spoke to "young, hip Leftist" women like themselves, The New Women were interested in organizing traditional women around issues of daycare and job discrimination.[237] The members described themselves as sixteen "very political women," most of whom had children and had been active in "the union, peace, and civil rights movements." In what seems a rejection of the radical feminist position in NYRW, they argued that the "particular . . . form of brainwashing to which we are subject" could not be solved "through discussion alone—but only through group action, especially as involves working-class and poor women." While the group certainly tackled issues that were important to the vast majority of women, they received little publicity and apparently had very little impact within the women's liberation movement.

The situation in NYRW probably would not have deteriorated so rapidly were it not that the Atlantic City protest flooded the group with new members. According to Baxandall, the sudden growth was "too much for us."[238] The fluid, unstructured meetings to which the regulars had grown accustomed no longer worked now that there were fifty to one hundred women crammed into the tiny SCEF office. The "mob meetings" that fall were, by many accounts, unwieldy and frustrating,[239] made infinitely more trying by the sectarian left women who began frequenting NYRW meetings in the wake of the protest. Their relentless attacks on radical feminists as "man-haters" convinced many in NYRW that the leftist newcomers were more interested in disrupting the group than in building a women's movement. In fact, many NYRW members believe that these women had been instructed by their leftist groupuscles or possibly by some agency of the government to obstruct NYRW. Barbara Mehrhof, who joined the group immediately before the pageant action, claims that "there was always a provocateur who would get up and berate us for being so self-indulgent [as] to talk about our situation as women." To Patricia Mainardi it seemed that

> As the movement grew, so did the number of women whose commitment to the women's liberation movement was more tenuous. Your feeling was that these were people who were there to stop anything from happening. I would not be the slightest bit surprised [to discover] that there were agents and reactionaries there.[240]

No doubt, some of the left women who showed up that fall at NYRW meetings had been ordered to direct or, failing that, to subvert the group. Much of the left felt that the growth of the women's liberation movement could only weaken the left. Nor, according to Mainardi, did it require much finesse or skill to obstruct a NYRW meeting:

> It was a problem made worse by a superdemocratic structure where we would have to listen to the [left women] forever. And, the next week somebody new would come in. You'd have to say, "the floor's your's. Bore me again." . . . If you were committed to letting everybody talk, that's what you got.[241]

Dissatisfaction with the meetings was considerable, and by mid-December a number of women proposed dividing the group into smaller groups. The majority of women voted to reorganize into three groups which would be randomly configured by lot. However, not everyone was concerned about the group's swollen size. Hanisch contends:

> Almost all the founders wanted to keep the large group, or split along lines of the people one wanted to work with, *if* such a split was necessary. . . . [But] people were afraid it was "elitist" to want to work with certain women with whom they shared a common political direction.[242]

Indeed, Anne Forer recalls that "nobody had the nerve to say that they didn't want to do it by lot, that they wanted to be with their friends."[243] Rather than challenge the division by lot, many women simply ignored their lot assignments. But, as Forer observes, it made little difference whether or not women were abiding by their lot assignments because at that point NYRW ceased to exist as a single organization. Mainardi suggests that splitting by lot was "an attempt to avoid splitting on ideological grounds."[244] Moreover, it was probably a way to prevent members of the old guard from grouping exclusively with each other—a scenario that would have formalized the hierarchy, which, despite their efforts, already existed, and that would have concentrated all the power in one, or possibly, two groups. A number of women also suspect that left saboteurs played a role in the reorganization of NYRW.[245]

Many women believe that the division had a deleterious effect on the group. Although the meetings may have been less chaotic after the split, they lacked the vitality of the big meetings. Hanisch wrote that the split divided the "original militants into several groups where we were less effective."[246] Peslikis argues that it "reinforced sectarianism because [NYRW] was the one place where any woman in New York was welcome."[247] Mainardi maintains that although "people had different positions before [the split] . . . they were at least talking to each other."[248] Another woman who was active in the group claims that "it was a movement at that point; but when it broke up into groups, you became this little group that didn't relate to anything."[249]

But while there may have been a movement in New York, it was a seriously fractured movement. There were tensions between politicos and feminists, WITCHes and more traditional leftists, advocates of consciousness-raising and proponents of action, pro-woman radical feminists and advocates of the conditioning thesis, and, finally, those who defended the "quiet women" and those who wanted to talk at will. NYRW survived only about six months after the reorganization. After the formation of the radical feminist action group Redstockings in early February 1969, NYRW was reduced to an umbrella group for the growing number of feminist groups. But at least some of the women who formed Redstockings had been dissatisfied with consciousness-raising as early as November 1968, suggesting that the problem was less the reorganization than proliferating political differences.[250] While the decision to reorganize undoubtedly hastened NYRW's demise, left obstructionism, the group's cumbersome size, and, perhaps most important, the growing polarization between politicos and feminists were already destroying the group. But, as Mainardi points out, there was a silver lining to this cloud. For "in falling apart [NYRW] seeded itself."[251]

****

From the beginning, the women's liberation movement was internally fractured. In fact, it is virtually impossible to understand radical feminism without referring to the movement's divided beginnings. Radical feminism was, in part, a response to the antifeminism of the left and the reluctant feminism of the politicos. Radical feminists' tendency to privilege gender over race and class, and to treat women as a homogenized unity, was in large measure a reaction to the left's dismissal of gender as a "secondary contradiction." Moreover, the politico-feminist schism was so debilitating that it seemed to confirm radical feminists' suspicions that difference and sisterhood were mutually exclusive. In the next chapter we will follow this debate as it moves out of New York City and takes on the dimension of a national struggle.

3

Breaking Away from the Left

Although our focus thus far has been on individual women's liberation groups, these groups were not atomistic cells. From the moment the Chicago group formed in the fall of 1967, radical women intended to create a national women's movement. While most of their effort went into building their own groups, they tried to coordinate national meetings and actions as well. For instance, women from Chicago, New York, and Washington, D.C. planned the first national women's liberation conference outside Chicago in November 1968. And in January 1969, women from New York, Washington, D.C., Boston, and Cleveland collaboratively organized a feminist protest at the leftist Counter-Inaugural demonstration. But while these events dissolved the geographical barriers separating women's liberationists, they did not succeed in bridging the ideological differences. The Thanksgiving conference was far more successful than the abortive D.C. protest, but both events were marked by heated battles between radical feminists and politicos. This chapter will examine these early conferences and protests, and will further explore the Movement's continued antagonism toward women's liberation—an antagonism which in early 1969 persuaded New York radical feminists that their energies would be better spent organizing an explicitly radical feminist movement outside the new left.

The Sandy Springs and Lake Villa Conferences

When radical women met at the Jeannette Rankin Brigade protest, they discussed the possibility of holding a series of regional conferences.[1] Instead, a group of twenty women from New York, Washington, D.C., Chicago, Baltimore, and Gainesville, Florida met at the Friends School in Sandy Springs, Maryland for three days in early August 1968.[2] The Sandy Springs meeting marked the beginning of Kathie Sarachild and Carol Hanisch's partnership with Judith Brown and Carol Giardina of Gainesville. According to Hanisch, there were "constant battles between politicos and feminists" at the conference.[3] Indeed, in reading over the conference transcript it seems as though almost every discussion led back to the critical question—is the enemy capitalism or men?[4] One of the most divisive discussions centered around whether the women's liberation movement should assume an explicitly anti-capitalist stance. Some women maintained that a system such as ours could easily accommodate some women's demands for equality, thereby co-opting the movement. One woman argued that the history of the woman suffrage movement demonstrated that growing consciousness about male chauvinism would not automatically foster a critical consciousness about capitalism. To these women it was essential that the movement define itself as explicitly and unequivocally anti-capitalist from the very beginning.[5] But to others who believed that "women's liberation" would be "intrinsically impossible in a capitalist culture," the question was not of critical importance.[6] Others went further, agreeing with the woman who said, "I'm not too concerned about socialism per se because I know that we could push socialism and not get anything out of it."[7]

Apparently, a "big controversy ensued" when Roxanne Dunbar of the Boston group, Cell 16, read aloud excerpts from Valerie Solanas's *SCUM Manifesto* and proclaimed it "the essence of feminism."[8] Solanas's *SCUM* (Society for Cutting Up Men) *Manifesto*, which she wrote in 1967, was one of the earliest, wittiest, and most eccentric expressions of second-wave feminism.[9] Solanas's unabashed misandry—especially her belief in men's biological inferiority—her endorsement of relationships between "independent women," and her dismissal of sex as "the refuge of the mindless" contravened the sort of radical feminism which prevailed in most women's groups across the country. Solanas was a maverick who sold mimeographed copies of *SCUM* to passersby on the streets of Greenwich Village. Radical feminists in NYRW knew next to nothing about Solanas until she shot and nearly killed Pop artist Andy Warhol in June 1968.[10] Solanas, who had appeared in one of Warhol's films, claimed she shot him because he had appropriated her ideas. After the shooting, Solanas's case became something of a *cause célèbre* among radical feminists. Ros Baxandall declared her "our movement's Victoria Woodhull."[11] Dunbar visited her in jail, while Ti-Grace Atkinson and others attended her trial. In the wake of the shooting, *SCUM* was finally published and it became obligatory reading for radical feminists. However, not everyone at the Sandy Springs meeting agreed with Dunbar that Solanas's polemic was "the essence of feminism." Marilyn Webb remembers finding *SCUM* interesting, but feeling politically distant from both Solanas and Dunbar.[12]

One of the more difficult discussions of the weekend occurred when someone suggested that Elizabeth Sutherland (of NYRW, and formerly of SNCC) contact Kathleen Cleaver, communications secretary of the Black Panther Party, to see if she knew of any radical black women's groups that might want to attend the upcoming Lake Villa Conference. Interestingly, women from D.C. resisted making such overtures on the grounds that militant black women "think [women's liberation] is a pile of shit."[13] One woman argued that it would be counterproductive to invite radical black women because they would simply use the opportunity to berate the audience for being white and middle class:

> Having experience with a black welfare group that had white women in it, I know that black militant women rule the day. They set the tone and they manage to completely cow white women in welfare organizations. I've seen it time and time again. I understand the problem. But they hold the cards on oppression . . . and they let white women know it. I don't want to go to a conference and hear a black militant woman tell me she is more oppressed and what am I going to do about it.[14]

Another speaker favored asking radical black women whose ideas on women's liberation mirrored theirs. However, she opposed inviting black women who believed that "women should go back into the home and give support to [the men] because they've never had that kind of support before.''[15] Other women, reportedly of the pro-woman faction, attacked as ''racist'' the suggestion that the only black women who should be included were those whose definition of women's liberation dovetailed with that of white women.[16] They conceded that black women would articulate a different version of women's liberation, but they maintained that to develop an understanding of the commonalities and differences in women's situation it was crucial that the movement not be all-white. ''It's absolutely essential for our ideology that we have militant black power women in on the formation of our ideology. It's for our own good that we need it.''[17] Some women offered as a compromise finding a radical black woman who already was a feminist to sit on the conference planning committee. However, others quickly attacked this idea as tokenism. The issue was apparently resolved (although not to everyone's satisfaction) when it was proposed that Sutherland and Cleaver be contacted at a later date about planning a conference on black women and women's liberation.[18] This conference, however, never materialized.

This drama would be played out many times in the future, for the issue of black women's relationship to women's liberation continued to haunt the movement.[19] The D.C. women were right that black women who identified with black power were typically unsympathetic to women's liberation. Even black women who spoke out against sexism felt that racism was by far the more pressing issue. Ironically, the rise of black power, so important in fostering feminist consciousness among white women, had very different consequences for black women. Black power, as it was articulated by black men, involved laying claim to masculine privileges denied them by white supremacist society. Within the black liberation movement black women were expected to ''step back into a domestic, submissive role'' so that black men could freely exercise their masculine prerogatives.[20] For instance, Angela Davis, one of the best-known black activists of the '60s, contends she was attacked as ''domineering'' by black men who feared that she was out to ''rob them of their manhood.''[21] And Kathleen Cleaver claims that she had to ''genuflect'' to the men in the Black Panther Party to be listened to.[22] Frances Beale of

SNCC, who was among the black women who openly challenged this "black macho," pointed out that while the black militant male was quick to renounce many white cultural values, "when it comes to women he seems to take his guidelines from the pages of *Ladies Home Journal.*"[23] In this climate where "sexism [was] promoted as a cure for racism" merely having leadership qualities, not to mention feminist sympathies, could make one suspect.[24] Given these circumstances it is extremely unlikely that black women, had they been approached, would have chosen to participate.

Had black women attended the conference it is possible that they would have guilt-tripped the white women, making it difficult for white women to feel that they could legitimately focus on their own oppression. For within the Movement black people had the power to turn the tables, to reverse the equation of white power and black powerlessness. Here, if nowhere else, they could prevail. But the decision against making overtures to black women was, of course, a terrible mistake. The presence of black women would have "muddied up the issue," as one woman regrettably put it.[25] But this is precisely why black women should have been invited. Had black women participated, white women would have been less inclined to rely solely on their own experiences when theorizing about women's oppression. However, it seems less clear how black women would have benefited. Indeed, they would have been in the position of having to explain to white women that some of the experiences that they were claiming as common to all women were more particularistic than universal. Once again, blacks would have had to assume the role of educating whites about racism.

Despite their considerable differences, the women who gathered at Sandy Springs decided to plan a national conference to commemorate the 120th anniversary of the first women's rights convention at Seneca Falls. The planning committee consisted of Marilyn Webb of D.C. Women's Liberation, Helen Kritzler of New York Radical Women, and Laya Firestone of the Westside group.[26] Webb succeeded in securing a $1,500 grant for the conference from the Institute for Policy Studies in D.C. Of course, radical feminists in NYRW were suspicious of the politicos in D.C. and Chicago. In fact, Kritzler recalls that Sarachild expected her to keep a watchful eye on the politicos and to oppose Webb, if necessary.[27] Interestingly, Bunch contends that the D.C. women invited the New York women to participate in the planning sessions to mitigate New York-D.C. factionalism. "We knew that the New York people didn't trust anybody else and we tried to . . . involve them in it to . . . build those bridges."[28] Despite the history of distrust, the conference planning sessions were remarkably free of conflict.

Unfortunately, the conference was as volatile as the planning sessions were tranquil. Almost 200 women from thirty cities in the U.S. and Canada gathered at Camp Hastings, a YMCA summer camp in Lake Villa, Illinois during Thanksgiving weekend of 1968.[29] The conference began with a brouhaha over the presence of a reporter at the event. Elizabeth Fisher came to report on the conference despite knowing that the organizers had decided to bar all members of the press from the proceedings. Fisher was not, however, a typical reporter from the mainstream press. Like her good friend Ruth Hershberger, author of the feminist classic *Adam's Rib*, Fisher was a middle-aged Village bohemian and feminist who had attended a couple of NYRW meetings. The organizers had established a "no-media" policy because they felt that the presence of reporters would inhibit candid discussion and could possibly facilitate FBI and CIA surveillance.[30] Moreover, they did not want their movement "sensationalized and raped by the press" as they claimed other movements had been.[31]

Women's liberationists were especially sensitive about the press after the slick radical magazine *Ramparts* published a cover story on "women power" which barely mentioned women's liberation, and then, it seemed, only to dismiss it.[32] The magazine's cover—a picture of a woman (or, rather, a close-up of her torso shot in such a way as to accent her cleavage) dressed in a skintight leotard wearing a "Jeannette Rankin for President" button—said it all. As one letter writer observed, "If you had a cover on Black Power like your cover on Women Power, it would be a picture of a sharecropper with a harmonica in one hand and a piece of watermelon in the other."[33] The article focused on the principals involved in the Jeannette Rankin Brigade, but concluded with a condescending discussion of the "the prettiest girls" in the Brigade, the members of "the miniskirt caucus," the authors' term for the women's liberation movement. They were "the stylish ladies who graduated from college with majors in the civil rights fights and campus free speech revolutions of the early '60's."[34] The article's emphasis on the women's good looks and sartorial preferences—"miniskirts, high boots and bright colors"—and its trivialization of their concerns infuriated politicos and radical feminists alike. Evelyn Goldfield of the Westside group characterized *Ramparts* as "the *Playboy* of the Left, exploiting sex and radical politics to make a buck."[35] With coverage like this from their "brothers," the conference planners were in no mood to be accommodating to any reporter, no matter how well-intentioned.

But for the most part their problems that weekend stemmed from internal differences, not from so-called interlopers. The conference was characterized by bitter factional fighting at the plenary sessions and by groundbreaking, exhilarating discussions during the workshops. One of the participants, Marlene Dixon of Chicago, noted:

> The character of Women's Liberation as a powerful and politically original movement appeared in workshops, while the defensive, Movement-trained quality of women's liberation dominated the plenary sessions. The workshops often left one elevated, while the plenary sessions left one depressed.[36]

Charlotte Bunch, who had the misfortune to chair one of the pugilistic plenary sessions, contends that the "plenaries were completely and totally impossible."[37] Bunch had a reputation as a fair and effective facilitator, but even she felt powerless to chair this discussion. Bunch maintains that there were four or five women in the audience who seemed determined to obstruct the proceedings. At the time, she felt that many of the conflicts were factitious and wondered if some of the divisiveness was the work of agents.

Most of the quarreling at the conference occurred between pro-woman radical feminists of New York and Gainesville—Judith Brown, Carol Giardina, Carol Hanisch, Kathie Sarachild, and Irene Peslikis—and politicos from across the country. Sarachild went to considerable lengths to ensure that the pro-woman line faction would be well represented at the conference. For instance, Sarachild reportedly lent Peslikis money to attend the conference with the expectation, or so Peslikis believed, that she would support Sarachild "to the end" in her battle against the politicos. To Peslikis, who was politically inexperienced and was not acquainted with the other pro-woman feminists, "it felt like it was Kathie and me against the whole country."[38] Indeed, a number of radical feminists from NYRW resisted Sarachild's attempts to get them to proselytize on behalf of the pro-woman line. When Sarachild approached Baxandall for support, she demurred because she "didn't think the movement should take a line at that point."[39]

Marlene Dixon wrote that radical feminists, whom she called "wildcat women," demonstrated "complete contempt" toward those women unable to dismiss the "invisible audience" of leftist male heavies. But Dixon was equally critical of the "Movement women" who she said "counter-attacked by rejecting 'consciousness-raising' as 'bourgeois counter-revolutionism.' " She also decried the "suspicion of leaders" which, she argued, pervaded the conference and "bordered on the pathological." Dixon claimed that Marilyn Webb, in particular, had been unfairly attacked for being a leader. However, Bunch contends that the attacks against Webb stemmed less from her status as a leader than from the fact that the pro-woman faction perceived her as the leader of the opposition faction. Overall, Dixon argued that the conference had been derailed by factionalism:

> The conference ended in the atmosphere in which it had begun: suspicion, envy, arrogance bred from the sure knowledge that . . . consciousness-raising or . . . socialist ideology was the single truth. No national organization, no journal or newsletter, no communication network, nothing of the structural framework for a movement did or could have emerged from the Chicago conference.[40]

However, for those women who chose to stay out of the fray, the conference was not about divisiveness and factionalism, but about connection and solidarity because it afforded them their first opportunity to meet with women's liberationists from other cities. While Heather Booth acknowledges that there were "lots of arguments," she remembers the conference for the "political breakthroughs and the wonderful warmth" it generated.[41] And Baxandall, who skipped the divisive plenaries, has only fond memories of the conference perhaps because it marked the first time she met other feminists with children. As a rule, women who avoided the plenaries and attended the workshops found the event inspiring.

The most memorable of all the workshops seems to have been the workshop on sex organized by Anne Koedt with help from Ti-Grace Atkinson. Baxandall remembers women exchanging "wonderful, detailed stories about sex" during the workshop. Indeed, these discussions reportedly continued long into the night. They shared their sexual fantasies, including those—especially sado-masochistic and lesbian fantasies—which a number of women seemed to find unsettling.[42] Many women also expressed their deep dissatisfaction with the cultural dichotomization of sex and affection. Much of the discussion centered around Koedt's "The Myth of the Vaginal Orgasm," an early version of which she distributed to the participants.[43] In this highly influential piece, Koedt maintained that although orgasm originates in the clitoris, women "have been fed a myth of the liberated woman and her vaginal orgasm" because "women have been defined sexually in terms of what pleases men." She advised women to "discard the 'normal' concepts of sex and create new guidelines which take into account mutual sexual enjoyment." According to the conference summary, Koedt's thesis was embraced by most of the women at the workshop.

But the breaking down of old prescriptions sometimes engendered the creation of new ones. For instance, one woman remembers feeling mortified when her friend revealed to the entire workshop that she claimed to have had vaginal orgasms. After her exposure, she dutifully "apologized to my sisters." Then there were arguments about celibacy. Amy Kesselman remembers debating the merits of celibacy with Dana Densmore of Cell 16. According to Kesselman, Densmore urged women to practice celibacy rather than "squander their energy on men and sex." Kesselman felt ambivalent about the Cell 16 women whose militancy she admired but whom she found "antiseptic and rigid." She remembers objecting to the celibacy line because "I didn't think that you could build a mass movement around celibacy. You have to promise people a better life, not a narrower life."[44]

According to the conference report, there were also "heated reactions" to the suggestion—probably Shulamith Firestone's—that pregnancy is physically debilitating and inevitably oppressive. And there was further evidence that new, constricting norms were emerging. Corinne Coleman, who had several children, had the temerity to oppose Firestone's view of pregnancy as "barbaric," and to suggest that many women not only remained completely healthy throughout their pregnancy but enjoyed being pregnant. Coleman claims that Firestone simply ignored her objections.[45] Later at the plenary, Firestone reportedly objected when someone asked that the audience applaud the efforts of the child-care attendants. Instead, she declared that mothers should have left their children at home.[46]

In the "alternative lifestyles" workshop, women agreed that there should be alternatives to marriage, but argued against "any new rigidity which would eliminate marriage as an option for the 'liberated women.' "[47] They also discussed the possibility of forming support groups to help women in "liberated marriages" or in "cooperative living arrangements" to withstand the pressure to conform. However, they questioned whether subcultures were not, by nature, confining and prescriptive. The workshop posed a question which would assume critical importance to the movement:

> Can there exist . . . a subculture which would act as a support group to allow individuals to choose from a variety of lifestyles, without imposing a rigidity to survive?

In a workshop entitled, "Cruising: Or the Rationalization of the Pursuit of Men," Naomi Weisstein and Marlene Dixon of Chicago argued that the frequent discussions of alternative lifesyles—"bisexuality, celibacy and communes"—ignored the fact that "most single women returning from the conference would still be in a private struggle to 'get a man.' "[48] They suggested that women form "syndicates" to "add dignity and control [to the] pursuit of men." Weisstein, who had helped organize such a group while in graduate school at the University of Chicago, argued that the group would not only "blacklist any man that messes some woman up," but "would [allow them to] approach men they wanted to meet." While women were interested in exploring alternatives to the "degradation of waiting to be 'chosen,' " they were not persuaded that the syndicate was practicable or desirable. Some pointed out that it could only work while women were in college, and that "it didn't remove women from the degradation of being sexual objects."

Of course, some of the most interesting discussions occurred outside the workshops and plenaries.[49] Shortly after the conference, Dolores Bargowski of Detroit wrote a letter to the *Voice of the Women's Liberation Movement* recounting a conversation she had with several other women about "matriarchal culture" and Helen Diner's book *Mothers and Amazons*. Bargowski explained that Diner's book inspired her to conceive of "Moon Women," whom she described as:

> those women today, having reached a certain consciousness about women in relation to this oppressive patriarchal society, who choose to reject its definitions and look elsewhere to affirm the values this society has repressed. This other place is the matriarchal culture which preceded the patriarchal when woman was recognized for her inherent creative potentials.[50]

Bargowski was not the first feminist to discuss matriarchy. Peggy Dobbins, whom Baxandall dubs the "original matriarchist," discussed matriarchy much earlier that year in NYRW meetings.[51] In fact, Dobbins's Wednesday night group explored anthropological and historical studies for evidence that society was once female dominated. Although most women were not especially interested in uncovering or celebrating matriarchy, a minority were. Unlike the majority of radical feminists and politicos who opposed biologically based explanations of gender, matriarchists seemed interested in revaluing women's reproductive capability.

Some women at the conference also discussed the upcoming Counter-Inaugural demonstration to protest Nixon's inauguration. The action was being organized by the National Mobilization Committee to End the War in Vietnam (Mobe). Webb and Baxandall, in particular, had ties with people in the Mobe. In fact, Webb's husband, Lee Webb, had informed her that there was a slot available on the program for a women's liberation speaker. Barbara Mehrhof reports that during the car ride back from Lake Villa, Firestone, Atkinson, Koedt, Margaret Polatnik, and she discussed the proposed action. According to Mehrhof, all the women agreed that consciousness-raising, as it was practiced in NYRW, was leading to more consciousness-raising rather than to action. They discussed reorganizing the group, making it "more action and theory-based." Margaret Polatnik suggested that they "give back the vote" at the Counter-Inaugural protest, and the others agreed.[52] According to Ellen Willis, the action was intended to demonstrate that "suffragism"—which they contended had eviscerated the first wave of feminism—was dead and that "a new fight for real emancipation was beginning."[53] They announced the action at the next meeting of NYRW and welcomed others to join them in planning the protest. Firestone, Willis, Peslikis, Mehrhof, Kearon, Forer, Baxandall, Linda Feldman, Barbara Kaminsky, and Sheila Cronan were among those involved in planning the protest. Although some WITCH women attended the Counter-Inaugural, they did not participate in these planning sessions.

The Counter-Inaugural Protest

The Counter-Inaugural was a traumatic experience for virtually all the women involved in organizing the feminist action. Many of the problems stemmed from the difficulties inherent in planning an action from four different cities. According to Webb, it was decided that plans should be made at the local level and finalized when the women arrived in D.C., two days before the action.[54] However, the very looseness of this arrangement rekindled the old antagonism between New York and D.C women's liberationists. The New York women feared that the D.C. women might sell out women's liberation in their negotiations with the Mobe organizers. And the D.C. women worried that the New York women might be planning an action which would alienate large segments of the Movement.

The New York women felt their fears were justified when they met with a chilly reception from the New York Mobe office, and when they discovered that Mobe had failed to mention women's liberation in the *Guardian* ad for the Counter-Inaugural.[55] They became even more suspicious when they learned that Webb had decided that men should be included in their planned action.[56]

The New York women had proposed that women destroy a large mock-up of a voter registration card and then burn their voter registration cards in unison. However, Webb thought that men should burn their voter registration cards too. The New York women objected to the change which, they argued, transformed the action from a "repudiation of suffrage as a sop for women to a protest against the electoral process."[57] Webb claims that she proposed the alteration to allow men to show their solidarity with the women.[58] But the New York women believed it was further evidence that the D.C. women were "cowardly" feminists who would go to any lengths to avoid alienating Movement men.[59] The New York women were even more upset when they discovered that Webb had scheduled the final planning session for Friday night, a full day before most of them would be in D.C.[60]

Fearing that the protest's feminism would be too attenuated, the New York women produced their own leaflet and Firestone wrote a speech for the action. Baxandall, who knew Dave Dellinger and others in Mobe and saw the D.C. women as allies rather than adversaries, informed Marilyn Webb that the New York women were planning a separate action. Baxandall says she felt compelled to notify them because the D.C. women were, after all, responsible for getting women's liberation on the agenda.[61] Three days before the protest, someone from the New York group called Webb to get the D.C. women's approval of their leaflet. Webb suggested that they delete the final sentence which read, "Women's liberation is the final revolution." Webb proposed that they acknowledge that both an economic and a cultural revolution were needed, and that the latter was only possible given the former. According to Webb, the person on the other end responded by declaring that the D.C. women could write their own leaflet and plan their own action, and then hung up.[62]

By the time the New York women arrived on Saturday afternoon the situation had degenerated even further. The New York contingent learned that Webb had arranged with Mobe that she would speak for women's liberation during the serious part of the rally, but had, in Firestone's words, scheduled the New York women "after the rally and even after the whole march . . . as a kind of dessert performance, a tap dance at the end of the show."[63] The New York women demanded that the workshop planned for that evening be cancelled and an emergency meeting held so that they could alter the plans for Sunday's action. As a compromise, it was agreed that both Webb and Firestone would deliver speeches during the rally. However, many women felt that Webb's speech was too conciliatory and that Firestone's was too antagonistic toward Movement men.[64] Webb's speech was decidedly politico and she carefully avoided criticizing Movement men:

> We, as supposedly the most privileged in this society, are mutilated as human beings so that we will learn to function within a Capitalist system. So that we will reinforce that system. We will not! Our minds have been permanently drugged—the media controls our thoughts. . . . This will stop!

Firestone's speech, by contrast, excoriated radical men and derogated the politico explanation of women's oppression:

> And it isn't just nasty capitalism doing it all either. Though certainly that must be eliminated if we are to get it pulled out at the root. But let's start talking about where you live, baby, and wonder whether capitalism and all those systems of exploitation might not just begin there . . . at home. Because you've got it ass backwards. And you won't have your revolution 'till you start seeing straight. . . . We women often have to wonder if you mean what you say about revolution or whether you just want more power for yourselves. This time we aren't going to wait for your revolutionary clarity . . . we've learned better.[65]

The situation grew more complicated and divisive when the WITCH women arrived in D.C. They appropriated some of the "Feminism Lives" chest banners that the New York radical feminists had designed and crayoned "WITCH" on the other side because it "sounded a lot less pompous."[66] It was also rumored that the WITCH women planned to drag Firestone from the stage to prevent her from delivering her speech.[67] Although the WITCH women also felt that Firestone's speech was far too critical of Movement men, they were not aligned with the D.C. women. Indeed, WITCH and D.C. Women's Liberation represented different kinds of left feminism. According to Helen Kritzler of NYRW, the WITCH women were wild and irreverent, while the D.C. women, "wore very short skirts, were very pretty, and *very* careful about their politics."[68]

Mobe's casual attitude toward the women's action didn't improve relations between the factions. Mobe slighted the women by not listing the women's protest on the day's program, and then, by moving the women's action from early to late in the program. Finally, when Dellinger introduced Webb, he announced, "the women have asked all the men to leave the stage except for the Vietnam vet who has earned the right to be there." As Jane Addams of SDS pointed out, Dellinger's announcement "implied that this was an assertion of 'Woman Power.' " In fact, the women had merely requested that people not associated with their action leave the stage because it was too rickety to hold anyone other than the women involved in the protest.[69]

But, while the Mobe planners felt that women's liberation was an issue to which they had to pay lip service, the audience was actively antagonistic to the women. Firestone claimed that "a football crowd would have been . . . less blatantly hostile to women."[70] Almost as soon as Webb began speaking some men began chanting, "Take it off!" and "Take her off the stage and fuck her!"[71] Webb recalls, "it was like a riot was breaking out."[72] The crowd became even more feral when Firestone spoke. But rather than rebuking the hecklers, as he did when the previous speaker—one of the Fort Hood Three—was booed, Dellinger tried to get the women off the stage.[73] Webb remembers Dellinger asking her to "shut Shulie up."[74] So great was the pandemonium that the destruction of the voter registration cards went unnoticed. The men's unchecked hostility prompted Willis to ask, "If radical men can be so easily provoked into acting like rednecks, what can we expect from others?"[75] Although Webb was shocked by the crowd's behavior, she maintains that there were some men in the audience who were opposing the hecklers.[76]

The women's liberation activists who took part in the Counter-Inaugural demonstration drew different conclusions from it. Shortly after the action, Jane Addams of SDS observed that "at the time many of us who had been at or near the stage felt intense anger and bitterness—a 'you can take your movement and fuck yourselves with it'—a feeling that certainly had justification given the intense hostility of the crowd." However, upon reflection she began to think that the action's vagueness was partially responsible for the heckling.[77] And unlike the radical feminists from New

York, Addams argued that it was unrealistic to expect that the left would immediately embrace women's liberation. She contended, "we should realize that we will meet hostility and ridicule from rather large segments of the audience."[78] At the time, Webb maintained that three distinct positions on women's liberation emerged from the D.C. protest: that women's liberation should be independent of the left; the SDS position that it should be integrated into the larger Movement; and her own middle-ground position that it should "remain as a separate arm of the revolutionary struggle." Webb contended that women's liberation groups "should work with other groups in struggles that help to end a capitalist system, but it should also develop forms that will destroy a superstructure of capitalist definitions of family, work, consumption, leisure, 'lady-likeness' and male supremacy."[79]

But, in a seething rejoinder, Willis, Mehrhof, Cronan, and Feldman asked mockingly, "Are we to be the 'arm' of a revolution, as Marilyn suggests, without asking *who is the head?*"[80] And Firestone claimed that there were two, not three positions on women's liberation: "Women for women all the way, and women who are afraid to be for women all the way."[81] Willis and the others further criticized Webb's characterization of the family as a "cultural superstructure:"

> The family is not a "cultural superstructure" but an *economic* class structure, intertwined but distinct from the capitalist structure. Women's sexual, reproductive and maintenance functions are economic functions, and the ideology of male supremacy upholds an exploitative economic arrangement.[82]

For women like Firestone, the D.C. experience deepened their resolve to build an independent women's movement outside the left. Immediately following the action, Firestone wrote a letter to the *Guardian* in which she declared:

> We say to the left: in this past decade you have failed to live up to your rhetoric of revolution. You have not reached the people. And we won't hitch ourselves to your poor donkey. There are millions of women out there desperate enough to rise. Women's liberation is dynamite. And we have more important things to do than to try to get you to come around. You will come around when you have to, because you need us more than we need

> you. . . . The message being: Fuck off, left. You can examine your navel by yourself from now on. We're starting our own movement.[83]

Some in NYRW who before the Counter-Inaugural had believed that women's liberation should be closely tied to the larger Movement now concluded that women needed to organize their own autonomous movement. The only women apparently unmoved by the events in Washington were the women of WITCH. In a letter to the *Guardian* repudiating Firestone's position, WITCH argued that women's liberation "is part of a general struggle; we are as essential to the movement as it is to us." In contrast to Firestone, WITCH declared the ruling class its enemy, and all oppressed people its allies. WITCH not only reprimanded Firestone for attacking men, especially radical men, but suggested, as Pam Allen had earlier, that "directing ourselves against men, as Shulamith's letter does, only reinforces the oppressive pattern of women defining themselves through men."[84]

The Counter-Inaugural had consequences for women throughout the nascent movement. As a result of the protest, Ellen Willis and Shulamith Firestone decided to organize Redstockings, "an action group based on a militantly independent, radical feminist consciousness."[85] The core of this new group consisted of those New York women who had participated in the Washington action. Although the D.C. women's liberation activists wanted to remain closely allied with the left, the Washington SDS collective wanted nothing more to do with them. After Webb returned home that evening from the protest, she received a phone call from a woman in SDS who warned her that if she or anyone else "ever gives a speech like that again, we're going to beat the shit out of you wherever you are." Although the caller did not identify herself, Webb recognized the voice immediately and claims the caller was Cathy Wilkerson, a woman who later became prominent in Weatherman. Webb was devastated by the experience:

> They cut me out of the Movement. At the time I didn't realize that they were going to cut themselves out of SDS, and out of life. . . . As far as I was concerned I had nothing more to do with SDS in Washington.

Although Webb acknowledges that their expulsion from the SDS community in D.C. forced them to forge their own politics, she also feels that it deprived the women's liberation movement of an organizational base.[86] Reflecting on the Counter-Inaugural experience, Webb says:

> There was a lot of support from the left. . . . I could see that there was enormous energy around this issue . . . and obvious tension. But the left may or may not have been our enemy. The left could have been a base and was a base, because that's where we all came from. Shulie's attack on the left cut off that possibility.[87]

"Men of Steel"

Relations between the women's liberation movement and the new left continued to deteriorate throughout 1969. As the Counter-Inaugural amply demonstrates, Movement recognition, when it occurred, came slowly and was usually token in nature. Women's liberationists were unprepared for the resistance they encountered in Movement circles. In a recent retrospective of the radical feminist movement, Willis writes:

> It's hard to convey to people who didn't go through that experience how radical, how unpopular and difficult and scary it was just to get up and say, "Men oppress women. Men have oppressed *me*. Men must take responsibility for their actions instead of blaming them on capitalism. And, yes, that means *you*." We were laughed at, patronized, called frigid, emotionally disturbed man-haters and—worst insult of all on the left!—apolitical.[88]

Most Movement men trivialized, patronized, or ridiculed women's liberation activists. Some men, like the Berkeley leader who declared, "let them eat cock!" were actively hostile.[89] As late as spring 1969 consciousness about sexism was still so low that one SDS chapter published a pamphlet which advised other activists, "the system is like a woman; you've got to fuck it to make it change."[90] Moreover, those male radicals who supported the new movement often seemed to do so because they assumed that women would attack capitalism rather than male supremacy. For example, in January 1969, Julius Lester hailed women's liberation as "one of the most significant developments of the past year." However, Lester envisioned the movement organizing women in their capacity as housewives to protest the high cost of groceries. "As prices continue to rise," Lester contended, "it is not pipe-dreaming to think of women sending bricks through supermarket windows."[91]

Ideological developments within the new left certainly contributed to tension between the two movements. Neither Weatherman nor the Progressive Labor Party—the dominant factions within SDS in the late '60s—was sympathetic to women's liberation. In their atavistic embrace of the labor metaphysic, PL'ers insisted that race and gender were "secondary contradictions" which would be resolved by socialist revolution.[92] In Weatherman's apocalyptic vision the system would be brought down by the Vietnamese abroad and black militants at home (with support from white revolutionaries and the white youths they organized).[93] For Weatherman, women's liberation was not only liberal and bourgeois, it was a dangerous diversion from the main event. In March 1969, Bernardine Dohrn of Weatherman declared:

> Most of the women's groups are bourgeois, unconscious or unconcerned with class struggle and the exploitation of working women. . . . Instead of integrating (not submerging) the struggles of women into the broader revolutionary movement, these women are flailing at their own middle-class images . . . their direction leads to a middle-class single issue movement—and this at a time when the black liberation movement is polarizing the country, when national wars of liberation are waging the most advanced assaults on U.S. imperialism, when the growth of the movement is at a critical stage.[94]

However, SDS was under considerable pressure to give at least token support to some version of women's liberation. At the December 1967 National Council meeting, three months after the NCNP Convention, SDS had passed a resolution on women's liberation. But while the resolution emphasized the importance of organizing women, it stressed that "women's liberation lies in building the anti-imperialist movement in this country." In other words, women were to be organized, but once again to fight someone else's battle. Indeed, the resolution endorsed "female discussion groups" that focused on "imperialism, the draft . . . [and overcoming] the fear women have of participating intellectually at meetings." Finally, the resolution argued that it was *women's* responsibility not only to "organize a political program for their liberation," but "to take the initiative to discourage male supremacism in interpersonal relationships with both men and women."[95] [emphasis mine] Of course, as radical feminists were quick to point out, SDS would never dare argue that it was incumbent upon blacks to challenge white racism.

One year later, the National Council went further by passing a resolution which at long last acknowledged that "all strata of women suffer under male supremacy" and that "the struggle for the equality of women is a revolutionary task." In contrast to the earlier resolution, it challenged the idea that "the fight for equality is solely the business of women, and that only women have the right and the responsibility to oppose male domination." But the resolution conceded that the primary contradiction was between the working class and the bourgeoisie, and cautioned that women's liberation "doesn't stand apart from the fight against capitalism in our society, but rather is an integral part of that fight."[96] The resolution was the source of acrimonious fighting between PL'ers, who opposed it, and the SDS regulars (those belonging to either Revolutionary Youth Movement I—or Weatherman—and Revolutionary Youth Movement II) who sponsored and supported it.[97]

However, when the resolution came before the SDS membership at its June 1969 convention, it was defeated. This time around the opposition was not limited to PL'ers. The June Conference was the scene of internecine factional fighting between PL and the SDS regulars-fighting from which SDS never recovered.[98] SDS had been the site of factional struggles before, but nothing like this, as both sides pulled out all the stops. The RYM factions, hoping to discredit PL on the basis of its anti-nationalist stance, enlisted the support of the Puerto Rican group, the Young Lords, the Chicano organization, the Brown Berets, and the Black Panther Party. Representatives of each group were scheduled to speak so that they could denounce PL.

According to Kirkpatrick Sale, everything went as planned until the third speaker, Rufus ("Chaka") Walls of the BPP, midway through his speech, inexplicably declared that the Panthers supported free love and "pussy power." When the audience began chanting, "fight male chauvinism!" Walls compounded his error by yelling back, "Superman was a punk because he never even tried to fuck Lois Lane." At this point the chanting, especially from PL quarters, was so loud that Walls was forced to relinquish the podium. This was to have been RYM's triumphant moment; instead, their strategy was in shambles. What made this especially embarrassing was that RYM members had been trying to gain support by assailing PL's stance on women's liberation. RYM leaders hastily conferred and decided to ask another Panther leader, Jewell Cook, to speak. Cook might have salvaged the evening for RYM had he not returned to the topic of women's liberation. But before he had finished, he managed to repeat Stokely Carmichael's by now infamous one-liner about women's position in the movement. The heckling and chanting became deafening because this sort of undisguised and public contempt for women's liberation was no longer acceptable in SDS circles. In the confusion a PL leader grabbed the microphone and lectured the crowd on the superiority of PL's stance on women's liberation and black liberation. Naomi Jaffe of RYM II (and WITCH) finally calmed the crowd by proclaiming that "women's liberation would not be used as a political football."[99]

The struggle with PL ended when the RYM factions, after staging a walk-out, declared themselves the real SDS and expelled PL on the grounds that it was "objectively anti-communist."[100] According to Andrew Kopkind, when they returned to the hall, Bernardine Dohrn, "flanked by a dozen SDS delegates (chicks up front) who stood Panther-style on the podium," read the bill of particulars against PL.[101] While it is certainly the case that PL had been "gearing up . . . to take control of SDS's organization," the expulsion nevertheless represented a major departure from SDS's long-standing policy of non-exclusion.[102]

After purging PL, the two RYM factions jointly elected officers and voted on a series of resolutions. However, Weatherman opposed the RYM-2 resolution on women's liberation which had been passed by the National Council only six months earlier. According to *Guardian* writer Margie Stamberg, Barbara Reilly (who had spoken in favor of the resolution at the December NC) and Howie Machtinger of Weatherman

> objected to "struggling for equality with men" and argued that no change in the status quo could occur until socialism was achieved. They objected to fighting for day-care centers . . . [and to] increases in welfare allowances, saying that fighting for democratic rights—even if these rights were seen to be serving real needs of the people—was not sufficient.[103]

The two Weathermen very cleverly attacked the resolution for its liberalism rather than its feminism. Commenting on its defeat, one SDS woman observed that "some of the worst male chauvinists in the movement can rap down the best line on women's liberation."[104] To Kopkind, who was covering the convention for the radical paper *Hard Times*, it seemed that SDS'ers found the women's liberation movement "immensely important."[105] But this was not an opinion shared by the women's liberation activists in attendance who discerned that SDS's interest in women's liberation was primarily opportunistic. Stamberg reported that the one three-hour slot set aside for the women's caucus had been scheduled for the same time that delegates were to have had their credentials certified. Then some women "effectively sabotaged" the caucus by voting to allow men to participate in it.[106] This sort of callous manipulation, so emblematic of the whole event, angered and saddened many people who attended SDS's last convention. Richard Flacks, a founding member of SDS, argued that by the time of the convention America's leading new left group had

> turned into the very opposite of what its founders had intended. SDS had begun with the intention of avoiding dogma, doctrine, top-down discipline, factional warfare, and sectarian style and language. Its purpose was to create the basis for a left that could appeal broadly to the American people. By its final convention in 1969, SDS had not only fallen prey to all the supposed failures of the Old Left, it had become an incredible caricature of its worst excesses. Monolithic, slogan-chanting factions met in open combat over obscure points of dogma, beyond any hope of intelligibility to the uninitiated.[107]

The expressive politics of the old SDS had been under attack since 1967, but the rise of Weatherman and PL obliterated it.

The roots of Weatherman lie in the action-faction—the driving force behind the Columbia University student rebellion of 1968. The group took its name from a line in Bob Dylan's "Subterranean Homesick Blues," which goes, "you don't need a Weatherman to know which way the wind blows." The action-faction was contemptuous of the SDS old guard who they felt favored ponderous intellectual debate and ineffective mass protest over aggressive confrontations with the powers-that-be. Disdainful of base-building, the people who formed Weatherman believed in "bringing the war home." Indeed, Kathy Boudin, Bernardine Dohrn, and Terry Robbins of Weatherman claimed that the street fighting during the 1968 Democratic Convention in Chicago had done "more damage to the ruling class . . . than any mass peaceful gathering this country has ever seen."[108] Like a number of other leftists, they no longer envisioned the U.S. experiencing a "social revolution at the hands of its own people," but, rather, imagined it succumbing to a "military defeat at the hands of twenty, thirty many Vietnams—plus a few Detroits."[109] To Weatherman, it seemed that the times required that radicals repudiate "part-time radicalism" and engage in heroic action to bring the system to its knees.[110] If students wanted to be part of the revolution, they would have to "de-studentize their lives," in the words of Weathermen Cathy Wilkerson, Les Coleman, and Mike Spiegel.[111]

If students seemed hopelessly timid and bourgeois to Weatherman, the blacks who were staging "insurrections" in America's ghettoes seemed fully capable of demolishing the system. By the time of the June convention, Weatherman even declared that "Blacks can do it alone."[112] For Weatherman the sole role available to white radicals was to "support the blacks in moving as fast as they have to and are able to." Any white who disagreed was denounced as "objectively racist."[113] In late 1969, Weatherman member Shin'ya Ono, Yoko Ono's cousin, argued that "organizing whites around their perceived oppression (whether it be women's liberation, student power, the draft and the stockades . . .) is bound to lead to a racist and chauvinist direction."[114] Staughton Lynd and Greg Calvert were among the few whites who continued to criticize the "white-support-for revolution" mentality that so characterized the white movement in the late '60s.[115] But many white radicals found it difficult to resist abdicating authority to black radicals whose apparent willingness to "pick up the gun" seemed the essence of revolutionary commitment.

To many white leftists it seemed that no group was engaged in more heroic action than the the Oakland-based Black Panther Party which was formed by Huey Newton and Bobby Seale in October 1966.[116] The Panthers counseled black Americans, who they defined as an "internal colony," to refrain from rioting and engage instead in armed self-defense and urban guerrilla warfare against the police, or the "white occupying army."[117] By opening a front against American imperialism in the "Mother Country," blacks would destroy the "imperialist system which suppresses the world-wide revolution of colored people."[118] (Considerably less grandiose was the Panthers' free breakfast program for inner-city children—a program which won them support among white liberals.[119]) What set the Black Panthers apart from black nationalist groups was their conviction that the problem was one of class as well as race, their belief that the enemy was the white ruling class, not "whitey." And perhaps most crucial from the standpoint of white radicals, the Panthers were not averse to forming alliances with them.[120] In fact, the Panthers encouraged white radicals to assume the role of support troops for the black movement. In June of 1968, Bobby Seale told the *Guardian*:

> Huey [Newton] said . . . that if any white person wants to act in the manner of a John Brown and in accordance with the needs of black people, then we can work with him. We're not going to jive, we're going forth. If they want to support the liberation struggle—beautiful. We let them ride. We let them work and produce.[121]

Weatherman, eager to establish its revolutionary credentials, responded with the slogan, "John Brown, live like him!"[122]

Some white leftists argued that the Panthers were typically more incendiary in their rhetoric than in their actions. For instance, Andrew Kopkind maintained that

> Panthers would shout "off the pig," and while it may have been a promise or a metaphor to ghetto people, uptight whites took it literally. As a matter of fact, the Panthers never formulated—or practiced—an aggressive strategy against the cops. For all the

> reported "gun battles" between Panthers and police, there are no cases of armed forays by Panthers, or even sniping. Huey had said at the start: "It's not in the panther's nature to attack anyone first, but when he is attacked and backed into a corner, he will respond viciously."[123]

Although the Panthers were undeniably the victims of unprovoked police attacks, they were, it seems, not completely without blame. For instance, in 1980 Eldridge Cleaver (then a born-again Christian) claimed that at least one of the Panthers' shoot-outs with the Oakland police was the result of a Panther ambush of the police.[124] Of course, even though the Panthers may have generally followed the example of the black panther, it mattered little to the government which took them at their word when they yelled, "off the pig." Indeed, the Panthers found themselves victimized by their own rhetoric as twenty-six Party members were killed between between April 1968 and the end of 1969.[125]

Weatherman's obsequiousness toward the Panthers peaked at the July 1969 United Front Against Fascism conference. The UFAF was organized by the Panthers and both RYM factions, and was generously funded by the Communist Party. While no one expected a return to the beloved community of SNCC circa 1963, many white and black radicals hoped it would mark the beginning of a coalition effort to resist government repression of the Movement, especially the BPP. Of course, each group also had its own self-interested reasons for supporting such a coalition. Without a base in the black community and beseiged by police and government agents, the BPP was anxious for allies in the progressive white community. The leaders of the Communist Party, believing that the Panthers enjoyed a strong base in the black community, hoped the Panthers would provide them with a much-needed entree into that community. The SDS regulars hoped that the conference would cement their partnership with the Black Panther Party and thereby establish their status as the vanguard of the white left. According to Jon Grell of *Rat*, the white radicals at the conference completely apotheosized the Panthers:

> From the opening night that amazing spirit emanating from whites to the Panthers was something like, "PLEASE, you are the vanguard, and PLEASE LEAD US TO THE REVOLUTION." And the Panthers in a way dug what was happening, rapping with

> tones like, "OKAY, HONKIES, WE'RE GONNA SHOW YOU WHERE IT'S AT, AND YOU'D BETTER DIG IT."[126]

But unity proved as elusive in 1969 as it had in 1967 at the NCNP. First of all, the ambience of the conference left something to be desired as armed Panthers patrolled the auditorium in what seemed a purposefully menacing manner.[127] Most white radicals were more than willing to accept anything the Panthers decreed, but even the Weatherman faction was unprepared to support the Panthers' proposed petition campaign for community control of the police. When they reluctantly opposed the concept of community control in *white* neighborhoods on the grounds that it would most certainly result in greater repression, the Panthers excoriated them. Panther leader David Hilliard announced:

> We don't see SDS as being so revolutionary. . . . We'll beat those sissies, those little schoolboys' ass if they don't straighten up their politics. So we want to make it known to SDS and the first motherfucker that gets out of order had better stand in line for some kind of disciplinary actions from the Black Panther Party.[128]

The Panthers' attacks on SDS not only convinced many Weathermen that the Panthers were unreliable allies, but suggested the possibility "that it was really Weatherman that was the vanguard of the revolution, after all."[129]

As with the abortive NCNP conference, the UFAF conference was also marked by divisiveness over women's liberation. The conference planners added a women's panel "only after last-minute pressure from Bay Area women's groups." According to Al Haber, the Panthers did not want to let a white woman from the "bourgeois women's movement" speak, but they reluctantly decided she could.[130] However, the women's panel was almost cancelled when the keynote speaker, Herbert Aptheker of the Communist Party, reading from his latest pamphlet, "droned on into the late hours, cutting into the time reserved for the women's panel."[131] Al Haber insists that this was not the result of poor preparation. "Aptheker is clearly doing this under direction. This is a man who has been around; he did not just happen to find himself halfway through his pamphlet." Women (and some men) in the audience, tired of having the women's panel at left events shunted to the end of the program or cancelled altogether, staged a spontaneous floor demonstration. According to Haber, who describes himself as one of the most vocal dissidents that evening:

> the goons, the Panther and SDS security, came around and intimidated everybody who was standing up: "You sit down and shut up or you're in trouble!" Two goons came and stood right in front of me, pressed against me, and pushed me down.[132]

Stamberg of the *Guardian* reported that "tempers flared" and that several female protestors were physically ejected from the auditorium. Explaining their expulsion, the BPP minister of education, Ray Masai Hewitt, said:

> The Black Panther Party is in the vanguard when it comes to the emancipation of women. Only a pig would attack the conference. If you want to act bad, you're gonna get treated bad.[133]

The women's panel was held, but many women remained angry. The next day, a group of women met to discuss movement chauvinism, and possible responses to the expulsion. Some women proposed writing a leaflet declaring that equality between the sexes was a bottom line for their participation in any united front. But, women in Weatherman and RYM II opposed any criticism of the Panthers, however qualified, as "objectively racist." Before a vote could be taken, women from Weatherman broke up the meeting. Stamberg wrote that the women disrupted the meeting with chanting and shouting. But Barbara Haber, who was active in Berkeley's independent women's movement, claims that the Weatherman contingent "turned over our chairs and knocked us around on the ground."[134] Writing about the event in 1970, Marlene Dixon maintained that it was "surely one of the ugliest exchanges between women to date." To Stamberg, the UFAF, with its relentless rhetoric and rancorous debates over women's liberation, seemed depressingly similiar to other left gatherings that year.

Had Weatherman been a less dominant force within the Movement the rift between the new left and women's liberation would probably not have grown so wide. But Weatherman alienated radical and left feminists alike. At the very time when women's liberationists were arguing that women should stop serving others and organize instead around their own oppression, Weatherman was urging radicals to secure guns so they could serve in the white auxiliary of the black liberation struggle. While politicos and radical feminists were struggling to devise ways to make the women's movement more egalitarian, Weatherman was scrapping participatory democracy for authoritarianism.[135] Whereas many radical and left feminists argued that the left needed to be more connected to the American people, Weatherman was choosing actions designed to confound if not alienate the vast majority of Americans. To Boston politico Meredith Tax, "they were so macho and their notion of how to make a revolution was so remote from anything that I could imagine happening. I just hated them."[136]

Then there was the October 1969 "Days of Rage" action in which 300 Weathermen attempted to "bring the war home" by directly engaging the Chicago police in battle. The action not only decimated their ranks—approximately 200 were arrested, including most of the leadership—but failed to win them the respect of the Panthers, who condemned the action as "Custeristic."[137] In fact, radical activist and Chicago Seven defendant Dave Dellinger contends that a mere twenty-four hours before the action, Chicago Seven lawyer William Kunstler and three Black Panthers, including Fred Hampton, met with four Weatherman leaders to try to persuade them to scuttle their plans. Hampton apparently told the Weathermen, "Bobby Seale's life is at stake. Revolution is no motherfucking game with us. The black community has too many martyrs already." The black community gained two more when Panthers Fred Hampton and Mark Clark were gunned down in a police raid on the Panther's Chicago house two months after the Days of Rage.[138]

Most of those involved in the women's movement, including politicos, rejected the vanguardism favored by Weatherman and other groups. Indeed, it pushed many politicos like Marge Piercy away from the left. In 1969, Marge Piercy wrote:

> The word "cadre" as something to caress in the mouth and masturbate over has gone whoosh to the top of the pole in the last year. Cadre has meaning when a movement has really gone underground, when its members have been through training that has attempted to change their characters, when groups have shared violent and harrowing experiences over time so that they

> know they can trust each other. Cadre applied to the white Movement in the United States at this time is elitist bullshit. Our big problem is learning how to reach all kinds of people and we haven't invented any training yet that helps much on that score.[139]

But by 1969, many leftists like Weatherman had abandoned all hope of ever reaching the people. In fact, in early 1970 Weatherman went underground to conduct its war against "pig Amerika." As former SDS president Todd Gitlin noted, "in the absence of revolutionary conditions, revolutionary will spilled forth to take up the slack."[140] Indeed, some white radicals began to argue that by using "sabotage," they could "stem the gap from pre-revolutionary conditions to a truly revolutionary situation."[141] The repression that would follow would help the movement grow, was, in fact, necessary for it to grow.[142] Sabotage, by making continued apathy impossible, would force people to "choose sides."[143] Many black and white radicals appeared indifferent to the possibility that most Americans might choose the wrong side. In fact, they seemed to assume that they would be on the other side of the barricades. By the time of the Days of Rage, Weatherman's alienation was so total that their new line was, "Fight the People."[144]

Having found the system guilty, only its immediate demolition would suffice. In this "climate of totalism" all reforms were repudiated as attempts to co-opt the Movement.[145] Those who criticized the idea of "raising the level of struggle" were attacked for clinging to white-skin privilege. Huey Newton embraced "revolutionary suicide," and David Hughey a white radical later convicted of several New York City bombings, argued that "challenging the existing order means putting that thing which they call life on the line and probably losing it in the process."[146] In an effort to explain what he terms "almost a politics of hate," Tom Hayden ventures that when "you get driven into a corner, you react like an animal in some ways."[147]

Revolutionary nihilism of this sort was at odds with the enthusiasm felt by many women's liberation activists. Indeed, one of the most attractive features of the women's liberation movement was its potential to politicize large numbers of previously apolitical women. Baxandall argued that feminists could "talk to women in ways that the left never can. We can reach women who are out of the universities, who are secretaries, waitresses, nurses who would never run into the left."[148] While feminists wanted to reach those women whose lives had been untouched by the Movement, many leftists were opting for vanguardism and insularity. This estranged radical feminists and politicos alike. For instance, at the Chicago Democratic Convention of 1968, Amy Kesselman tried to persuade a group of male radicals—most of whom later helped establish RYM-II—that the Movement should try to educate rather than reject the young people supporting Eugene McCarthy's presidential campaign. This was not an unreasonable idea since the police riot in the streets and the machinations on the convention floor caused many "McCarthy kids" to question the wisdom of working within the system. But, one of the men turned to her and announced, "McCarthy kids suck. Get it?" When she persisted, she was told, "Listen, if you don't stop talking I'm going to bite off your nipple." She turned for support to the one man in the group who was part of the SDS old guard, but he stood there impassively. Kesselman was not yet ready to abandon the left. But after several more "horrific" encounters with leftist men, Kesselman decided that she would "let the left eat itself into a cannibalistic corner."[149]

Finally, while many women's liberationists did not object to violence per se, they did object to the machismo which accompanied Movement militance. Richard Flacks observed that "as the movement became more militant, many males found it an excellent arena for competitive displays of virility, toughness and physical courage."[150] The Movement had always been competitive, but women had a greater chance of gaining recognition when intellectual rather than physical prowess was admired. By 1969, with SDS in the hands of Weatherman, it had become what Ann Arbor SDS'er Barry Bluestone had feared back in 1967—"a political jock . . . with strong limbs, but a dull mind."[151] Weatherman, more than any other group, was obsessed with smashing "honkieness" and "wimpiness"—two words which seemed linked in the Weathermind.[152] Anxious that Weatherman not be "part of a sissy movement," as Mark Rudd put it, the group's inner circle or "Weather Bureau" renounced all vestiges of the old expressive politics, including participatory democracy.[153] According to Meredith Tax, who was well acquainted with Boston Weatherman, the Weather meeting style was similar to PL's in that they were "extremely brutal and authoritarian." But she maintains that although the Weathermen were "not more obnoxious than PL, they were more macho." Indeed, to Tax "they were bullies."[154]

But at the same time that Weatherman was railing against wimpiness, it claimed to be struggling against male chauvinism as well. The group supported efforts to cultivate female leadership and advocated organizing women—for the anti-imperialist struggle, of course. Weatherman also attacked monogamy as male ownership of women and encouraged women (and men) to experiment with same-gender sex. But for Weatherman women's liberation (at least the version they found acceptable) involved women transforming themselves into street-fighting women, or women of steel. According to their 1969 position paper, "Honky Tonk Women," women's liberation meant women's metamorphosis "from passive wimps, afraid of blood or danger or guns, satisfied with the limitations set on us by hated slave relationships with one man."[155] As the politico group Bread and Roses pointed out, the women who were seen as "right on" in Weatherman were those who were "tougher" and fought better than the men, not those who were struggling for women's liberation. In fact, one Weatherman collective reportedly expelled a woman it deemed insufficiently militant for "male chauvinism."[156] Some women embraced the group's macho posturing, perhaps because it allowed them to be transgressive and to lay claim to male turf. In January 1970, a Weatherwoman wrote of the need to avenge Fred Hampton's murder:

> There can be no life—no culture—without the gun. We can be nothing but scared ass honkies if we can't face the pig and with the power of cosmic consciousness put a bullet in his racist belly.[157]

Weatherman's obsession with eliminating "wimpiness" culminated on March 6, 1970, when an anti-personnel bomb that Weatherman Terry Robbins was assembling exploded in his hands, killing not only him, but Diana Oughton and Ted Gold as well.[158] (Nine months after the explosion, Weatherman repudiated its earlier "glorification of the heavier the better," terming it "the military error."[159])

Although Weatherman certainly had the support of many on the left, it was opposed by equal or greater numbers, especially after the Days of Rage fiasco. Former SDS'er Jeff Shero decried their "militant masochism" and observed that while "most want to end the war, SDS offers the unprepared a new war at home."[160] And, "you don't need a rectal thermometer to know who the assholes are," became a popular joke in certain Movement circles.[161] Writing in the aftermath of the 1969 SDS convention, former SDS president Carl Oglesby noted:

> On every quarter of the white Left, high and low, the attempt to reduce the New Left's inchoate vision to the Old Left's perfected remembrance has produced a layer of bewilderment and demoralization which no cop with his club or senator with his committee could ever have induced.[162]

And as Al Haber was being bullied by Panther and SDS security at the UFAF, he remembers feeling:

> This was clearly no longer anything I wanted to be part of. I'm sure there were a lot of agents there. . . . There could have been more of them than us, who knows? But I didn't want to be in *their* movement. God, it did not feel good.[163]

Haber was but one of many radicals who wanted out of "their" Movement. By mid-1969 many were beginning to take up the task of "self-repair," or to engage in more hopeful kinds of left activity, or, in the case of many women, to join or commit themselves more fully to the women's liberation movement.[164]

****

The sense of revolutionary urgency, growing government repression, and the unending war contributed to the Movement's hostility to women's liberation. In 1969 Piercy observed:

> It is not necessary to recount the history of the last two years to figure out what happened. Repression brings hardening. It is unlikely that the Movement could have gone along with the same degree of involvement in personal relationships. An excessive amount of introspection and fascination with the wriggles of the psyche militate against action. . . . But there is also a point be-

> yond which cutting off sensitivity to others and honesty to what one is doing does not produce a more efficient revolutionary, but only a more efficient son of a bitch. We are growing some dandy men of steel nowadays.[165]

But most important, Movement men were not anxious to divest themselves of male privilege. The fight against male supremacy was considerably less abstract than the struggle against racism, in which white radicals could win points by reciting Panther rhetoric. Fighting sexism required that men make tangible changes in their lives, such as sharing the housework. During the '70s, sectors of the nonsectarian left did begin to acknowledge the validity of at least some feminist claims. However, for many women the change came much too late. Repeated encounters with antagonistic or indifferent Movement men persuaded many women like Marge Piercy and Robin Morgan, who had been politicos, that they would have to go outside the left to build a women's movement.[166]

Because most early radical feminists believed that feminism expanded rather than contradicted a left analysis, they did not typically criticize women who chose to remain personally involved in the male-dominated Movement. Indeed, as we have seen, many of them continued to participate in leftist groups and projects. But over time the idea that feminism was intrinsically revolutionary—that it included a left perspective—gave way to the conviction that feminism and the left were antinomies. Ann Snitow remembers that some of the other women in the founding brigade of New York Radical Feminists believed that feminism and the left were incompatible.[167] Barbara Haber, who was active in the new left and women's liberation, maintains that "the tension between being a radical and being a feminist was widespread in the early '70s."[168] And by 1973, cultural feminists were beginning to make non-involvement with the so-called male Movement a precondition for feminist acceptance.

Clearly, the continued sexism of large segments of the left contributed to many feminists' estrangement from it. The growing animosity toward the left was also fueled by sectarian left groups like the Socialist Workers Party, which many feminists believed were trying to colonize the women's movement. But this overly global rejection of the left created a great deal of emotional turmoil for those women who wanted to participate in the women's movement without forsaking the left or a left analysis. Barbara Epstein, who belonged to both the Communist Party and SDS, and later became involved in the feminist movement, "experienced the feminist movement as telling me that I was no longer allowed to belong to the left. I really felt the women's movement tore apart the home I had made for myself [in the left]."[169] Heather Booth felt it was "both wrong and too difficult" to make women choose between movements.[170]

Those women who wanted to remain more connected to the left and who rejected the idea that "feminism includes socialism," that it automatically contains a critique of class relations, were responsible for articulating another strain of feminism, socialist-feminism. Some socialist-feminist groups merely recycled old politico arguments, but socialist-feminism often represented a step toward feminism from the earlier politico position. Whereas politicos generally tried to mobilize women around the war, imperialism, political repression, and class oppression, socialist-feminists were committed to "organizing women simultaneously around the issues of gender and class." Of course, in this respect they were still quite different from radical feminists who organized women solely around the issue of gender. Indeed, many socialist-feminists today concede that Marxism was too often the dominant partner in this marriage. Barbara Ehrenreich, one of the architects of socialist-feminism, admits that in trying to "fit all of women's experience into the terms of the market," socialist-feminists were "too deferential to Marxism."[171]

By the mid-'70s there was a small but dynamic socialist-feminist movement as socialist-feminists established women's unions throught the country. The Chicago Women's Liberation Union (CWLU), the first and most successful women's union in the country, was genuinely committed to fighting both the sexual and economic class systems.[172] Socialist-feminists did important political work, especially in the areas of reproductive rights and day-care. Indeed, the most fascinating of all the CWLU projects was an underground abortion clinic named Jane. Jane began as an abortion referral service in 1969. In the pre-*Roe* period, one could find feminist abortion referral services in most major cities. But the women running Jane, tired of sending women to illegal abortionists who grossly overcharged them, decided to teach themselves how to perform abortions. From 1969 until mid-1972 when the clinic was busted, the clinic performed 100 illegal abortions a week, and almost in full view of the police.[173]

However, socialist-feminists' proximity to the left made them vulnerable to attack by sectarian leftists who felt that their feminism was diverting women from the real class struggle. In fact, Barbara Ehrenreich contends that between the years 1975 and 1977 Marxist-Leninist and Maoist groups virtually destroyed the flourishing network of socialist-feminist women's unions. Ehrenreich claims that these groupuscles either attacked from outside or joined and harassed from within over twenty socialist-feminist women's unions across the country, "dragging almost all of them to their deaths in arcane squabbling over the 'correct line.' "[174] As a result, socialist-feminism is today a tendency primarily confined to the academy.[175]

Radical feminists' decision to organize women outside the left allowed them to organize a movement largely unimpeded by the left. By contrast, socialist-feminists who chose to remain connected to the left became hopelessly bogged down in internecine battles with sectarian leftists. But as the next chapter suggests, radical feminists' decision to divorce the left, while absolutely necessary, was not without costs to the movement. In the process of getting the left "off [their] backs," they separated radical feminism from the very social radicalism out of which it had formed.

4

Varieties of Radical Feminism—Redstockings, Cell 16, The Feminists, New York Radical Feminists

The radical feminist groups discussed in this chapter agreed that gender, not class or race, was the primary contradiction and that all other forms of social domination originated with male supremacy.[1] Radical feminists' commitment to an independent and autonomous women's movement and their conviction that male dominance was not a mere by-product of capitalism put them at odds with early socialist-feminists.[2] Nor did radical feminists feel much of an affinity with liberal feminists whose efforts to eliminate sex discrimination in the workplace they supported, but whose assimilationist goal of bringing women into the mainstream they opposed. To radical feminists, NOW's narrow focus on formal equality with men not only ignored the fundamental problem—women's subordination within the home—it assumed that equality in an unjust society was worth fighting for. However, as this chapter suggests, radical feminism was anything but monolithic. While Redstockings, The Feminists, New York Radical Feminists, and Cell 16 were all radical feminist groups, they were divided on critical questions. By late 1969, there had emerged different, and sometimes widely divergent, strains of radical feminism.

Redstockings

When Ellen Willis and Shulamith Firestone founded Redstockings in February 1969 it was with the intention of establishing "an explicitly radical feminist group, as opposed to a group [like NYRW] that had radical feminists in it along with other people."[3] They envisioned Redstockings as a "very militant, very public group," one which would be committed to action as well as to consciousness-raising.[4] They chose the name Redstockings

> to represent a synthesis of two traditions: that of the earlier feminist theoreticians and writers who were insultingly called "Bluestockings" in the 19th century, and the militant political tradition of radicals—the red of revolution.[5]

As Willis remembers it, "it was Shulie and I who decided on the group, Shulie and I who made up the name, and we who invited other people."[6] Besides Willis and Firestone, the earliest members of Redstockings included Kathie Sarachild, Irene Peslikis, Pat Mainardi, Barbara Mehrhof, Pam Kearon, Linda Feldman, Sheila Cronan, and Barbara Kaminsky. Carol Hanisch did not join the group because she moved to Gainesville, Florida to organize women for the Southern Conference Educational Fund (SCEF) and to work in Gainesville Women's Liberation with her friends Judith Brown and Carol Giardina. Sarachild attended several early Redstockings' meetings, but in March she moved to Gainesville for a month to work on a consciousness-raising handbook.[7] However, when Sarachild returned in April she became one of the group's key members.[8] Ros Baxandall, Barbara Leon, and Alix Kates Shulman joined later that spring.

For its first action, Redstockings decided to address the issue of abortion. By the late '60s sentiment within the medical profession and family-planning organizations was shifting in favor of reform (and in some cases repeal) of abortion laws. Beginning with Colorado in 1967, a number of states started to reform these laws. Unfortunately, these so-called reform bills were little better than the laws they replaced. The new laws did make therapeutic abortion legal, but "punitive therapeutic abortion committees put women through intense and often moralizing inquiries to determine whether their abortion request was truly justified on 'health' grounds." For instance, California and Colorado not only required written consent from two doctors and the hospital committee, but made the procedure more expensive by mandating that it be done on an inpatient basis. Restrictions such as these forced poor women who "lacked the personal connections to private doctors and the funds necessary to obtain a safe hosptial abortion" to use back-alley abortionists.[9] Seeing the less than liberating effects of abortion reform, radical feminists like Cindy Cisler, a founder of New Yorkers for Abortion Law Repeal, contended:

> Proposals for "reform" are based on the notion that abortion must be regulated, meted out to deserving women under an elaborate set of rules designed to provide "safeguards against abuse. . . . " Repeal is based on the . . . idea of *justice*: that abortion is a woman's right and that no one can veto her decision and compel her to bear children against her will.[10]

Indeed, as Willis points out, when feminists began to push for the repeal of abortion laws, "our first target was the 'reformers' who sat around splitting hairs over how sick or poor or multiparous a pregnant woman had to be to deserve exemption from reproductive duty."[11]

New York was among the states considering reforming its abortion law. When it was announced that the state would be holding legislative hearings on abortion reform on February 13, 1969, and that fourteen men and one woman—a nun—had been selected as expert witnesses for the hearing, women's liberationists and NOW members alike decided to picket the hearing. A group of about seven women's liberationists resolved to do more than merely picket. Determined that those fifteen witnesses would not be the only ones allowed to discuss under what conditions women might be permitted abortions, they decided to disrupt the hearing.[12] After one of the witnesses, a judge, recommended that abortion be made legal for women who had "'done their social duty' " by having four children, Kathie Sarachild stood up and shouted, "'Alright, now let's hear from some *real* experts—the women.' " According to a *New York Times* reporter, the committee members just "stared over their microphones in amazement" at what was happening. Sarachild continued talking and urged the legislature to repeal all abortion laws "instead of wasting more time talking about these stupid reforms."[13] Then Willis stood up and began to testify. Exasperated, one legislator pleaded with the protestors to "act like ladies," but to no avail.[14] Finally, the committee adjourned and moved to another room to meet in executive session. Shortly after the protest, in an interview for the *Guardian*, Willis explained:

> We broke up the hearings to push a political debate. We wanted to expose how the system operates in a male-supremacist way. We are particularly interested in exposing the concept of expertise, as opposed to letting people make decisions about their lives. This is the same stuff they tried to push over on the black movement.[15]

Inspired by the success of this action, the newly formed Redstockings decided to hold their own hearings on abortion. Although many women refused to testify about their abortions for fear of possible repercussions, Peslikis and Kaminsky managed to line up twelve speakers for the March 21 speak-out.[16] Mehrhof recalls that members of Redstockings wore skirts and red stockings to the event. In an effort to "confront the spurious personal-political distinction," the assumption that abortion was somehow not political, the women decided to talk about themselves rather than talk in theoretical terms. Writing shortly thereafter, Willis maintained that they had been correct to talk in personal terms for it "evoke[d] strong reactions . . . empathy, anger, pain" from the 300 or so people who attended. So successful was the speak-out that its organizers hoped that the idea of speak-outs would "catch on and become the equivalent, for the women's movement, of the Vietnam teach-ins."[17] In fact, their speak-out inspired others to speak out on the issue. As part of their campaign to overturn abortion laws, French feminists enlisted the support of a number of prominent French women (including de Beauvoir) who risked fines and imprisonment by publicly declaring, "I have had an abortion."[18]

In early April, Sheila Cronan proposed that for their next action the group hang a banner which would read "Liberty for Women: Repeal All Abortion Laws" from the Statue of Liberty. However, Cronan and her allies encountered technical problems in constructing the banner, and opposition to the action when Sarachild returned to the group. Sarachild argued that the action was poorly conceived and that the group's energy would be better spent writing a manifesto.[19] When the group voted in mid-June to scuttle the action, the discussion reportedly "broke down into great recriminations."[20]

The Statue of Liberty action became a point of contention because members disagreed about the importance of consciousness-raising. Not everyone in the group was as committed to consciousness-raising as Sarachild, Peslikis, and Mainardi. Certainly, Mehrhof, Kearon, Cronan, and Linda Feldman—who eventually left Redstockings to join The Feminists—felt that consciousness-raising should be de-emphasized. Even Firestone reportedly wanted the group to be more action-oriented. There were also disagreements about the pro-woman line. Mehrhof, Kearon, Cronan, and Feldman were its most vocal detractors. But Willis contends that both she and Firestone were far more psychologically oriented than Sarachild, Peslikis, and Mainardi of the pro-woman faction.[21]

The tensions over consciousness-raising and the pro-woman line seem to have been exacerbated by Sarachild's re-entry to the group. She reportedly let the group know that she was returning to Redstockings despite her differences with the group.[22] She then reportedly tried to recruit to the group women who she thought shared her political vision. Baxandall, who was at that time in a study group with Anne Forer, Judy Thibeau, and Helen Kritzler, was among those Sarachild succeeded in recruiting. Baxandall asserts that Sarachild told her that she was shifting the group's focus from action to consciousness-raising and that the meetings were, as a result, much improved.[23] Indeed, the group became less action-oriented following the March 1969 abortion speak-out. The group did disrupt another all-male abortion panel at Cooper Union and helped to organize a number of joint actions.[24] But from the spring of 1969 until its demise in the fall of 1970, the group devoted most of its time to consciousness-raising, organized c-r groups for new women, drafted its manifesto, and distributed movement literature.[25]

Redstockings, as the name implies, was strongly influenced by the left. Although the group rejected Marxist theorizing on the "woman question," it appropriated Marxist methodology in an effort to construct a theory of women's oppression. For instance, Firestone argued that in developing an analysis of male supremacy, feminists could

> learn a lot from Marx and Engels: Not their literal opinions about women—about the conditions of women as an oppressed class

> they know next to nothing . . . —but rather their analytic *method*.[26]

The pro-woman faction, the dominant faction in Redstockings, articulated what Willis has described as "a kind of neo-Maoist materialism," which put them at odds with many other radical feminists.[27] According to the pro-woman line, women's behavior was the result of immediate external conditions and not, as many other feminists argued, the result of their conditioning. Or in the words of their manifesto, "women's submission is not the result of brainwashing, stupidity, or mental illness but of continual, daily pressure from men."[28] It rejected as false all psychological explanations of women's behavior. For instance, while many feminists argued that women marry because they are brainwashed into believing that they must, pro-woman feminists argued that women marry because remaining single is "truly difficult" and requires that one work at a "boring and alienating job."[29] Carol Hanisch, one of the main proponents of the pro-woman line, even argued that looking pretty and acting dumb were survival strategies which women should continue to use until such time as the "power of unity" could replace them. Willis maintains that the pro-woman line

> did tend to put power issues into very sharp focus. If you simply ignored the complicated psychological issues which [the pro-woman line faction] didn't agree existed and just talked about the particular power relations that were happening . . . you still learned a lot.[30]

Moreover, in arguing that there were no personal solutions, but, rather, "elements of resistance and accommodation" in all choices, Redstockings tried to avoid making moralistic judgements about other women, especially non-Movement women.[31] Indeed, for some Redstockings the pro-woman line was also a way to address the issue of class. In the spring of 1970, Barbara Leon argued:

> to advocate that women "liberate themselves" by giving up marriage reflects a strong class bias in automatically excluding the mass of women who have no other means of support but a husband.

To Leon all the talk of conditioning or brainwashing

> falsely divides women into two groups—those who are "militant" and those who are still "brainwashed," thus keeping us apart and preventing us from realizing our common oppression. Talk about brainwashing ensures domination of the feminist movement by college-educated white women: the majority of women whose struggles we must join (welfare mothers, black and brown women fighting for their liberation, working women and housewives) are too involved in matters of survival to listen to mythical abstractions about damaged psyches or internalized images.[32]

As Leon's statement suggests, Redstockings assumed that their "common oppression" united women more than class or race divided them. In their manifesto, Redstockings tried to mitigate class and race divisions by "defin[ing] our best interest as that of the poorest, most brutally exploited woman," and by "repudiat[ing] all economic, racial, educational or status privileges that divide us from other women."[33] Redstockings' analysis suggested that a multi-class and multi-racial movement could be achieved if white, middle-class women would simply renounce their privileges and altruistically identify with women who were less privileged than they. It was a nice fantasy, but as we shall see, it did not materialize.

Pro-woman feminists not only defended married women against charges of brainwashing, they claimed that marriage represented the best bargain for women—a position which was somewhat anomalous among radical feminists. Patricia Mainardi claimed that in consciousness-raising sessions

> it became obvious that the entire alternative lifestyle revolutionary subculture was in some ways a giant step backwards for women, despite its attractive aspects and the hopes some women had for it being an improvement over "traditional marriage."[34]

Mainardi went further and argued that both men and women "would like love, security, companionship, respect and a long-term relationship."[35] And in a 1971 speech, Sarachild argued "most women wouldn't join a movement that called for 'free love' . . . because they know that isn't freedom (for women) or love (for women)."[36] In explaining women's preference for monogamous relationships, Leon stressed "the dangers of venereal disease, unwanted pregnancy, or forcible rape that a woman exposes herself to in casual encounters.''[37] Not everyone in Redstockings agreed that sexual fidelity was preferable to "free love." Willis recalls having had "terrible fights" with Sarachild about monogamy.[38] While Willis admits that consciousness-raising revealed that most women favored monogamous relationships, she claims that the group was unable to reach a consensus about why this was so:

> There were a lot of arguments about how to interpret that material (did it represent these women's true desires, their objective interest given a sexist culture, or the psychology of the oppressed) and what to make of the minority who disagreed (was the difference in their situation or their emotional makeup, did they have false consciousness, or what).[39]

Sarachild proposed in 1969 that women "use marriage as the 'dictatorship of the proletariat' in the family revolution. When male supremacy is completely eliminated, marriage, like the state, will disappear."[40] Indeed, Sarachild reportedly declared at one Redstockings meeting, "we won't get off the plantation until the revolution!"[41] The irony of all this is that most of the women in Redstockings did not reside on "plantations." For instance, Sarachild, despite her protestations about staying on the "plantation," had never married. In fact, Willis claims that most of the women in Redstockings "came out of the counter-culture and continued to hang out with counter-culture men." Willis notes that "there was this rebellion and resentment against the lives that in many ways we were, in fact, living."[42]

But if the pro-woman feminists of Redstockings were highly critical of the sexual revolution and free love, they were not anti-sexual in the way Cell 16 and The Feminists were. Like a number of other radical feminists, they criticized the repression of female sexuality and "took for granted women's desire for genital sexual pleasure."[43] To feminists who doubted that heterosexuality for women was either fully chosen or truly pleasurable, the Redstockings' position smacked of false consciousness. Indeed, Atkinson reportedly attended one Redstockings meeting where she and Willis got into a disagreement over whether women really needed sexual relationships. Willis recalls at one point in the debate "Ti-Grace saying very patronizingly that [sexual desire] was all in my head."[44]

Redstockings' analysis of sexual politics had more than a little to do with their conviction that heterosexuality could be deployed on women's behalf. Indeed, in 1968 Sarachild argued, "We're saying that for most of history sex was, in fact, both our undoing and our only possible weapon of self-defense and self-assertion (aggression)."[45] Redstockings envisioned women directly confronting the men in their lives, much as the women did in William Hinton's *Fanshen*, a widely read and influential book among feminists and leftists which documents the revolutionary transformation of the Chinese village of Long Bow.[46] According to Willis, the idea behind Redstockings' "vision of direct confrontation between sexual classes" was that if all women demanded equality and refused to " 'scab' " men would be forced to treat women as equals.[47] But as Willis notes, there was a strong "heterosexual presumption" here which ran counter to Redstockings' claims that they did not elevate one lifestyle or sexual preference over another:

> It was tacitly assumed, and sometimes explicitly argued that men's need for sexual love from women was our biggest weapon in both individual and collective struggle—and that our own need for *satisfying* sexual love from men was our greatest incentive for maintaining the kind of personal confrontation that feminism required.[48]

Lesbians, who were seen as withdrawing from the sexual battleground rather than engaging men in struggle, were irrelevant to Redstockings' vision of class struggle between men and women.

In their manifesto, Redstockings contended that "*all men*"—not just the ruling class men whom politicos typically targeted—"receive economic, sexual and psychological benefits from male supremacy." Indeed, according to their manifesto, "*All men* have oppressed women." Redstockings rejected an institutional analysis of women's oppression because they felt it allowed men to evade responsibility for their role in maintaining male supremacy. Thus, the manifesto contended that "institutions alone do not oppress; they are merely tools of the oppressor."[49] Willis, who finds fault with Redstockings' anti-institutional analysis, explains:

> The idea that systems (like the family or capitalism) are in some sense autonomous, that they operate according to a logic that in

> certain ways constrains the rulers as well as the ruled, was rejected as a mystification and a way of letting men off the hook. To say, for instance, that the family oppressed women was to evade the fact that our husbands and fathers oppressed us.[50]

To Pat Mainardi, for instance, the problem was not marriage, but, rather, the "male supremacy and sex roles within marriage."[51] Not all members agreed with this analysis; in their individual writings both Willis and Firestone stressed the centrality of marriage and the family to women's oppression.[52] For example, in *The Dialectic of Sex*, Firestone called for the elimination of the family structure, "the vinculum," she argued, "through which the psychology of power can always be smuggled."[53] If all men were their oppressors, all women were automatically assumed to be their allies, or sisters. Thus Redstockings pledged that they would "always take the side of women against their oppressors."

By spring 1969, only several months after Redstockings' founding, group members found themselves increasingly divided on ideological, structural, and strategic questions. Kearon, Mehrhof, Cronan, and Feldman constituted the minority that pushed for more action and theory, separatism in personal as well as political life, and a more egalitarian group structure. They resented Sarachild's attempts to reinstitute consciousness-raising, an activity they felt resulted only in more consciousness-raising, never in action.[54] Even before the disintegration of NYRW, Mehrhof had argued that "consciousness-raising has the ability to organize great numbers of women, but to organize them for nothing."[55] Mehrhof and others wanted to organize actions in order to make their ideas public and to test themselves. To Kearon consciousness-raising seemed dangerously static:

> The mass of woman want facts and statistics. We also want training in consistent principles of feminism. We want to change and remold ourselves. Talking about our personal problems is not enough.

And, in what seems a reference to Sarachild, Kearon pointed out that it "is not for any well-educated woman to declare that education is unnecessary or undesirable. It is essential for all women to be politically educated."[56]

This faction also opposed the pro-woman line which they argued underestimated women's revolutionary potential and thus "kep[t] [women] from moving out . . . from going on the offensive." In particular they objected to Redstockings' position on marriage and sex. Kearon criticized the assumption that "it is natural for men and women to be dependent on each other." She excoriated the pro-woman line faction for being concerned with ensuring male fidelity "instead of encouraging women to break off their relationships with men."[57] According to Willis:

> The struggle [over separatism] was between women who took for granted that being with men was desirable and those who wanted nothing to do with men and were angry at women who they felt were too male-oriented.[58]

For this minority faction, the goal was to wean women from debilitating relationships with men, not to encourage them to engage their lovers or husbands in battle. They argued that heterosexuality inhibited female solidarity and encouraged female dependence. And, like Atkinson, Kearon chided pro-woman feminists for being so concerned with sex:

> Sex is considered a necessity of life (Who says so? Well Sigmund Freud and Paul Krassner seem to think so). And by sex they mean heterosexual sex not masturbation, not lesbianism. It is considered "dangerous" to one's health to go without it for long periods of time. Exactly what kind of symptoms one can expect from it is never mentioned. But the very vagueness of the disease makes "sex starvation" a heavy threat, and is just another device, originated and propagated by men to keep women bound to them.[59]

For Kearon and her allies, heterosexual desire was nothing more than a male fabrication designed to keep women enslaved to men.

Mehrhof, Kearon, Feldman, and Cronan also opposed what they felt was the inegalitarian structure of Redstockings. They argued that the group automatically assumed that those women with skills, such as writing or public speaking, should be the group's spokeswomen. This became an issue almost immediately when Willis and Firestone were extensively quoted in a series of *Guardian* articles on women's liberation.[60] Some women felt that they should not have identified themselves as Redstockings members without first informing the group that they were being interviewed. Others resented their access to the media. At a March 25 meeting, Kearon and others criticized Firestone and Willis for "hoarding" the creative work and dominating the meetings.[61]

The "equality" proponents learned that Atkinson's group, The October 17th Movement (later to be re-named The Feminists) had adopted the lot system whereby work was divided into two categories—creative and routine—and was determined by lot rather than expertise or familiarity.[62] By April, they had succeeded in getting Redstockings to vote in the lot system. In early June, Mehrhof and Kearon raised the issue of class, claiming that those women with skills had not obtained them by accident, but by virtue of their class background. Mehrhof and Kearon were of working-class or lower middle-class origins, but this was something they shared with several other members, including Willis, Peslikis, and Sarachild.[63] The equality issue—or the class issue, as it later became—caused a great deal of tension in the group. Willis, who wrote a column on rock music for *The New Yorker*, admits that writers had a certain power in the movement because they could get their ideas across much more easily than other women. Their power contravened the ideology, especially characteristic of Redstockings, of women's shared powerlessness. The influence enjoyed by writers in the movement suggested that some sisters were indeed more powerful than others.

Those accused of elitism handled the criticism differently. In 1984, Willis wrote that she "tried to respond to the criticism by echoing it and withdrawing from [her] leadership role, in classic guilty liberal fashion."[64] But Willis recalls that Firestone was very "impatient with all the noodling over egalitarianism" and did nothing to disguise it:

> I remember one meeting where Shulie refused to do any typing. She said that was what she had always had to do and she hadn't joined the women's movement to do more typing. She was very snarky about that.

In the end, Willis believes that Firestone "took it personally and felt betrayed by people whom she felt were trying to derail the movement." She claims that Firestone "was always under attack" for elitism and feels that it was "aimed as much at her good qualities as her bad qualities." Willis admits that Firestone could be "bossy and domineering," but contends that she was also "a leader with good ideas."[65] According to Mehrhof's notes of the March 25 meeting, Firestone, upon being attacked, said, "the same thing happened in Radical Women—you are trying to castrate me."[66] In the *Guardian* article, Firestone attributed the "decapitation of leadership" to a "terror of carrying [feminism] to its logical conclusions."[67] But, at least in principle, Firestone was not opposed to internal democracy. In *The Dialectic of Sex*, she maintained that the movement's commitment to "establishing an egalitarian structure" set it apart from other movements which "are unable to practice among themselves what they preach."[68]

Sarachild was also attacked for being too dominant, too much of a leader. Willis, like many others who worked with Sarachild, acknowledges that she could be "really obstreperous and not listen to people." However, she feels that Sarachild was "attacked unmercifully for being 'too male, too unsisterly, too argumentative, and too judgmental.' "[69] As usual, Sarachild was attacked for her confrontative method of consciousness-raising. This time, Joyce Betries, who later joined the sectarian left group Youth Against War and Fascism, challenged Sarachild's leadership. Betries succeeded in getting the group to adopt a set of consciousness-raising rules designed to minimize the power differential within the group. According to Cellestine Ware, a black woman who helped found New York Radical Feminists, the rules even prohibited members from commenting on another's experience.[70]

The issue of expansion was yet another tension in the group. Until the summer of 1969 the group had been closed except to those who were recruited by members. Many of the founders preferred to recruit women who agreed with the group's program. Baxandall contends that Sarachild "wanted people who had developed a line to be in the group together and to recruit other people based on that. She was in the process of becoming a Leninist."[71] Their reservations about expansion stemmed in large part from fears that new members would weaken the group's analysis.[72] However, other women felt that the group, by remaining closed to all but those who already agreed with its analysis, was wasting an opportunity to organize large numbers of women. In late June, Redstockings announced that it would begin organizing groups for new women. According to one estimate, there were about 200 women in Redstockings at its height.[73] By establishing new groups, Redstockings expanded, and avoided diluting the politics of the original group, Group X.

But there was tension between the new women, who were forever suggesting that the manifesto be changed, and the founders, who saw any revision as a vitiation of their manifesto.[74] Karla Jay was among the new women who felt that the founders expected them to embrace their program and analysis "as though they were the Ten Commandments."[75] Yet one can appreciate how the founders felt. Many of the new women lacked their experience in radical politics. In fact, Peslikis contends that many of the women who joined Redstockings lacked any class analysis.[76] Over time the new groups grew more autonomous from the founding group.

Redstockings continued to function until the fall of 1970. But the battles over separatism, consciousness-raising, elitism, and expansion wore people down. Mehrhof, Kearon, Feldman, and Cronan left Redstockings for The Feminists between the spring and fall of 1969. Firestone grew increasingly impatient with the pro-woman line and the consciousness-raising program of the dominant faction and was increasingly at odds with the minority faction that was pushing the "equality issue."[77] She was also becoming more involved in writing her book, a fact which undoubtedly made some women resentful. Mehrhof noted that by late June, Firestone was "slipping out of the group."[78] Within a few months she would begin to organize New York Radical Feminists with Anne Koedt. In fall 1969, Willis moved to Colorado to participate in the GI Coffeehouse movement and to try to initiate a radical feminist movement there. Shortly after Redstockings accepted Betries' consciousness-raising rules, Betries left the group. Somewhat later, Sarachild left the group, and with Barbara Leon and Colette Price started *Woman's World*, "a New York City-based newspaper of feminist analysis."[79] Peslikis and Mainardi left to start Redstockings artists, and later, the journal *Women and Art*.

Why did Redstockings dissolve? The group's detractors maintain that Redstockings was derailed by its dogmatic commitment to the pro-woman line and consciousness-raising.[80] Peslikis contends that Redstockings had fulfilled its purpose by writing its manifesto and disseminating movement literature.[81] And Hanisch and Leon attribute Redstockings' demise to newcomers who joined the group despite disagreeing with the group's philosophy.[82] However, the group's most vocal dissidents had been with the group from the outset.

Redstockings left its mark on the movement. It popularized consciousness-raising, invented the speak-out, and radicalized thousands of women by distributing movement literature—at first free of charge. Redstockings' insistence that all men oppress women and its nonjudgmental stance toward non-Movement women were valuable correctives to the prevailing left analysis which attributed women's oppression to the "system" or to women's "false consciousness." Nevertheless, the pro-woman line was in many respects problematic, especially as it was elaborated by Sarachild and others. Both consciousness-raising and the pro-woman line assumed that women's experiences and interests were uniform, or as Sarachild put it, "that most women were like ourselves—not different."[83] In assuming the universality of their experiences, they seriously underestimated the class and racial differences dividing women. Even as late as 1973, Sarachild maintained that "what was moving behind radical women was that we understood that we were basically the same as other women and therefore what would turn us on would turn other women on."[84] But despite their sincere efforts to identify with those women most victimized by the system, the movement remained largely white and middle-class. The vast majority of working-class and third-world women were not "turned on" by their feminism.

Their assumption that most women were like themselves also led them to underestimate the difficulty of achieving female solidarity. The Chinese women of Long Bow may have built "a strong united sisterhood," but as Willis points out, "America is not a Chinese village."[85] Their declaration, "we will always take the side of women against their oppressors," ignored the possibility that women's interests might in fact be oppositional.[86] Their insistence on pursuing "only what is good for women," rather than what is " 'revolutionary' or 'reformist,' " echoed Stokely Carmichael, who in 1968 had declared "it is not a question of right or left, it's a question of black."[87] While this was clearly a reaction to those left feminists who were forever criticizing feminism as intrinsically reformist, it seemed to imply that "reformist" and "revolutionary" were male categories which did not apply to women's liberationists—a point later amplified by cultural feminists. Perhaps this is why pro-woman feminists were initially so restrained in their criticism of liberal feminists whose feminism was more self-interested and who lacked Redstockings' commitment to "the poorest, most brutally exploited women." For example, it was not until 1971, long after other radical feminists, that Sarachild acknowledged that

> N.O.W. was always afraid to support the principles of all-female groups, despite the absolute necessity for an oppressed class to organize out of earshot of the oppressor and build an independent base of power. The classy N.O.W. ladies were too afraid of labels like "man-hater."[88]

And in contrast to most radical feminists who dismissed *Ms.* magazine when it began publishing in the spring of 1972, Sarachild hailed it as "a molotov cocktail that looked like a martini." She lavished praise on the magazine, claiming that its "feminist, political content, in some important ways, is better than most of what the women's liberation movement has yet come up with."[89] Although she conceded that *Ms.* seemed "rather nervous about its association with the real, breathing women who comprise the feminist movement," she argued:

> Of course, *genuine* support from the "prominent" and "respectable" type of women could be a real aid to *Ms.* and to the feminist movement as a whole. The defeat of male supremacy is, after all, in our common interests and such women may have access to sources of information and money which would otherwise be unavailable for feminist use.[90]

Sarachild's early defense of *Ms.* is ironic because by 1973 she was charging *Ms.* with opportunism and calling the magazine "the Teamsters of the women's movement." Sarachild argued that *Ms.* had "moved in on the women's movement the way the Teamsters moved in on the Farmworkers Union. They don't break hard ground themselves. They only go where people have been."[91] In 1973 Sarachild, Hanisch, Leon, and Price re-established Redstockings, and in 1975 accused Gloria Steinem, *Ms.* magazine's chief editor, of having had ties with the CIA.[92] They further insinuated that the CIA was using the magazine as a pawn to supplant radical feminism with liberal feminism. For the re-formed Redstockings, the movement's decline was the work of "agents, opportunists, and fools."[93] They did not acknowledge that their faith in a universal sisterhood might have been misplaced.

If pro-woman feminists were slow to criticize liberal feminists they took little time in denouncing women who chose alternative lifestyles. Their conviction that the search for alternative lifestyles would promote "personal solutionism," and would distance the movement from the masses of women led them to validate traditional over rebellious lifestyles. Sometimes they even seemed more interested in preserving traditional strategies than in carving out new ones for women. Jennifer Gardner, an early proponent of the pro-woman line who had moved from New York City to the Bay Area and worked on the *Women's Page*, attacked the small-group concept which Pam Allen, now another Bay Area resident, had pioneered:

> The small group is . . . simply a counter-institution. It works by diverting women's energy from revolutionary activity to attempts to live an alternative life style. In small groups . . . we are supposed to create a new morality right in the middle of the same old objective conditions. The implication is that we are to blame for our oppression, that all we need to do is "change" ourselves, and things will be fine.[94]

With the emergence of the gay liberation movement and lesbian feminism, Redstockings' "heterosexual presumption" developed into an antagonism toward lesbian feminism that verged on homophobic. To the pro-woman faction the growing numbers of women exploring same-sex relationships seemed to jeopardize the struggle against male supremacy, at least as they had envisioned it. In mid-1971, Sarachild and Leon claimed that within the

> "left" flank of the so-called feminist organizations (in "women's liberation" and "radical lesbians") there were and still are all those incredible claims of groovy and liberated all-female "alternative lifestyles," of women who were so "strong" they no longer "cared" about men even though they were still living in the same world as men, the man's world, in fact.[95]

Women who experimented with celibacy, lesbianism, bisexuality, and women's communes were accused of retreating from the sexual battlefield. And in 1975 the recomposed Redstockings blamed lesbians, in partnership with "pseudo-leftists," for the movement's decline.[96] For example, Pat Mainardi contended:

> The leftist women thought of us as support troops for their dogma; the lesbians as potential sex partners, the sum of these two attitudes—followers, supporters and sex partners—is exactly the same as men's attitudes towards all women. It is easy to see the derivation of the left-lesbian alliance—they need each other, as two sides of the same coin.[97]

Redstockings' fears about personal solutionism were not unfounded, for experimentation with nontraditional lifestyles was often accompanied by diminished political activism. Some women did become more interested in making internal changes—"changing their heads"—than in struggling to change external conditions. Yet many women in the movement did not find the prospect of relentless struggle with recalcitrant men appealing. Moreover, to many it seemed that women would have more energy to fight male supremacy if they were no longer entangled in emotionally draining relationships with men. In fact, many radical feminists, including a few Redstockings, were exploring alternatives to heterosexuality. Although radical feminists were committed to collective struggle, they were hardly uninterested in improving the quality of their personal lives. Beyond a point, the Redstockings' solution of engaging men in personal and collective struggle seemed more tiring than inspiring to many women.

Just as the pro-woman faction argued that no lifestyle was preferable to another, they contended that no man was better than any other. But the idea that all men were intransigent heels was, as Willis explains:

> contradictory to the fact that we were all trying to pressure the men to be better. For what improvements men did make were a choice on their part, because they could find women who were not in the movement if they wanted to.[98]

If men were irredeemably sexist, unwilling as members of the oppressor class to part with their privileges, women were ineluctably their victims. Their contention that "women act out of necessity, . . . not out of choice" reduced women to helpless victims unable to act upon the world. For instance, in 1970 pro-woman line advocate, Judith Brown wrote:

> The current trend toward unisex and female aggressiveness in bed is not a sign of female liberation. In Unisex [*sic*] the male is coopting [*sic*] the few ornaments women have to make themselves more attractive in the necessary race for a man. Urging women to take more responsibility in bed is an attempt to extend her sphere of emotional responsibility to love-making; now the man doesn't even have to take the risk of initiating sex.[99]

The assumption seemed to be that men were imposing new fashion and sexual standards upon women. But, of course, many women were interested in playing a more active role during sex and welcomed the less constricting clothing afforded by unisex fashions. By the same logic, it could be argued that abortion laws were liberalized to maximize men's sexual access to women.

Even Patricia Mainardi, who was very much in the pro-woman camp, today acknowledges that the pro-woman line may have exaggerated men's power and women's powerlessness.[100] In an effort to discourage women from seeking personal solutions, pro-woman feminists depicted women's oppression as so total that individual women were unable to resist. Pro-woman feminists made women's oppression seem monolithic and immutable in much the same way that certain feminists today do. Indeed, Willis maintains that Redstockings' tendency to see men as "a monolithic mass" and women as powerless victims set the stage, quite unintentionally, for the sort of analysis articulated by Andrea Dworkin.[101] The major differences being that pro-woman feminists attributed women's acquiescence to material conditions rather than to false consciousness, and men's resistance to the attachment of any oppressor class to its privileged status, not to some peculiarly male predilection for power.

The pro-woman line became a much maligned tendency within certain movement circles. For instance, Judith Hole and Ellen Levine accused the pro-woman line of fostering "female 'cultural nationalism' " by glorifying feminine behavior.[102] And feminist playwright Anselma dell'Olio claimed that the pro-woman line revalued femininity, and thus encouraged attacks on strong, assertive women.[103] However, Sarachild and others would never have condoned attacks on strong women. In fact, they were constantly under attack for being too vociferous and "unfeminine." Moreover, the pro-woman line faction was interested in validating women's traditional survival strategies, not femininity. Redstockings did apotheosize women, but for the political acumen and cunning which they believed women had developed as members of an oppressed class. In contrast to cultural feminists, they would have attributed male belligerence and female pacifism to men's power and women's powerlessness, not to biological differences or different value systems. For Redstockings, it was a question of power relations, not values.[104]

Cell 16

To Susan Brownmiller, the women of Cell 16 were the "movement heavies."[105] Nor was Brownmiller the only one who felt this way. After members of Cell 16 visited a NYRW meeting in 1968, Corinne Coleman remembers having thought, "wow, they're very strong!" Certainly, Cell 16 with their program of celibacy, separatism, and karate seemed the quintessential radical women's liberation group. Cell 16's political perspective became well known within the movement because the group published one of the very earliest radical feminist journals, *No More Fun and Games*—a title that captures all too well the essence of the group's message. Roxanne Dunbar formed Cell 16 in the summer of 1968 after moving to Boston from the West Coast where she had been active in the new left. She recruited women to the group by placing an ad in an underground paper. Besides Dunbar, Cell 16 consisted of Dana Densmore (whose mother, Donna Allen, was a founder of Women Strike for Peace), Jeanne Lafferty, Lisa Leghorn, Abby Rockefeller (of *the* Rockefeller family), Betsy Warrior, and Jayne West. They reportedly read Valerie Solanas's *SCUM Manifesto* "as their first order of business."[106]

Cell 16 initially avoided the feminist-politico schism because it was a small group in which membership was contingent upon agreement with the group's politics.[107] In fact, when Meredith Tax and Linda Gordon—who later helped found the Boston socialist-feminist group Bread and Roses—tried to join, they were turned away. Dunbar conceived of Cell 16 as a vanguard cadre group. In the first issue of *No More Fun and Games*, published in October 1968, Dunbar proclaimed:

> A vanguard of women must operate to show women the possibility of a new society. . . . Our means, other than our educational efforts and the formation of communes will be secret. We shall not fight on the enemy's grounds—on his streets, in his courts, legislatures, "radical" movements, marriage, media.[108]

And, in February 1969, Dunbar declared that at some point "warfare (guerrilla style)" would be necessary.[109] Despite the group's avowed commitment to egalitarianism, Dunbar was Cell 16's leader and major theoretician until she left the group in early 1970. Tax believes that Dunbar "wanted to be a charismatic leader in that very male style of charismatic leader. She basically believed that she was Lenin. And she was certainly very good."[110]

But while Cell 16 impressed many women as the most militant of all women's liberation groups, their theoretical efforts were, initially at least, sometimes more leftist than radical feminist. Indeed, Dunbar's thinking was a strange mélange of Marx, Mao, de Beauvoir, and Solanas. Group members agreed that men oppressed women and that all women, not just working-class women, were their victims. But unlike most radical feminists who maintained that Marxist thinking on the "woman question" was of limited use in understanding male dominance, Dunbar declared that "Marx, Engels, Bakunin, Lenin, and Mao have analyzed woman's condition and place in history accurately." According to Dunbar the problem with the new left's analysis of women's oppression was not its blind reliance upon Marxist theorizing, but, rather, its failure to follow Marx and Engels closely enough.[111] Following Engels, Dunbar argued that the family was the cornerstone of male supremacy and that women, by virtue of their status as "household slaves," represented the "proletariat" within the family.[112] But Dunbar did not identify those aspects of Engels's or Marx's thinking that contradicted her feminism, particularly their privileging of class over gender. And in contrast to most radical feminists, Dunbar at first seemed to envision women's liberationists taking over the larger Movement rather than establishing an independent women's movement. Indeed, she seemed to share politicos' concern that feminism be connected to other movements and not fought on "an exclusive, narrow front":

> Ultimately, we want to destroy the three pillars of class (caste) society—the family, private property, and the state—and their attendant evils—corporate capitalism, imperialism, war, racism, misogyny, annihilation of the balance of nature.[113]

Whereas Redstockings argued that women's behavior was determined by their material conditions, Cell 16 attributed women's behavior to their sex-role conditioning. To Cell 16, women's interest in sex, fashion, make-up, and children demonstrated not only the extent to which they were damaged, but the extent to which they collaborated with the system.[114] For instance, Lisa Leghorn contended that "one can only be conditioned insofar as one desires to be accepted by those who condition."[115] Dana Densmore maintained that men would be unable to oppress women if women stopped believing in their inferiority:

> If the minds of the women are freed from these chains, no man will be able to oppress any woman. No man can, even now, in an individual relationship; all the woman has to do is walk out on him. And ironically enough, that is exactly what would force the men to shape up fastest. . . . All that's needed is for the woman to learn enough respect for herself to be unwilling to live with a man who treats her with contempt.[116]

While Redstockings believed that men rather than women needed to change, Densmore argued that "it is the situation that men and women find themselves in, the structures of society and the attitudes of women, that make it *possible* for men to oppress."[117] For Cell 16 the problem was women's diffidence and their dependence upon men, and the solution lay in women "unconditioning" themselves by taking off the accumulated emotional and physical flab that kept them enthralled to men. They exhorted women to swear off sex and relationships with men, to learn karate, and to live in communes—in all-female communes for those who were smart enough to still be single. With karate and celibacy, women, if not completely invulnerable and impenetrable, could at least achieve a degree of self-sufficiency and control over their lives.

As one might expect from exponents of the conditioning thesis, Cell 16 opposed biological explanations of gender differences. In the first issue of *No More Fun and Games*, Densmore maintained:

> Men have constructed an elaborate rationalization of why women are naturally suited to their role. This is the whole fantasy of WOMAN'S NATURE: gentle, loving, unaggressive, tender, modest, giving, patient, naive, simplistic, simple, irrational, instinctual, home-centered.[118]

In the same issue, Dunbar attacked the ideology of maternalism:

> The female human has no more maternity than any other animal. The characteristics usually attributed to women are the personality traits of Slaves—not the nature of the female. We have learned materialism and maternalism not from our closeness to reproduction, but from our experience as Slaves to men and children, our closeness to shit.[119]

However, by February 1969, when the second issue of their journal was published, Cell 16 seemed unsure whether feminism implied a repudiation of roles or a revaluation of femininity. Dunbar called on "men and women to reject their programmed roles," and in an editorial the group suggested that women who wanted children had "not achieved sufficient maturity and autonomy and [are] seeking a hopeless fulfillment through neurotic channels."[120] But Dunbar also defined feminism as "the liberation of the female principle in all human beings—the worldview which is maternal, materialist, and peaceful (noncompetitive)." Whereas Dunbar had equated maternity with slavishness only four months earlier, she now argued that women's programming for motherhood would "allow the female principle to take ascendance over the male principle."[121] This was in marked contrast to other radical feminists who held that women's socialization for motherhood ensured their subordination.[122]

For Dunbar, feminism involved the supplantation of the male principle by the female principle. Indeed, she preferred the term "female liberation" to women's liberation because it suggested that the movement's goal was the liberation of the female principle. Since Cell 16 defined maleness as the problem, they worked at banishing it from their midst. According to Dunbar, "much of the meeting is spent in reminding ourselves to stop 'acting like men.' All of us seem to have been infected with the phallic structures to some extent."[123] Dunbar even maintained that poor, third-world women would make better leaders than college-educated women because they were less likely to have been contaminated by masculine ideology.[124]

While Cell 16 was obsessed with avoiding male behavior, their style was anything but stereotypically feminine. They pioneered the popular movement look of khaki pants, work shirts, combat boots, and short hair. In fact, at the November 1969 Congress to Unite Women in New York City, Cell 16 horrified many feminists in the audience when one member of the group ceremonially cut off Dunbar's long hair as a protest against male-defined standards of beauty. Their performance distressed many in the audience who felt that the length of one's hair had very little to do with one's feminism.[125] Susan Brownmiller, among those in attendance who found their repudiation of femininity somewhat troubling, remembers someone shouting from the audience, "Men like my breasts, too. Do you want me to cut them off?"[126]

Although Dunbar was careful to define masculinity and femininity as socially constructed rather than biologically determined, some of the group's members were moving toward a biologistic understanding of gender. For instance, in an article that borrowed heavily from Solanas's *SCUM*, Betsy Warrior argued that if men wanted to preserve the planet they would "have to control and subdue their inner nature as they have outer nature." She condemned men's "aggressive, destructive drives" and contended that those "qualities make [men] unfit for life today."[127] After Dunbar's departure from the group in early 1970, Cell 16 shifted slowly from constructionism to essentialism. Nowhere is this plainer than in the group's writings on sexuality. Originally, Dunbar had argued that sexual "needs" are "conditioned needs" which can be "unconditoned."[128] Densmore suggested that "healthy (free) people would engage in the act of sex only for reproduction." Densmore held that "happy, healthy self-confident animals and people don't like being touched, don't need to snuggle and huggle. They are really free and self-contained and in their heads."[129]

However, by April 1970, the argument was becoming gendered. Densmore contended that while men do indeed experience a release from sex, for women "most of whom don't have orgasms at all . . . this physical issue is much less clear."[130] Moreover, Densmore argued that women have sex because they desire "human kindness, communication, back-to-the-womb merging and oblivion," not sexual pleasure.[131] While Densmore had argued in 1968 that people—male or female—who desired affection were the victims of mothers who had "trained [them] to be insecure and crave reassurance," by 1970 she found affection the only justifiable reason for sex. And in May 1973, Abby Rockefeller declared that "the real issue is simply that women *don't* like [sex] either with the same frequency or in the same way as men."[132] She maintained that the origins of men's hypersexuality and women's hyposexuality were hormonal. As though this constitued scientific proof, she contended:

> Even men who have no inclination to have sex with a reluctant woman find themselves experiencing a strong independent need for it. Many claim to experience physical discomfort to the point of pain if this need is not satisfied.[133]

In a 1971 issue of *No More Fun and Games*, Densmore's mother, Donna Allen, attributed male supremacy to genetic differences between the sexes:

> Being XX, a woman feels with total security that she is female. But the normal XY man does not have this same inner security about his identity. Vacillating between gentleness and aggressiveness, being genetically both, he tends to let himself be defined from outside.[134]

Cell 16's growing reliance upon essentialist explanations of gender was not altogether unpredictable. Almost from the beginning Cell 16 had a schizoid position on sex roles—calling for their elimination, yet paradoxically making maternalism the cornerstone of their feminism. In this respect the group departed from other radical feminists who believed that feminism required the explosion or deconstruction of gender differences. For instance, Firestone maintained that

> just as the end goal of socialist revolution was not only the elimination of the economic class *privilege* but of the economic class *distinction* itself, so the end goal of feminist revolution must be, unlike that of the first feminist movement, not just the elimination of male *privilege* but of the sex *distinction* itself: genital differences would no longer matter culturally.[135]

And Kate Millett declared that a feminist revolution entailed "unisex, or the end of separatist character structure, temperament and behavior, so that each individual may develop an entire—rather than a partial, limited, and conformist—personality."[136]

Cell 16 prefigured cultural feminism not only in its essentialist formulations of gender, but in its antipathy toward sex. From the first issue of *No More Fun and Games*, Densmore argued that sex is "inconvenient, time-consuming, energy-draining, and irrelevant."[137] She contended that "sex is actually a minor need, blown out of proportion, misunderstood."[138] And Dunbar called for liberation from sex:

> With all the talk of sexual liberation, one rarely hears talk of the liberation from sexuality, which many women privately voice. Such a sentiment reveals, so men say, "frigidity," "coldness," Brave New World surrealism. Yet for most women, right now, sex means brutalization, rape, submission, someone having power over them, another baby to care for and support.[139]

Dunbar echoed Solanas when she declared that "[t]he person who has been through the whole sex-scene, and then becomes by choice and revulsion, a celibate, is the most lucid person."[140] However, by July 1969, less than a year later, the argument shifted somewhat—sex wasn't merely energy-draining and dangerous for women, it was deleterious to the movement as well. Warrior argued that women "won't be able to clearly analyze our position and we will have a vested interest in not making males too hostile," unless women forsake "personal relationships and group situations with men."[141] In contrast to Redstockings' assumption that women's heterosexual needs would ensure their commitment to feminism, Cell 16 argued that women's hyposexuality was essential to the cause. Thus Densmore observed that "if it were true that we needed sex from men, it would be a great misfortune, one that might almost doom our fight."[142]

Cell 16 was probably the first group to propose that women withdraw from men personally as well as politically. Although Cell 16's heterosexual separatism helped establish the theoretical foundation for lesbian separatism, the group never advocated lesbianism. For Cell 16, the fundamental problem with homosexuality was that "like heterosexuality it suffers from being sexuality." Densmore argued that homosexuality was a response to the perversity of heterosexuality, and strongly implied that homosexuality was "unnatural."[143] Dunbar and Leghorn advised women to separate "from men who are not consciously working for female liberation," but warned them against seeking refuge in lesbian relationships. "Homosexuality," they argued, "is nothing more than a personal 'solution.' "[144] When lesbian-feminist activist Rita Mae Brown criticized Dunbar in February 1970 for ignoring the issue of lesbianism, Dunbar reportedly replied, "What I want to do is get women out of bed. Women can love each other but they don't have to sleep together."[145] Dunbar also articulated what was probably the earliest feminist critique of pornography, which she maintained, "expresses a masculine ideology of male power over females."[146] Like current feminist anti-pornography activists, she maintained that pornography *is* violence against women, and likened pornography to the lynching of blacks. In fact, Dunbar's excoriation of pornography sounds remarkably contemporary.

Cell 16's proto-cultural feminism co-existed rather awkwardly with its Marxist analysis. However, after Dunbar left Cell 16 in early 1970, the group moved away from a Marxist analysis as they elaborated Dunbar's notion of "the female principle." They devoted their energies to attacking "the male concept" rather than the family or the state. For instance, in April 1970, Leghorn identified "the male concept" as the source of all systems of domination:

> The assertion of the male concept has created a chaotic world—massive powers destroying each other in the quest for more power, economies dependent upon wars of aggression, masses of oppressed peoples caught in intricate hierarchies of caste and class and ineffectual bureaucracies intent on the preservation of centralized modes of decision-making. Hierarchy, centralization and the patriarchal family are all manifestations of aggression.

Moreover, Leghorn maintained that these "male patterns of hierarchy" were unknown in matriarchal cultures.[147] The group also elaborated upon Dunbar's analysis of women as a classless caste. Densmore even asserted that "the unity of women exists already" because she claimed "[t]here are no classes among women."[148] Cell 16's shift from Marxism might have been related to the Socialist Workers Party's (SWP) attempted take-over of the group sometime after Dunbar's departure. According to one account, two of the original members of Cell 16 became involved in the SWP while still involved in the group.[149] A schism arose and the group decided to disband amicably rather than allow themselves to be ravaged by factionalism. However, the non-SWP members discovered that the SWP women had tried to appropriate the files, mailing lists, and some funds from *No More Fun and Games*. At this point the non-SWP women circulated a letter throughout the movement alerting women to the SWP's efforts to "infiltrate" feminist groups. They re-established Cell 16 and resumed publication of *No More Fun and Games*. The group continued to function until 1973.

Interestingly, after Dunbar left the group, she became more committed to Marxism. She moved to New Orleans where she tried to organize southern women into the women's liberation movement. She formed the Southern Female Rights Union and then the New Orleans Female Workers' Union which was committed to building a "working-class base for the women's movement." In mid-1971 Dunbar's group, the Southern Female Rights Union, parroting the standard left line on the women's movement, proclaimed that the "programmatic demands" of the women's movement "were essentially white and middle-class demands designed to 'free' the typical single, white and middle-class woman from the tribulations which her working-class and Third World sisters cannot escape."[150] And in mid-1970, Dunbar even came out against legalized abortion, which, she argued, would be used to facilitate the genocide of black people. She asked an audience in Berkeley, "What are our individual lives (white women dying from illegal abortions), compared to the genocide of a whole people?"[151] In subsequent years, the mercurial Dunbar became involved in organizing first Appalachian, and then Native American women.[152]

In its revaluation of femininity, villainization of maleness, emphasis on personal rehabilitation, and belief in a global sisterhood, Cell 16 was the prototypical cultural feminist group. And, although Dunbar probably came to regard Cell 16's perspective as class- and race-bound, the seeds of that analysis were in Dunbar's original analysis, especially her equation of feminism with "the female principle."

The Feminists

One cannot discuss The Feminists without first discussing its founder, Ti-Grace Atkinson. Her biography is relevant not only because she so dominated the group while a part of it, but also because it can help illuminate why it was that Atkinson was so invested in being the most radical of all radical feminists. Atkinson was raised in an upper-class, Republican family in Louisiana. After marrying at the age of seventeen, she attended the University of Pennsylvania where she received her B.F.A. While living in Philadelphia she helped establish that city's Institute of Contemporary Art and wrote art criticism for *Art News*. She and her husband divorced in 1961, and in the mid-'60s she moved to New York and enrolled in Columbia's graduate program in political philosophy.[153] When she joined NOW in 1967, at the age of twenty-eight, she was a registered Republican with no prior political experience.[154] However, Atkinson was no novice to feminist ideas. She had read Simone de Beauvoir's *The Second Sex* in 1962 and, like so many other other women who helped spark the second wave of feminism, she was profoundly affected by it.[155] Feeling isolated, she wrote to de Beauvoir in 1965, who suggested that she write to Betty Friedan. Atkinson did contact Friedan, who initially viewed her as her protégé. Indeed, Friedan claims that it was she who pushed Atkinson into NOW's leadership for she felt that Atkinson's "Main Line accent and ladylike blond good looks would be perfect . . . for raising money from those mythical rich old widows we never did unearth."[156] Before long, however, Friedan discovered that Atkinson was anything but an obedient acolyte.

Atkinson's turbulent relationship with NOW began in February 1967, when she attended the first organizational meeting of the New York chapter. In December 1967 she was elected president of New York NOW, by far the largest and the most radical of all the NOW chapters. Although there were forty-five other chapters, the New York chapter contained thirty percent of the organization's membership.[157] Kate Millett, author of the 1970 bestseller *Sexual Politics*, feminist playwright Anselma dell'Olio, and civil-rights lawyer Florynce Kennedy were among the more radical women who belonged to this chapter. As a result of her involvement in NOW, Atkinson met women who politicized her about other forms of oppression and who introduced her to the "more radical factions" at Columbia University during the strike of 1968.[158] As Atkinson puts it, "my *feminism* radicalized me on other issues, not vice versa."[159]

But as Atkinson became more radical she grew disillusioned with NOW, and the NOW establishment grew increasingly apprehensive about her. From the beginning, Atkinson wanted the organization to take "unequivocal positions . . . on abortion, marriage, the family"—the very issues which many members were anxious that NOW avoid. Increasingly, Atkinson staked out positions that were on the cutting edge of feminism. For instance, abortion-rights activist Cindy Cisler contends that it was Atkinson who first pointed out the inconsistency of supporting both the repeal and the reform of abortion laws.[160] Moreover, Atkinson's involvement with controversial figures like Valerie Solanas and abortion advocate Bill Baird made the NOW establishment extremely uneasy.[161] Her very public show of support for Valerie Solanas in the aftermath of the Warhol shooting infuriated many NOW officers who feared that people might think the organization actually condoned the act.[162] Years later, Friedan was still furious about Atkinson's behavior. "No action of the board of New York NOW, of National NOW, no policy ever voted by the members advocated shooting men in the balls, the elimination of men as proposed by that SCUM Manifesto!"[163] Of course, Atkinson's outrageousness delighted the press who seemed to hang on her every word. As early as March 1968, a *New York Times* reporter labeled Atkinson the movement's "haute thinker."[164]

The situation came to a head on October 17, 1968, when Atkinson and other "younger dissenting" members tried to bring participatory democracy to NOW. They proposed that NOW scuttle elections and instead choose officers by lot and rotate the positions frequently to equalize power within the organization. However, the New York chapter defeated the proposed by-laws by a two-to-one margin. Atkinson claimed that the speeches given by those opposing the democratization of NOW

> revealed unmistakably that the division in N.O.W. as well as in the feminist movement as a whole is between those who want

> women to have the opportunity to be oppressors, too, and those who want to destroy oppression itself.[165]

To Atkinson, the lopsided vote demonstrated beyond a doubt that NOW was part of the problem rather than the solution. She resigned that night as New York chapter president and from her four other NOW offices as well. In her press release, Atkinson explained that the dissidents wanted

> to get rid of the positions of power, not get up into those positions. The fight against unequal power relationships between men and women necessitates fighting unequal power everyplace: between men and women (for feminists especially), but also between men and men, and women and women, between black and white, and rich and poor.[166]

Although several other NOW members apparently had vowed that they too would resign from the organization if the proposed by-laws were defeated, only two other women besides Atkinson left the organization in protest.[167]

With those two women, Atkinson formed the October 17th Movement, "named in honor of the day both of our departure from the rest of the Movement and our inception."[168] However, the October 17th Movement hardly represented a movement. As Atkinson herself remarked in 1971, she left NOW "essentially alone."[169] Indeed, within several months Atkinson was the only founding member left in the group. But by late winter, Anne Koedt from NYRW started attending meetings, and in the spring of 1969, when disaffected Redstockings members started to join, the group began to cohere. By early summer the group consisted of ten to fifteen core members including Atkinson, Koedt, Lila Karp, Nanette Rainone, Anne Kalderman, Sheila Cronan, Pam Kearon, Marcia Winslow, and Linda Feldman.[170] By June 1969, the group renamed itself The Feminists.[171] That fall they were joined by Barbara Mehrhof, another malcontent Redstockings member. Interestingly, many of the women in the group—with the obvious exception of Koedt—came to the women's liberation movement with no prior experience in other movements for social change.

In January 1969, the group undertook its first action—a demonstration at New York City's Criminal Court to support local abortionist Dr. Nathan Rappaport and to demand the repeal of all abortion laws.[172] They did not stage their next action until September 23, 1969, when five members stormed into New York City's Marriage License Bureau to charge its officials with fraud. They distributed a leaflet at the action which asked women:

> Do you know that rape is legal in marriage? Do you know that love and affection are not required in marriage? Do you know that you are your husband's prisoner? Do you know that, according to the United Nations, marriage is a "slavery-like practice?" So, why aren't you getting paid? Do you resent this fraud?[173]

According to *Rat* writer Jane Alpert, they then descended upon City Hall to confront Mayor Lindsay "as an official representative of male society which uses force to suppress women into monogamous relationships dangerous to their individual identities."[174] The one question which reportedly fascinated the media was whether or not any of the demonstrators were married. Unable to elicit an answer from the five women, one reporter covering the protest noted that "Miss or Mrs. Atkinson had runs in her stockings."[175]

As should be obvious from the foregoing passage, Redstockings and The Feminists developed very different positions on marriage. They parted company on many other issues as well. (Indeed, the two groups even wrote differently, as The Feminists developed a style as turgid and abstruse as the Redstockings' was straightforward and accessible.) While Redstockings appropriated Marxist categories and concepts, The Feminists appropriated much of the style and the rhetoric of the new left. In fact, The Feminists embraced the very aspects of the new left (or certain sectors of it) which Redstockings found most deplorable—its elitist stance toward non-Movement people and its vanguardism. Moreover, The Feminists rejected Redstockings' view that theory and action should follow from consciousness-raising. Instead they argued that consciousness-raising with its "detailing of reactions and feelings" and its "eschewal of judgment as moralistic" was retarding the movement's growth.[176]

For Redstockings the problem was one of power—who had it and who lacked it; for The Feminists it was a matter of sex roles—who conformed and who refused.[177] Thus to dismantle the system of male dominance, feminists would have to, in the words of their manifesto, "annihilate" the sex-role system.[178] In contrast to Redstockings' materialism, The Feminists developed a highly psychological analysis of male supremacy. They proposed that men oppress women "to extend the significance of their own existence as an alternative to individual self-creativity."[179] While Redstockings argued that men oppress women for the material benefits they received, The Feminists' analysis suggested that men oppress women out of some undefined psychological need. And by contrast to Redstockings who believed that women's behavior was the result of material necessity, The Feminists believed it was largely the result of internal coercion. In other words, "women were messed up" as well as "messed over" because they had internalized their oppression.[180]

Thus Atkinson contended that if women wanted to change their situation they would have to "eradicate their own definition," would have to "commit suicide," would, in effect, have to stop acting like women.[181] Indeed, for The Feminists the problem was, in a very real sense, women themselves and the extent to which they collaborated in their oppression. What this meant was that The Feminists spent most of their time upbraiding women for their quiescence and urging women, not men, to shed their role. For instance, at the February 1969 disruption of the New York legislative hearing on abortion reform Ellen Willis recalls having had a "huge argument with a member of [The Feminists] who was yelling at the committee's female secretaries and clerks that they were traitors for not walking out on their jobs and joining us."[182]

But to The Feminists, the pro-woman line's contention that all choices represented compromises of one sort or another was nothing more than a cop-out that allowed women to feel allright about not taking the necessary steps to change themselves.[183] They argued that radical feminists "must not only deal with what women want; we must change women's ideas of themselves and in that way change what women want."[184] But as we shall see, The Feminists seemed to think that the most effective way to get women to transform themselves was by "setting standards" for what constituted proper feminist behavior.

Like Redstockings, The Feminists rejected biologistic explanations of gender differences. They named men the enemy, but they maintained that "it is the male role . . . that must be annihilated—not necessarily those individuals who presently claim the role."[185] And Atkinson contended that "the sex roles—both male and female—must be destroyed, not the individuals who happen to possess either a penis or a vagina, or both, or neither."[186] But despite this explicit social constructionism, there were essentialist underpinnings to their analysis of sexuality. The Feminists maintained that the institution of heterosexuality, with its emphasis on the apochryphal vaginal orgasm, existed to ensure that women reproduce and mother:

> It is in the interest of the male in the sexual act to emphasize the organ of reproduction in the female because it is the institution of motherhood, in which the mother *serves* the child, which forms the pattern (submission of her will to the other) for her relationship to the male.[187]

They also believed that heterosexuality, in Atkinson's words, "acts as a reassuring reminder" of men's "class supremacy" and as a "convenient reminder to the female of her class inferiority."[188] Mehrhof and Kearon made the argument even more explicitly in their 1971 article on rape:

> There is, then, no unique *act* which affirms the polarity Aryan/Semite or white/black. Sexual intercourse, however, since it involves the genitals (that particular difference between the sexes selected by the Ideology of Sexism to define superiority/inferiority), provides sexism with an inimitable act which perfectly expresses the polarity male/female. The Reality created by the Ideology makes the sexual act a renewal of the feeling of power and prestige for the male, of impotence and submission for the female.[189]

Their understanding diverged sharply from Anne Koedt's pioneering analysis of normative heterosexuality in "The Myth of the Vaginal Orgasm." Koedt attributed the cultural obliteration of the clitoris to men's preference for penetration and their fear of becoming sexually expendable. Most important, Koedt distinguished between the institution of heterosexuality and heterosexual sex; for The Feminists the two were essentially indistinguishable from each other. Finally, Koedt advocated the exploration of new sexual techniques that would maximize women's sexual pleasure, while The Feminists maintained that masturbation would fulfill any sexual needs women might have. For The Feminists the fact that "physical pleasure can be achieved in both sexes through auto-eroticism" demonstrated that the major function of sex "as a social act" is to reinforce male dominance and female subordination.[190] And to those who argued that "sexual contact" is a "biological need," Atkinson replied that it was "formerly only the means to satisfy the social need of the survival of the species."[191]

Nor did The Feminists advocate lesbianism as an alternative to heterosexuality. Atkinson contended that lesbianism

> is based ideologically on the very premise of male oppression: the dynamic of sexual intercourse. Lesbians, by definition, accept that human beings are primarily sexual beings. If this is the case (that human beings are primarily sexual), one would have to grant that women *are*, in some sense, inferior.

Inferior, according to Atkinson, because " 'sex' is based on the *differences between* the sexes." [her emphasis][192] Atkinson even suggested that feminism and lesbianism might be oppositional, "that lesbianism, in fact *all* sex, is reactionary, and that feminism is revolutionary."[193] As Irene Peslikis notes, their point "wasn't to give up men for women, it was just to give it up!"[194] Indeed, The Feminists argued that once male supremacy had been defeated, opposite and same-sex "physical relations . . . would be an extension of communication between individuals and would not necessarily have a genital emphasis."[195] But if the problem were one of ideology not biology, as Mehrhof and Kearon suggested, why would genitally-oriented sex remain suspect even after the elimination of male dominance? As Willis observes, the implication that genital sexuality was merely a function of male supremacy seemed rooted in the "unconscious acceptance of [the] traditional patriarchal assumption . . . that lust is male."[196] But to The Feminists, it was *they* who had broken through the confines of patriarchal thinking; those other feminists who thought female sexual pleasure important failed to see that men had deceived them into believing it was. In other words, it was a problem of false consciousness.

The Feminists' analysis of sexuality, especially their equation of sexual desire with maleness, owes more to Valerie Solanas than to Anne Koedt who was, of course, briefly a part of the group.

One finds little, if any, evidence of Koedt here because she withdrew from the group before it articulated its stance on sexuality. The debt to Solanas is, by contrast, quite clear. In fact, Atkinson began her November 1968 article, "The Institution of Sexual Intercourse," with a short quotation from Solanas's *SCUM Manifesto*. And in 1974, she characterized Solanas's polemic as "the most important feminist statement written to date in the English language."[197] In *SCUM*, Solanas had declared:

> Sex is not part of a relationship; on the contrary, it is a solitary experience, non-creative, a gross waste of time. The female can easily—far more easily than she may think—condition away her sex drive, leaving her completely cool and cerebral and free to pursue truly worthy relationships and activities. . . . When the female transcends her body, rises above animalism, the male, whose ego consists of his cock, will disappear.[198]

For Solanas, Cell 16, and The Feminists sex was something that women needed to be liberated from. It is important to note that this was not the position typically taken by radical feminists. Radical feminists agreed for the most part that the sexual revolution had done little to liberate women. Women may have the right to have sex, but do they have the right to say "no," they asked? They maintained that by transforming sex into a duty, the sexual revolution had only made women more exploitable. Nor had it really challenged the male-centered bias of normative heterosexuality. Indeed, radical feminists tended to ignore the ways in which the sexual revolution expanded women's sexual horizon and instead focused on the increased sexual exploitation that accompanied it. But if most radical feminists were highly critical of the sexual revolution, they did not believe that freedom lay in the denial of women's sexuality. Rather, they were convinced that the repression of female desire was central to women's oppression, and sexual liberation essential to women's liberation. Firestone maintained that in a feminist society "humanity could finally revert to its natural polymorphous sexuality—all forms of sexuality would be allowed and indulged."[199] Boston feminist Karen Lindsey warned feminists against rejecting casual sex out of their frustration with the sexism of the sexual revolution.[200] Kate Millett declared that women's liberation would bring about "an end to sexual repression."[201] And, of course, the reason abortion loomed so large in the early radical feminist agenda was that without it there could be no such thing as sexual freedom or self-determination for women.

Much of The Feminists' theorizing had to do with how the movement might develop "standards" of feminist behavior. From the beginning, The Feminists used the lot system in an effort to equalize power within the group. However, by the summer of 1969, some members, including Atkinson, were pushing for The Feminists to become a disciplined, revolutionary, vanguard group with strict membership and attendance regulations and even more draconian rules to ensure egalitarianism. They maintained that the group should take precedence over all else. To test members' allegiance to the cause, they even proposed that the group begin meeting for social purposes every Saturday night in addition to the weekly business meeting. Other members objected on the grounds that the Saturday night meeting would exclude those women who were unable or unwilling to attend, especially those who were involved in primary relationships. Of course, this was in some sense the point, for if they couldn't part with their husbands or lovers for one night, what kind of feminists were they?

The group had discussed taking a break from meetings that summer, particularly because Koedt, Karp, and several others were leaving town during the last part of summer. However, those who wanted The Feminists to become a vanguard cadre felt that the group should forge ahead and construct an analysis because the movement was constantly accused of lacking one. Indeed, they believed that the group must exploit the historical moment, must "seize the time," in the vernacular of the day, and they resented that others had gone on vacation at so critical a time. So despite the fact that half the membership was absent, the group drafted most of its manifesto and passed a series of membership requirements.[202] The manifesto stated:

> Membership must be a primary commitment and responsibility; no other activity may supersede work for the group. . . . Outside study, participation in discussions, completion of individual assignments *and* attendance at actions are equally important and compulsory.[203]

The manifesto put a premium on "maintaining discipline" and even provided for the expulsion of refractory members. If a member missed more than one-quarter of the meetings in any given month, she forfeited her voting privileges "until the third consecutive meeting of [her] renewed attendance." And if this happened three times in a three-month period, the woman would be expelled from the group.

Moreover, all tasks were to be distributed by lot. Women with writing or speaking skills were encouraged to withdraw their names from the "privileged" lot where those tasks were assigned so that others could cultivate these skills. Koedt and the other vacationing members reportedly denounced the rules as fascistic.[204] According to one insider, Koedt maintained that the rules would effectively silence those members, like herself, who were just beginning to find their voices.

The Feminists voted in another membership requirement that summer which sent shockwaves throughout the New York movement. Contending that the institution of marriage was "inherently inequitable" and that "the rejection of this institution both in theory *and in practice* [was] a primary mark of the radical feminist," they decreed that:

> no more than one-third of our membership can be participants in either a formal (with legal contract) or informal (e.g., living with a man) instance of the institution of marriage.[205]

Of all their many rules and requirements, the quota was surely the most controversial. It was widely condemned in other parts of the movement, and the group lost a number of its most vital members when Koedt, Karp, and Rainone—all of whom opposed the rule—decided to quit.[206]

Most radical feminists felt that the quota wrongly attacked married women rather than the institution of marriage. However, one of the members who pushed for the quota denies that it in any way implied that married women were less trustworthy feminists. She claims that the quota was adopted to spare married members participating in the Marriage License Bureau demonstration from ridicule by the press. But if this were the case, why did the demonstrators refuse to reveal their marital status to those reporters who inquired? Indeed, others in the group dispute this explanation. For instance, Nanette Rainone contends:

> There were those who said that marriage was debilitating to women, therefore we couldn't have a lot of married women in our group because they would be damaged and would affect the thinking of the group. They felt that married women would cause the group to compromise.[207]

Kearon admits that the quota was "a bit of an embarrassment" for married members, but thinks that it was good to have "as few of those women" as possible who would go home to discuss the meetings with their husbands. She believes that those who supported the quota wanted the group to take more militant positions, which they felt married women might oppose.[208] Mehrhof, who joined the group immediately following the group's marriage action in September, corroborates Kearon's view:

> In those days, which you have to remember were very, very different, we were incredible fanatics. It might be a terrible thing to say, but we just felt that some women were more prepared to move out than others. We had to take the responsibility of saying we can only have a certain percentage of women who are married and locked into men in the group.[209]

In their view, feminism was synonymous with separatism and marriage with collaboration. In fact, Kearon argued that "men are able to exert a powerful and constant pressure on their wives which can be dangerous to the movement."[210] At about the time the quota was established, Kearon wrote:

> In rejecting marriage we are setting up a standard for ourselves based on what we believe feminism must be in order to succeed. In rejecting marriage and fidelity to the male, we are cutting off our retreat from radical feminism and *creating* the necessity for female unity and trust.[211] [her emphasis]

But the policy engendered feelings of mistrust and betrayal, not the solidarity and trust they had hoped for. By the time Mehrhof became a member that fall, there were no longer any married women left in The Feminists. Redstockings member Irene Peslikis, who is married, briefly joined The Feminists in the spring of 1970 in part to challenge the quota.[212] She recalls that "it was an incredibly humiliating experience to have people condescend to you." Peslikis found their condescension especially galling since "they didn't speak on national televison about their abortions," as she courageously had following the Redstockings' abortion speak-out.[213]

Atkinson's writings suggest that she may have had other things on her mind besides shielding the group's married members from criticism by the press. Atkinson, who referred to married women as "hostages," maintained that "the proof of class consciousness will be when we separate off from men." To Atkinson, marriage, or for that matter any relationship with a man, was perilous for women:

> The price of clinging to the enemy is your life. To enter into a relationship with a man who has divested himself as completely and publicly from the male role as possible would still be a risk. But to relate to a man who has done any less is suicide.[214]

But Atkinson appears to have been more concerned with the movement's image than with the welfare of those feminists who continued to "consort with the enemy."[215] Atkinson desperately wanted the movement to be taken seriously, to be regarded as revolutionary, yet she felt that "so far, the feminist movement has, primarily, been women coming together to complain."[216] And in her view, radical feminists who continued to associate with men undermined the movement by making it appear ludicrous:

> The basic issue is consistency between belief and acts. Of course, you know that every woman in the movement is married to the single male feminist existing. That's why we're funny. Contradiction is the heart of comedy. A woman saying men are the enemy with a boy friend sitting next to her is both humiliating and tragic.[217]

Atkinson herself refused to appear with men in public when it might be construed that they were friends. She made an exception for any man who had "disassociated himself from the male role and from the male class as much as possible."[218] Later, she reportedly refused to appear with *any* man in public except to engage in a "class confrontation."[219]

Atkinson seems to have been motivated not only by a desire to demonstrate the movement's seriousness, but by the desire to establish The Feminists as the most militant radical feminist group. In April 1969, Atkinson referred to the October 17th Movement as "the first radical feminist group."[220] In February 1970, she claimed that the group had "formed the radical feminist wing of the movement."[221] And a month later she made the incredible claim that "the most radical feminists [from NYRW] came to The Feminists."[222] Perhaps The Feminists' vanguardism was a hypercorrection for their inexperience with radical politics. Or perhaps they mistook militant vanguardism for radicalism because they lacked any real background in other radical movements for social change. Whatever the reason, the quota made married women feel as though they were the enemy.

The Feminists' fondness for rules didn't subside after the summer. In fact, the rules seemed to proliferate, thus bearing out Koedt's pessimistic prophecy that the group was moving toward fascism. Although the group professed its commitment to "individual self-development," the rules and the equalizing techniques seemed designed to obliterate differences. At some point in the group's history, Mehrhof and Kearon even proposed that the group adopt a uniform as an equalization measure. But as long as Atkinson, the famous feminist, remained in the group, the differences between them would remain annoyingly obvious.

Sometime in the fall or winter of 1969, the group established the disc system to facilitate equal participation during discussion. Each member was given a designated number of chips at the beginning of the meeting and was required to throw a disc in the middle of the room every time she spoke. Once a member had exhausted her supply of chips, she could no longer participate in the discussion. Mehrhof and Kearon admit that the group instituted the disc system largely because of Atkinson's loquacity. Atkinson technically abided by the system, "but now," according to Kearon, "each time she spoke, she spoke for so long."[223]

Despite the plethora of rules and systems, the problem of who wrote the papers and who initiated the ideas apparently persisted. So, in the winter of 1969–70, the group decided to form the Creativity Workshop to tackle the problem. Atkinson writes that the workshop was established "to encourage and support individual members in seeking out and developing their creative potentialities."[224] People were expected to analyze and write about issues of particular interest to them. However, the Creativity Workshop lasted but two meetings before it was transformed into the Class Workshop.

The Class Workshop, which was instigated by Mehrhof and Kearon, quickly decided that Atkinson should be excluded from the group because she was upper class. Atkinson's writings indicate that she was initially supportive of the Class Workshop. In February 1970, she proudly claimed that in contrast to the rest of the women's liberation movement, "The Feminists . . . with the exception of myself . . . are lower- or lower-middle-class and/or black."[225] And Atkinson began to explore class differences among women. Although she denied that women belonged to any other political class but their sex class, she claimed that women "do evidence certain expressions characteristic of the members of power classes in relation to subordinates."[226] She conceded that women who were attached to upper or middle-class men lacked power within the economic class system, but she maintained that they could exploit other women within their own sex class.

Mehrhof elaborated upon Atkinson's ideas about class. She, too, argued that the "secondary class system," by which she meant the economic class system, failed to give any real power to women. "Women," Mehrhof argued, "will always be defined by their minor position in the primary class structure."[227] However, she contended that class differences would assume importance as women organized themselves. In fact, she maintained that the women's liberation movement "has become the occasion whereby these class antagonisms will make themselves known." Mehrhof's analysis reduced the problem of class to male values. In fact, she attributed all forms of social domination to "the male value system," and argued that women who exploit other women in the movement have "internalized male values."[228] Here we see the identification of power with maleness. While this analysis acknowledged the existence of class differences among women, it viewed them as inauthentic, as male derived and defined. Thus, upper- or middle-class women derived tangible benefits, but not real *power*, from their fathers' or husbands' position in the class system. The problem for The Feminists was that these women would undermine female solidarity by pretending, as Atkinson put it, to be "kings" when they were really "beggars."[229]

During the winter and spring of 1970 relations between Atkinson and the Class Workshop worsened. "What happened," Mehrhof asserts, "is that we began to challenge her on theory. Ti-Grace felt that she was The Feminists' theoretician."[230] Then, on April 5, 1970, The Feminists passed a resolution which criticized Atkinson for allowing the media to define her as the group's leader.[231] They argued that Atkinson had circumvented and undermined the lot system by distinguishing her activities as a group member from her activities and appearances as an individual. They contended that Atkinson's growing stature in the media made a mockery of The Feminists' much-vaunted egalitarianism. Finally, they declared that " 'feminist ideas' arise out of the common condition of women and are not therefore the exclusive property of any individual."

To ensure that the group was truly "leaderless," they resolved that "*all* contact with the media on feminist issues by a member of The Feminists is to be decided upon by the group and chosen by lot." The resolution warned that flagrant disregard for the rule would result in expulsion from the group. An addendum to the resolution required that all members "appearing on the media" be identified by their group affiliation rather than by name. Two days after it was passed, Atkinson condemned the resolution as "wrong on principle," and withdrew from the group.[232] Both Mehrhof and Kearon insist that the group did not want Atkinson to resign and were surprised when she did.[233]

The resolution was probably prompted by a March 1970 *Newsweek* article which described Atkinson as the group's spokeswoman. *Newsweek* wasn't the only magazine or newspaper heralding Atkinson as a movement leader. By 1970, both the movement and Atkinson were receiving a great deal of publicity. Atkinson's high profile confounded the group's attempts to erase all power differentials between members. All their egalitarian measures could not prevent the press from singling out Atkinson as a leader. If all members were truly equal, why was it that only Atkinson was pursued by the press and sought after for speaking engagements? Why were they treated like ciphers? Since The Feminists could deal with differences only by muting them, the celebrity in the group had to be muzzled. Atkinson was an anomaly, a constant reminder of difference and privilege. Kearon even suggests that "Ti-Grace functioned . . . as our man in The Feminists. I don't know how upper-class she was, but she certainly gave off that she was, and that comforted a lot of people."[234] Of course, it is more than a little ironic that the very thing the group was struggling against was what enthralled them.

After Atkinson's departure, the group passed more rules. Members were penalized for tardiness; digressions were no longer permitted during meetings; liquor and drugs were not to be used during or before meetings; and members were encouraged to develop "personal living habits . . . consistent with good health." A year later, in 1971, the group voted to exclude *all* married women from membership in The Feminists.[235] This last decision was prompted by Mehrhof, Kearon, and Cronan's participation in the Detroit Radical Feminist Conference in the spring of 1971. The Feminists' proselytizing on behalf of separatism upset both conference planners and attendees. In the midst of one heated exchange, Robin Morgan, who opposed the separatist strategy, pointed out that even The Feminists allowed one-third of their members to be married. Upon their return to New York, Cronan promptly proposed that the group bar all married women to establish complete consistency between theory and practice.[236]

In the post-Atkinson era, The Feminists did not diverge from the group's original analysis of sexuality. At a December 1972 Lesbian-Feminist Conference at Columbia University, members contended that "aside from rape, prostitution and marriage, sex just is not all that important." In other words, sexuality was important only insofar as it was used against women. They argued that "ethically and morally, feminists must strive to love each other and not be confused with the distractions that sex offers."[237] If women were to have sex, The Feminists urged them to embrace "Amazon Virginity," "where you have sex but don't take it real seriously."[238]

After Atkinson's withdrawal, The Feminists seemed to lose interest in being a vanguard group. Instead, they committed themselves to developing a female "counter-reality" and counterculture. In October 1971, Kearon and Mehrhof contended:

> The first step toward breaking the debilitating hold on us of the Sexist Ideology is the creation of a counter-reality, a mutually guaranteed support of female experience undistorted by male interpretation.[239]

The group succumbed to essentialism as it explored matriarchy and developed a "female religion." Kearon and Mary Lutz developed a religious rite in which wine and marijuana were the sacraments and the chant was "Momma." They constructed an enormous and anatomically correct, papier-mâché man which they tore apart during the ritual.[240] In 1973, The Feminists maintained that "a female religion could provide the same 'faith' that Marxism, humanism, and liberalism provide: a sense that we are not doomed to failure. Someday women will rule the world."[241] Kearon argues that the ritual was an important outlet for women's misandry and insists that regardless of whether or not matriarchy ever existed, "it was a good thing for women to harken back to a world of their own."[242]

The Feminists continued to function until late 1973. By the time of its dissolution, Mehrhof, Kearon, and Cronan were no longer with the group. Cronan was the first to leave, dropping out in 1971 to enter law school. Mehrhof and Kearon stayed long enough to become victims themselves of the equality issue. They believe that they were resented because they lacked Atkinson's "aura" and "prestige."[243] They, apparently, weathered the attacks, but had a falling-out. Mehrhof left the group in June 1972 and Kearon followed suit sometime within the year to attend law school.[244] After Kearon left The Feminists, the group became even more absorbed in the question of matriarchy. In June 1973, The Feminists "presented the case for matriarchy" at a New York NOW-sponsored panel discussion entitled "Matriarchy vs. Humanism." At the event, the group proposed a "new plan for feminist revolution [which included] the long-term goal of building permanent institutions which would move away from personal, humanistic solutions."[245]

The Feminists' interest in female mysticism, matriarchy, and female counter-institutions—all of which were predicated upon an essentialist view—certainly prefigured cultural feminism. But the Feminists would never have followed this trajectory had Atkinson remained active in the group. Atkinson would not have tolerated the group's explorations into female mysticism and matriarchy because, unlike Mehrhof and Kearon, who sought "the restoration of female rule," Atkinson had always doubted that women would wield power differently from men.[246] Indeed, by 1970 Atkinson had grown so cynical about sisterhood that she proclaimed, "Sisterhood is powerful. It kills sisters."[247] Moreover, Atkinson believed that feminism entailed confrontation, not retreat into spirituality. In 1974, Atkinson declared:

> whenever "religion"—whatever its alleged genesis—has resurfaced in a Movement, it has historically been a sure sign of decadence and reaction. *Any* religion is too much religion![248]

Finally, Atkinson was moving away from implicitly essentialist explanations of male dominance which, she contended, had blinded feminists to women's capacity to oppress others. In fact, in 1971 Atkinson confounded virtually everyone when she became involved with the Italian-American Civil Rights League, an organization formed by Mafia kingpin Joseph Columbo. In August 1971, shortly after Columbo was gunned down, Atkinson participated in a panel discussion on violence in the women's movement. When it was her turn to speak, Atkinson taped a picture of the slain Columbo to the podium and harangued the audience of feminists for having failed to support "Sister Joseph Columbo."[249] This was not what the audience expected of Atkinson, and many women in the auditorium jeered her. To them Columbo was nothing more than a gangster who trafficked in drugs and prostitution. But Atkinson claimed, much to their dismay, that Columbo was a revolutionary committed to building a working-class movement in America. In fact, Atkinson suggested that it was he who was the revolutionary whereas women's liberationists were hopeless "phonies" who talked about violence instead of "hanging out" in "the street with people [who were] fighting for their own asses."[250] Again we have the familiar refrain—the women's movement has radical pretensions, but no real revolutionary substance. Several days later, Atkinson wrote:

> The irony of it! . . . I, the Super-Feminist, Extremist, Man-Hater, divorced you [the women's movement] over the picture

> of a working-class, uneducated, criminal, second-generation immigrant, male corpse. I stood by the irrefutable evidence of his Revolutionary spirit, *in spite of* his maleness.[251]

Kate Millett later observed that Atkinson "is the best teacher we have—she will give us the hardest case, a Mafia boss, and impose his humanity upon us. Rub our noses in his bullet wounds. Teach us humanity."[252] But Atkinson was doing more than simply imposing Columbo's humanity on the audience, she was excoriating women's liberationists for failing to "pick up the gun." This was, of course, what Weatherman was saying to the rest of the left, and it is not coincidental that Weatherman was the one leftist group Atkinson singled out for praise in her speech. This was a militant vanguardism that seemed to grow out of a contempt for the people, that indeed made an enemy of the people.

In important respects, though, The Feminists' proto-cultural feminism followed from the group's and Atkinson's original conceptualization of the problem. Atkinson admitted that while she had always "tried to maintain the distinction between *men* (as biological entities) being the enemy, and the *behavior* of men being the enemy," that even she at times had lost sight of the distinction.[253] Moreover, by identifying female acquiescence as a large part of the problem, The Feminists made the process of re-creating oneself the central feminist task. Their conflation of the political and the personal made lifestyle synonymous with political struggle. But while The Feminists invoked "the personal is political" in the interests of intensifying the struggle, it could also be invoked by those escaping political struggle. And over time, personal transformation did become a substitute for political action.

The Feminists were the first of many radical feminist groups to interpret "the personal is political" prescriptively. For The Feminists, one's personal life was a reflection of one's politics, a barometer of one's radicalism and commitment to feminism. While The Feminists proscribed heterosexual relationships rather than heterosexual sex, it was just a matter of time before the standard became even narrower and more confining. Indeed, The Feminists' advocacy of separatism established the theoretical foundation for lesbian separatism.

New York Radical Feminists

By mid-1969, one of the most pressing problems facing the women's liberation movement was, paradoxically, its success. In New York City alone, there were thousands of women clamoring to become involved in the movement. Yet none of the existing radical feminist groups seemed ready or willing to organize them. The Feminists, as an avowedly vanguard group, was obviously for women who were combat-ready, rather than for neophytes. And after months of debate on the advantages and disadvantages of expansion, Redstockings was just beginning to undertake organizing groups for new women. Most radical feminists feared that vitiation would accompany expansion. But as interest in women's liberation grew, some women realized that the movement had to face the challenge. Minda Bikman, who joined a Redstockings group in July, remembers Shulamith Firestone, whom she knew from Washington University in St. Louis, complaining that Redstockings was missing the opportunity to organize masses of women.[254] Of course, Firestone was also deeply dissatisfied with Redstockings' dogged commitment to consciousness-raising and the pro-woman line. Rather than remain in the group, Firestone decided to form a new group with Anne Koedt, who had recently departed The Feminists.

When Shulamith Firestone and Anne Koedt launched New York Radical Feminists (NYRF) in the fall of 1969, it was in the hope that they were building "a mass-based radical feminist movement."[255] Ann Snitow remembers Firestone explaining at an early planning session that this group would "seed itself," rather than remaining closed and self-contained like other radical feminist groups.[256] Firestone and Koedt were also anxious that this group avoid what they considered to be the Redstockings' and The Feminists' ideological and organizational flaws.[257] To that end, Koedt wrote the group's manifesto and Firestone its organizing principles, and they virtually "hand-picked" the members of their new group. Snitow attended the group's first formal organizational meeting and remembers it as "an ecstasy of discussion. These were the people who were going to be the new group. We were there with the understanding that this would be better than whatever had been."[258]

During October and November a group of about five women met to plan NYRF. By the end of November, the group consisted of seven women—Minda Bikman, Diane Crothers, Marsha Gershin, Ann Snitow, Cellestine Ware, Firestone, and Koedt. All of its members—with the exception of Snitow, who had been in England for two years—had been involved in other feminist groups. The founding "brigade" of NYRF took the name, the Stanton-Anthony Brigade. (They had planned to call their cell groups "phalanxes" until someone astutely pointed out that the fascists had called themselves "phalangists" in the Spanish Civil War.[259]) On December 5, 1969, Koedt and Firestone presented a draft of the group's manifesto and organizing principles to a group of forty women.[260] The first group to be organized, West Village-1, contained a number of writers, including Grace Paley, Susan Brownmiller, Sally Kempton, and, later, Alix Kates Shulman. The group's organizing efforts were made considerably easier when writer Vivian Gornick announced the formation of NYRF and listed a contact phone number in a November issue of the *Village Voice*.[261] Soon the group was swamped with mail from women all over the country. By February, there were eleven brigades, three of which were in the Village.

The group's manifesto, "Politics of the Ego," favored a highly psychological analysis of male supremacy, not unlike that of The Feminists. The Feminists had argued that men oppress women "to extend the significance of their own existence as an alternative to individual self-creativity." Koedt stated the same idea with considerably less obfuscation in NYRF's manifesto:

> We believe that the purpose of male supremacy is primarily to obtain psychological ego satisfaction, and that only secondarily does this manifest itself in economic relationships.[262]

The manifesto's sole reference to economic factors was thus largely dismissive. According to the manifesto, male supremacy was a psychological dynamic in which men dominate women "out of a need for a sense of power."[263] The root of the problem was what Koedt called the "male ego identity" which sustained itself by destroying women's egos. Koedt even suggested that the more powerless a man, the more likely he would be to oppress women. Although Koedt rejected biologism—she described femininity, for instance, as a "skill"—her contention that men oppress women for "ego fodder," that the services men extracted from women were "services to the male ego," implied that the desire for power was singularly male. As Willis observes:

> NYRF proposed in essence that men wanted to exercise power for its own sake—that it was intrinsically satisfying to the ego to dominate others. According to their formulation men do not defend their power in order to get services from women, but demand services from women to affirm their sense of power.[264]

NYRF's explanation of male dominance, clearly an elaboration of The Feminists' analysis, conceptualized the problem as one of maleness rather than of unequal power relations. Indeed, the manifesto's "ahistoricism and timeless categories of inequality" so concerned both Snitow and her friend Evelyn Frankford that they proposed revising the manifesto. However, when they broached the idea at the December 5th meeting, they encountered resistance from Koedt, Firestone, and others as well. Interestingly, Snitow thought that she and Frankfort had succeeded in carrying the majority, but concedes that the final, published version of the manifesto makes no mention of history.[265] Willis contends that NYRF's analysis implied that "men, by virtue of their maleness, had an inherent predilection for power."[266] While it is true that NYRF targeted maleness as the problem, I think the group conceptualized maleness as culturally constructed rather than biological determined. It is true, however, that the manifesto's conflation of male supremacy with maleness did set the stage for essentialist explanations of male supremacy. In other respects their manifesto departed from The Feminists' analysis. For instance, in contrast to The Feminists, Koedt did not suggest that either heterosexuality or love were intrinsically demeaning or oppressive to women. The problem for Koedt was the compulsory nature of heterosexuality which prevented women from viewing sex as "just a voluntary act which [women] may engage in as an expression of [their] general humanity."[267]

The manifesto was also an explicit repudiation of the Redstockings' pro-woman line. Although Koedt conceded that alternatives to the female role were both "prohibitive and prohibited," she maintained that women have also, unfortunately, come to see themselves as men's inferiors. Indeed, she argued that "it is precisely through the destruction of women's egos that they are robbed of the ability to act." According to the manifesto, the female socialization process was so thoroughgoing that woman's "ego is repressed at all times to prepare her for this future submissiveness."[268] As Willis pointed out, the NYRF manifesto treated women like "passive recipients of social indoctrination."[269] Koedt concluded the manifesto by exhorting women to "destroy the notion that we are indeed only servants to the male ego . . . by constructing alternate selves that are healthy, independent and self-assertive."[270]

Although the manifesto stressed the importance of personal transformation, NYRF's organizing principles made it clear that the organization's primary goal was to effect radical structural change. NYRF's organizing principles were an implicit repudiation of The Feminists' organizational rigidity:

> we have proposed a structure designed to promote the development of an organic group cohesion as opposed to a cohesion forced by external rules and regulations: a group in which people will become radicalized feminists of their own accord and at their own pace rather than being pressured into it by a group line imposed from above; a group women will attend because they need to and want to, and not because they fear the consequences of missing a meeting; a group which will enrich its members personally and not just drain them for the sake of The Cause.[271]

Firestone designed NYRF as an umbrella group which would consist of geographically based, "nuclear leaderless/structureless" cell groups, or brigades. Each brigade would be named after a different radical feminist or, if possible, a "team of radical feminists," like Elizabeth Cady Stanton and Susan B. Anthony, the Grimké sisters or the Pankhursts. The brigades would consist of no more than fifteen women to achieve "a working internal democracy" and to engender intimacy and a common political consciousness. Firestone favored the small group for she felt it allowed women to "seal up the gaps between them." She encouraged women within the new brigades to pair off in order to give each other positive reinforcement. She maintained that the "Sister System," as she called it, had been used by first-wave feminists and had proven useful as well in the Stanton-Anthony Brigade.[272]

To ensure that NYRF would be composed of *radical* feminists, new brigades were subject to a six-month probationary period. During this "formative period," the "conditional brigades" were expected to spend three months doing consciousness-raising and another three months reading and discussing feminist literature from the first and second waves. Firestone envisioned consciousness-raising as a crucial component of NYRF's program. But in contrast to the Redstockings who argued that the purpose of consciousness-raising was to change the system not to change women, Firestone recommended consciousness-raising:

> to increase personal sensitivity to the various levels and forms that the oppression takes in our daily lives. We have all, in order to adjust to our condition, had to develop elaborate blinkers. . . . Before we can remove the structures of oppression, we must remove our own accommodations to them.[273]

Firestone hoped that this intensive course of study and consciousness-raising would give new members an adequate grounding in feminist theory and history, and an understanding and appreciation of radical feminism. At the conclusion of this six-month period, the brigade could apply for full membership in NYRF. Acceptance was contingent on approval of the brigade's name and each individual's signature to the manifesto, "Politics of the Ego." It was also expected that new brigades would elect delegates to NYRF's Coordinating Body, research and produce a booklet biography of the feminist whose name they had chosen, and initiate an action from beginning to end. At this point a brigade had "full autonomy and independence to begin the serious work of an experienced brigade."[274]

Koedt and Firestone believed that they had devised an organization which would prove that a "mass-based radical feminist movement" need not be oxymoronic. However, their enthusiasm was not universally shared. Their first action—a protest against the sex-role stereotyping of Christmas toys—had to be abandoned because of conflicts and disorganization.[275] Moreover, many of the "conditional" members objected to the probationary period and felt "colonized" by the Stanton-Anthony Brigade. Brownmiller, for one, felt that Stanton-Anthony members took the position that "they were the feminists, the rest of us were the colonies. We all thought that we were equal, and already full members." In fact, many women reportedly wanted their brigades to be named Stanton-Anthony.[276] Snitow thinks that the probationary period might have been excessively long given those hypertrophied times when revolution seemed around the corner:

> So great was the explosion of both interest and commitment that to tell someone who had been in NYRF three months that they couldn't yet vote was insulting because you could remake the world in three months.

However, she stresses that the impulse behind the membership rules had more to do with political education than with vanguardism. According to Snitow, they believed that membership restrictions were necessary to ensure that "everyone would be an experienced feminist, everyone would have thought through the enormous implications of feminism." Snitow recalls that "Shulie, in particular, was so tired of square one."[277] Although Stanton-Anthony envisioned its leadership as temporal, the brigade nonetheless assumed leadership of the organization, and this at a time when all leadership was seen as nefarious. Snitow suspects that Stanton-Anthony was also resented by the others because they were seen as "the fancy girls," "the flashy bunch," whose brigade was "a thrilling intellectual cauldron."[278] Indeed, Stanton-Anthony was quite a dazzling group. Firestone and Koedt, as founders of the women's liberation movement in New York, were the best known. Both had written influential articles, and people within NYRF knew that Firestone's book *The Dialectic of Sex* would be out that fall. Snitow regularly did feminist reviews for radio station WBAI's "Womankind" program. However, Brownmiller claims "we didn't resent Stanton-Anthony. As Sally Kempton always used to say, 'They add a lot of class to our group.' "[279] But it was precisely Stanton-Anthony's "class" and authenticity that engendered the resentment. The rules, which formalized the distinction, came to symbolize Stanton-Anthony's authenticity and the newcomers' status as acolytes.

Tensions finally exploded in early summer of 1970—about six months from the date of the organization's founding—at a general meeting of NYRF when Stanton-Anthony was attacked for its alleged elitism, and the rank and file abrogated the membership rules. Snitow recalls the meeting was like "a palace revolution. We were really being drawn up. They were throwing out their leaders."[280] Brownmiller thinks that "Anne and Shulie decided they were victims of a putsch led by me." Brownmiller admits that she may have spoken out against the rules, for she believed that the very notion of a "vanguard brigade was unnecessary, extraordinarily presumptuous, and silly and demeaning to the rest of us." But Brownmiller maintains that she was not attempting to wrest control of the organization from its founders:

> Shulie and Ann thought I was a comer whom they couldn't control. They were probably right about this, but wrong about my scheming to snatch the leadership from their hands. I never thought in those terms. But neither did I believe that they were the leaders and that I and the rest of us were the followers. They did think this, and so the seeds of destruction were there.[281]

Certainly, this revolution was aided by those within the palace. Both Bikman and Crothers—who had bonded with each other over their problems with Koedt and Firestone, respectively—spoke in favor of rescinding the membership rules. In fact, Brownmiller claims that it was Diane Crothers who accused Firestone and Koedt of being "dictatorial" and "elitist."[282]

Immediately following the vote, Stanton-Anthony retreated to the basement to figure out how to respond to the rebellion. Snitow remembers that they all felt "exhausted and burned up" by this "intense and incandescent period" of activism. But Firestone, for one, was more than exhausted. She was fed up with NYRF and, according to Snitow, had been disenchanted with the group for some time:

> Shulie was more globally furious at the [newer members] for not being good, or for being off. She felt the new groups were vitiating and adulterating. This wasn't the organization she had planned.[283]

Firestone wanted to let the membership know how she felt, she wanted to harangue them. But Snitow counseled against it for she "was terrified of the rift." She also suspects that she was "protecting some fantasy I had of the group's need not to be utterly repudiated by its founders." Snitow prevailed, but she now regrets having "quelled" Firestone for she thinks that Firestone probably "knew a lot about the ways in which the movement was being vitiated."[284] When they returned to the meeting, they launched no tirades, but simply announced that they were disbanding their brigade and withdrawing from the organization. Brownmiller contends she was shocked by their pronouncement and maintains that "most of the people in the room, including me, wanted them to stay."[285]

For most of those attending the tumultuous meeting, it was an issue of elitism and powermongering, not an issue of the movement's attenuation. However, Firestone's concerns were not unwarranted. As in Redstockings, many of the middle-class and upper-middle-class women joining NYRF seemed more interested in self-improvement than in the radical restructuring of society. Their feminism was narrower, more individualistic, and more self-interested. The newcomers often lacked the founders' radical perspective on other forms of social domination. For instance, Firestone, who was uncompromising in her criticism of the organized left's sexism, nonetheless maintained that radical feminism "refuses to accept the existing left analysis not because it is too radical, but because *it is not radical enough*."[286] Although radical feminists did not think that socialism was sufficient to liberate women, neither did they believe that feminism was compatible with capitalism. Indeed, Firestone called for a "feminist socialism."[287] Radical feminists assumed that radical feminism would politicize newer women about other forms of social domination. But, as Willis points out, radical feminism made the newcomers aware of their oppression as women; it did not automatically transform them into radicals who were "committed to overall social transformation."[288] It was disillusioning for women like Firestone to see some of these new women grasping onto feminism as an ideology of self-improvement.

After the dissolution of Stanton-Anthony, West Village-1 became the unofficial leadership brigade of NYRF. By early 1971 the group totaled 400 members.[289] NYRF did important educational work, especially around the issue of rape. Their January 1971 speak-out and April 1971 conference on rape were enormously successful in raising consciousness about the issue. Susan Brownmiller was a driving force behind these events and they helped inspire her landmark book on rape, *Against Our Will*.[290] However, NYRF was now quite different from what its founders had envisioned. With the abolition of the three-stage membership structure, the group was no longer the rigorous, demanding, cadre-like organization Firestone and Koedt had imagined. In fact, Hole and Levine contend that "without any formal structure through which to measure their growth, define and refine their politics, and initiate actions, most of the groups lost any sense of the larger organization."[291] Although NYRF continued to sponsor conferences through 1974, the remaining brigades had dissolved by the beginning of 1972.

With the break-up of the founding brigade, the organization moved in a different political direction as well, sometimes accepting rather than challenging dominant cultural assumptions. The December 1971 prostitution conference which they co-sponsored with The Feminists was a case in point. From the beginning, the few prostitutes who attended the conference complained that the organizers assumed a judgmental stance toward them. Most incredible of all from the prostitutes' standpoint was that the organizers had entitled one panel, "Toward the Elimination of Prostitution," and yet had failed to include one prostitute on it. The place finally erupted when a member of The Feminists declared herself an "honorable woman" because she lived in a tenement, worked as a secretary, and yet refused to sell her body. As Millett noted, "the accusation, so long buried in liberal goodwill and radical rhetoric—'You're selling it; I could too, but I won't'—was finally heard. Said out loud at last."[292] Alix Kates Shulman found the conference organizers' moralizing "untenable," and Kathie Sarachild criticized the conference for "veering away from feminism . . . into some kind of social work."[293] Sarachild took the planners to task for assuming that they could theorize about prostitution without consulting the women with first-hand experience—prostitutes themselves. Snitow was also critical of the conference and doubts that such a conference could ever have emerged from Stanton-Anthony.[294] Despite the fact that many feminists were critical of the conference, the organizers insisted on attributing the dissension to leftists, particularly those from the sectarian group Youth Against War and Fascism. According to Sarachild, the organizers claimed that

> "The prostitutes weren't *really* the kind of feminists they were putting themselves forward to be. Actually they were 'Leftists' who had been sent by their underground groups to disrupt the conference."

While Sarachild acknowledged that "sections of the male supremacist pseudo-left" might have played a role in the tumult, she maintained that women's participation in the left "does not *in itself* contradict that they are feminists."[295]

The dissolution of Stanton-Anthony marked the end of Firestone and Koedt's involvement with the organized movement. Reportedly they felt they had been deposed because their analysis was too radical. By the time Firestone's book was published in October 1970, she had already dropped out of the movement. Koedt co-edited *Notes from the Third Year* in 1971 and the aboveground anthology *Radical Feminism*, which was published in 1973, but she kept her distance from the movement. Brownmiller believes that

> there is no other explanation for [Firestone and Koedt's departure] except the phenomenon of certain kinds of personalities that are brilliant and prescient about starting things, but then leave when the movement becomes popular (and no longer in their control).[296]

Brownmiller's analysis suggests that Koedt and Firestone sought personal control. But it seems just as likely that they wanted the power to define the movement and prevent its attenuation. However, by 1970, this was a power the founders were rapidly losing.

For many veteran radical feminists in New York City, the most striking evidence of the movement's attenuation was the March 18, 1970 *Ladies Home Journal* sit-in. Although the sit-in was organized by a group called Media Women—to which both Kempton and Brownmiller belonged—women from Redstockings, The Feminists, and NYRF actively participated in planning and carrying out the action. Between 100 and 200 women poured into editor-in-chief John Mack Carter's office and presented him with a lengthy list of demands which included:

> that Carter be replaced by a woman; that all editorial sales and advertising personnel be women; that black editorial workers be hired in proportion to black readership; that a daycare center be established on the premises for working mothers—to be run as a collective by the mothers; that the policy of the magazine be changed to: eliminate all degrading and useless advertising . . . and focus on the real issues facing women today; that the *Journal* publish an issue on women's liberation written by members of the movement.[297]

Not surprisingly, Carter proved intransigent. After hours of arguing, the women had made no headway whatsoever. Firestone, Atkinson, and Ros Baxandall were by this point extremely frustrated with the imperious Carter and with the demonstration's organizers who seemed uninterested in making contact with the clericals who worked at the *Journal*. Firestone took it upon herself to speed up the negotiations process by climbing onto Carter's desk and shredding copies of the *Journal*.[298] Firestone's dramatic gesture apparently provided Carter with the incentive he needed to negotiate. However, Carter refused to negotiate with a group larger than twelve. A small delegation did confer with him over the objections of many women who felt that all the protestors should be present during the negotiations.[299]

The radicals' worst fears were realized when the delegation emerged from hours of negotiations having secured only one of their fourteen demands—the publication of an eight-page supplement on the movement to be penned by the protestors. The women had also succeeded in wrangling $10,000, joint editorial control of the supplement, and collective by-lines from Carter.[300] But many women felt that the negotiating team had allowed itself to be cleverly manipulated by Carter. After all, they reasoned, hadn't many major women's magazines already run articles on the new movement? And wouldn't the *Journal* stand to profit from the publicity surrounding the sit-in? Some women also thought that the action was self-aggrandizing, perhaps a way for some writers to "break into print and get themselves known to a few top editors."[301] Indeed, the organizers' willingness to abandon their more radical demands suggested to many radicals that the action was merely a "group job interview."[302] Baxandall even claims that some women showed up for the sit-in with their vitaes in hand.[303] At the time Baxandall harshly criticized the action:

> I was at the *Ladies Home Journal* action and it was repulsive in that several professional writers were conducting job interviews and convincing the man they were expert writers, furthering their careers. This turned me off and severed the solidarity. . . . When some of us objected to this type of elitism and individualism we were put down for not being sisterly. Who are our sisters—what does it mean to say we define our best interest as that of the poorest, ugliest and most brutally exploited?[304]

One *Rat* writer argued that the action was "effective as publicity," but suggested that Media Women "would do well to examine their commitment to the liberation of all sisters, in order to assure their interest in fame or fortune do not take precedence." She also contended that the demonstration proved that "it is not feasible for radicals to participate in joint actions with those who do not share our understandings [*sic*] about the nature of the power structure."[305] Even Karla Jay, a member of Media Women who praised aspects of the action, contended that they had

> folded under the offer of a few goodies! Somewhere, despite all our good intentions, the action had become elitist. What good had we done? Aside from the publicity . . . we had only succeeded in getting Vassar girls higher paying jobs in publishing.

And Jay noted that as the day wore on, the protestors had "started more and more to appeal to [Carter's] capitalist self-interest—how much money he would make on a women's liberation issue."[306] A number of movement veterans were disenchanted with the action. Baxandall remembers resolving to leave the movement after the action because she was so angry at Media Women for ignoring the secretaries at the *Journal*.[307] Nor was Atkinson or Firestone pleased with the action.[308] According to Bikman, Koedt "hated" the sit-in.[309] And novelist Alix Kates Shulman believes the action demonstrated that the "movement had reason to worry about writers coming in and ripping off the movement."[310] For veteran radical feminists who had always maintained that no woman would ever be free until all were free, the sit-in raised disturbing questions.

****

In the early '70s radical feminism seemed to be flourishing. Certainly, the women's liberation movement was having an enormous impact on the nation. In July 1970, New York State liberalized its abortion law, making it the most progressive in the country. Three years later, in *Roe v. Wade*, the U.S. Supreme Court ruled that state laws forbidding abortion violated the consitutional right to privacy. In August 1970, the House of Representatives, after only an hour of debate, passed the Equal Rights Amendment; it was subsequently passed by Congress in March of 1972. And on August 26, 1970—the fiftieth anniversary of woman suffrage—feminists staged the largest demonstration for female equality in American history. The Women's Strike for Equality drew between 35,000 and 50,000 women in New York City alone.[311] Talk of women's liberation (or more often, women's lib) was everywhere. There was an explosion of radical feminist literature—both aboveground and underground. Kate Millett's *Sexual Politics*, Firestone's *The Dialectic of Sex*, and Robin Morgan's anthology *Sisterhood is Powerful* were all published in 1970 and were all best-sellers. Radical feminist groups and projects cropped up everywhere, not only in major urban centers.

But by 1973, the radical feminist movement was actually in decline. The groups responsible for making the important theoretical breakthroughs were either dead or moribund. Certainly, The Feminists, Cell 16, and NYRF had evolved in ways which their founders had never intended—Cell 16 and The Feminists toward cultural feminism, and NYRF toward liberal feminism. A number of movement pioneers had withdrawn from the movement, often, as Sarachild and Leon observed in mid-1971, as a result of being attacked as "elitist," "middle class," or "unsisterly."[312] In fact, in the summer of 1970 a small group of self-named "feminist refugees," among them some of the women responsible for establishing the first women's liberation groups in the country, met in New York to discuss the leadership "purges."[313] Then there were the divisive struggles over class, elitism, and sexual preference which started to consume the movement in 1970. By 1972, the women's movement was so fractured that it made, in the words of Nora Ephron, "the American Communist Party of the 1930's look like a monolith."[314] The radical feminist wing of the movement became so absorbed in its own internal struggles that it sometimes found it difficult to look outside itself, to focus on the larger problem of male supremacy.

Among some of the founders, there was a growing uneasiness about the movement's direction. For instance, Sarachild, Hanisch, Leon, Mainardi, and Colette Price revived Redstockings in December 1973, in large part because they believed that while "the trappings of the early radical upsurge remain . . . the content and style have been watered down. Operating on its initial momentum only, the movement is slowing down."[315] A few of the founders even began to question certain initial premises of the movement. Roxanne Dunbar was among those who moved decisively toward Marxism. And in mid-1973, Ellen Willis criticized the increasingly popular movement idea that women constituted a classless caste. In fact, Willis maintained that women's liberation required an "economic revolution" and could be achieved only through an alliance with men.[316]

By 1973 radical feminism was beginning to give way to cultural feminism and liberal feminism. In the early '70s liberal feminism broadened its analysis as it moved away from Friedan's economistic and legalistic approach and embraced aspects of radical feminism. In contrast to Friedan, who had disparaged radical feminists' focus on the "personal," many liberal feminists came to agree with radical feminists that there was a political dimension to personal life. NOW chapters even began to establish consciousness-raising groups for interested women. But liberal feminists remained determinedly individualistic and in this respect their feminism diverged from radical feminism. While radical feminists were committed to social transformation, liberal feminists spoke of self-improvement. *Ms.* magazine, which began publishing in 1972, was quite successful in promulgating this "pull-yourself-up-by-your-bootstraps" brand of feminism and many women came to embrace it.[317] Equally attractive to many women was that liberal feminists indicted sex roles rather than men. From the beginning Friedan had presented feminism as a sex-role revolution in which both men and women would benefit. Indeed, for Friedan feminism was but "a stage in the whole human rights movement."[318] And in 1970, Gloria Steinem, *Ms.* editor and the best-known exponent of this new liberal feminism, deployed radical rhetoric, but like Friedan implied that women's liberation was men's liberation as well. "Men will have to give up ruling class privileges, but in return they will no longer be the ones to support the family, get drafted, bear the strain of responsibility and freedom."[319]

Women joining the movement turned to NOW for a variety of reasons, not the least of which was its liberalism. But NOW was also nowhere nearly as fractious as most radical feminist groups, and it was considerably more accepting of women who did not yet know that in some feminist circles high heels and make-up were evidence of collaboration.[320] And by comparison to radical feminists who must have seemed as though they were engaged in a long and tedious encounter session with each other, liberal feminists seemed models of efficiency and effectiveness. Of course, to many women's liberationists it seemed that the legislative and judicial victories that liberal feminists were claiming were nothing but concessions designed to co-opt the movement. For instance, in September 1970 The Feminists sent a message to the Senate Subcommittee on Constitutional Amendments denouncing the ERA and advising feminists "against squandering invaluable time and energy on it."[321] A delegation of Washington, D.C. feminists invited to testify about the ERA before the same committee, declared, "We are aware that the system will try to appease us with their [*sic*] paper offerings. We will not be appeased. Our demands can only be met by a total transformation of society which you cannot legislate, you cannot co-opt, you cannot *control*."[322] And Firestone went so far (in fact, further than many other radical feminists) as to dismiss child-care centers as attempts to "buy women off" because they "ease the immediate pressure without asking why the pressure is on *women*."[323] But the totalism of radical feminism's vision and its cynicism toward reform struck many women as futilitarian.

Although cultural feminism was still quite inchoate in 1973, there was within the radical feminist wing of the movement more talk of essentialism and a greater antagonism toward the left. One also finds the emphasis shifting in certain quarters from political confrontation to personal transformation and the construction of a specifically female culture and community. There was less activism, especially around abortion and child care—two issues central to early radical feminism. But this followed in large part from the way in which radical feminism was defined by groups such as The Feminists and Cell 16. If radical feminism required separation from men in one's personal life, those issues that seemed very connected to women's relationships with men were no longer the burning issues. Beginning in 1971 the focus of radical feminist activism started to shift to the issue of rape. Previously when radical feminists spoke of violence, they were often referring to, in the words of Ann Snitow, "the violence of the mind."[324] In demonstrating against beauty pageants, women's magazines, and the media, feminists were challenging the cultural representation of women which, they argued, caused untold psychic damage to women. And while radical feminists sometimes acknowledged the role played by physical violence in maintaining male supremacy, they tended to emphasize other factors—marriage, the family, normative heterosexuality, women's economic dependence, and lack of reproductive freedom.[325] Feminist philosopher Alison Jaggar suggests that as the enormity of the problem of male violence became known, some radical feminists began to turn to biologistic explanations of male dominance.[326]

Although cultural feminism was fundamentally distinct from radical feminism as it was articulated by Firestone, Atkinson, Sarachild, or even Dunbar, the seeds of cultural feminism were in all the varieties of radical feminism. The characterization of "woman" as a unitary category, the depiction of men as irrevocably sexist and of women as powerless victims, and the conviction that feminism was the single transformative theory—all helped to pave the way for cultural feminism. And although radical feminism was unalterably opposed to personal solutions, its frequent conflation of the personal and the political made it easy for the cultural feminist commitment to personal transformation or the liberal feminist concern with self-improvement to be defined as political. While the radical feminist movement as a whole was social constructionist and committed to maximizing women's sexual pleasure, there were radical feminists whose views of gender and sexuality prefigured cultural feminism. In fact, the tendency of some radical feminists to blame maleness rather than power relations not only encouraged essentialism, but also helped shift the focus away from confronting men to building a female counterculture as a refuge from contaminating maleness. Yet radical feminism's demise did not follow inevitably from either its theoretical shortcomings or even the increasingly conservative cli-

mate of the '70s. To understand the decline of radical feminism and the ascendance of cultural feminism, we must look more closely at the period of 1970–1973 when the movement was ravaged by intense factionalism over the issues of elitism, class, and lesbianism.

5

The Eruption of Difference

The first wave of radical feminism was, as Ann Snitow observes, characterized by the belief that "we are one, we are woman."[1] But by 1970, the rhetoric of universal sisterhood had given way to wrenching discussions of women's differences, as lesbians and working-class women challenged the assumption that there was a uniformity to women's experiences and interests. From 1970 onward, excoriations of the movement as racist, classist, and heterosexist became routine if not obligatory at feminist gatherings. Some feminists, like Robin Morgan and Kathleen Barry, reacted by claiming that class was a male-defined category irrelevant to women.[2] Barry even argued that the women raising it were interlopers from the "male left" intent upon sabotaging the women's movement.[3] Similarly, the reorganized Redstockings alleged that the women pressing the issue of lesbianism were politicos who had initially disparaged women's liberation and were now using lesbianism "to replace feminism or eliminate it, or else . . . dilute it."[4] While it is true that leftist women stressed class, the women who initially questioned the movement's class dynamics were veteran radical feminists, not outside agitators. Nor was Redstockings' depiction of lesbian feminists as antifeminists accurate. Although the most influential early lesbian-feminist collective, The Furies, was composed of former politicos, the conjoining of feminism and lesbianism proved logical and compelling to many radical feminists as well. However, those feminists who believed in a global sisterhood found it easier to attribute the conflicts to political adversaries than to acknowledge the formidable obstacles to female unity. As this chapter demonstrates, these issues caused enormous upheaval within the movement in the early '70s. The "gay-straight split," in particular, crippled the movement, ending long-term friendships, partnerships, and groups. But the issues of class and sexual preference would undoubtedly have proven less explosive had the movement from the outset been less nervous about exploring women's differences.

Class and Elitism

From the beginning both radical feminists and socialist-feminists went to great lengths to try to avoid reproducing the "macho leadership" that prevailed in the new left by the late '60s.[5] As we have seen, they often tried to achieve egalitarianism by eschewing leadership and formal structure. Meredith Tax recalls that at the first planning sessions for the Boston politico group Bread and Roses, one of the biggest concerns was "how to have an organization that wouldn't have an authoritarian structure that would create a few hotshots." But, as Tax readily admits, "there was a certain denial of reality in this because that's what the people in this room were, and that's why they were there."[6] Indeed, there was a certain denial, but it was necessary to preserve the fiction of absolute equality. Unfortunately, the movement's fondness for egalitarian and collective forms often inhibited its effectiveness.[7] Tax recalls that it was a struggle just convincing many of the women in Bread and Roses that their meetings—which sometimes numbered 200 women—would run more smoothly with the assistance of a chair:

> It wasn't clear if anyone should raise their hands, because it wasn't clear if anyone was chairing. I would often end up chairing, and I wouldn't know what to do. I mean I didn't want to be the bad authoritarian, but it was such a mess that I couldn't stand it. . . . The meetings were a total turn-off. If we had known more we could have done better. The one thing I learned from that is that I never want to be a leader without clear-cut responsibilities and structure again. I was clearly one of the people in the leadership and it was totally de facto. What that meant was that my phone never stopped ringing for two years.[8]

The editors of the SDS newspaper *New Left Notes* chose to print this cartoon next to the statement put forth by the Women's Liberation Workshop at SDS's June 1967 convention.

Florika chained to the "Amerika-Dollie" in a guerilla theater skit at the August 1968 Miss America protest. Photo: *Voice of the Women's Liberation Movement.*

Shulamith Firestone (left) and Ros Baxandall (right) at the January 1969 Counter-Inaugural protest in Washington, D.C. Photo: Redstockings Women's Liberation Archives.

Redstockings' disruption of New York state's legislative hearings on abortion reform in February 1969. Ellen Willis is on the left holding papers. Photo: Dan Hogan Charles, *The New York Times*.

The March 1970 *Ladies Home Journal* demonstration. Susan Brownmiller is in the foreground gesturing with papers. Photo: Jack Manning, *The New York Times*.

Jane Alpert and David Hughey demonstrating outside Women's House of Detention in late 1969. Photo: Steven Rose, *Rat*.

Shulamith Firestone, 1970. Photo: Michael Hardy.

May 1972 rally to oppose the recriminalization of abortion in New York. Photo: Bettye Lane.

Ti-Grace Atkinson (foreground with "Impeach Nixon" sticker on her forehead) and Florynce Kennedy (behind her) take part in an October 1972 Women Against Richard Nixon demonstration. Photo: Bettye Lane.

From left to right: Gloria Steinem, Arlie Scott, Robin Morgan, Kate Millett, and Jean O'Leary at a 1978 conference. Photo: Bettye Lane.

Kathie Sarachild and James Forman (formerly of SNCC) at a January 1981 Counter-Inaugural demonstration. Photo: Redstockings Women's Liberation Archives.

Women's International Terrorists' Conspiracy from Hell (WITCH) demonstrate their secret powers on the street as they read their manifesto. Photo: 1988 © by Fred W. McDarrah.

Although the situation in Bread and Roses seems particularly extreme, there was within the movement very little tolerance of anything that seemed even vaguely hierarchical.

As the movement became more newsworthy, it became more phobic about leaders. For instance, in late 1969, Marilyn Webb was expelled from the coordinating committee of D.C. Women's Liberation on the grounds that she permitted the press to single her out as a leader. The issue apparently arose when Webb was interviewed by the press during a demonstration protesting D.C. General Hospital's "genocidal practices" toward black women. Although Webb gave a speech at the rally, many women felt she should not have allowed the press to treat her as the protest's spokeswoman because she had not done her share of the "shitwork" for the demonstration. Webb maintains that she exempted herself from the organizational work because she was seven months pregnant at the time. After the demonstration, Webb was summoned to a meeting where she was asked to leave D.C. Women's Liberation:

> To a person they asked me to leave the women's liberation movement because I had taken leadership when I didn't deserve it. It was like a witchhunt. They voted me out of the movement. I had even found the office to rent in which I was voted out. I cried for days.[9]

Of the eighteen women sitting in judgment, only three voted against Webb's expulsion. Webb was devastated, but she decided to remain involved in the movement and with several other women—including those who had supported her during the meeting—Webb established the feminist newspaper *off our backs*.[10]

In retrospect, Webb's expulsion seems extreme to say the least. Why did women's liberationists attack each other in this way? First of all, as Willis observes, the emergence of leaders contradicted the premise that this was a nonhierarchical movement of equals:

> When you're used to being on the bottom of a hierarchy everyplace and now you have your own movement, and you find the hierarchy being reproduced, it creates a special kind of rage. Plus it so contravened our very overly naive and optimistic

> ideas about sisterhood, and how transcendent sisterhood was going to be. So, it was, somehow very much more disillusioning.[11]

Indeed, there was enormous resentment toward those who seemed to be benefiting from their involvement in the movement. Helen Kritzler felt "what we were doing was making a women's movement. We were not out to make individuals involved in that movement famous."[12] But despite the movement's ultra-egalitarianism, some women were beginning to acquire names for themselves. Of course, the one thing that feminists could peddle were their ideas, and as a consequence, women writers were especially mistrusted. Even dedicated movement veterans like Shulamith Firestone whose book, *The Dialectic of Sex*, was a tremendous contribution to radical feminist theory, were reportedly criticized for trying to "cash in" on the sudden trendiness of the women's movement.[13] The distrust of writers was so great that Alix Kates Shulman recalls being "terrified" that she might have to choose between being a writer and being an activist in the movement.[14]

It was not until Barbara Mehrhof and Pam Kearon organized the Class Workshop in the winter of 1970 that class became implicated in the question of leadership or elitism. The Class Workshop included women from both The Feminists and Redstockings. Mehrhof and Kearon were joined by Irene Peslikis, Linda Feldman, Judy Duffett, Judy Thibeau, Ina Clausen, and Page Dougherty. With the exception of one woman, the women in the Class Workshop were raised in lower-middle-class and working-class families.[15] Kearon maintains that the issue of class was originally but "a wrinkle in the equality issue."[16] However, before long the two issues became inalterably linked as the problem of inequality became redefined as a problem of class. In the spring of 1970, the women of the Class Workshop issued a statement explaining that they had established the group

> because of the exclusion of most working-class women from the women's liberation movement, as a reaction to the oppression we as women of the working class experienced in the movement, and because of the leadership of upper-middle class women within the movement. The feminist movement began because we were tired of being led by men. But neither do we want to be led by women.[17]

Many people assumed that the Class Workshop was exclusively Marxist in orientation. Susan Brownmiller, for one, felt that the women of the Class Workshop had "just discovered Marxism."[18] Some did want to acquaint themselves with Marxist theory, but others, like Mehrhof and Kearon, opposed any "veering towards leftism."[19] In fact, as a former student of Marxist scholar Herbert Aptheker, Brownmiller was probably more familiar with Marxist theory than anyone in the Class Workshop. Certainly, the members of the Class Workshop were more interested in challenging movement elitism than in rethinking radical feminism's conviction that gender was the primary contradiction. Nor did the group actually try to organize women around the issues of class and gender. Whereas socialist-feminists tried to reach out to working-class women outside the movement, the women of the Class Workshop confined themselves to exploring their own class backgrounds and to critiquing the movement's class and racial biases.

The Class Workshop began on a conciliatory note by devising a questionnaire designed to clarify class differences among women. However, they were anything but conciliatory at the strife-torn second Congress to Unite Women in May 1970, where they pushed the issues of class and race, and attacked professional women writers.[20] According to one account, on the second day of the conference some members of the Class Workshop burst into the evening plenary session

> demanding that the discussion be devoted exclusively to that issue, and that race and class were the only relevant issues. As a result of this and resulting confusion, most workshops could not be reported out to the plenary, action proposals went undiscussed, and no continuing structure for Congress participants was established. And under the pretext that the Congress was using male forms of organization (Roberts Rules of Order), the groups that disrupted virtually prevented any fruitful discussion from taking place among the women as a whole—even on the issues they felt should be the focus of discussion for the group![21]

The Class Workshop tried to persuade the assembly to adopt a series of resolutions on the media. In the preface to their proposals, they declared "*everyone* in the movement must be in groups which operate COLLECTIVELY (i.e., use the LOT SYSTEM) and

WORK IN THE INTERESTS OF THE MOST OPPRESSED WOMEN." (The extensive capitalizing was, of course, a carryover from The Feminists.) And, they proclaimed, "Ideas don't belong to *any* individual." The following were among their proposals:

> 1. Anyone who appears in the media is to be drawn by lot from her group. . . . The lot is to be rotating. No one is to participate in the media alone. 2. Women's Liberation is getting popular enough that the media needs us as much as we need them, We can and must dictate our terms to them: present prepared statements and refuse to give personal information. From now on anyone who refuses to follow this policy must be assumed to be doing so for her own personal aggrandizement. 3. No member of a group can appear as an independent feminist—whether for fame or money. 4. No individual or group can earn a living by writing or speaking about women's liberation. 5. Anyone who wants to write should write for the movement, not for the publishing industry. 6. Any individual who refuses collective discipline will be ostracized from the movement.[22]

The Class Workshop went so far as to propose that the Congress pass a resolution attacking Susan Brownmiller and Lucy Komisar, two feminist writers who helped organize the *Ladies Home Journal* action. According to Brownmiller, the resolution read, "We condemn Susan Brownmiller and Lucy Komisar for seeking to rise to fame on the back of the women's movement by publishing articles in the establishment press." After the resolution had been read, Brownmiller shot up out of her seat and shouted, "You're using my name, sister," to her assailant, Judy Thibeau.[23] Fortunately, the resolution did not pass. The Class Workshop also passed out a leaflet at the Congress attacking professional women writers, and Media Women in particular. Their vilification of women writers was precipitated in large part by the *Ladies Home Journal* action which had occurred only two months earlier. Their leaflet read:

> On the other side we have the professional writers—the "liberals" and "reformists" who claim that by working for an oppressive system, somehow, women would be less oppressed. These are the Susan Brownmillers and Lucy Komisars—the "media women"—who at the *Ladies Home Journal* action assured the male editor that they were not "on a Dyke trip,"—that they were "professionals"—"some of the best writers in the

> country"—and that they would help him sell his magazine because Women's Liberation was really the up and coming thing.[24]

To a great extent the Class Workshop was a response to the media's growing fascination with the women's liberation movement. Ann Snitow recalls that the media blitz "was a wind in our ears. . . . Everyone was an intellectual and underpaid. Careerism was still a somewhat distant concept, but there was a rush."[25] Indeed, there was a rush and some people were, of course, profiting professionally from the movement. Certainly, one of the reasons Brownmiller was singled out was that she had recently published an article on the women's movement in *The New York Times Magazine*.[26] Unfortunately, both radical feminists and politicos tended to respond to the media's clamoring for leaders by throttling individual expression. What happened to Atkinson in The Feminists happened time and time again to other feminists. Writing about her women's group, Elinor Langer observed that "[n]o one could be smarter than anyone else, or prettier, or more talented, or make more money, or do anything significant on her own."[27] For instance, in the spring of 1969, Naomi Weisstein was asked to give a speech in Berkeley. However, her husband, Jesse Lemisch, contends that her women's group in Chicago nixed the engagement:

> Naomi had already displayed extraordinary oratorical skills, moving large audiences with a mutuality and responsiveness which I had previously seen only in the black movement. Fearing that she would acquire a national reputation and become a "star," her group told her that she should turn down the invitation to speak at Berkeley, as well as all future speaking invitations.

According to Lemisch, Weisstein was "hoist on her own petard" because she had whole-heartedly supported those egalitarian measures—the skills-sharing and speaker rotation—that rationalized the "quashing" of her skills.[28]

But the movement's policy against cooperating with the establishment press did not prevent the media from promoting certain women as movement leaders and spokespersons. Instead, it prevented the movement from exercising any control over who was proclaimed a movement leader. As Frances Chapman notes, the anti-leader line, gave "enormous power to unnamed leaders.

We allowed the reformists and careerists to take over the movement simply because we refused to let any of us lead it."[29] Ironically, the movement's self-imposed silence empowered the media, allowing them to choose Gloria Steinem—a talented journalist sympathetic to feminism, but a virtual unknown in movement circles—as a movement spokesperson. Nor did the movement's eschewal of formal structures resolve the problem of power; rather, as Jo Freeman noted, it "became a way of masking power."[30] Moreover, the struggle over elitism had a debilitating effect on the movement as women with skills were discouraged from using or even sharing them. In fact, the attacks on leaders went a long way toward wiping out the movement's original leadership. Patricia Mainardi recalls the attacks:

> Every time you opened your mouth someone told you to shut it. Every time you tried to write something someone told you you shouldn't. So, finally you went away. . . . That first generation of people got really burned. I feel like I got really burned. You were out on the front lines and people turned against you.[31]

In early 1972, lesbian-feminist activist Rita Mae Brown, who had earlier championed the equality cause, suggested that the movement's equality line had "become a tyranny of personal conformity. Imagination, inspiration, and efficient political organization are suspect and throttled."[32] Although the women who raised the issues of class and elitism were challenging the movement to acknowledge women's differences, their remedy entailed suppressing those differences by eliminating individual initiative and expression. They were seduced by the chimera of a transcendent sisterhood, as were their lesbian-feminist sisters to whom we will now turn.

Lesbianism

Until late 1969, opponents of women's liberation were more apt to raise the issue of lesbianism than were radical feminists—many of whom were initially befuddled by the conjoining of these seemingly disparate issues.[33] Of course, some radical feminists did allude to sexual preference, if only abstractly and obliquely in the context of sexual liberation. While most early radical feminists believed that the sexual revolution of the '60s was in many respects more exploitive than liberating, they nonetheless envisioned feminism dismantling the edifice of sexual repression. For instance, in the widely circulated "Sexual Politics: A Manifesto for Revolution," Millett contended that feminism would bring about freedom of sexual expression and "bisex, or the end of enforced perverse heterosexuality."[34] And in *The Dialectic of Sex*, Firestone declared that a feminist revolution would bring about a reversion to "natural polymorphous sexuality—all forms of sexuality would be allowed and indulged."[35] Anne Koedt, of course, made the earliest and most explicit connection between the institution of heterosexuality and women's oppression. Koedt suggested that men suppress the truth about the clitoral orgasm because it "would indicate that sexual pleasure was obtainable from either men *or* women, thus making heterosexuality not an absolute, but an option."[36]

But many radical feminists, especially those who viewed women's liberation and sexual liberation as mutually exclusive, were often skittish if not hostile toward lesbianism. Most commonly, they dismissed lesbianism as sexual rather than political. Thus Roxanne Dunbar of Cell 16 argued that the task of feminism was to get women out of bed rather than change the gender of their partners. And Abby Rockefeller maintained that lesbianism "muddles what is the real issue for women by making it appear that women really like sex as much as men—that they just don't like sex *with* men." (her emphasis)[37] Many radical feminists also objected to the role-playing which they assumed was endemic to lesbian relationships. Atkinson spoke for many when she pronounced:

> Because lesbianism involves role-playing and, more important, because it is based on the primary assumption of male oppression, that is, sex, lesbianism reinforces the sex class system.[38]

And in 1970 Brownmiller reportedly refused an invitation to speak to the staid lesbian organization, the Daughters of Bilitis (DOB), because she thought lesbians hypersexual and oppressively male.[39] A number of radical feminists agreed with Brownmiller and Atkinson that lesbians were too attached to sex roles, in the form of butch-femme roles, to be likely or desirable recruits to feminism. Many also feared that lesbianism could become a refuge from feminist activism.

But at the same time that many radical feminists were rushing to disassociate feminism from lesbianism, many others—both politicos and radical feminists—were discovering that they felt sexually attracted toward one another. For instance, Marilyn Webb remembers that in D.C. "we were putting our energy into each other and slowly falling in love with each other as well." Although Webb maintains that "we didn't think of it as gay at the time," other women clearly did consider their feelings lesbian.[40] Baxandall claims that among New York radical feminists

> Lesbianism wasn't a big thing because virtually everyone was experimenting with it. We'd go away to write something and almost everyone would sleep together. We even drew lots [to determine who would sleep with whom] and then cheated.[41]

Although the specific scenario that Baxandall describes was most likely atypical, there was certainly widespread experimentation with lesbianism. Peslikis, who became involved with another woman before lesbians began to push for movement recognition in Spring 1970, contends that at least in New York, many radical feminists were open to lesbianism. While many lesbian-feminists claim that heterosexual radical feminists resisted lesbianism, Peslikis asks sarcastically, "Like who was ready for whom?" For Peslikis, as for many others, lesbianism was "a natural extension of all my feelings about women."[42] Of course, this was what Judith Brown had predicted in 1968 when she wrote:

> Women who turn away from men for a time, to look to each other for political relationships, movement thinking, and an organizational milieu, are bound to see here and there someone they love. The slightest measure of female liberation will bring with it an ability to perceive again the precise qualities and degree of responsivity that inhere in other women.[43]

While women's liberationists were divided on lesbianism, many reformist feminists were unalterably opposed to any discussion of lesbianism. Friedan reacted defensively to the early stirrings of lesbianism, labeling it a "lavender menace," and warning that it could undermine the credibility of the women's movement.[44] The NOW leadership was so reluctant to deal with the issue that it reportedly omitted the lesbian group DOB from the press release listing the institutional sponsors of the November 1969 Congress to Unite Women which New York-NOW had organized.[45] Shortly thereafter, Rita Mae Brown, who had been trying to raise the issue of lesbianism within NOW, was inexplicably relieved of her duties as the editor of New York-NOW's newsletter. Brown was so angered by the organization's homophobia that she resigned from her other NOW offices, taking two other lesbians with her. The three women promptly issued a statement detailing the homophobia within the organization:

> The leadership consciously oppresses other women on the question of sexual preference—or in plain words, enormous prejudice is directed against the lesbian. Lesbian is the one word that can cause the Executive Committee a collective heart attack. This issue is dismissed as unimportant, too dangerous to contemplate, divisive or whatever excuse could be dredged up from their repression. The prevailing attitude is, and this is reflected even more on the national level, "Suppose they (notice the word, they) flock to us in droves? How horrible. After all, think of our image."[46]

The charismatic Rita Mae Brown probably did more than any other individual to raise feminists' consciousness about lesbianism. Beginning in late 1969, Brown set about organizing a lesbian-feminist movement. Brown joined a Redstockings' consciousness-raising group, which she soon quit after deciding that Redstockings "was not too pro-woman when it came to Lesbians."[47] After leaving Redstockings, Brown moved on to the Gay Liberation Front (GLF), where she managed to persuade some of the women to form consciousness-raising groups and to make common cause with lesbians from women's liberation. As a result of Brown's visit, Lois Hart, Suzanne Bevier, Ellen Bedoz, and Arlene Kisner of GLF formed a group with Sidney Abbott, Barbara Love, Michela Griffo, and March Hoffman—all of whom had been active in radical and reformist feminist groups.[48] Brown and gay activist Martha Shelley, the former president of NY-DOB, also formed a consciousness-raising group, but it soon dissolved.

Meanwhile, Brown had established contact with a small group of Vassar undergraduates that included Jennifer Woodul, among others. With Cynthia Funk (an early NYRW member), March Hoffman, Michela Griffo, and the Vassar students, Brown traveled to various feminist gatherings where she raised the issue of lesbianism from the audience. Woodul recalls:

> We started travelling around with Rita to women's liberation conferences. There were usually about four or five of us from Vassar, and Cynthia, March, maybe Michela from New York, and Rita, of course. We would go to these women's liberation conferences and push the issue of lesbianism. I say "we" because what would happen is that Rita would push the issue of lesbianism and we would support her. Sometimes we would do it in a straightforward way and sometimes we would do it in a planned way, seating ourselves strategically around the room and acting like we hadn't come there together.[49]

Coletta Reid, who later worked with Brown in the Washington, D.C. lesbian-feminist collective, The Furies, claims that Brown borrowed this particular tactic from the Trotskyites.[50] Brown and her retinue challenged a number of feminists, including Roxanne Dunbar and Marlene Dixon who appeared together on a panel in Boston in early 1970.[51] After Brown's opening salvo, Cynthia Funk told the panelists:

> I'm tired of hearing about the oppression of women. . . . Let's look at the oppression right here in this room. You women on the panel have used your heterosexual privilege to silence the topic of love—especially love between women, which would seem to me to be critical to the movement.

According to Brown, after several seconds of "stunned silence," Dixon ventured that some of her best friends were homosexual.[52] Dunbar's response was that women did not have to sleep together to love each other. Then she declared that homosexuality was simply not that important because "homosexuality is a chosen oppression whereas being a woman is the root oppression."[53]

However, these were isolated skirmishes. The issue of lesbianism really exploded on May 1, 1970, opening night of the second Congress to Unite Women, when forty lesbians pre-empted the scheduled proceedings to raise the issue of lesbianism. (The divisiveness over class and lesbianism prompted some women to dub this the "Congress to Divide Women.") The action was planned by a group that included Brown, Funk, Hoffman, Hart, and Bedoz.[54] The following account of the "Lavender Menace" action appeared in the women's underground paper *Rat*:

> On May 1st, at 7:15 p.m. about 300 women were quietly sitting in the auditorium of intermediate school 70 waiting for the Congress to Unite Women to come to order. The lights went out, people heard running, laughter, a rebel yell here and there, and when those lights were turned back on, those same 300 women found themselves in the hands of the LAVENDER MENACE. . . . Seventeen of the Radical lesbians wore lavender t-shirts with LAVENDER MENACE stenciled across the front. These women were the first wave of the action and the ones who took over the auditorium.[55]

The other demonstrators were dispersed throughout the audience and were supposed to declare their support for the action and join the women on stage. Once on stage, they would reveal both their Lavender Menace t-shirts and their lesbianism. However, as Woodul explains, the demonstrators needn't have acted as "pigeons" in the audience for "as soon as the floor was taken, women by the droves began to come up on stage."[56] For two hours the protestors held the floor as they talked about what it was like to be a lesbian in a heterosexist culture. The final assembly of the Congress adopted the set of resolutions advanced by "The Lavender Menace: Gay Liberation Front Women and Radical Lesbians." The resolutions read:

> 1. Women's Liberation is a lesbian plot. 2. Whenever the label lesbian is used against the movement collectively or against women individually, it is to be affirmed, not denied. 3. In all discussions of birth control, homosexuality must be included as a legitimate method of contraception. 4. All sex education curricula must include lesbianism as a valid, legitimate form of sexual expression and love.[57]

One of the most important things to come out of the Congress action was the Radicalesbian position paper, "The Woman-Identified Woman," copies of which were distributed to women in the audience.[58] Like the action, the paper was designed to assuage heterosexual feminists' fears about lesbianism. In fact, Jennifer Woodul contends that the "Menaces" decided to use the term "woman-identified" because they hoped it would prove less threatening to heterosexual women:

> I was there when the ideas for "Woman-Identified Woman" were beginning to take shape. We were trying to figure out how to tell women about lesbianism without using the word, lesbian, because we found that at these conferences we kept freaking people out all the time. And I believe it was Cynthia [Funk] who came up with this term, "woman-identified." At least, that was the first time I had ever heard it. So what we were trying to do was make women realize that lesbians were not different from other women in any sort of strange way.[59]

To legitimize lesbianism, Radicalesbians had to persuade feminists that lesbianism was not simply a bedroom issue and that lesbians were not male-identified "bogeywomen" out to sexually exploit other women. They accomplished this by redefining lesbianism as a primarily political choice and by locating the discourse within the already established feminist framework of separatism. They criticized as "divisive and sexist" the tendency to characterize lesbianism "simply by sex." Moreover, they suggested that far from being male-identified, lesbians, by virtue of their distance from contaminating maleness, were actually more likely to be woman-identified than heterosexual women who were "dependent upon male culture for their [self]-definition:"

> Only women can give to each other a new sense of self. That identity we have to develop with reference to ourselves, and not in relation to men. . . . Our energies must flow toward our sisters, not backward toward our oppressors. As long as women's liberation tries to free women without facing the basic heterosexual structure that binds us in one-to-one relationship with our oppressors, tremendous energies will continue to flow into trying to straighten up each particular relationship with a man. . . . This obviously splits our energies and commitments, leaving us unable to be committed to the construction of the new patterns which will liberate us.

Although the paper's tone was not antagonistic—for instance, they avoided defining heterosexual women as collaborators—the assumption was that feminism required lesbianism:

> It is the primacy of women, of women creating a new consciousness of and with each other, which is at the heart of women's liberation, and the basis for the cultural revolution.

"The Woman-Identified Woman" was not the earliest expression of lesbian-feminism. Both Rita Mae Brown and Martha Shelley had angrily denounced movement homophobia in the pages of *Rat* and *Come Out*, respectively.[60] But what set "The Woman-Identified Woman" apart from these earlier pieces, what made it so significant, was that it redefined lesbianism as the quintessential act of political solidarity with other women. By defining lesbianism as a political choice rather than a sexual alternative, Radicalesbians disarmed heterosexual feminists. Of course, the knotty problem of sexuality remained. Even Radicalesbians had to admit that lesbianism involved sex:

> Until women see in each other the possibility of a primal commitment which includes sexual love, they will be denying themselves the love and value they readily accord to men, thus affirming their second-class status.

The introduction of sex troubled many heterosexual feminists who had found in the women's movement a welcome respite from sexuality. Ellen DuBois was just one of many heterosexual feminists who initially resented the intrusion of sexuality into the movement:

> I felt finally I had found a movement where I didn't have to worry about whether or not I was attractive or whether or not men liked me. . . . And just as I was beginning to feel here at last I could forget all of that, sex once again reared its ugly head.[61]

Lesbians faced the formidable task of persuading heterosexual feminists that lesbianism offered women something substantially different from the familiar heterosexual pattern of dominance and submission. They tried to accomplish this by reassuring heterosexual feminists that lesbianism involved sensuality rather than sexuality, "communication" rather than "conquest." For instance, in a widely reprinted article, "Smash Phallic Imperialism" (which the leftist Liberation News Service retitled "The Sensuous Woman," thus prompting an angry letter from its author), Boston lesbian-feminist Sue Katz contended:

> For me, coming out meant an end to sex. . . . Physical contact and feelings have taken a new liberatory form. And we call that *sensuality*. . . . Physicality is now a creative non-

> institutionalized experience. It is touching and rubbing and cuddling and fondness. . . . Its only goal is closeness and pleasure. It does not exist for the Big Orgasm. It exists for feeling nice. Our sexuality may or may not include genital experience. . . . The sensuality I feel has transformed my politics, has solved the contradiction between my mind and my body because the energies for our feminist revolution are the same as the energies of our love for women.[62]

And another lesbian-feminist ventured:

> What we have to learn is that being with, loving, and sexually relating to women is an entirely different reality—a different situation and that old fears are not really relevant. Lesbian women know this . . . straight women don't. So many straight women get very uptight and threatened by Lesbians: they feel that they are now sexual objects for the whole human race . . . that the safety they had with women is gone because of Lesbianism. But stop for a moment—that fear reveals more about the character of the heterosexual world.[63]

However, to break lesbianism's association with maleness, lesbian-feminists often reinforced dominant cultural assumptions about women's sexuality. They spoke platitudinously about the differences between women's (and, by extension, lesbian's) diffuse, romantic, and nurturing sexuality and men's aggressive, genitally oriented sexuality. Brown contended that "the male seeks to conquer through sex while the female seeks to communicate."[64] A member of Gay Women's Liberation in Berkeley maintained, "Men who are obsessed with sex are convinced that lesbians are obsessed with sex. Actually, like other women, lesbians are obsessed with love and fidelity."[65] In a July 1971 issue of the Los Angeles feminist newspaper *Everywoman*, written and edited by gay women's groups, one writer contended:

> Fortunately, Lesbianism never really had anything to do with men, despite all attempts at interference, and as a consequence remains the only viable pursuit left on earth as pure as snow, ego-free, and non-profit.[66]

If sex between women was as "pure as snow," heterosexual sex was thoroughly corrupted and inevitably oppressive.[67] Of course, in this respect, lesbian-feminists were merely echoing The Feminists and Cell 16. By presenting lesbianism as the political solution to women's oppression, and by invoking essentialist ideas about female sexuality, lesbian-feminists managed to sanitize lesbianism. But, as we shall see, this formulation of lesbianism had serious consequences for lesbian and heterosexual feminists alike.

Most heterosexual feminists who witnessed the Lavender Menace action seemed not to have felt threatened by it. In fact, Kearon recalls that in the aftermath of the second Congress, women would say to her, "the lesbians are so full of love and you [the women of the Class Workshop] are so full of hatred."[68] Baxandall thought the action was "funny and wonderful," and Snitow appreciated the "wit and vaudevillian charm" with which it was done.[69] But the action, in contrast to the paper, was really a plea for movement acceptance rather than an assertion of vanguard status. And, while the "Woman-Identified Woman" dismantled the ideological impediments to lesbian acceptance, it could not eliminate the emotional barriers.

The situation heated up considerably when the media seized upon the issue. In December 1970, *Time* magazine ran a short piece entitled, "Women's Lib: A Second Look," which not only revealed to the world that Kate Millett was a bisexual, but suggested quite hopefully that the revelation would discredit the movement.[70] Feminists, including Atkinson, Steinem, Brownmiller, and Florynce Kennedy, responded by holding a press conference in which they declared that women's liberation and gay liberation were "struggling towards a common goal"—a society in which people would no longer be categorized on the basis of their gender or sexual preference.[71] The decision to embrace rather than repudiate lesbianism succeeded in silencing the press. But there was no calm in New York-NOW where a purge mentality set it. In fact, Betty Friedan reportedly spearheaded a successful effort to prevent lesbians from being elected or re-elected to office in the 1970 New York-NOW elections. According to former New York-NOW President Ivy Bottini, Friedan succeeded in large measure because she received the support of two closeted NOW members.[72] In fact, a number of former NOW members contend that the organization's homophobia was not unrelated to the large number of closeted lesbians within the organization who felt they might be exposed as lesbians if the issue were openly discussed.[73]

Until mid-1971 when NOW finally passed a resolution supporting lesbianism "legally and morally," anyone within the organization who advocated lesbian rights was vulnerable.[74]

Women's liberation groups did not fall victim to the paranoia that seized NOW because they had always eschewed respectability. But the issue of lesbianism was still enormously divisive. From the period 1970–1972, the movement was convulsed by the gay-straight split, and nowhere was the conflict more acrimonious than in Washington, D.C., the birthplace of the lesbian-feminist group The Furies.

The Emergence of Lesbian-Feminism in Washington, D.C.

The women's liberation movement in D.C. was still more or less politico in orientation, even in 1970. The leftist think tank, The Institute for Policy Studies (IPS), remained central to the women's movement. Charlotte Bunch, Judy Coburn, and Betty Garman, all of whom were active in the movement, were fellows at IPS.[75] The D.C. movement continued to be largely a movement of friends. It was also extraordinarily vital, with twenty-four discussion groups and fourteen projects by 1970.[76] That same year both the left and the women's movement in D.C. shifted their attention somewhat from the war to the government's campaign of repression against the Panthers. For instance, women's liberationists there reportedly discussed the possibility of kidnapping Martha Mitchell to obtain the release of jailed Panther leader, Erica Huggins.[77]

Things changed when three women associated with the Chicago Seven defendants moved to town. (The Chicago Seven—or "The Conspiracy" as they mockingly called themselves—were accused of having incited a riot at the 1968 Democratic National Convention.) Tasha Peterson, Dave Dellinger's daughter, Susan Gregory, Rennie Davis's lover, and Susan Hathaway, Davis' former lover, moved to D.C. with Davis in the spring of 1970 following the conclusion of the Chicago Seven trial.[78] The three women moved in with Betty Garman—IPS fellow, Mobe leader, and Conspiracy supporter. Although Peterson, Hathaway, and

Gregory were apparently relative newcomers to the left, theirs became "the high-powered leftist house" in D.C.[79] And, although their feminism was, by all accounts, highly underdeveloped, Hathaway and Peterson began working at *oob* that summer.[80] Of course, *oob* in this period was highly politico, its pages filled with reports of women in third-world liberation struggles. Some movement veterans resented the Chicago women who were immediately treated as trusted comrades rather than the parvenus many felt they were. Bunch admits that the Chicago women, who identified themselves as "anti-imperialist women" rather than as feminists, were "very arrogant."[81]

Webb claims that many women were especially angered by the fact that the Chicago women were asked to participate in an experimental two-week women's commune to which many movement old-timers had not been invited. At the conclusion of the commune, the group decided to form a permanent women's commune. To some in the larger left community, the decision proved that "all their terrible fantasies were true. We'd decided to leave our husbands."[82] However, many women ended up backing out for one reason or another.[83] Garman, Peterson, Hathaway, and Gregory did establish a women's house which became known in D.C. as the "anti-imperialist women's house."

Webb recalls that the two-week commune was a "very intense shared experience, almost a religious experience," for the nine or ten women who participated:

> What we actually did on the retreat was talk theory and practice, eat, clean, cook, take one group mescaline trip, which had the effect of welding us together in an intense and inexplicable closeness. Lesbianism was not on the agenda, although in retrospect it should have been obvious that homosexuality would be a future result for some of us.[84]

An account of the women's commune appeared in the July issue of *oob*. The writers advocated all-women's communes as a refuge from "sexual mindfucks:"

> Many women have become alienated from the sexual functions of their bodies because sex has been used to keep us in our place. As a step toward wholeness, mustn't we withdraw from the oppression of sexual mindfucks and build all female collectives? Some may include sex between women, but for many,

> these collectives will probably be a period of celibacy—probably the first time in most women's lives.[85]

But, another participant recalls that their discussions of sexuality were largely confined to talk of "smashing monogamy."[86] The concept of "smashing monogamy" was very much in vogue among leftists and left feminists who argued that monogamy was an evil that originated with private property. Jean Tepperman recalls that "among left feminists it was almost assumed that the desire for sexual fidelity was a bourgeois hang-up."[87] Barbara Haber contends that in her first consciousness-raising group, Cathy Wilkerson of SDS and Weatherman attacked her for wanting to stay married. "She said that emotional security was a horrible, right-wing thing to want."[88] Indeed, much of the talk about monogamy originated with the Chicago women who were influenced by Weatherman's anti-monogamy line.[89]

Although D.C. women's liberationists were debating the virtues of nonmonogamy and celibacy and were establishing all-women's communes, there was still little discussion of lesbianism.[90] In contrast to the New York women, some of whom were already experimenting with lesbianism, the D.C. women remained very apprehensive about it. As late as the summer of 1970, Marilyn Webb, Coletta Reid, and Nancy Ferro criticized the mass media for depicting the typical women's liberationist as "a total weirdo—a bra burner, man-hater, lesbian, sickie!"[91] Things began to change in the fall of 1970 when women from D.C. traveled to Philadelphia to participate in the Panther-sponsored Revolutionary People's Constitutional Convention (RPCC). The RPCC, held over Labor-Day weekend, attracted at least 6000 people who wanted to have a role in writing a new constitution that would "represent all oppressed people."[92] Each workshop (Third World, GI, Women, Gay Liberation, etc.) was supposed to draw up a list of rights necessary for that group to achieve its self-determination. However, as had happened at the United Front Against Fascism Conference one year earlier, the Panthers seemed suspicious of the women's liberation activists in the audience. According to one report, the Panthers repeatedly canceled the women's workshop.[93] When the women finally did meet, it was under the direction of Panther women and under the paranoid eye of Panther security guards. The women's workshop was attended by about twenty lesbians from New York—many of whom, like Rita Mae Brown and Martha Shelley, were involved in Radicalesbians—who had earlier in the conference devised a list of lesbian demands. Angry at the Panthers' attitude toward women's liberationists and lesbians, and unable to make the workshop's demands more "woman-identified," they decided to leave the convention.

Given the lesbians' list of demands, it is little wonder that they clashed with the Panthers. They called for an end to the sexual programming of children, the destruction of the nuclear family, and the establishment of communal child-care facilities under the control of "woman-identified women." And, not incidentally, they demanded that women be given "complete control of our social system." However, the printed report of the convention reduced the workshop's demands to the following:

> That women have the right to choose heterosexuality, bisexuality, or homosexuality. That crash programs in the technology relevant to women be made available to them, i.e., child care.

While the lesbians obviously failed to make much of a dent in the Panthers' male chauvinism, they had a profound effect on many D.C. women's liberationists. Coletta Reid was unable to attend the conference, but many of her friends made the journey to Philadelphia. She remembers women returning from the conference "thinking maybe lesbianism was the big thing these days."[94] Joan E. Biren (also known as JEB) did attend the conference, and remembers that in the midst of a heated discussion in the women's workshop:

> this woman stood up and identified herself as a radical lesbian. I nearly fainted dead away. . . . I ran up to her afterwards and said, "What you said was the most wonderful thing I ever heard. I really want to talk to you some more." She gave me her name and address and subsequently I went up to New York by myself.

What impressed Biren about the New York lesbians was that "they were able to make the connection that lesbianism wasn't just about sex, but that it was about extending the thinking of feminism."[95] Soon Biren and Sharon Deevey, another veteran of D.C. Women's Liberation, had resolved to form an all-lesbian commune. Their first recruit was Ginny Berson, a friend of Biren's from Mount Holyoke who wrote occasionally for the leftist periodical *Hard Times*. Not knowing any other lesbians in D.C., they set about to recruit lesbians from New York to live in their collective house.

Coincidentally, at the same time they were recruiting lesbians for their house, Radicalesbians was disintegrating under the pressure of political and personal antagonisms.[96] Two of the most central women in the group, Rita Mae Brown and Cynthia Funk, decided to move to D.C. By late fall, there was much more talk of lesbianism, fueled in part by the pairing off that was occurring among some members of the women's community.[97] This process was accelerated by the second meeting of the RPCC, held in D.C. over Thanksgiving weekend. Reid contends that the RPCC was:

> really important because all these women came in from out of town. And it was the first time that I really got the sense that women's liberation was dominated by lesbians. The main thing was that the women who came to the Panther convention were radicals, whereas *oob* [where Reid was a staff member] had been associated with lots of different kinds of women. It was clear that these women were really radical and that ninety percent of them were lesbians.[98]

Of course, lesbians did not dominate the movement in late 1970, but lesbians apparently dominated the feminist caucus at the RPCC. Wendy Cadden, Pat Parker, Judy Grahn, and Nancy Adair were a few of the lesbians who attended the convention. In December 1970, Reid declared herself a lesbian and organized a women's house with Helaine Harris, co-founder with Adair of the Southwestern Female Rights Union, and Lee Schwing, a Goddard work-study student at *oob*.

In February 1971, Biren and Deevey succeeded in establishing the first all-lesbian house in D.C. They formed the house, which they named "Amazing Grace," with Cynthia Funk, Nancy Myron, and three other women who had recently moved from New York, and Berson of D.C. Biren and Deevey had high expectations of Amazing Grace which they hoped would mark the beginning of an explicitly lesbian movement in D.C. Biren recalls:

> Sharon and I had this plan of having a collective house of lesbians. We had spent so much time arguing with men or arguing

> with women about their men that we were sure that the answer was to have a lesbian house. That would solve so many problems.[99]

But they discovered that many problems remained, especially the problem of class. Amazing Grace, which had been painstakingly planned over a two-month period, ended "brutally and abruptly" after only one week.[100] The experiment collapsed when some of the working-class women balked at the communal organization of the household. To Berson it was

> an extreme case of class conflict. It was so clear. . . . Here were these two Mount Holyoke girls and a Swarthmore girl who stayed home and didn't hold wage jobs and these three other women from South Boston who went to straight jobs every day and worried about money while the middle-class women just assumed our financial needs would always be taken care of by a generous world.[101]

Most of the middle-class women wanted the group to banish the concept of private property, while most of the working-class women rebelled against such an arrangement. One of the working-class women explains:

> I did not want to have a communal room with all our clothes in it, where I picked out a pair of underwear in the morning. We were all supposed to share our clothes and sleep in the same room. Come on, come off of it!

Biren and Deevey, whose idea it was, were devastated by the group's dissolution.

Two women conspicuously absent from Amazing Grace were Rita Mae Brown and Charlotte Bunch.[102] Annoyed that they had not been included, Brown and Bunch started their own group in February 1971, which they called "the lesbian come-out c-r group." The group consisted of about ten women from the D.C. women's community who had either recently come out or were contemplating doing so. To Berson it seemed that the group was "mostly straight women who were trying to be lesbians, and Rita."[103] Besides Bunch and Brown, the group included Tasha Peterson, Susan Hathaway, and Susan Gregory of the anti-imperialist women's house, and Coletta Reid, Lee Schwing, and Helaine Harris of the second women's house.[104]

Although there were tensions between the founders of Amazing Grace and the women in the c-r group, both groups were feeling increasingly embattled within the local feminist movement. Rather than renouncing heterosexuality and converting to lesbianism, most heterosexual feminists were resisting the lesbian-feminist presumption that feminism required lesbianism. A number of incidents occurred that winter and spring which further polarized the community along gay-straight lines. On New Year's Eve, the Women's Center held a dance which would have remained uneventful had not several lesbians objected when one woman arrived with her four-year-old son in tow. The community became convulsed over the issue of whether or not male children should be permitted into "women's space."[105]

By early spring, many heterosexual feminists were accusing lesbians of taking over the movement, and cutting them out. That spring, *oob* printed an article which likened lesbian-feminist politics to the "sexual fascist politics" of Norman Mailer.[106] In April, Reid, Hathaway, Peterson, and Schwing resigned from *oob*, claiming that their work was being censored.[107] Moreover, a split was brewing at the feminist day-care center which Reid had helped establish. Some members reportedly began to question whether Reid and her lesbian friends were appropriate role models for the children. Reid claimed that one woman even suggested that lesbian day-care workers might molest the young girls in their care.[108] In response, Reid and the other women who were to form The Furies submitted a list of demands to the day-care collective. Their leaflet, published in *Rat*, demanded the following changes:

> 1)The heterosexual bias of the center has got to go. There must be a continual gay presence so children can see women loving women and men loving men. 2)The daycare center must be run on communist principles. . . . The primacy of the parent-child relationship can no longer be assumed. Those who belong to the daycare center must be moving towards collective living themselves. 3)Adult chauvinism must be struggled with, along with class and race. 4)The nuclear family prejudice must end. Single women and lesbians with children must be the top recruiting priority. 5)Men who are not struggling with their sexism must leave. The women will decide who can stay. The men who stay must be in men's consciousness-raising groups that help them

> express their homosexuality. 6)The kids should be encouraged to explore their own bodies and the bodies of each other and to masturbate.[109]

When the collective met without Reid and decided that they wanted their children to be bisexual rather than homosexual, Reid resigned from the collective. The antagonism between lesbian and heterosexual feminists had a good deal to do with deeply engrained homophobia, but as these incidents suggest, it was certainly aggravated by the dogmatism of lesbian-feminists.

The hostility that lesbian-feminists encountered had the effect of diminishing the differences between them. However, it took a woman suspected of being a government agent to bring the two groups together. This woman had been involved in politico circles in D.C., Boston, and New York, and had aroused people's suspicions by advocating violent actions, fingering others as agents, and passing on sensitive information indiscriminately. Bunch, who now regrets the whole episode, contends that they were concerned about agents because "as a group we had some contact with Weatherwomen who were underground at the time. And, among all of us we had contact with a variety of women across the country."[110] In fact, the Chicago women had even considered going underground, not because they were guilty of any illegal activity, but because they had come to believe in the necessity of armed struggle. (Moreover, the Chicago women had reason to believe that they had already been infiltrated by another informer, who worked for the Chicago police. This woman, who claimed to have borne Panther leader Fred Hampton's baby, had already followed them to D.C. and moved into their house before they suspected she might be an informant.[111])

So in late April the lesbian c-r group invited Biren, Deevey, and Berson to a meeting to discuss the woman in question, who was, in Harris's words, "affecting all of us, *whatever* our politics were."[112] The group spent about three weeks trying to determine whether or not she was an agent, and at one point even kept her under a twenty-four watch to prevent her from reporting in to her agency.[113] The D.C. women went so far as to publish an article—accompanied by FBI-like mugshots of her—naming her as an agent in the pages of *Rat*.[114] Eventually, the group began to focus less on her and more on the relationship between the left, feminism, and lesbianism in "an exchange of ideas," which Harris identifies as "cataclysmic."[115] Cataclysmic, because these discussions led to the formation of the lesbian-feminist group The Furies.

The Furies Collective

By early May of 1971, the group had formed a living collective called "Those Women" and had moved into two houses. The group consisted of Bunch, Biren, Brown, Deevey, Berson, Harris, Peterson, Hathaway, Reid, and Schwing. They decided to call themselves "Those Women" because heterosexual feminists were forever referring to them as "those women" apparently because they could not yet bring themselves to say the word "lesbian."[116] For most of its existence The Furies were actually known as Those Women. It wasn't until January 1972 when the group began publishing a newspaper called *The Furies* that they decided to change the name. It should be pointed out that while The Furies was by far the most famous lesbian-feminist collective, it was perhaps not the most representative group. Other groups were less absolutist and zealous.[117] But they were not nearly as influential as The Furies. It wasn't simply that they produced a newspaper, but that it contained some of the most powerful and insightful writing to be found anywhere in the movement.[118] Certainly, when one thinks of lesbian-feminist theorists, one thinks immediately of Charlotte Bunch and Rita Mae Brown. And while The Furies failed to persuade most lesbian-feminists that they should form a separate lesbian-feminist movement, they nonetheless set the terms of the debate.

As their first action, The Furies decided to push the issue of lesbianism at a retreat which had been called to determine the future of the foundering D.C. women's center. Bunch, who with Deevey was one of the center's founders, claims that the center was in disarray largely because a number of the center's key people "were increasingly moving into the lesbian issue."[119] Approximately 100 feminists attended the retreat, which despite its bucolic setting was anything but serene. According to Harris, who characterizes the group's style at the retreat as disruptive and dogmatic:

> The Furies went as a lesbian-feminist front. Someone from the group attended each workshop and tried to steer the discussion onto lesbianism. Basically we were telling women that we really believed that they should leave their husbands and boyfriends and become lesbian-feminists. [We contended] that was the only choice that they really had.[120]

Bunch corroborates Harris's account:

> We decided that the issue at the retreat was going to be lesbianism and that every workshop and everything that happened was going to have to deal with that issue. We would make everybody—the straight women, the menshevik lesbians, and the apolitical lesbians—address the lesbian issue. And we did. The entire retreat was us ranting and raving in every corner.[121]

Woodul, who had moved to D.C. that fall, but had only recently re-established contact with Brown, recalls that Brown

> had told me she was working with these women and that things were going to happen at this conference. She told me that I should come to this workshop with her and support what was going to happen. So, I figured it was going to be the same thing that we always used to do when I was at Vassar, which was pushing lesbianism. And my role was always to stand over there and go, yeah, yeah. But, I didn't know, since I hadn't been around the [local] women's movement very much, how big a deal it was going to be. By the end of the day, there was a huge split between lesbians and straight women.[122]

Indeed, Bunch remembers that at the end of the retreat "we announced that we would no longer have anything to do with the women's center until it officially dealt with this issue. We were, in essence, leaving the organized women's movement."[123] Their tendentiousness alienated not only many heterosexual feminists, but even some lesbians who stood up in the general meeting and criticized them.[124]

Most of The Furies saw themselves pursuing a separatist strategy at the retreat. Berson, for example, believed that "our goal had been to make it real clear where we stood, to see who would come with us, and to cut out anybody who wouldn't. I felt that we totally succeeded, and that although hardly anybody came with us, at least we had been real clear about what we wanted."[125] Woodul, who joined The Furies later that year, felt that the action resulted in a "self-imposed isolation. My feeling about it—which was probably because I had known Rita before—was that it was just another tactic of isolation to form this elite group."[126] However, Reid's account of the retreat suggests that she experienced it as an imposed rather than a self-imposed exile:

> I remember [someone] getting up and saying we were taking over the women's movement. I remember sitting there and thinking to myself, now how would we go about doing that? And the only thing I could think of was that we would confiscate the key to the women's center. How could anybody take over somebody's movement? That's an interesting concept, isn't it? God, it was awful! As far as I can tell that was when we were thrown out of the women's movement. I felt that everybody whom I had been friends with and who was straight, and whom I had known for so long, was really against me.[127]

The women's liberation movement in D.C. was decimated by the split. To many Furies members, the movement's dissolution merely proved the indispensability of lesbian energy. Bunch maintains:

> What's most important to me, and what I've always commented upon was that when we left, the women's liberation movement in the city fell apart. It was very dramatic for when we finally pulled out of all the projects, everything except *oob* fell apart. The women's center closed a couple of months later. They accused us of destroying the projects, and I said, "If I were you I would have been out to prove that we were wrong, that you could keep the women's movement going without lesbian energy." But they couldn't. . . . As a cohesive entity, the women's liberation movement fell apart for awhile.[128]

Reid contends that before the split the "most energetic women" in the D.C. movement were those "who had been straight and were now lesbians. We were the ones staffing the women's center and leading the demonstrations."[129] It is true that The Furies' disassociation from the movement had an enervating effect on the local women's liberation movement. However, this was probably as much a testimony to the debilitating effects of the debate as it was to the power of lesbian energy. One of the reasons that the issue so crippled the D.C. movement was that it occurred in a politico community where radical feminism had made little headway.[130] Lesbian-feminism was an implied rejection of the politics which had remained uncontested in D.C. since the movement's inception. But even though the women in D.C. were politicos, they still saw themselves as committed women's liberationists. The debate certainly had a dispiriting effect on heterosexual feminists, who found their commitment to feminism suddenly challenged. And, although homophobia was certainly a factor in the split, so was the lesbian chauvinism of The Furies, most of whom had been heterosexual themselves until very recently. Heterosexual feminists understandably resented their attempts to mandate and prescribe proper sexual behavior. Moreover, it must have really rankled veteran feminists to have Peterson, Hathaway, and Berson, who had until recently seen the women's movement as peripheral to the larger Movement, denigrate their commitment to feminism.

Indeed, one of the most puzzling parts of The Furies' story is the transformation of the anti-imperialist women from reluctant feminists to die-hard lesbian separatists. Why would they have found lesbians like Brown so attractive when they had so little appreciation for the women at *oob*? According to Harris, lesbianism was appealing "because of the energy, commitment, and charisma that these women had." Harris also believes that they found lesbian-feminists "more radical" than the feminists at *oob*.[131] "More radical," perhaps, because they had renounced heterosexual privilege in much the same way that members of Weatherman had abdicated their "white skin privilege." And, as "outlaws," lesbians had a special cachet for the would-be Weatherwomen that heterosexual feminists lacked. If the revolution would be led by the most marginalized, outcast groups, then it was, of course, reasonable to think that lesbians were the vanguard of the revolution.

Rita Mae Brown has characterized The Furies as "feminist-socialist" in perspective.[132] While The Furies were avowedly anti-capitalist, the group's politics was certainly not typical of socialist-feminists, most of whom would have objected to the Furies' view of heterosexuality as the cornerstone of male supremacy and lesbianism as "the greatest threat" to its continued existence.[133] And while most socialist-feminists were still demonstrating against the war in 1971, The Furies were generally boycotting such protests. The Furies' analysis could be more accurately described as a mélange of Radicalesbian, radical feminist, and Weatherman politics. In contrast to Radicalesbians who tried to achieve conciliation, The Furies sought out conflict. In the January 1972 premier issue of *The Furies* newspaper, Berson declared that feminists had but one choice—to come out. "Lesbianism is not a matter of sexual preference, but rather one of political choice which every woman must make if she is to become woman-identified and thereby end male supremacy." Moreover, she argued that "[l]esbians must get out of the straight women's movement and form their own movement in order to be taken seriously, to stop straight women from oppressing us, and to force straight women to deal with their own Lesbianism."[134] And while Radicalesbians spoke of lesbianism "creating a new consciousness," The Furies conceived of lesbianism as a way to intensify the struggle against male supremacy. For instance, Bunch contended:

> Lesbianism is a threat to the ideological, political, personal and economic basis of male supremacy. . . . The Lesbian's independence and refusal to support one man undermines the personal power that men exercise over women. Our rejection of heterosexual sex challenges male domination in its most individual and common form. We offer women something better than submission to personal oppression. We offer the beginning of the end of collective and individual male supremacy.[135]

Finally, while Radicalesbians avoided explicitly impugning heterosexual feminists' radicalism, The Furies portrayed heterosexual feminists as the movement's albatross. Brown maintained:

> Straight women by virtue of being tied to men don't understand Lesbians or the political meaning of Lesbianism. Straight women don't know what our lives are like. They can't think like we do. We understand their lives because we were all raised to be straight. It is one-way communication. Straight women are confused by men, don't put women first. They betray Lesbians and in its deepest form, they betray their own selves. You can't build a strong movement if your sisters are out there fucking with the oppressor.[136]

For The Furies, "coming out" became the feminist equivalent of "picking up the gun," the barometer of one's radicalism. Coming out, which they maintained involved breaking the final tie to male privilege, became a way to separate the serious revolutionaries from the dilettantes and the dabblers. Of course, The Feminists and Cell 16 had set the precedent for this analysis by exhorting women to renounce men. But The Furies raised the ante considerably by demanding that women come out, irrespective of erotic or economic considerations. For some women, the loss of heterosexual privilege was more than offset by the exhilaration of coming out. Bunch recalls:

> My sense of excitement of what we were going to do was much greater than the sense of sacrifice. . . . I had always sacrificed the legitimacy of one group to explore something new, and I'd never regretted it.[137]

For many, the transformation seems not to have caused any great emotional upheaval. Harris contends that "the right politic came down the road at the right time for us, and we identified with something that personally we would have identified with if there hadn't been a politic."[138] Perhaps the ease with which they became lesbians led them to believe that many others would follow in their footsteps. Bunch admits that "in some ways we thought that everyone would become a lesbian, too, even though we didn't intellectually think that. But we didn't think it would be so hard."[139] Most women, however, did not experience this confluence of ideological and erotic imperatives.

When most feminists failed to follow them, The Furies simply concluded that only they were serious revolutionaries. Like The Feminists and Cell 16, but perhaps most like Weatherman, The Furies conceived of themselves as a vanguard cadre. Biren remembers The Furies having "a whole image of ourselves being a revolutionary cadre."[140] Harris contends that "we really did feel that we were the vanguard, that we had a heightened level of consciousness."[141]

Like most vanguard groups, The Furies led a hermetic existence. Although The Furies were planning to connect cadres of like-minded women across the country, they never managed to do so. In fact, the only real outreach The Furies accomplished—

and this was certainly not insignificant—was at a distance, through their newspaper. And they remained very aloof from the larger D.C. feminist community. Indeed, The Furies managed to make themselves marginal within an already marginalized community. During its existence the group admitted only two new members, Jennifer Woodul and Nancy Myron. Harris believes that most D.C. feminists regarded them as "arrogant."[142] Bunch suspects that The Furies

> were hated in Washington for all kinds of reasons. We were closed, elitist, very intense and very smart. We dressed up when everyone was downwardly mobile. We championed the idea of leadership when the movement was anti-leadership. We were proud to be unpopular.[143]

Although The Furies were especially resented by heterosexual feminists, they were not exactly embraced by the lesbian community in D.C. either. Many lesbians, especially those for whom lesbianism was primarily a sexual choice, mistrusted The Furies' brand of political lesbianism.[144] Since The Furies' arguments for lesbianism were based upon political rather than erotic considerations, some lesbians believed that their sexual proclivities might shift with the political climate. The Furies did have their admirers though. Beverly Manick (then known as Fisher) contends that the group to which she belonged, George Washington Women's Liberation, greatly admired The Furies.[145]

Bunch believes that The Furies' "arrogance" had a great deal to do with "self-preservation":

> We had a sense that we were against the world and that we had to believe in ourselves. You also have to realize what was going on inside the group. It was so wrenching.[146]

Indeed, life in The Furies was wrenching. First of all, privacy was virtually nonexistent, according to Brown:

> All clothing rested in a common room. We slept together in [sic] mattresses on the floor in the same room. We had desks together if we wanted desks. . . . The only time you could be left alone was in the middle of the night.[147]

To ensure that everyone's consciousness was sufficiently evolved they engaged in grueling "criticism-self-criticism sessions." During these "struggle sessions"—a concept borrowed from Weatherman—Furies members would take each other to task for their racism, classism, heterosexism, and ageism. Brown has written that "The Furies began to create within ourselves the dynamic of a fascist state. . . . We kept the language of the revolution, but the procedure of the Inquisition."[148] According to Harris, people were so anxious to avoid attacks that they would often keep their feelings to themselves:

> The set of politics was formed very early in the Furies, and the rest of the time was spent codifying them and translating them into lived experience. Later on, there was not a lot of genuine struggle or discussion because people were afraid to be wrong. People's most creative instincts were squashed.[149]

Those who disagreed with the dominant line were not encouraged to stay. As the group was beginning to take shape, one woman let it be known that she had misgivings about The Furies' separatism, especially their stance on male children.[150] (In fact, The Furies had the feminist community in an uproar when they declared that women should not waste their energies on male children and should relinquish custody to the father. This is precisely what Reid did with her two-year old son. Like many feminists, Marilyn Webb, who had been close to Reid, "thought they were nuts."[151]) She was reportedly made to feel that her doubts reflected a lack of revolutionary resolve. This woman's departure did not mark the end of conflict. In fact, the situation only became more conflictual as class became the next battleground.

Bunch suggests that class was an especially explosive issue in The Furies because of the strong anti-materialist ethic that the anti-imperialist women brought to the group.[152] The Furies certainly intended their analysis, which focused on concrete behavior and attitudes, as a corrective to the left's abstract analysis of class. Their analysis of class was in large measure a rebellion against the left's romanticization of poverty and practice of "self-proletarianization" or downward mobility.[153] In her 1972 article "The Last Straw," Brown ridiculed middle-class feminists' attempts to erase class differences through downward mobility:

> I know that for many middle class women, downward mobility was a first attempt at trying to change their ways. However,

> those women must realize that the irony of downward mobility, its fatal flaw, is that they could *afford* to become downwardly mobile. Their class privilege enabled them to reject materialism. For those who grew up without material advantages downward mobility is infuriating—here are women rejecting what we never had and can't get![154]

The Furies, and Rita Mae Brown in particular, deserve a great deal of credit for analyzing class dynamics within the women's liberation movement. They understood that class differences among women were authentic, not the result of "false consciousness," as many feminists claimed. The group even tried to rectify inequality within the collective by developing a "graduated income tax based upon one's past privilege and current ecomonic status."[155] This "privilege-sharing" enabled some working-class Furies members to attend school.

However, their analysis of class was often oversimplified. Even Harris, who considers The Furies' exploration of class one of the group's greatest achievements, contends that their analysis often caricatured working-class and middle-class women. Working-class women were portrayed as direct and confrontational; middle-class women as indirect, querulous, and psychologically manipulative. Harris recalls:

> We used to make fun of another women's collective that in writing dropped their 'g's and cursed a lot in order to write like and identify with the working class. But, I think that class wasn't always treated any less superficially by The Furies. At one point it was even argued that working-class people hit their kids and middle-class people didn't.[156]

Moreover, despite their protestations to the contrary, The Furies were organized around a hierarchy of oppression. That is, those who were the most oppressed—working-class, old-gay [those women whose coming-out predated the women's movement], or young—enjoyed the most legitimacy within the group. In theory, The Furies maintained that "no one is to blame for the economic or class position into which she was born."[157] But, in practice, the working-class women routinely castigated the middle-class women. Harris claims that Hathaway was always "on the hot seat," not only because she did not deal especially well with the issue of class, but because her parents were upper-class. Harris recalls feeling "very lucky to be the youngest member of the group, as well as a high-school drop-out who was involved with a working-class woman."[158] As was too often the case with '60s movements, the politics of *ressentiment* prevailed.

The issue of class exploded when The Furies debated whether or not to exclude all children—not just male children—from the collective. Because the group was collectively organized, every member was responsible for child care. According to Bunch, the middle-class women generally wanted to keep the children but "were told that we had the privilege to spend time with children." The working-class women maintained that they had spent their whole lives raising children and were not going to raise children now. Bunch, Reid, Biren, and Deevey, all of whom opposed the expulsion of children, were "class-tripped" out of their position. Bunch claims that she and Reid capitulated to keep the group from breaking up. She believes that Biren and Deevey, who were raising the baby Fred Hampton had allegedly fathered, agreed to the expulsion to avoid being expelled themselves. Bunch contends that the group "became anti-children and covered it up with class."[159] Harris contends that some members simply didn't want to be around children and rationalized their banishment on political grounds. Harris believes that "the effects of establishing as correct the exclusion of children were immense and lasting."[160] Despite their capitulation, Deevey and Biren were purged from the group for "classist behavior." Fearing the purge would further alienate some feminists, the group told Biren and Deevey to keep quiet about their expulsion.

Some Furies members contend that others in the group used the issue of class opportunistically. While characterizing the Furies' work on class as a "naive but important effort to try to figure out how class affects the interaction of women," Bunch admits that "some people shaped a lot of the analysis to fit their own needs."[161] One of the working-class members of the group contends that the issue of class "stalemated" The Furies because Brown used the issue to further establish her power base within the group. Harris believes that "the group allowed itself to be manipulated by Brown," and she faults the group for failing to counter Brown at different points. However, like many other Furies members, Harris is quick to point out that Brown was an important and positive force in the group for she was enormously bright, creative, and committed.

Estranged from the larger feminist community, The Furies grew increasingly isolated and insular. In March 1972, the group challenged Brown on her imperious style. Brown considered it a purge, while others claim Brown left before she could be expelled.[162] Bunch contends that Brown's departure set in motion a "dynamic of backbiting and internal fighting," which Bunch felt would continue unabated unless the group disbanded. The Furies dissolved in April 1972, a month after Brown's departure, and only a year after its founding. However, several Furies members continued to put out the newspaper until the summer of 1973. Both Bunch and Harris believe that The Furies' complete isolation was a major factor in the group's demise. Bunch felt "we were turned completely inward; cannibalism was the next step."[163] Another member recalls that the "bitter end was very bitter."

It is somehow appropriate that The Furies began with the rooting out of a suspected agent, for they seemed always to be on the look-out for suspected contaminants. Yet, it is ironic that The Furies, who did so much to advance the movement's understanding of women's differences, were completely unable to tolerate differences among themselves.

****

Lesbian-feminists like The Furies forced heterosexual feminists to acknowledge that sexuality is socially rather than biologically constructed, and to understand the centrality of institutionalized heterosexuality to women's oppression. Feminists were forced to rethink their assumptions about lesbianism. Some even came to regard lesbians as the vanguard of the women's movement. For instance, Ti-Grace Atkinson, who had earlier declared that "feminism is a theory, lesbianism is a practice," now contended that "feminism is the theory, lesbianism the practice."[164] By challenging the stigmatization of lesbianism, lesbian-feminists not only made lesbianism a viable option, but, in Frances Chapman's words, "taught individual women that they could live in the world as *people*."[165]

But the recasting of lesbianism as a political imperative, the characterization of it as the logical outcome of one's feminism, was problematic. Lesbian-feminism exacerbated the feminist tendency to conceptualize sex in service to the movement—which, as Deirdre English has pointed out, was merely a variation on the old theme of "sex in service to society."[166] This prescriptivism had deleterious consequences for both lesbian and heterosexual feminists. The movement's acceptance of lesbianism was always conditional—contingent upon lesbians' willingness to de-emphasize sexuality and conform to a "female" sexual standard. Lesbianism was never really legitimated on sexual grounds. But, of course, at some level (especially at the level of practice as opposed to rhetoric) lesbianism is about sex—a fact that bothered some heterosexual feminists. For instance, Atkinson, one of the most vocal proponents of political lesbianism, says that she was "surprised" by the "heavy sexualization that went on as lesbians became a real force in the movement. That was kind of a shock. I was disappointed that it was not more different from heterosexual relationships."[167] And if lesbianism grew out of political conviction rather than sexual desire, what to do when sexual desire failed to mirror political doctrine? Of course, it was assumed by all women's liberationists that one's sexuality should reflect one's politics, but this was particularly so for lesbians whose sexuality was believed to be an extension of their feminism. Moreover, in an effort to distinguish lesbian from heterosexual relationships, lesbian-feminists often depicted lesbian relationships and sexuality as completely unproblematic. The admission of sexual problems was taboo for it threatened the ideological edifice of lesbian-feminism. For instance, Harris remembers that in The Furies "there was no room for discussing problems in your sexual relationship. There weren't any discussions of sexuality. It was assumed that your sexuality was successful."[168]

For heterosexual women who did not come out, the situation was perhaps worse. Whereas lesbianism was valorized, heterosexuality was disparaged. Indeed, heterosexuality and feminism were often presented as antinomies. Since heterosexual desire was defined as "male identified," heterosexual feminists often felt compelled to conceal or renounce their desires. In fact, heterosexual women were made to feel like the movement's backsliders. Their inability or refusal to make a "primal commitment" to other women, as Radicalesbians put it, made their feminism suspect. As Webb points out, "women who weren't gay were treated like second-class citizens."[169]

The gay-straight split had an enormous impact on the women's liberation movement. As lesbianism became coterminous with radical feminism, many heterosexual women left the movement. Some heterosexual feminists like Jean Tepperman found the "turmoil too painful" and "edged" their way out of the movement.[170] Others decided to leave the movement to avoid being treated like "second-class citizens." Mainardi contends that many heterosexual women "were driven out of the movement [when] lesbianism became the only issue and the only solution."[171] Some women became more involved with the left and specifically with socialist-feminist groups. Other women became involved in more mainstream forms of political activism—organizing clericals and hospital workers, and participating in reform groups like NOW and the National Abortion Rights Action League. Of course, some heterosexual radical feminists remained involved in radical feminist groups, but by 1975 the radical wing of the movement was predominantly lesbian. Although efforts at rapprochment were made, mistrust often remained. For instance, in 1973, Bunch and Brown tried to initiate a local project which would have involved both heterosexual and lesbian feminists. The project, called "Yes, we have no bananas," was an attempt to have the local movement provide women with essential services. Brown proposed that they begin by opening a meat market. However, the second meeting was filled with so much antagonism between lesbians and heterosexual women that by the third meeeting there were virtually no heterosexual women present. Out of that group emerged the feminist publication *Quest*, but no rapprochment.[172]

The Furies believed that lesbianism would inevitably lead to an intensification of the struggle against male supremacy, but it did not. With the rise of lesbian-feminism, the conflation of the personal with the political, long in the making, was complete and unassailable. More than ever, how one lived one's life, not one's commitment to political struggle, became the salient factor. One can even see this illustrated in the increasingly popular term "woman-identified," which seemed to suggest that one's attitude and behavior mattered more than one's political philosophy and stance. Thus, one could take all the right positions, that is, be a feminist, and still be judged male-identified. Moreover, the focus shifted from building a mass movement to sustaining an alternative women's culture and community. Brownmiller contends:

> The influx en masse of non-political lesbians into the women's movement and . . . the emotional feeling around them that they somehow were heroines of the women's movement because they were women who had no truck with men moved the movement away from confrontation with male power into alternative lifestyles.[173]

Those issues, like abortion and child care, which had the power to mobilize large numbers of women were often disparaged as "straight women's" issues.[174] For instance, lesbian-feminist Julia Penelope Stanley pronounced:

> Only a lesbian can have *no* stake in the social system. . . . Straight women, even those who call themselves 'feminists,' are still tied to men and dependent on their tolerance and goodwill, which is why they cling to issues like equal pay and birth control. A woman who has no vested interest in men wouldn't bother.[175]

And Sharon Deevey railed against the heterosexual presumption which she argued permeated the women's liberation movement. "Everything around me was, and of course, always had been, heterosexual . . . especially Women's Liberation: birth control, bad fucks and abortions."[176] Of course, this just exacerbated a tendency begun earlier by some radical feminists.

In some respects, the emergence of lesbian-feminism, edged the movement closer to cultural feminism. Its emphasis on a female counterculture and its essentialist arguments about female sexuality were quintessential cultural feminism. But, lesbian-feminism was an affront to the cultural feminist idea of a universal female experience. Even though their goal was to obliterate differences, lesbian-feminists insisted that lesbians were different from heterosexual women. In fact, cultural feminism's ascendance within the movement is in large measure attributable to the turmoil created by lesbianism and class. As the next chapter suggests, cultural feminism seemed to offer an alternative to all the divisiveness generated by these debates.

6

The Ascendance of Cultural Feminism

Radical feminism remained the hegemonic tendency within the women's liberation movement until 1973 when cultural feminism began to cohere and challenge its dominance. After 1975, a year of internecine conflicts between radical and cultural feminists, cultural feminism eclipsed radical feminism as the dominant tendency within the women's liberation movement, and, as a consequence, liberal feminism became the recognized voice of the women's movement.

As the preceding chapters have shown, there were prefigurings of cultural feminism within radical feminism, especially by 1970. This nascent cultural feminism, which was sometimes termed "female cultural nationalism" by its critics, was assailed by radical and left feminists alike. For instance, in the December 1970 issue of *Everywoman*, Ann Fury warned feminists against "retreating into a female culture":

> Like other oppressed [*sic*], we have our customs and language. But this culture, designed to create the illusion of autonomy, merely indicates fear. Withdraw into it and we take our slavery with us. . . . Furthermore when we retreat into our culture we cover our political tracks with moralism. We say our culture is somehow "better" than male culture. And we trace this supposed superiority to our innate nature, for if we attributed it to our powerlessness, we would have to agree to its dissolution the moment we seize control. . . . When we obtain power, we will take on the characteristics of the powerful. . . . We are not the Chosen people.[1]

Similarly, in a May 1970 article on the women's liberation movement in Britain, Juliet Mitchell and Rosalind Delmar contended:

> Re-valuations of feminine attributes *accept* the results of an exploitative situation by endorsing its concepts. The effects of oppression do not become the manifestations of liberation by changing values, or, for that matter, by changing oneself—but only by challenging the social structure that gives rise to those values in the first place.[2]

And in April 1970, the Bay Area paper *It Ain't Me, Babe* carried an editorial urging feminists to create a culture which would foster resistance rather than serve as a sanctuary from patriarchy:

> It is extremely oppressive for us to function in a culture where ideas are male oriented and definitions are male controlled. . . . Yet the creation of a woman's culture must in no way be separated from the political struggles of women for liberation. . . . Our culture cannot be the carving of an enclave in which we can bear the status quo more easily—rather it must crystallize the dreams that will strengthen our rebellion.[3]

But these warnings had little effect as the movement seemed to drift almost ineluctably toward cultural feminism. Cultural feminism seemed a solution to the movement's impasse—both its schisms and its lack of direction. Whereas parts of the radical feminist movement had become paralyzed by political purism, or what Robin Morgan called "failure vanguardism," cultural feminists promised that constructive changes could be achieved.[4] To cultural feminists, alternative women's institutions represented, in Morgan's words, "concrete moves towards self-determination and power" for women.[5] Equally important, cultural feminism with its insistence upon women's essential sameness to each other and their fundamental difference from men seemed to many a way to unify a movement that by 1973 was highly schismatic. In fact, cultural feminism succeeded in large measure because it promised an end to the gay-straight split. Cultural feminism modified lesbian-feminism so that male values rather than men were vilified and female bonding rather than lesbianism was valorized, thus making it acceptable to heterosexual feminists.

Of course, by 1973 the women's movement was also facing a formidable backlash—one which may have been orchestrated by the male-dominated New Right, but was hardly lacking in female support. It is probably not coincidental that cultural feminism emerged at a time of backlash. Even if women's political, economic, and social gains were reversed, cultural feminism held out the possibility that women could build a culture, a space, uncontaminated by patriarchy. Morgan described women's art and spirituality as "the lifeblood for our survival" and maintained that "resilient cultures have kept oppressed groups alive even when economic analyses and revolutionary strategy fizzled."[6] There may even have been the hope that by invoking commonly held assumptions about women and men, anti-feminist women might experience a change of heart and join their ranks. The shift toward cultural feminism also suggests that feminists themselves were not immune to the growing conservatism of the period. Certainly, cultural feminism's demonization of the left seemed largely rooted in a rejection of the '60s radicalism out of which radical feminism evolved.

Female Culture as the Fourth World

"The Fourth World Manifesto" was an embryonic but highly influential expression of cultural feminism. It should be read as a transitional work, one that straddled the line between radical and cultural feminism. The original "Manifesto" was drafted by a group of women's liberationists from Detroit (including Barbara Burris, Kathleen Barry, and Joanne Parrent) shortly before a spring 1971 conference which brought together North American anti-war women with Indochinese women in Toronto.[7] It was later revised by Burris and was subsequently published in both *Notes from the Third Year* and *Radical Feminism*. The paper was an excoriation of the left, especially the anti-imperialist women who had helped to organize the Toronto conference.[8] The Detroit women criticized the conference organizers for calling it a "women's liberation" conference when, in fact, women's liberation was barely addressed. To them it seemed yet another attempt to "turn the independent women's movement" into an "adjunct to the anti-war and anti-imperialist movements."[9] There was, of course, nothing new in this criticism—as early as the Jeannette Rankin Brigade protest Sarachild and Firestone had opposed all efforts to organize women around anything other than their oppression as women.

But in other respects the "Manifesto" strayed a bit from the radical feminism of Firestone and Sarachild as it exaggerated certain tendencies within radical feminism. The "Manifesto" claimed that the struggle for women's liberation was inherently anti-imperialist because women constituted a colonized group—what they termed the "Fourth World." Some radical feminists had earlier argued that the struggle for women's liberation would undermine capitalism. But while it was precisely this thinking that informed the "Manifesto," there was a subtle difference. Burris et al. were not arguing that women's liberation would subvert the American empire. Rather, they were redefining imperialism in an effort to claim the experience of colonization as their own. And while some radical feminists had suggested that the desire to dominate others was somehow peculiarly "male," most did not reduce war and imperialism to male supremacy, as did the Detroit women who argued that war and imperialism were rooted in "male supremacist society."[10] Furthermore, while most radical feminists ignored women's differences, "The Fourth World Manifesto" went further, defensively denying them. Responding to the left's dismissal of the women's movement as white and middle-class, the authors of the "Manifesto" maintained, quite correctly I think, that the ranking of oppression so pervasive in both the left and the women's movement promoted little but guilt-mongering. However, they also argued:

> A woman's class is almost always determined by the man she is living with. . . . Class is therefore basically a distinction between males, while the female is defined by her sexual caste status. . . . As the Female Liberation Movement must cut across all (male-imposed) class, race and national lines, any false identification of women with privileges that are really male (such as whiteness or class, etc.) will be fatal to our Movement.[11]

According to this view, the debates over class and race were nothing but a male invention. Indeed, in their view, all the talk about class and race was the work of "the male Left," which wanted to "manipulate" these "male-imposed" differences to thwart the women's liberation movement.[12] Finally, the authors of the

"Manifesto" contended that the goal of feminism should be the assertion "of the long suppressed and ridiculed female principle." They characterized female culture—which they attributed to women's colonization, not to their biology—as one of "emotion, intuition, love, personal relationships, etc, as the most essential human characteristics [*sic*]."[13] While this echoed the work of Cell 16, it stood in contrast to most radical feminist thinking on gender.

In 1969 when Dunbar first proposed that the task of feminism was the resurrection of the female principle, most women's liberationists remained unconvinced. But by 1971, many more found this logic persuasive. Of course, there was opposition to the "Manifesto." One writer in *Rat* criticized it for "glossing over all the real barriers that exist." This same writer observed that the celebration of femininity involved the recycling of stereotypes:

> The female principle is nothing but the negative counterpart of the male principle. . . . Several years ago when women used their head [*sic*], you were called unfemine [*sic*]; now you are called male-identified. And armed struggle should not be reserved for men by calling it macho.[14]

In fact, by 1973 Barbara Burris had grown sufficiently apprehensive about the way in which the article was being used that she added a postscript claiming that it had been distorted by others:

> This "Manifesto" was never intended to be a glorification of the female principle and culture. . . . Recently there has been an unfortunate reaction among some women's liberationists . . . to call anything they do not like 'male.' It would be a tragedy if women were to make our oppressed state into a virtue and a model of humanity and the new world. . . . There is a danger that the women's movement will help destroy its own ends if the split between the female and male is made into a new feminist orthodoxy.[15]

A Voice from the Underground

In contrast to "The Fourth World Manifesto," Jane Alpert's controversial article, "Mother Right: A New Feminist Theory," was anything but tentative.[16] Where the "Manifesto" rejected a precultural analysis of femaleness, "Mother Right" breathlessly embraced a biologistic explanation of gender differences. Alpert was still a fugitive when she wrote "Mother Right" in the spring of 1973. With David Hughey, Pat Swinton, and her lover Sam Melville, Alpert had taken part in bombing a number of military and war-related corporate buildings in Manhattan between July and November 1969.[17] They were not affiliated with any leftist group, but, rather, like a number of leftists at that time, felt the need to escalate the struggle against the "war machine." However, their group had the bad fortune to be infiltrated by George Demerle, a former member of the extreme right-wing group the Minutemen, who had offered to inform on leftist groups for the FBI. Alpert, Melville, and Hughey were apprehended by FBI agents on November 12, 1969. But Swinton managed to escape and went underground. Primarily to reduce Melville's sentence—he faced up to 195 years in prison—Alpert and Hughey agreed to plead guilty to the lesser offense of conspiracy to destroy government property. The prosecution agreed that if the defendants pleaded guilty rather than going to trial, Melville would be sentenced to no more than eighteen years in prison, and Hughey and Alpert to no more than five years. According to her memoir of the period, *Growing Up Underground*, Alpert was less than ecstatic about following this strategy but apparently did so because her codefendants desired it.[18] However, in May 1970, before she was to be sentenced, Alpert skipped bail and went underground.

Before Alpert went underground she had been marginally involved with the women's liberation movement. She had attended several NYRW meetings, but was very much on the politico side of the politico-feminist divide. Alpert wrote for the underground paper *Rat* and was instrumental in the women's take-over of the paper. After the female staff members assumed control in late January 1970, they called around the city to recruit feminists to the paper. The first woman Alpert called was Robin Morgan, the one woman with whom she had had "scintillating discussions about the left and feminism."[19] Alpert worked on the women's *Rat* until she went underground. In her poem to Alpert, "Letter to a Sister Underground," Robin Morgan claims that while Alpert was still aboveground she confided to Morgan that she knew she was "a mercenary in someone else's revolution—that of men—

paid with the coin of male approval.''[20] But if Alpert was moving toward feminism before becoming a fugitive, it was only after going underground that she became a committed feminist. That Alpert turned to feminism was a testimony not only to the growing irrelevance of Weatherman—the leftist group with which she had contact while underground—and to the women in the consciousness-raising group she had joined. It was also a testimony to Robin Morgan who took it upon herself to ''recruit'' Alpert to feminism.[21]

In her widely published article ''Mother Right,'' Alpert renounced the left and proclaimed her ''conversion'' to radical feminism. The first part of the article was written as an open letter to her ''sister-fugitives'' in the Weather Underground. Here she detailed the sexism of Weatherman, in particular the sexism of her lover, Sam Melville. Her embarrassingly intimate revelations about Melville struck many as inappropriate, especially given that he had been among the prisoners murdered during the September 1971 uprising at the Attica Prison.[22] Alpert also presented herself as Melville's unwilling accomplice in the bombings:

> I was very much pressured, against my own sense of tactics and timing, into playing the role I did in the group of radical bombers Melville half-led, half-dragged along with him. The pressure was of the kind peculiar to male-female relationships: he constantly threatened to leave me if I backed out.[23]

While it seems likely that Alpert did object to Melville's carelessness and capriciousness, her writings from that period reveal someone who seemed to be committed to armed struggle. In her account of the eight days she spent at the Women's House of Detention, she had argued:

> The movement moved outside the law some years ago, but we're still hung up on our middle-classness and we've got plenty to learn from people who've been outside the system far longer than us. I never felt like a special case in the House of D. All of us were in there for essentially the same reason. We had been chosen to be locked up because none of us can deal with the system and the system couldn't deal with us outside the jails. Someday soon it won't be able to deal with the sisters in jail either. What I heard most in the House of D was ''Hey, Conspiracy, I know you had nothing to do with those bombs, but if

> you can find that girlfriend of yours who split, tell her to come back and *blow this motherfucker up*!"[24] [her emphasis]

To those familiar with Alpert's writing at the time of the bombings, her depiction of herself as Melville's victim seemed at best overdrawn. But what most shocked many leftists and women's liberationists was Alpert's callous proclamation at the conclusion of the open letter:

> And so, my sisters in Weatherman, *you* fast and organize and demonstrate for Attica. Don't send me news clippings about it, don't tell me how much those deaths moved you. I will mourn the loss of 42 male supremacists no longer.[25] [her emphasis]

This declaration earned her the enmity of many leftists and feminists who were horrified at Alpert's suggestion that the prisoners' sexism made their slaughter insignificant.

Had "Mother Right" been only a tirade against the left it is unlikely that it would have generated quite the controversy it did. But the article was also an ambitious attempt to fashion a "new feminist theory." In it Alpert contended:

> For centuries feminists have asserted that the essential difference between men and women does not lie in biology but rather in the roles that patriarchal societies (men) have required each sex to play. . . . However, a flaw in this feminist argument has persisted: *it contradicts our felt experience of the biological difference between the sexes as one of immense significance*.[26] [her emphasis]

Alpert traced the "power of the new feminist culture [and] the powers which were attributed to the ancient matriarchies" to female biology, specifically women's reproductive capacity:

> The unique consciousness or sensibility of women, the particular attributes that set feminist art apart, and a compelling line of research now being pursued by feminist anthropologists all point to the idea that *female biology is the basis of women's powers*. Biology is hence the source and not the enemy of feminist revolution. [her emphasis]

She maintained that all women, not just mothers, possess maternal qualities because "motherhood" is a "potential which is imprinted in the genes of every woman."[27] In fact, for Alpert, women's shared maternalism was the solution to the crisis over women's differences. She argued that in a society where motherhood empowered women there would be no divisions among women because "motherhood cuts across economic class, race, and sexual preference."[28] And in another stark reversal of radical feminism, Alpert argued that a feminist revolution would resemble the Reformation or the "Christian revolution" rather than the Cuban or Chinese revolutions in that "economic and political changes" would "follow rather than precede sweeping changes in human consciousness." Alpert contended that "the ripples spread through the institutions from the masses of people, rather than the other way around.[29] Morgan would invoke Alpert's "ripple" metaphor two years later in her article, "Rites of Passage":

> I think our feminist revolution gains momentum from a "ripple effect"—from each individual woman gaining self-respect and yes, power, over her own body and soul first, then within her family, on her block, in her town, state, and so on out from the center, overlapping with similar changes other women are experiencing, the circles rippling more widely and inclusively as they go. This is a revolution in consciousness, rising expectations, and the actions which reflect that organic process.[30]

As this suggests, cultural feminism's vision of social change was profoundly individualistic and far removed from the collectivist impulse that informed radical feminism.

But for Alpert feminism did not merely resemble a religious movement; rather, it was a religious movement:

> The feminist revolution will be at its root a religious transformation of society, in which society-wide recognition of the creative principle as female will take the place of worship of the modern (male) God, and women will simultaneously gain not merely respect but true power.[31]

Indeed, for Alpert the end goal of feminism seemed to be the aversion of nuclear annihilation and ecological disaster through the "resumption" of matriarchy:

> Could it not be that just at the moment that masculinity has brought us to the brink of nuclear destruction or ecological suicide, women are beginning to rise in response to the Mother's call to save Her planet and create instead the next stage of evolution? Can our revolution mean anything else than the reversion of social and economic control to Her representatives among

> Womankind, and the resumption of Her worship on the face of the Earth?[32]

In its unabashed essentialism, anti-leftism, and idealist notions about social change, "Mother Right" represented a dramatic departure from radical feminism. Most important, by contesting the negative valuation of femininity rather than femininity itself, "Mother Right" reaffirmed rather than challenged dominant cultural assumptions about women. Whereas radical feminists objected to feminism's subordination to the left, Alpert suggested that feminism and the left were intrinsically incompatible. It is interesting to note that today Alpert regrets "the transcendental, mystical quality of "Mother Right" and "the virulence of its anti-leftism."[33]

Although Alpert was underground at the time she wrote it, "Mother Right" was hardly written in a vacuum. It is clear from Alpert's memoir that while she was underground Morgan was her mentor, if not her lifeline. In the days of NYRW Morgan had been an unapologetic politico. However, by the time of the women's seizure of *Rat*, Morgan had concluded that leftist politics contradicted radical feminism.[34] In fact, the first women's issue of *Rat* included Morgan's tour de force, "Goodbye to All That." Like most of Morgan's writing it was a very cleverly and powerfully written piece. But one can see foreshadowings of cultural feminism in it—rancor toward the left (perhaps a hypercorrection for her earlier commitment to the left), and an unwillingness to see women as anything other than men's victims. And there was the essentialism—the claim that women were by nature ecologists, and the suggestion that if leftist men refused to relinquish their "cock privilege," that they be divested of their "cocks."[35]

According to Alpert, Morgan played a fairly large role in shaping "Mother Right." Morgan not only encouraged Alpert to write it, she also collaborated with Alpert on the article's title. And upon reading an early draft of the piece, Morgan sent Alpert "a letter longer than the piece itself" with suggested revisions.[36] It was Morgan who pushed Alpert to re-evaluate her relationship with Melville and urged her to see her relationship with him as paradigmatic of women's relationship to the left. And Morgan sent Alpert Elizabeth Gould Davis's book *The First Sex*.[37] Davis's book claimed to offer incontrovertible evidence of ancient gynocracies and female biological superiority, which Alpert used to support her thesis.[38]

"Mother Right" was the most fully developed articulation of cultural feminism to date, but it was not wholly original. One finds echoed in it the false universalism and anti-leftism of "The Fourth World Manifesto" and "Goodbye to All That." Nor was the characterization of women's liberation as a spiritual movement entirely new. In 1971 Mary Daly, a theologian and NOW member, declared the women's movement "a spiritual movement," one which "has the potential to awaken a new and post-patriarchal spiritual consciousness."[39] Daly amplified these ideas in *Beyond God the Father*, her 1973 book which both Morgan and Elizabeth Gould Davis praised.[40] And, as we have seen, others, including Cell 16, Mehrhof and Kearon of The Feminists, and Morgan, had already moved toward essentialism and matriarchalism. In fact, in the summer of 1972, Morgan's self-defined "faggot-effeminist" husband, Kenneth Pitchford, drawing upon the work of Cell 16, argued:

> To be shockingly blunt, it is the male principle in human beings that has brought us historically to the verge of extinction; if we are to survive it will be because the female principle, once omnipotent in pre-history, is returned to power so that our warped existence can be set right again after being awry for ten thousand years.[41]

So, although Alpert put it all together, these ideas were very much in the air by 1973.

Morgan reportedly predicted that "Mother Right" would outlast *Das Kapital*.[42] Although it did not, it was, nonetheless, extremely influential among feminists. Shortly after its publication, long-time pacifist Barbara Deming argued that Shulamith Firestone, who had advocated artificial reproduction, had "failed to see what Jane Alpert sees: the capacity to bear and nurture children gives women a special consciousness, a spiritual advantage rather than a disadvantage."[43] The Feminists (minus Atkinson) praised Alpert for calling upon feminists to devote themselves to the "restoration" of matriarchy, but predictably took issue with Alpert's contention that one could be a "serious feminist and live with or relate to a man or men."[44] Although Betsy Warrior of Cell

16 questioned the religious overtones of "Mother Right," she lauded Alpert for attacking the left and revaluing motherhood.[45]

As these endorsements suggest, there was no single reason why "Mother Right" resonated for many women. Some found the article compelling because it offered feminists a retreat from the turbulent activism and marginality that many had embraced in the '60s. Certainly, this is a large part of the reason that Alpert was such a willing convert to Morgan's brand of feminism. In *Growing Up Underground*, Alpert concedes that "Robin and her version of feminism were leading me back to my family, to the friendships I'd formed in college, and to the world of middle-class values I had violently rejected in 1969."[46] Moreover, "Mother Right" invoked powerful cultural assumptions about gender differences, especially their immutability and incontrovertibility. Many were persuaded by this feminist essentialism particularly because it suggested that women were by nature peaceful, democratic, and benevolent—the idea that "woman is wonderful," as French feminist Monique Wittig has put it.[47] Finally, many found Alpert's contention that women were united by their common biology enormously tempting given the factionalism within the movement.

Indeed, if one looks at the writings of those women who were articulating cultural feminism in this period, it is clear that they were motivated in part by a desire to put an end to the painful and often immobilizing discussions about women's differences. Their hostility toward the left derived in large measure from its obvious commitment to analyzing class and race differences. Thus we find Robin Morgan and Kathleen Barry, two women who played a very important role in the articulation of cultural feminism, assailing feminists who wanted to explore questions of class, race, and sexual preference. For instance, at the schismatic 1973 West Coast Women's Studies Conference in Sacramento, California, Robin Morgan pleaded with the audience to recognize that "the point is that we as feminists must search . . . for the connectives between women. It is The Man who looks for the differences."[48] Barry, who helped organize the conference, denounced the women who raised the issues of class, race, and imperialism as saboteurs who "must be treated as the enemy from within" the movement. Barry was especially upset with Rita Mae Brown, whom the organizers had very reluctantly asked to lead a workshop on class:

> What does it mean when Rita Mae Brown, in a class workshop at this Women's Studies Conference, asks women to separate themselves into groups based on their class? It is perhaps the most hideous form of mimicry of the male class system of thought and politics. It is presuming that women are somehow responsible for the class men have provided for them. And above all, it negates the reason for us being together—to identify female first, with ourselves, with each other.

Barry counseled feminists to bury their differences and concentrate instead on building a female culture. In a rehash of Alpert's recently published "Mother Right," Barry contended:

> We must look to our matriarchal past for guidance in defining a culture that is a logical extension of nature. With the essence of motherhood and a sense of the preservation of life imprinted in our genes, matrilineal descent will naturally become the organization of the society we envision.[49]

Morgan had assumed the same stance earlier that year at the West Coast Lesbian Feminist Conference in Los Angeles in April 1973. Here, Morgan railed against leftist women, especially members of the Socialist Workers Party. According to one of the conference organizers, Morgan even tried to prevent the socialist-feminist workshop from meeting.[50] Devoting much of her keynote talk to the gay-straight split, Morgan argued that the split had been "created by our collective false consciousness" and had been exacerbated and exploited by "The Man."[51] For some time, Morgan had been trying to mitigate tensions between heterosexual and lesbian feminists by emphasizing their commonalities. For instance, in a spring 1972 speech to D.C. feminists, she declared that "a lesbian is any woman who has ever loved another woman. By that definition every women in this room is a lesbian."[52] At the Los Angeles conference, Morgan, repeating what Atkinson had argued in 1971, maintained that the real test of feminist commitment was not whether one slept with women, but whether one would be at the barricades. Morgan also argued that the real enemy facing the feminist movement was neither heterosexual women nor lesbians, but rather "the epidemic of male style among women."[53] She contended that those lesbian feminists who advocated nonmonogamy, accepted transvestites and transsexuals as allies, and listened to the rock group the Rolling Stones had adopted a "male style [which] could be a destroyer from within" the women's movement.[54] Of course, the conjoining of masculinity and lesbianism was still sufficiently prevalent at least outside the movement that this accusation seemed almost calculated to stir up feelings of guilt. By defining the pursuit of relationships as female and the pursuit of sex as male, Morgan then tried to intimidate her lesbian audience back into the familiar terrain of romantic love:

> Every woman here knows in her gut the vast differences between her sexuality and that of any patriarchally trained male's—gay or straight. That has, in fact, always been a source of *pride* to the lesbian community, even in its greatest suffering. That the emphasis on genital sexuality, objectification, promiscuity, emotional noninvolvement, and coarse invulnerability was the *male style*, and that we, as women, placed greater trust in love, sensuality, humor, tenderness, commitment.[55] [her emphasis]

Morgan was trying not only to forestall the spread of "maleness" throughout the lesbian community, but also to persuade lesbians that they shared a consciousness and political agenda with heterosexual feminists. Morgan concluded her speech by calling upon women to create a "gynocratic" society:

> If we can open ourselves *to* ourselves and each other, as women, only then can we begin to fight for and create, in fact reclaim, not "Lesbian Nation" or "Amazon Nation"—let alone some false state of equality—but a real Feminist Revolution, a proud gynocratic *world* that runs on the power of women.[56] [her emphasis]

Although Morgan's critique of egalitarianism was quite cryptic, it was a significant statement. Tentatively, but increasingly, Morgan was suggesting that the left was dangerous not only because it was sexist and posited the primacy of class, but because it promoted egalitarianism. By the summer of 1972, Alpert maintains that Morgan was "beginning to reject not just the sexism of leftist men, but the very social democratic principles from which the [left] movement had developed."[57]

Many radical and left feminists disagreed with this emerging cultural feminism, but there was very little vocal opposition. Responding to "Mother Right," Ann Froines wrote:

> I don't want to be defined exclusively as Mother, whose source of knowledge and understanding comes welling up mysteriously from my reproductive organs and glandular excretions. Such ideas contradict mine, and most women's experiences, and, as such, are reactionary and anti-women, though they are disguised as vehemently feminist. . . . I cannot see either how understanding the "essential oneness of the universe" has ever, in history, helped formulate a strategy for progressive change or revolution. Every religion has instead postulated the existence of believers, and non-believers have been shunned, exiled or murdered since the beginning of time.[58]

But radical feminists, enervated from years of struggle, were unable to organize any collective opposition to cultural feminism. Their lethargy finally ended, however, when Jane Alpert surrendered to federal authorities on November 14, 1974, four and one-half years after going underground.

Alpert's surrender became a major media event because she was among the first radical fugitives to surface, and, even more important, because her lawyer announced her "renunciation of radical activities and her conversion to the feminist movement."[59] The media loved this story of the contrite ex-radical, the apostate, for it seemed to presage a return to more quiescent days. But Alpert's case troubled many leftists and feminists who believed that feminism entailed a commitment to social radicalism. For instance, upon reading of Alpert's surrender, *oob* reporter Madeleine Janover asked presciently, "What does this mean for radical feminism?"[60] Many more leftists and women's liberationists began asking themselves this question when District Attorney Paul Curran proudly proclaimed that Alpert was "cooperating fully" with FBI investigators "in providing details of her years underground."[61] Curran's talk of Alpert's cooperation, her lawyer's emphasis on her repudiation of her radical past, and her earlier dismissal of the Attica slaughter convinced many that she was informing on fellow fugitives.

By early 1975 feminists were circulating petitions and letters denouncing or supporting Alpert. The first petition, signed by nearly 100 women—primarily socialist-feminists and women with ties to Weatherman—assumed that Alpert was acting as an informant and asked feminists to deny her entrance into the feminist movement:

> We cannot welcome her into our organizations, communities, and movement. How can anyone in the name of feminism willingly cooperate with a bunch of corrupt men in the Department of Justice? Informing on sisters and brothers is not part of the feminist movement.[62]

Soon afterward, a letter signed by Ti-Grace Atkinson, Florynce Kennedy, Susan Sherman, and Joan Hamilton was circulated. Although they did not directly accuse Alpert of informing, they did accuse her of betraying the Movement:

> It is not war that destroys us, but betrayal. For betrayal destroys the heart and soul of our revolution. We are in crises. Our honor, our integrity, our good faith are our primary weapons. We must not, can not, will not lose them. Our comrades underground are the seeds of our future. They are our pride. It is to these comrades in struggle we owe our deep and abiding loyalty. We can understand the pressures of the struggle and the traps it holds for us, but we reject anyone who betrays this loyalty as incapable of guiding or leading us.[63]

They then argued that there existed two systems of justice in America—one for people like Alpert and another for people like Assata Shakur, an imprisoned black activist. And they proposed that the movement would be aligning itself with both class and race privilege if it supported Alpert. They concluded with the declaration, "We are Attica, or we are nothing." Atkinson and the others never tried to solicit signatures for their letter. If they had, it is unlikely they would have interested many radical feminists in signing it. Even those who opposed all cooperation with the state and deplored Alpert's pronouncement on Attica would have had trouble imagining that Weatherman contained "the seeds of [their] future."

Their letter prompted other feminists to solicit signatures for a petition affirming the movement's support of Alpert. To those who claimed that Alpert had provided the FBI with information on the whereabouts of other fugitives, they responded that Alpert had only slight contact with the underground before the publication of "Mother Right," and had none since its publication. They further criticized the letter's attempt to "reactivate guilt politics" and declared:

> We have an organic commitment to all oppressed peoples—but we affirm our own priorities as women. To do otherwise is indeed a betrayal of feminism, one which would send us all back to the ladies' auxiliaries.[64]

But, of course, Alpert's detractors had every right to question her (and, by extension, her supporters') commitment to the struggles of other oppressed peoples. Interestingly, the petition did not repudiate cooperation as antithetical to feminism, but maintained instead that Alpert's "conduct under enormous pressure was and continues to be that of a woman with great integrity and strong feminist commitment." This petition was also signed by almost 100 women, including Morgan, Barry, Mehrhof, Kearon, Adrienne Rich, and Gloria Steinem.[65] Some leftist feminists signed the petition too, for although they opposed collaboration with the state, they believed that Alpert had been unfairly accused.[66]

Many of the women who signed this petition probably did not do so out of the conviction that the left was as much women's enemy as the state. However, this appears to have motivated at least some of the women who circulated the petition. Of course, if the left were equally to blame for women's oppression, then collaboration against the "male left" was not inconsistent with feminism. For instance, Susan Rennie and Kirsten Grimstad, who compiled both the *New Woman's Survival Catalogue* and *The New Woman's Survival Sourcebook* and were two of Alpert's fiercest defenders, observed that "many feminists feel the entire issue [of collaboration] is irrelevant since both the established authorities and the male left are oppressive to women; it is a choice between oppressors."[67] Of course, statements such as these from her supporters did little to enhance Alpert's credibility.

Throughout the saga, Alpert maintained that " 'cooperation' means simply supplying the Government with details of my *own* life as a fugitive." [her emphasis] Morgan defensively claimed that "cooperative meant Jane played the 'Shirley Temple' act with them. When questioned, she wore a skirt and didn't call the cops 'pigs.' "[68] But, in fact, the FBI expected quite a bit more from Alpert than good manners. They knew from Alpert's "Mother Right" that she had been in contact with other radical fugitives and they expected her to provide them with detailed accounts of those meetings. Although Alpert wanted a lighter sentence, she maintains that she was not anxious to divulge information about other fugitives. Alpert decided to placate the FBI by giving them a fabricated account of her life underground. Moreover, she decided to give her lawyer the same fictionalized account. Alpert claims that she pursued this "deluded" strategy because Morgan "put a great deal of pressure" on her to do so. Alpert believes that Morgan pushed her to follow this strategy because Morgan wanted to live vicariously through her:

> I think that the fantasy of being a feminist fugitive who turned the tables on the FBI and who had all of these FBI agents and the law snared in her web was very enticing to her. I don't think she could resist playing it out through me. It's what she would have wanted to do in those circumstances.[69]

Although Alpert's characterization of Morgan's motives may be correct, it reveals, as did her account of the bombings, a certain confusion about her agency in these events.

Almost immediately after being released on bail, Alpert regretted having broken with the long-standing leftist principle of noncooperation.[70] Alpert especially regretted having admitted to using a certain alias which she later realized could lead the FBI to her co-conspirator, Pat Swinton. Indeed, one of the reasons the left had always opposed talking with the FBI was that history had demonstrated that even seemingly benign and unconnected pieces of information could prove pernicious to others. Alpert now admits that the strategy of trying to outsmart the FBI was "bad for the movement, Pat and me."[71]

Many people suspected the worst of Alpert when authorities arrested Swinton on March 12, 1975, in Brattleboro, Vermont. Swinton's lawyer, Fred Cohn, alleged that Alpert was responsible for Swinton's apprehension.[72] Suspicions remained even after a spokesperson for the Department of Justice claimed that information about Swinton's whereabouts was provided by ex-fugitive Barry Stein.[73] Although Swinton (who began calling herself Shoshana after going underground) denied that Alpert had turned her in, she did contend that Alpert had "unwittingly given them enough information for the authorities to find me. Moreover, Swinton emphasized, "there is no such thing as a 'little cooperation.'"[74]

But, ironically, it was Swinton's lawyer, and not Alpert, who revealed that Alpert and Swinton had lived together while fugitives. Alpert apparently did lie to the authorities about her underground contact with Swinton and Swinton's role in the bombings. And when the time came for Swinton's trial, Alpert refused to testify against Swinton, pleading "personal integrity," the Fifth Amendment, and "self-preservation." "Self-preservation" because a prisoners' liberation newsletter, *Midnight Special*, had alerted women in Alpert's prison that they had "a traitor in their midst."[75] Swinton was acquitted on September 26, 1975, in large part because Alpert and David Hughey refused to testify against her.[76] Although the prosecutor decided against charging Alpert with making false statements, both she and Hughey were charged with civil contempt for their refusal to testify against Swinton. As a result of the civil contempt charge, Alpert was incarcerated for two full years rather than twenty-one months. In fact, it is not obvious that Alpert's initial cooperation with the FBI earned her a lighter sentence. As she pointed out in her memoir, David Hughey received approximately the same sentence in 1970 at a time when there was considerably more pressure on the government to deal harshly with radicals.

The question of whether the movement should embrace or censure Alpert continued to polarize the feminist community. In the fall of 1975, Robin Morgan organized a support group for Alpert called the Circle of Support for Jane Alpert. Barbara Mehrhof was the coordinator of the Circle whose members included Pam Kearon, Kirsten Grimstad, Susan Rennie, and Florence Rush. To gain support from feminists who might object to her involvement in armed struggle, they maintained that Alpert had been forced by Melville to take part in the bombings.[77] Moreover, they asserted that Alpert was really attacked not because she informed—which they claimed she had not—but because of her "strong opposition to the underground left and her insistence that the Marxist cause is as much an adversary of women as the establishment right."[78] On the lecture circuit in Michigan, Morgan insisted that Alpert was "a victim of the Left."[79] One of Alpert's staunchest supporters,

Gloria Steinem, commented, "No one minded when [Alpert] was planting bombs in offices where secretaries worked. Now they're upset because they suspect her of informing on radical men."[80] (Of course, Alpert was suspected of having informed on radical women as well.) But, these dismissals did not satisfy feminists who believed that feminism implied an oppositional rather than a cooperative stance toward the state. The Alpert affair confirmed Atkinson's worst fears about the movement's lack of revolutionary resolve. She reportedly remarked that the feminist movement might go down in history as the "stoolie movement" as a result of Alpert's actions.[81] Many radical feminists maintained that the movement should more actively resist the system rather than disavow militant action. To demonstrate their support for noncooperation, a group of feminists, including Atkinson, former *Rat* staffer and radical activist Sharon Krebs, black feminist and journalist Margo Jefferson, and writer and anti-war activist Grace Paley formed a defense committee for Pat Swinton.[82]

Susan Saxe's Capture

The debate became more volatile when leftist fugitive Susan Saxe was arrested in Philadelphia on March 27, 1975. Saxe had been underground since October 1970, when she and four others robbed the Brighton branch of Boston's State Bank and Trust and absconded with $26,000. During the robbery, a policeman was shot and killed. Saxe and the others were charged with another bank robbery and with the bombing and burglarizing of a U.S. Army armory in Newburyport, Massachussetts. (In fact, the armory raid netted Saxe's group classified documents which revealed that the army had contingency plans, called Operation Geronimo Bravo, for counter-insurgency operations against Boston's civilian population.[83]) Some time after going underground, Saxe came out as a lesbian; she was involved in Philadelphia's lesbian-feminist community at the time of her arrest. Saxe issued a statement following her arrest in which she declared:

> First, a greeting of love and strength to all my sisters—courage for our warriors, hope for our people and especially for all my sisters and brothers underground in Amerika. Keep on fighting,

> stay free, stay strong. I promise you a courage to match your own. For me this is not an end, but a new beginning. I intend to fight on in every way as a lesbian, a feminist and an amazon.[84]

Although Saxe identified herself as a feminist and a lesbian, the feminists who supported Alpert did not rush to embrace her. Had Saxe renounced the "male left" and presented herself as its victim, she probably would have received a very warm reception from Alpert's feminist supporters. But Saxe had emphasized that in her case feminism "was not a 'conversion,' but a process that followed my previous commitment as day follows night." Some lesbian-feminists reportedly argued that they would support Saxe as a lesbian, but not as an accused killer and bank robber. And others completely disavowed Saxe, on the grounds that "anyone accused of bank robbery is not a lesbian."[85] In a widely reprinted article, lesbian-feminist and *Village Voice* writer Jill Johnston made it clear that Saxe's continued identification with the left was a stumbling block to her acceptance among some feminists:

> [Saxe's] appeal strains the facilities [*sic*] and sentiments of sisters who extend warmth and support for every woman, especially those driven under any circumstances to extreme actions and who at the same time deny identification with actions committed by individuals under the banner of the male left or any violence committed in the name of lesbian/feminism.

Like many lesbian-feminists, Johnston blamed Saxe for the FBI's harassment of lesbian-feminist communities which the Bureau suspected of harboring other radical fugitives.[86] Many feminists attacked Saxe for identifying feminism with "criminal violence against the state." Johnston labeled Saxe's linking of feminism with the bank robberies a "telescopic deception" since Saxe was, she argued, merely acting in the "context of the patriarchal contest between fathers (right) and sons (left)."[87] Both Johnston and feminist writer Virginia Blaisdell contended that feminist declarations by unrepentant radical fugitives damaged the credibility of the women's movement. But Blaisdell's concern that feminism's association with "adventurist and suicidal . . . underground politics" might jeopardize the possibility of building a mass-based feminist movement, seems at least understandable. Johnston's objection to Saxe, however, grew out of her conviction that resisting the system was male:

> The lesbian/feminist movement is much subtler and more subversive than the male models of historical change. The women I know at least are not so dumb as to think there's anything worth taking over. Women with SDS and Weatherpeople were participating in male ideas of change. . . . As for reform within the structure itself, we root for our Bellas and our Chisholms, but we know that true revolution is a glacial process of unknown cell structures that will evolve out of shared bits of profoundly internalized consciousness.[88]

More incredibly, Johnston maintained that only "conventional women still relate to the oppressor by opposing him." Thus the true rebels were those who had transcended patriarchy rather than resisted it. Although Morgan did not go this far, she too denounced the "ejaculatory tactics" of the "boys' movement," her term for the new left.[89] Morgan had not always opposed confrontational or violent tactics. At a 1971 forum on violence in the women's movement, she reportedly argued that "violent rage was not necessarily a male trip."[90]

The idea that feminism was primarily an exercise in "changing one's head," rather than challenging the material barriers to women's liberation, was anathema to unreconstructed radical feminists. For instance, Susan Stein contended:

> Ideologically, Feminism today is whatever any woman who calls herself a feminist says it is. In fact . . . the bulk of feminist energies is going toward a cultural renaissance of women. . . . However, this concentration on . . . the rebirth of our soul easily becomes not only an excuse to abstain from genuine confrontation with any given oppressor . . . but worse: . . . the feminist begins believing that women's "spiritual resurrection," as Johnston puts it, is not only the goal of the Revolution, but is itself the political strategy by which we can eliminate our own, and all oppression.[91]

Cultural feminism's rejection of the left and confrontational politics troubled many feminists, especially those who believed feminism involved a deepening rather than a disavowal of radicalism. For instance, the staff of the Boston radical feminist journal *The Second Wave* urged feminists to reaffirm their opposition to the state:

> We must recognize our true enemies, otherwise we allow a very dangerous mentality to surface—the same mentality which identifies with the oppressors rather than the oppressed, looks out

> for number one and is quick to back down when supporting something stops being chic and starts being dangerous.[92]

And Atkinson specifically challenged Johnston's assumption that separatists were somehow impervious to the repressive power of the state:

> Separatism means "the state cannot touch me because I do not recognize the state." Jill Johnston's piece . . . very seriously makes this proposal: that the state has nothing to do with us. The state is on our backs! . . . We cut the state out of our existence by fiat? That just doesn't happen by choice. What happens is they come to us and we are totally unprepared: "I beg your pardon, but you don't exist because I have it in my little book here that you don't exist."[93]

The Redstockings and Gloria Steinem

In the brouhaha over Alpert, Swinton, and Saxe, radical feminists found themselves in a largely reactive position. However, in the spring of 1975, the reconstituted Redstockings went on the offensive in a desperate attempt to reassert radical feminist politics. On May 9, 1975, the group issued a press release accusing *Ms.* magazine editor Gloria Steinem of having once been involved with a CIA front.[94] Following as it did on the heels of the Alpert controversy, the Redstockings' revelations raised anew the question of feminism's relationship to the state.

This aspect of Steinem's past had already been made public in 1967 when *Ramparts* magazine revealed that the CIA had subsidized a number of domestic groups including the National Student Association (NSA) and the Independent Research Service (IRS), an organization which Steinem had helped found.[95] The IRS had been established in 1959 to encourage American students to participate in the communist-dominated World Festivals of Youth and Students for Peace and Freedom. Steinem had been the director of the IRS from 1959 through 1960 and had continued to work for the organization through 1962.[96] Redstockings alleged that the CIA established the IRS to organize an anti-communist delegation of Americans to disrupt the festival. They also claimed that Steinem and the IRS had been involved in gathering information on foreign nationals attending the festivals. However, Steinem's own account of the IRS's involvement in the festivals differed dramatically from the Redstockings' version. Shortly after the *Ramparts* article appeared, *The New York Times* published an interview with Steinem in which she admitted that she had known about the CIA funding, but claimed that she had never been asked to gather information on Americans or foreigners who participated in the festivals. According to Steinem, the IRS had encouraged Americans to attend the festivals in order to open up the lines of communication between the East and the West. In fact, Steinem maintained that the CIA's involvement was benign, if not enlightened:

> Far from being shocked by this involvement I was happy to find some liberals in government in those days who were far-sighted and cared enough to get Americans of all political views to the festival.

Steinem asserted that "the CIA's big mistake was not supplanting itself with private funds fast enough."[97]

But Kathie Sarachild, Carol Hanisch, and the other Redstockings members were not only concerned about Steinem's former relationship with a CIA front. They insinuated that *Ms.* magazine was part of a CIA strategy to replace radical feminism with liberal feminism. *Ms.* magazine had been a source of irritation to many feminists since its inception. A number of feminist writers were especially angry when *Ms.* first formed and went outside the movement for its writers and editors. (In fact, Susan Brownmiller, Nora Ephron, and Sally Kempton were struggling to establish a mass-circulation feminist magazine named *Jane* before *Ms.* was even conceived. When Brownmiller heard that Elisabeth Forsling Harris wanted to establish a feminist magazine, she suggested to her that the two groups work together. However, Harris reportedly insisted that Steinem was her editor and rejected Brownmiller's offer. Brownmiller's group was forced to scuttle its plans because they could not raise the necessary seed money.[98]) Generally, radical feminists complained of the magazine's liberal orientation and attributed *Ms.*'s denatured feminism to the magazine's commercial orientation. But Redstockings looked at *Ms.*'s "curious financing"—Warner Communications put up virtually all the money for the magazine but relinquished corporate control by taking only twenty-five percent of the stock—and asked:

> We are wondering whether all this curious financing is connected to the lesson Gloria Steinem said she learned in 1967: "The CIA's big mistake was not supplanting itself with private funds fast enough." The *Ms.* editors should come forward with more information about their unusual stockholders.[99]

Redstockings contended that the formation of *Ms.* magazine had given Steinem a strategic position from which "feminist politics can be influenced." And they alleged that "information can and is being gathered on the personal and political activities of women all over the world."[100]

Steinem, reportedly devastated by the Redstockings' accusations, decided against responding to the charges. However, this decision backfired as some feminists thought her silence suggested that she might, in fact, have something to hide. Betty Friedan, never a big fan of Steinem's, reportedly declared that the CIA had infiltrated the women's movement and called on Steinem to answer the Redstockings' charges.[101] Steinem's vocal support for Alpert and her own refusal to repudiate her past involvement with the IRS made many feminists, like Ellen Willis, curious about her stance on cooperating with the state. In fact, Willis resigned her position as part-time contributing editor at *Ms.* on June 30, 1975. In her statement of resignation, Willis emphasized that the Redstockings' accusation solidified, but did not precipitate, her decision to resign. Willis explained that she was ending her two-year association with *Ms.* because of political differences with the magazine—including its promotion of "conservative, anti-left feminism." Willis was particularly angry that despite assurances that the magazine would publish an article on the Alpert debate, no such article appeared. Instead, *Ms.* published an article by Morgan which emblematized the conservative, anti-left feminism Willis deplored. Indeed, she claims that Morgan's article, "The Rights of Passage," was "rushed into production in record time before everyone who wanted to had a chance to read it."[102]

Newspaper accounts of the festivals would seem to support the Redstockings' contention that the CIA's actions were neither "far-sighted" nor "liberal." Further substantiation comes from Eugene Theroux, an NSA leader knowledgeable about the IRS's recruitment of students for the festivals, who reports that the Americans went to "cause trouble."[103] However, the Redstockings' analysis ignored the fact that throughout the '50s and most of the '60s liberalism and anti-communism were coterminous. Indeed, some liberals, including Allard Lowenstein, reportedly cooperated with the "good-wing" of the CIA which looked to social democrats rather than right-wing dictators to defeat communism.[104] Moreover, Redstockings presented no evidence to support their insinuation that Steinem and *Ms.* were currently in league with the CIA.

The members of Redstockings were right to feel that radical feminism was being supplanted. As they pointed out, the enormously influential *Ms.* magazine generally did promote liberal and cultural feminism rather than radical feminism in its pages. By attacking Steinem and *Ms.*, Redstockings were attempting to reestablish radical feminism as the dominant theoretical strain within the women's liberation movement. Redstockings did not succeed in staving off radical feminism's decline, but their charges helped to form the battle lines.

Nowhere were the battle lines more tightly drawn than at Sagaris, the fledgling feminist educational institute, which had recently been awarded a *Ms.* Foundation grant.[105] The Sagaris collective had accepted a $5,000 grant from the foundation during its first semester. They approached the foundation again when they discovered that the school was underenrolled and thus underfunded for its second semester. But many faculty members and students objected when the collective announced that the school had received an additional $10,000 grant. The dissenters argued that the collective should refuse to accept the money because Steinem had not yet responded to the Redstockings' allegations. When the issue was put to a vote, the majority of the faculty and one-third of the students opposed accepting the money. Immediately following the vote, four faculty members—Ti-Grace Atkinson, Alix Kates Shulman, Susan Sherman, and Marilyn Webb—and about twenty students seceded from the school to form the August 7th Survival Community. Shortly after their secession, Steinem issued a rejoinder to the Redstockings' accusations.

But even after Steinem responded to their charges, Redstockings continued to challenge her account of her past. Many radical feminists had initially supported Redstockings because they believed that the group was raising important issues about feminism's relationship to the state and was presenting a powerful and incisive critique of *Ms.* magazine. Over time, however, sympathy began to shift toward Steinem, who many felt was the object of an ad feminem attack.[106] Moreover, the homophobic edge to Redstockings' analysis (available in their recently published book, *Feminist Revolution*) persuaded few feminists that this was the group to put the movement back on the right track.[107]

Female Culture and Feminist Businesses

Cultural feminism did not succeed simply because it manipulated women's anger at the left or promoted the idea of universal sisterhood. Indeed, not everyone who advocated women's culture did so out of the conviction that it would discourage conflict among women or rid feminism of "leftover leftism."[108] Rather, a large part of what made cultural feminism so appealing was that it offered women a refuge from male supremacy (and, for some, the vicissitudes of political struggle) and, seemingly, a conduit out of subordination.

The concern with alternative institutions was hardly unique to feminism. Both the new left and the black freedom movement established alternative institutions both to challenge the legitimacy of the system and to "structure power differently."[109] Among the first such efforts were the Mississippi Freedom Democratic Party and the Freedom Schools that were formed during Freedom Summer of 1964. In the aftermath of the 1964 Democratic Convention Bob Moses [Parris] of SNCC even suggested that the Movement attempt to form its own state government in Mississippi rather than try to integrate the Democratic Party.[110] And at roughly the same time, Tom Hayden proposed convening a constitutional convention of unrepresented people in Washington, D.C.[111]

However, as black radicals and new leftists confronted the unresponsiveness of the system, some began to conceive of alternative institutions somewhat differently—as islands of resistance completely and quite deliberately outside the system. By creating one's own culture, one could function uncontaminated by the dominant culture and without the risk of co-optation, or so it seemed. As early as 1966, SNCC's Atlanta Project contended that "true liberation" required that blacks "cut ourselves off from white people," and "form our own institutions, credit unions, co-ops, political parties, write our own histories."[112] Three years later, well-known poet and black nationalist Amiri Baraka (formerly LeRoi Jones) offered the following counsel to black radicals:

> But you must have the cultural revolution. . . . We cannot fight a war, an actual physical war with the forces of evil just because we are angry. We can begin to build. We must build black institutions . . . all based on a value system that is beneficial to black people.[113]

And in an article urging people to take part in the protest planned for the 1968 Democratic Convention, Tom Hayden argued:

> We are in the streets because no institution is changeable from within. We build our own free institutions—community organizations, newspapers, coffeehouses—at points of strain within the system where human needs are denied. These institutions become centers of identity, points of contact, building blocks of a new society from which we confront the system more intensely.[114]

To many in the new left and the black movement, counter-institutions seemed the next step in resisting the system.

In 1971 when Barbara Mehrhof and Pam Kearon of The Feminists called upon feminists to create a "counter-reality," they were among the first in the women's movement to do so.[115] But between the years 1973 and 1975 the idea became far more common. In 1973, Kathleen Barry maintained that

> the *process* of the struggle for liberation cannot be *only* one of negation and fighting. If in our battles we unleash the creative process in women to begin building a viable female culture, feminist revolutionary potential then becomes unlimited.[116] [her emphasis]

Speaking before the 1975 NOW Convention, Ann Pride reportedly declared women's culture the "third wave" of feminism.[117] Mary Daly argued that a female "counterworld" would contribute to the movement's growth because she reasoned that "[t]he power of presence that is experienced by those who have begun to live in the new space radiates outward, attracting others."[118] Daly dismissed those who criticized this "new space" as escapist:

> When sacred space is discovered, the possibility of deterioration into escapism or of absolutizing the space into a particular form is there. However, the real danger is that women will succumb to accusations of escapism or singlemindedness by those who do not see the transcendent dimensions of feminism.[119]

The contention that female culture was revolutionary, not diversionary or escapist, was a common theme in much of this writing. Susan Rennie and Kirsten Grimstad asserted:

> Woman-identified explorations are occurring today . . . in all of what we call "women's culture"—which is often more precisely lesbian culture made available to all women. This is perhaps the most profound and ultimately far-reaching expression of our politics—the incredibly difficult and moving discovery of a woman's world view that will inform the conception and reality of women's power to change their lives and their culture.[120]

Robin Morgan defended women's culture on the grounds that it would have a regenerative effect upon the movement:

> I don't think we can fight every minute of every day the way we have to as women without a culture and without a vision of what it is that we are fighting for. I think that women's culture is an absolute necessity. . . . It is not cultural nationalism, it is not self-indulgence, it is not any of the silly sophomoric things that socialist realists at times claim in their knee-jerk thinking. Culture is breath, it is oxygen to us as an oppressed people who have never before spoken in our own voice.[121]

Rita Mae Brown argued that feminists should turn their attention away from civil rights to building an alternative women's culture because "revolution is what counts." But Brown's notion of what such a culture might achieve was far more grandiose than Morgan's. Brown reportedly argued that feminists should follow the example of the Nazis, whom, she argued, succeeded because they constructed an alternative culture within the dominant culture.

> [The Nazis] organized an alternative culture within the German culture and they took over in ten years. It's shocking. Nazism

> was an alternative culture built on certain emotional things that already existed. This is a negative event, but the process worked.[122]

By 1973 feminist health centers, credit unions, rape crisis centers, bookstores, presses, and publishing companies were beginning to form across the country. Alternative institutions, however, were not the sole preserve of cultural feminists. Radical feminists, and to a far lesser extent socialist-feminists, were involved in running rape crisis centers, feminist health centers, credit unions, and newspapers. But in contrast to cultural feminists, they did not envision such work as part of a larger strategy of building a women's culture guided by "female" values. At first, alternative feminist institutions were run collectively and not for profit. In fact, there was virtually no discussion of feminist businesses until 1973 when Helaine Harris and Lee Schwing wrote an article in *The Furies* newspaper advocating feminist institutions as the "next step" toward creating a feminist society.[123] The idea that feminists would be involved in entrepreneurial activity was still so heretical in 1973 that Harris and Schwing referred to these businesses euphemistically as institutions. Harris and Schwing argued that feminist institutions would solve a variety of the movement's problems. Most important, feminists would be able to get paid for doing political work so that their energies would not be dissipated by "straight" nine-to-five jobs. No longer would feminist projects and study groups disintegrate because women were too busy working straight jobs to keep the groups afloat. Moreover, they maintained that these institutions would go a long way toward providing women with economic security, and would as a result help to dissolve the material barriers to coming out. Finally, they argued that feminist enterprises would benefit the least privileged because lesbians, working-class and third-world women would be given preference in hiring.

Harris and Schwing offered a compelling argument for feminist businesses, but the issue caused such disagreement among *The Furies'* staff that for the first time in the paper's history the collective printed a dissenting piece by collective members Loretta Ulmschneider and Deborah George. They questioned Harris and Schwing's assumption that women would "actually have more time to work on an ideology in a lesbian/feminist business than in a straight job." They argued that feminist businesses would most benefit middle-class women because they had the necessary resources and skills to begin such ventures. They criticized Harris and Schwing for not analyzing the relationship between alternative businesses and capitalism. Finally, they contended that alternative institutions cut people off from the larger struggle as people become "closed in on themselves" and absorbed with the problems and dynamics of their specific group.

But many feminists, including a number of former Furies members, found Harris and Schwing's arguments compelling. In fact, after the dissolution of The Furies collective quite a few Furies members became involved in establishing feminist businesses. Former Furies members founded Diana Press, Olivia Records, Women in Distribution, and *Quest/a feminist quarterly* which encouraged the development of feminist businesses.[124] In a 1974 *Quest* article, Coletta Reid, a founder of Diana Press, argued that "the most important goal of women's businesses is to put women in a position to gain and use economic power." However, Reid cautioned that feminist businesses should not mimic capitalist businesses. She maintained that "insofar as possible, the internal organization of women's businesses should be consistent with the goals of the future socialist economy they're working towards."[125]

Although former Furies members helped pioneer the idea of feminist businesses, they were by no means the only feminists promoting them. Often those who advocated the creation of feminist counter-institutions did so by counterposing them to what they claimed was the left's chronic ineffectiveness. Robin Morgan maintained that the "mushrooming" of feminist alternative institutions such as the Feminist Women's Health Centers and Feminist Credit Unions showed that feminists were "maturing beyond those . . . ejaculatory tactics [of the left] into a long-term, committed attitude toward *winning*."[126] Morgan even helped to finance these alternative groups and businesses through the profits of her best-selling anthology, *Sisterhood is Powerful*.[127] In 1975, Rennie and Grimstad hailed feminist credit unions as "the tinderboxes that will spark the real prairie fires."[128] In other words, unlike the Weather Underground which had produced a book entitled *Prairie Fire*, these feminist businesswomen were effecting real change. And in early 1974 Kathleen Barry, Mary Daly, Adrienne Rich, and Joan Hoff Wilson wrote:

> It is springtime, and while the male politics of the sixties grow less relevant in their rhetoric to people's lives, women move on. This is a period of rapid expansion and outreach for the Women's Movement as Feminism finds form in new health centers, community women's centers, women's studies programs, rape crisis lines, and similar projects.[129]

Feminist institutions and businesses appealed to women who wanted to bring about immediate and tangible change in women's lives. For instance, Jennifer Woodul of Olivia Records contended that "it's useless to advocate more and more 'political action' if some of it doesn't result in the permanent material improvement of the lives of women." To those who favored them, feminist businesses promised women self-sufficiency and self-determination. No longer would large publishing houses decide which feminist writers were published. No longer would women be forced to see physicians who patronized and infantalized them. But advocates of feminist businesses often came to believe that this was the way to effect substantial structural change. For instance, Woodul, arguing that feminists businesses were the "wave of the future," claimed that they were "a way to get actual power for women":

> Over the past few years, we've discovered different ways to make our minds and bodies stronger—to take personal power. Olivia and other feminist businesses believe that we now need to take our economic power. State power is a ways down the road, but just because we don't start with it, that doesn't mean we're not on the way to getting it.

Kathleen Barry argued that feminist businesses would promote "economic self-sufficiency" which in turn "would allow women an economic as well as cultural context in which to become free of patriarchy."[130]

Women who discussed the obstacles to women's economic independence were frequently dismissed as naysayers afflicted with "leftover leftism" who would rather complain about women's oppression than formulate solutions. For instance,

Kathleen Barry maintained that those who opposed feminist businesses did so because they had become inured to their oppression and had succumbed to the " 'correct line' " thinking so indigenous to the political Left of the patriarchy."[131] And Morgan contrasted the optimism of those forming alternative institutions to the "failure vanguardism" promoted by veteran radical feminists:

> To succeed in the slightest is to be Impure. Only if your entire life, political and personal is one plummet of downward mobility and despair, may you be garlanded with the crown of feminist thorns. . . . Well, to such a transparently destructive message I say, with great dignity, "Fooey." I want to *win* for a change. I want us *all* to *win*.[132] [her emphasis]

Likewise, Rita Mae Brown contended:

> Big is bad. Feminists don't want anything to do with it because women will strangle in frozen hierarchies. . . . Perhaps what we don't acknowledge is that big means successful in America. Many feminists may die before they admit it but they are terrified of success. Failure in patriarchal terms, defines women. Success means you're a ballbuster, acting like a man.[133]

The radicalism of the '60s did sometimes succumb to defeatism and the hostility to hierarchy was sometimes psychologically motivated. But although Brown and Morgan were unwilling to admit it, those who dared oppose the heady optimism of cultural feminism had legitimate political concerns.[134] Radical feminists had rejected hierarchy out of a desire to "structure power differently," to avoid the "frozen hierarchies" of traditional organizations. Although this could be quite destructive when taken to the extreme, it was not a bad impulse. And radical feminists' skepticism about "success" stemmed not only from the conviction that American society needed to be overhauled rather than reformed, but from an understandable (if at points paralytic) fear of cooptation.

Of course, the idea that women could achieve real economic independence through alternative institutions was quixotic. Feminist businesses served a tiny fraction of the female population and employed an infinitesimal percentage of the feminist population. Moreover, those who proposed that feminist businesses would empower women economically ignored the structural barriers not only to women's economic independence, but to the success of these businesses. As with cultural feminism as a whole, the tendency was to treat women's culture as though it could and did exist entirely outside the larger culture.

Feminist businesses were originally conceived as a way to carry on the struggle. The women who formed Olivia Records did so in large part because they wanted "to bring women into some sort of feminist consciousness," and they saw music as "an incredible vehicle for slipping in under people's blocks."[135] Likewise the women who formed Women in Distribution did so to help disseminate movement literature, specifically books being published by small feminist presses. But when a group of feminist businesswomen established the unabashedly capitalist Feminist Economic Network, other feminists began to question whether their goal was to overthrow the system or share in its riches. The Feminist Economic Network (FEN) was the brainchild of the Oakland Feminist Women's Health Center (OFWHC) and the Detroit Feminist Federal Credit Union (DFFCU)—two organizations whose leadership favored hierarchy, centralized decision-making, and capitalist methods. Although many feminists hailed the California FWHC's and the DFFCU as model feminist organizations because they were "set up around solutions and women's strengths rather than crises and oppressions," both groups experienced considerable internal dissension.[136] The FWHC's working conditions and hierarchical structure and the DFFCU's expansionist designs prompted clinic workers and credit union members alike to question whether those in power had forsaken principle for pragmatism.[137] However, if internal opposition prevented the founders of the OFWHC and the DFFCU from "implementing [their] most creative feminist visions," FEN's structure ensured that they need remain accountable only to "those feminists who shared [their] visions."[138]

FEN grew out of a November 1975 conference organized to establish an information and resource-sharing network among feminist credit unions.[139] However, representatives from the OFWHC, DFFCU, and Diana Press arrived at the conference with the intention of establishing a corporate structure "to provide economic development and accept financial leadership for the

Feminist Movement."[140] These three organizations became the nucleus of FEN, but the principals were Laura Brown of the OFWHC and Joanne Parrent of the DFFCU. To achieve financial solvency for the movement, FEN would borrow money from feminist credit unions and lend it to those feminist businesses participating in FEN. According to Kathleen Barry, one of FEN's few vociferous supporters, the founders hoped that by enhancing women's economic independence, FEN would "bring Feminism to another level of confrontation with patriarchy."[141] However, that was not how most conference-goers saw it. The proposed FEN by-laws, which eschewed collectivity and accountability, so alarmed the majority of conference participants that they formed another organization, the Feminist Economic Alliance, rather than joining FEN. Even Beverly Manick, who considered herself a close political ally of the women at Diana Press, was shocked to discover the extent to which their views had come to diverge from hers.[142]

FEN's first and only achievement consisted of the acquisition and partial renovation of the once palatial Women's City Club in downtown Detroit during the winter of 1976. FEN acquired the building in a rather circuitous manner through $250,000 in loans from the DFFCU.[143] The FEN leadership viewed the City Club's renovation into the "world's largest womanspace" as the first step in their ambitious strategy to achieve "economic self-sufficiency for the Feminist Movement."[144] Their prospective income-generating projects included a plastic speculum factory and a women's inter-city helicopter service between Los Angeles and San Francisco.[145] However, criticism of FEN mounted as it began to take shape organizationally. Many DFFCU members felt that the purchase of the City Club had seriously jeopardized the credit union's solvency by depleting a quarter of its assets. And many of the women whom FEN had hired to renovate and manage the club felt exploited by the long hours and strenuous labor asked of them. The FEN leadership responded to the growing mistrust and resentment by hiring armed women to guard the building. Their presence only exacerbated tension, and violence erupted at the City Club on April 11, 1976, only two days after the building's grand opening. Several women who had been critical of FEN's policies were beaten and injured during the melee.

Mounting deficits and pervasive mistrust forced the dissolution of FEN in September 1976, less than a year after its founding.

FEN received much hostile attention from the feminist press because its founders repudiated the model of feminist businesses as it was originally articulated. Whereas Harris, Schwing, and Reid had emphasized that feminist busineses would be collectively and democratically run and accountable to the feminist movement, the women of FEN berated feminists for even raising these issues. In fact, the founders of FEN tried to disarm their critics by suggesting that their detractors were intimidated by the bold and visionary nature of their venture. They maintained that feminist commitment to the principles of collectivity and accountability simply reflected women's preference for powerlessness. For example, Kathleen Barry and several FEN founders argued that since "the beginning of the Women's Movement, women have found countless ways to avoid the challenge of daring to think beyond the confines of our oppression."[146] When Joanne Parrent was criticized for sitting on both the boards of the DFFCU and FEN, she responded:

> I think that's our petty, small narrow minds as women. . . . If you look at the male corporate world, you'll see many men who are on the Board of directors of many corporations and the reason for this is so that those corporations can work together, so there's liaisons between those corporations.[147]

But while the women of FEN were willing to adopt capitalist hierarchy from men, they condemned their critics for adopting the "male" concept of democracy. And they frequently dismissed proponents of democratic decision-making and collective organization as male-identified or as dupes of the "male left." For instance, Parrent contended:

> we recognize democracy as a patriarchal concept. It is merely the housekeeper of our capitalist economy. It was developed by men for men. . . . We will never make the immense changes that as feminists we see necessary by imitating the structures that men have created.[148]

Women who challenged the compatibility of feminism with capitalism were accused of parroting the "downward mobility" of the left, or as "aping" the "correct-line politics" and "trashing" style of the left.[149] The founders of FEN maintained that women could embrace capitalism and eschew democracy precisely because they were women and had common interests. They invoked the female principle—by definition beneficent—to justify their appropriation of capitalist and anti-democratic methods. Laura Brown maintained that because women have the same interests "each time an individual woman gets power, we all have more power."[150] And Debra Law of the OFWHC and FEN argued:

> I see no arbitrary separation between myself and working in a feminist institution and community, because I see no separation between my best interests and any other woman's best interest. . . . One of the most basic principles of feminism is that there is a basic commonality between women. It's an extremely important assumption . . . and the only one I can work on.[151]

Here we see the convergence of cultural with liberal feminism. In arguing that one woman's power empowers all women, cultural feminists were echoing what liberal feminists had been saying all along. This "trickle-down" approach to feminism demonstrated a stunning disregard for the material barriers to women's liberation. The struggle for liberation became a question of individual will and determination, rather than collective struggle. The problem, as Redstockings noted (if far too categorically), was that liberal and cultural feminists subscribed to the same "individualist line that denies the need for a movement, and implies that when women don't make it, it's their own fault."[152] And increasingly, one finds liberal and cultural feminists united by their common distaste for confrontational politics and their shared admiration of effectiveness and hierarchy. Thus, in "Rights of Passage," Morgan attacked radical feminist "oldies" as bitter and defeatist and lavishly praised Betty Ford as "that fine closet feminist."[153] Of course, there remained significant differences between these two stands of feminism, the most important that liberal feminism favored integration whereas cultural feminism advocated the construction of a separate female power base. However, for some cultural feminists like Morgan who advocated "pluralistic tolerance," this represented no stumbling block at all.[154]

With FEN, feminism became, as Laura Brown put it, "anything we say it is."[155] Of course, FEN represented an extreme example of cultural feminism. FEN received little public support from other cultural feminists perhaps because its founders so outrageously flaunted their disregard for established radical feminist norms.

FEN was short-lived and the damage it did was limited. But the larger shift toward feminist counter-cultural institutions and businesses had serious consequences for the movement. In 1975 Heather Booth and Naomi Weisstein argued that such enterprises provided "vision and hope," but suggested that they also comprised a "partially defeating strategy":

> Alternate institutions are, by their nature, limited, small, weak, and easily destroyed. They do not alter existing power relations. We use up all our miniscule resources to construct and maintain these institutions. This detours us from making claims on the vast resources of large institutions in society which should be providing us with what we need.[156]

Although there is much truth in what they said, their assessment was not entirely fair, for these institutions sometimes did make demands upon the system. For instance, rape crisis centers, although they were later co-opted, did much to change public opinion about rape and spurred liberal feminists to work for revised laws against sexual assault. And feminist health centers raised women's consciousness about medical procedures and drugs, and were instrumental in changing medical and nursing practices. Booth and Weisstein's argument is far truer of feminist businesses, which found themselves hopelessly enmeshed in a larger economic system which understood one thing—profit. Under these conditions feminist businesses had a difficult enough time merely surviving, much less resisting the system. Indeed, in the late '70s many feminist businesses either failed or were forced to jettison or drastically modify the initial egalitarianism and collectivism that were their hallmarks.[157] Over time politics necessarily took a back seat to profit. The owner of a women's music-distribution company recalls that in the "early '70's at our national meetings of distributors, all we did was talk politics. Sales? Who cared?" However, by the early '80s the emphasis had changed so drastically that she advertized for MBA's when she needed a Boston distributor.[158]

Then there was the problem of women's culture, the "new

space'' which Daly had predicted would become a magnet attracting others to it. In practice, women's communities were small, self-contained subcultures that proved hard to penetrate, especially to newcomers unaccustomed to their norms and conventions. In fact, with the ascendance of cultural feminism, the radical wing of the movement began to exist more as a community than as a movement. These largely self-enclosed communities provided support to those who belonged, but often seemed indifferent to those who did not. While the denizens of these communities used the language of sisterhood, they often assumed a patronizing stance toward those ''unliberated'' women who were still living in ''The Man's'' world. In 1979, Barbara Ehrenreich criticized ''a feminism which talks about universal sisterhood, but is horrified by women who wear spiked heels or call their friends, 'girls.' ''[159] Cultural feminism aggravated the tendency toward exclusivity, and the uncommitted, feeling themselves the objects of derision, often responded by avoiding rather than joining the movement. Finally, while women's culture was originally defended as a way to sustain the movement, it seemed instead to promote withdrawal from political struggle. Even Adrienne Rich, an early defender of women's culture, noted that ''woman-only space,'' while often a ''strategic necessity,'' had too often become ''a place of emigration, an end in itself.''[160]

The Radical Feminist Opposition to Cultural Feminism

The debates over Alpert, Saxe, Steinem, and FEN concerned the very identity and direction of the movement, and were, as a result, often acrimonious. Cultural feminists frequently railed against their detractors for appropriating what they termed the ''correct-lines'' and ''trashing'' style of the new left. However, cultural feminists were themselves often remarkably intolerant of dissent, branding it ''unsisterly.'' They routinely dismissed their feminist critics as anti-feminist and as ''dupes of the male left.'' In fact, cultural feminists tried to depict these conflicts as a tiresome re-play of the politico-feminist split. One rumour circulating at the time was that Atkinson, Shulman, and Sherman ''were sent to Sagaris by the 'male Left' to disrupt it.''[161] In their 1975 *New*

Woman's Survival Sourcebook, Susan Rennie and Kirsten Grimstad reported that *oob*, which had been critical of both Alpert and Steinem, had

> switched its emphasis from national news reporting with a radical feminist slant to focusing on intra-movement factionalism, from what appears to be a predominantly male left perspective.[162]

And Kathleen Barry attributed FEN's demise to the infiltration of leftist ideas into the women's movement and its presses.[163] But this was not always an effective strategy since many of cultural feminism's most vocal critics were veteran radical feminists like Willis, Atkinson, Hanisch, and Sarachild. So, cultural feminists sometimes depicted their radical feminist critics as hopelessly bitter, defeatist, and hypercritical. Indeed, Morgan went so far as to insist that veteran radical feminists were defending not the original meaning of radical feminism but "a bizarre new definition of 'radical feminist.' "[164] In fact, it was cultural feminists like Barry and Morgan who were trying to redefine radical feminism in a way that would rid it of its residual leftism. For them, Jane Alpert's vision of mother right, the matriarchal reorganization of society, was the feminist, or feminine, alternative to socialism.

But to many radical feminists cultural feminism represented a reversal, if not a betrayal, of much that was fundamental to radical feminism. For instance, in one of the earliest and most cogent critiques of cultural feminism, Willis maintained:

> The Jane Alpert debate has brought into focus the current strategy of women who seek to define feminism as a conservative, anti-left movement. In essence, they are attempting to exploit women's rightful anger at the sexism of the male-dominated left to discredit the very idea of leftist politics—i.e. economic class struggle—as a "male trip" irrelevant to women. For a radical feminist analysis of women's concrete, material oppression they substitute fantasies of lost matriarchies, female superiority and "mother right." They defend themselves against criticism with an appeal to a phony concept of sisterhood that stigmatizes disagreement as "divisive," or "anti-woman," or "self-hating."[165]

In the summer of 1975, Atkinson and Sarachild appeared together on a panel with Swinton at The School for Marxist Education and reportedly "spoke of feminism as part of a larger movement against an oppressive system."[166] Several months earlier Atkinson had declared mother right and matriarchalism "reactionary nationalism," and had argued that liberal feminism and matriarchalism were indistinguishable in that both advocated revising rather than eliminating the power structure.[167] In their 1975 article, "Will the Women's Movement Survive?," Naomi Weisstein and Heather Booth contended that changes in consciousness follow from "re-ordering power relations," rather than vice versa. They too criticized feminists' concern with female culture, matriarchies, and mysticism. And they warned other feminists that "without a movement to support it, consciousness veers off, turns inward toward self-hatred or destructive mysticism, and finally dies."[168] And that same year, in the Redstockings' publication *Feminist Revolution*, radical feminist writer Brooke Williams maintained that cultural feminism was threatening "to transform feminism from a political movement to a lifestyle movement."[169]

Even some prominent liberal feminists spoke out against the preoccupation with women's culture, although predictably their major criticism seemed to be what had irritated them about radical feminism—its separatism. Speaking before the 1977 NOW Convention, outgoing NOW President Karen DeCrow reportedly criticized advocates of women's culture for promoting separatism rather than integration and for encouraging a retreat into mysticism.[170] Friedan called cultural feminism "a schizophrenic retreat from the necessities and actual possibilities of the modern women's movement."[171]

Radical feminists' counter-offensive was in some respects quite successful, in the short term. Most underground feminist newspapers agreed that cooperation and capitalism were antithetical to feminism, and that the state was more inimical to women than was the left. But the newspapers may not have reflected the opinion of the rank and file. Moreover, many of those women calling themselves radical feminists may have opposed FEN, but not the essence of cultural feminism. Certainly, after the commotion died down the movement continued its drift toward cultural feminism. By the late '70s the idea that feminism involved the celebration of female difference was no longer remarkable. Indeed, the most startling aspect of Jane Alpert's analysis—her reclamation of female biology—had become almost commonplace.[172]

Nor was the conjoining of feminism and spirituality any longer controversial as the pages of feminist periodicals were filled with articles about matriarchies and goddess-worship.[173] As Brooke Williams has pointed out, one can see the shift from radical to cultural feminism reflected in the changing titles of feminist newspapers and journals. Whereas early women's liberation papers had titles such as *off our backs, Ain't I a Woman, No More Fun and Games, It Ain't Me, Babe, Tooth 'n' Nail*, '70s periodicals carried names like *Amazon Quarterly, The Full Moon, 13th Moon, Womanspirit*, and *Chrysalis*, the latter a self-described "magazine of woman's culture."[174]

****

By 1975 it was too late for a revival of radical feminism. The economic, political, and cultural constriction of the '70s and the collapse of other oppositional movements in this period made radical activism of any sort difficult. Much of the movement's original leadership had been "decapitated" during the acrimonious struggles over class and elitism.[175] And, of course, a number of the founders had retreated from the movement when lesbianism was advocated as the natural and logical consequence of feminism. Moreover, many of the new women who had flooded into the movement in the early '70s saw radical feminism as an ideology of self-improvement, not radical social transformation. This might not have been so great a problem had the founders not assumed that radical feminism would automatically politicize women about other systems of oppression. But as I have tried to demonstrate, radical feminism was derailed, at least in part, by its own theoretical limitations. Many of radical feminism's more problematic features—the false universalism, the contention that gender was the primary contradiction, and the conviction that feminism was *the* transformative social theory—derived largely from the left's antagonism toward women's liberation. Other deficiencies, such as the too-eager attribution of false consciousness and the prescriptive casting of the "personal is political," were faults that radical feminism shared with other '60s movements.

NOW was a major beneficiary of radical feminism's disintegration as first the schisms and later the countercultural focus encouraged some radical feminists to join an organization which they had initially disparaged. In 1975 NOW's membership elected a new slate of leaders who advocated bringing the organization "out of the mainstream and into the revolution." And a surprisingly radical list of demands was generated at the government-funded Houston Women's Conference of 1978, an event in which NOW members played a large role.[176] But liberal feminism has floundered without the benefit of a vocal radical feminist movement. For example, liberal feminists have failed to take an unapologetic stance on abortion rights. By speaking euphemistically of "choice" and refusing to acknowledge what radical feminists had always emphasized—that abortion is very much about women's sexual freedom—liberal feminists have conveyed both to the public and to their conservative adversaries their own ambivalence about abortion.[177]

That the radical feminist movement was unable to sustain itself is hardly remarkable. This is, after all, the fate of all social change movements. It was certainly the fate of the black freedom movement and the new left as well. But if radical feminism failed to survive as a movement, its effects were hardly evanescent. Although women's situation in the late 1980s falls far short of the radical feminist vision, the world today is nonetheless vastly different from what it was twenty years ago. While one can point to other factors—technological advances in birth control, the expansion of the tertiary sector, the "male revolt" against the bread-winner ethic, and the collapse of the family wage system, which has in turn made dual-income families a necessity—radical feminism was central to this transformation. By challenging the phallocentrism of normative heterosexuality, radical feminists have contributed to a restructuring of heterosexual sex. As a result of radical feminists' affirmation of female desire, women are today more apt to assert their sexual needs. Both the legalization of abortion and growing public awareness of rape as a serious crime (reflected in revised rape laws) have done a great deal to further women's sexual self-determination. By exposing the sexism of the medical profession, questioning the omniscience of the physician, and promoting self-help techniques, radical feminists have encouraged women to take a more active role in their health care.[178] Radical feminism's assault on the nuclear family and institutionalized heterosexuality has helped to make it possible (if not easy) for people to fashion alternatives to the nuclear family and heterosexuality. And while housework and child care remain far too much women's work, there has been some erosion of the sexual division of labor in the home—as a consequence both of changed economic conditions and of radical feminism. Finally, although gender is far from meaningless in our culture, our cultural definitions of masculinity and femininity are today far less rigid and constraining than was the case before the resurgence of feminist activism in the late '60s.

Epilogue

Much has happened since radical feminism dissipated in the mid-'70s. Rather than summarize the history of the women's movement over the past thirteen years, I will spend the next few pages exploring some of the continuities and disjunctures between second-wave feminism in the pre- and post-'75 period. I will focus on developments in three areas that have been particularly important: the meaning of feminism itself—whether its goal is gender equality or the affirmation of female difference; sexuality; and, finally, women's differences from one another.

In the period since 1975 we see that some issues which had previously proven problematic are no longer so and others which had seem resolved or had remained unexamined have become problematicized. For instance, the question of feminism's relationship to other progressive movements—the source of so much and such persistent tension in the late '60s and early '70s—is no longer the divisive issue it once was. This does not so much reflect a resolution of the question as it does the waning of other oppositional movements.[1] This is not to say that the dissipation of radicalism has benefited feminism. In fact, the women's movement would probably be stronger if there were other dissenting voices.

By contrast, the question of whether feminism entails the transcendence of gender or the affirmation of femaleness has become the new feminist faultline. The idea that feminism involves the preservation and celebration of femaleness rather than the transformation of gender is no longer unique to cultural feminism. Indeed, the valorization of femaleness has gained considerable currency in the '80s and has been taken up by a variety of feminists, some of whom disagree on many other issues. For instance, we find both Jean Bethke Elshtain and Betty Friedan, two feminists who hold diametrically opposed positions on a number of key questions, contending that feminists should acknowledge the deep significance of gender differences.[2] Moreover, some feminist scholarship of the last decade has claimed to show just how different men and women are.[3] Carol Gilligan's critically acclaimed book, *In a Different Voice*, which argues that women and men have different moral sensibilities, is a case in point.[4]

In fact, feminists who were once unequivocally committed to an equal rights approach now find themselves divided on many issues of public policy, including no-fault divorce, benefits for pregnant workers, and the rights of surrogate mothers. But these recent reappraisals of the equal rights strategy tend to stem less from an idealization of femaleness than from the realization that efforts to "mandate equality in circumstances of social inequality" can have unintended negative consequences for women.[5]

The idea of female difference now informs much feminist organizing, especially around issues such as militarization, ecology, and pornography. Eco-feminists and feminist pacifists have argued that women by virtue of their closeness to nature are in a unique position to avert ecological ruin or nuclear annihilation.[6] This thinking marks a further departure from radical feminism, which maintained that the identification of women with nature was a patriarchal concept. But, as we have seen, it is consonant with the thinking of cultural feminists like Jane Alpert and Robin Morgan.

If radical feminists defined ecology and militarization as human rather than feminist issues, this was not the case with pornography, which radical feminists attacked as early as 1969.[7] Like today's anti-pornography feminists, some early radical feminists contended that pornography caused violence against women. However, what was new about the feminist anti-pornography movement that developed in the late 1970s was the centrality of pornography to its analysis of male dominance.[8] Early radical feminists had attacked pornography, but did so along with other mass media representations of women.[9] In contrast to many of today's anti-pornography feminists, they favored boycotts and protests rather than using the legal machinery of the state to limit or eliminate pornography.[10] Nor did radical feminists—even those like Atkinson or Dunbar who were quick to define pornography as a feminist issue—identify pornography as the linchpin in women's oppression, as have some anti-pornography activists today.[11] Briefly, anti-pornography activists present a highly dichotomized view of male and female sexuality, one in which women seek reciprocity and intimacy in love-making, while men pursue power and orgasm.[12] Indeed, in current feminist indictments of pornography, maleness and femaleness appear as eternal and fixed categories—unchanging, and it would seem, unchangeable.[13]

Why, one might ask, was it that pornography became such a burning issue in this period? In part, it seems a reaction to the sexual revolution which increased women's sense of sexual vulnerability by acknowledging women's right to sexual pleasure while ignoring the risks associated with sexual exploration for women. Nor is it coincidental that the anti-pornography movement began in the late '70s, a period of intense backlash against feminism. As Ann Snitow has pointed out, feminists sustained a number of defeats in this period—the most significant the Supreme Court decision eroding women's right to abortion and the growing opposition to the ERA in state legislatures. Snitow asks if some feminists taking stock of the situation did not reason that men might be more responsive if they abandoned the ideology of gender equality for the ideology of difference.[14] There was also the hope, I think, that *women* might be more responsive to feminist arguments based on difference. By invoking traditional ideas about women's sexuality and manipulating women's anger at pornography, anti-pornography feminists hoped to unify the movement and to expand its base. For them pornography was the issue that could transcend race, class, age, sexual preference, and even ideology.[15]

But, ironically, anti-pornography feminists failed to mobilize women across those chasms, instead igniting a debate within the movement around sexuality that is only now beginning to cool down.[16] The pornography question exposed feminists' continuing disagreement over the nature and meaning of sexuality for women.[17] As we know sexuality has typically proven problematic for feminists.[18] One need only think back to that early Redstockings meeting where Atkinson and Willis disagreed over the authenticity of female desire. And although the terms of the debate have changed over the years, there are some striking parallels. Indeed many ideas associated with the current anti-pornography movement were first articulated by early radical feminists. For example, anti-pornography feminists maintain that although women may experience heterosexual sex as pleasurable, they cannot be said to consent under conditions of "compulsory heterosexuality."[19] According to this view, consent can take place only when the larger oppressive conditions no longer prevail; in other words, only after patriarchy is dismantled.[20] But this consignment of heterosexual desire to the realm of false consciousness was anticipated by The Feminists in the late '60s. Nor did anti-pornography feminists' presentation of sexuality, more specifically heterosexuality, as a domain solely of danger and victimization originate with them.

But there are crucial differences between the two periods. Even though individual radical feminists disagreed about sexuality in the pre-'75 period, the women's liberation movement as a whole was generally able to retain a stereographic view of sexuality—one which acknowledged that sexuality is for women a domain of both danger and pleasure. Thus feminists' concern with enhancing women's sexual pleasure was not typically seen as undermining the work of the anti-rape movement. In fact, this tension around sexuality was largely contained until the late '70s when the anti-pornography movement began to take shape.

But the most significant change in the post-'75 period involves the reconsideration of feminist ideas about sexuality, specifically, the problematizing of desire. In the period covered by this book it was generally assumed by radical feminists that female desire when liberated from male constraints and expectations would be untarnished by fantasies of dominance and submission. It was also assumed that one's sexuality could, with some work, be transformed into an unambiguous reflection of one's politics. But by the late '70s quite a few feminists had discovered that sexuality was neither that malleable nor so easily aligned with one's politics. The anti-pornography movement with its strictly egalitarian vision of sexuality pitched them into self-confrontation again. Some began to wonder if holding desire accountable to some abstract standard of political correctness didn't encourage us to renounce our sexuality as it is now. Nor did it seem so obvious anymore that certain sexual expressions are intrinsically liberated and others intrinsically degraded. Some even questioned what had been axiomatic for so long—that liberated sexuality requires the disentanglement of sexuality from power. Indeed, beginning in the late '70s, butch-femme roles and sado-masochism, both of which had been seen as expressions of false consciousness—were asserted as legitimate expressions of female desire.[21] By demonstrating the variety of women's sexual desires, the sex debate undermined the anti-pornography movement's contention that there is a uniformity to female desire.[22]

In the period under discussion in this book, women's differences from one another, when they were acknowledged, generally concerned sexual preference and, to a lesser extent, class. Although quite a few white women's liberationists were concerned about the relative absence of women of color in the feminist movement, their attempts at outreach too often remained token in nature. Indeed, the mad, last-minute scramble for a "black feminist" or a "woman of color" that characterized many feminist conferences and gatherings suggests that discussions of race were seen as both obligatory and peripheral. In stark contrast to lesbianism, race remained tokenized. But this has changed dramatically in the 1980s as growing numbers of women of color have become involved in the women's movement and have challenged the movement's silencing of women's differences. In fact, race has become as pivotal an issue as lesbianism was in the early and mid-'70s.

Of course, from the early days of the movement there were black women like Florynce Kennedy, Frances Beale, Cellestine Ware, and Patricia Robinson who tried to show the connections between racism and male dominance. But most politically active black women, even if they criticized the black movement for sexism, chose not to become involved in the feminist struggle. Efforts to generate a black feminist movement, which date back to 1973 with the founding of the short-lived National Black Feminist Organization, were less than successful.[23] Some attribute the

NBFO's demise to its inability to reach any workable consensus around what constituted a black feminist politic.[24] However, the organization suffered not only from internal factiousness, but also from its inability to mobilize black women around feminist issues. At its peak, in fact, the NBFO had no more than 400 members. Why is it that women of color are now joining a movement that in the past they had dismissed as diversionary and irrelevant to their struggles? Diane Lewis contends that as some blacks became upwardly mobile as a result of the civil rights movement, they moved into a public arena characterized by gender inequality.[25] Examining the comparative status of black men and women in education, employment, and elected political office, Lewis finds black women falling behind black men. Lewis suggests that this development, coupled with men's domination of the black freedom movement, has undermined the tradition of egalitarianism in the black community and eroded the centrality of black women in black public life. It has also, she argues, made black women more responsive to feminism. Lewis's argument is persuasive, although it fails to account for the growing presence of Asian and Hispanic women in the women's movement. Certainly it seems that the efforts of Audre Lorde, Cherríe Moraga, Barbara and Beverly Smith, and Bell Hooks, among others, have been crucial in remaking the women's movement so that it better addresses the needs and concerns of women of color.

In the past ten years we have witnessed an explosion of writing by women of color.[26] They have decried as a "deadly metonymy" the tendency of white middle-class feminists, who after all constitute but "part of the universe of women," to "speak for the whole of it."[27] This is the point of Lorraine Bethel's acerbic poem, "What Chou Mean *We*, White Girl?"[28] In itself, there was nothing new in this since black women, in particular, had from the beginning criticized white feminists for assuming that their experience was universal. But what is different today is the unwillingness of women of color to cede feminism to white women. In fact, some black feminists have even argued against the formation of separate black feminist organizations. For instance, Bell Hooks argues that black feminist groups unwittingly reinforce rather than challenge "the white feminist attempt to present them as an Other, an unknown, unfathomable element."

Hooks suggests instead that women of color "re-appropriate" feminism so as to provide "all women a feminist ideology uncorrupted by racism."[29]

Women of color have also maintained (as have white socialist-feminists) that gender oppression cannot be analyzed alone, as though it were unaffected by other systems of oppression. For example, the Combahee River Collective in its influential 1977 statement argued that the major systems of oppression must be understood as "interlocking," and analyzed as such.[30] Confronted with the "simultaneity of oppressions" women of color have encouraged feminists to see that other forms of oppression—especially those relating to race and class—are for many women equally salient.[31] Women of color have also called for a revision of feminist thinking about the family, one that acknowledges that for women of color the family is not only a source of male dominance, but a source of resistance to racism as well.[32]

****

In the period since 1975 feminism has been more notable for its theoretical achievements than for its political accomplishments. There are, of course, important exceptions: women's studies programs have continued to flourish, and important legal precedents have been established, especially in the areas of comparable worth, rape, abortion, and domestic violence. Although it should be noted that the movement's reliance on the courts would seem to underscore its inability to generate mass support for its program. Fundamental to feminism's decline in the political arena has been its failure to attract large numbers of younger women. As in the '20s—a decade to which the '80s bears some resemblance—feminists have discovered that many younger women are indifferent if not hostile to the women's movement.[33] They are, in the words of one journalist, "postfeminist."[34] Why has the women's movement which so successfully voiced many women's concerns in the late '60s and early '70s failed to attract younger women? To some extent feminism is the victim of its own success. If younger women see feminism as irrelevant, it is partly because the movement has managed to change the world, especially for those white middle-class women who have traditionally made up the bulk of its ranks.

But other factors are at work as well. The "postfeminism" of this period stems in part from the recuperation of feminism (emblematized by the advertizing slogan, "you've come a long way, baby") whereby equality is presented as a fait accompli, and feminism, as a consequence, rendered an anachronism.[35] Indeed, one of the most striking developments in the post-'75 era is the marginalization of feminism, especially when compared to the visibility enjoyed by feminists in the late '60s and early '70s. Today it is not unusual to see women's issues debated as though they were unrelated to feminism. In the last ten years feminists have found themselves demoted to the rank of "special interest group." Feminism's invisibility masks how irrevocably feminism changed our political discourse. Would we find conservative presidential candidates endorsing child care or the concept of equal pay had a feminist movement not existed? Would the much-discussed gender gap even exist without a prior feminist struggle? Of course, the situation is paradoxical. Politicians' eagerness to exploit women's issues points both to the tremendous gains that have been made over the past twenty years and to the extent of feminism's recuperation.

But feminists are not entirely blameless in all this. Liberal feminists' almost exclusive focus on the ERA, an amendment which it now seems may have had more symbolic than actual value, meant that other important issues such as child care, abortion, and the feminization of poverty were given short shrift.[36] And to the extent that cultural feminists have been politically active, they have been so around issues such as peace and ecology or in the struggle to end male violence against women and its repesentation in pornography. But while there exists among women of different ages, races, classes, and sexual preferences, considerable anger about misogynist pornography, a mass-based movement has not coalesced around this issue.

Despite the diminished level of activism in this period, there have been, as I have tried to show, positive developments, which should make for a stronger feminist movement when there is a revival of activism. First, there has been a welcome reconsideration of whether women's interests are best served by deploying an ideology which affirms gender differences and presents them as natural and immutable. At the same time, there has been a growing recognition that sometimes "sex-differentiated policies are necessary to achieve gender justice."[37] Equally important, the recent emphasis on analyzing the interaction of male dominance, capitalism, racism, and systems of sexual hierarchy would seem to suggest improved possibilities for coalition politics. Furthermore, the growing frustration with prescriptive politics may prepare the way for a more truly inclusive movement, one which would embrace women regardless of their sexual preference, marital status, or sartorial taste. Perhaps most crucial of all, the new-found acknowledgment of women's differences from one another has established the precondition for a multi-class, multiracial women's movement, which can, to paraphrase Audre Lorde, transform our differences into strengths.[38]

Notes

Notes

INTRODUCTION

1. The term "the Movement" refers to the overlapping protest movements of the '60s—the black freedom movement, the student movement, the anti-war movement, and the more self-consciously political new left. Throughout the book I will use this term when referring to this constellation of radical movements; I will use "movement" when referring to the women's liberation movement solely to minimize confusion.

2. Marlene Dixon, "On Women's Liberation," *Radical America* February 1970, p. 28.

3. Ellen Willis, "Sister Under the Skin? Confronting Race and Sex," *Village Voice Literary Supplement*, #8, June 1982.

4. For examples of radical feminism, see Shulamith Firestone *The Dialectic of Sex: The Case for Feminist Revolution*, rev. ed. (New York: Bantam, 1970); Kate Millett, *Sexual Politics* (Garden City, NY: Doubleday, 1970); Ti-Grace Atkinson's collected essays, *Amazon Odyssey* (New York: Links Books, 1974); *No More Fun and Games*, the journal published by the Boston radical feminist group Cell 16; and, perhaps most important of all, the annual New York journal *Notes*. *Notes from the First Year: Women's Liberation* was published by New York Radical Women in June 1968. *Notes from the Second Year: Women's Liberation* was edited by Shulamith Firestone and Anne Koedt (assistant editor) and published in April 1970. The final edition, *Notes from the Third Year: Women's Liberation* was edited by Anne Koedt, with Anita Rapone and Ellen Levine listed as assistant editors. It appeared in 1971. The anthology *Radical Feminism*, edited by Anne Koedt, Ellen Levine, and Anita Rapone (New York: Quadrangle, 1973) was intended to be a compilation of the articles from *Notes*. However, a number of feminists—including Kathie Sarachild (Amatniek), Ros Baxandall, Shulamith Firestone, Carol Hanisch, Pat Mainardi, Irene Peslikis, and Ellen Willis—withdrew their work from the anthology when it became clear that the anthology would not include the full spectrum of radical feminist ideas, especially the pro-woman line, a position espoused by the radical feminist group Redstockings. For this reason, it is not the most accurate guide to early radical feminism. However, it does contain many classic articles. See Kathie Sarachild, "Covering Up Women's History,

An Example—Notes from the First, Second and Third Years,'' in *Woman's World*, July-September 1972. (Kathie Amatniek began using the "matrilineal name form," Sarachild, at the first national women's liberation conference in November 1968. Outside the women's movement she is known as Amatniek.) Radical feminism, as it was originally defined, has died out; however there are individual feminists whose writing has remained informed by it. See, in particular, Ellen Willis, *Beginning to See the Light* (New York: Knopf, 1981). For an interesting critique of both liberal and cultural feminism, see Redstockings, eds., *Feminist Revolution* (New Paltz: Redstockings, 1975). An expurgated and expanded version was subsequently published by Random House in 1978.

5. Shulamith Firestone and Anne Koedt used the phrase "to dare to be bad" in their editorial statement to *Notes from the Second Year* (New York: Radical Feminism, 1970).

6. Ellen Willis, "Radical Feminism and Feminist Radicalism," in Sohnya Sayres, Anders Stephanson, Stanley Aronowitz, and Fredric Jameson, eds., *The '60's Without Apology* (Minneapolis: University of Minnesota Press, 1984), p. 91; Kathie Sarachild, "The Power of History," in Redstockings, eds., *Feminist Revolution*, p. 16. Willis contends that radical feminism showed every sign of becoming a mass movement; Sarachild claims that it already was a mass movement.

7. Friedan quoted in Judith Hole and Ellen Levine, *The Rebirth of Feminism* (New York: Quadrangle, 1971), p. 92.

8. Friedan called for the strike to commemorate the fiftieth anniversary of the ratification of the Nineteenth Amendment, which mandated woman suffrage.

9. The speech did not represent a total break with the politico politic because the group believed, in contrast to radical feminists, that the women's liberation movement should continue to struggle against the war. For the Bread and Roses speech, see "Revolutionary Feminism," *Rat*, v. 3, 7, May 22–June 4, 1970. As the '70s wore on, socialist-feminism absorbed larger and larger chunks of the radical feminist analysis. See the important 1972 manifesto of the Hyde Park chapter of the Chicago Women's Liberation Union, "Socialist Feminism: A Strategy for the Women's Movement," 1972, mimeo in author's possession; Zillah Eisenstein, ed., *Capitalist Patriarchy and the Case for Socialist Feminism* (New York: Monthly Review Press, 1979); Batya Weinbaum, *The Curious Courtship of Women's Liberation and Socialism* (Boston: South End Press, 1978).

10. Major cultural feminist writings include: Jane Alpert, "Mother Right," *Ms.*, August 1973; "Rights of Passage," "Theory and Practice: Pornography and Rape," "Lesbianism and Feminism: Synonyms or Contradictions?" and "The Proper Study of Womankind: On Women's Studies," in Robin Morgan's collection of essays, *Going Too Far* (New York: Random House, 1978); Barbara Burris, "The Fourth World Manifesto" in Koedt, Rapone, and Levine, *Notes 3*; Mary Daly, *Beyond God the Father: Towards a Philosophy of Women's Liberation* (Boston: Beacon, 1973) and *Gyn-Ecology* (Boston: Beacon, 1978); Adrienne Rich, *Of Woman Born* (New York: Norton, 1976); Susan Griffin, *Woman and Nature: The Roaring Inside Her* (New York: Harper and Row, 1978); Janice Raymond, *The Transsexual Empire* (Boston: Beacon, 1979); Kathleen Barry, *Female Sexual Slavery* (Englewood Cliffs, NJ: Prentice-Hall, 1979). For my analysis and critique of cultural feminism, see "The Taming of the Id," in Carole Vance, ed., *Pleasure and Danger* (Boston: Routledge and Kegan Paul, 1984), pp. 50–72.

11. Mary Daly, *Beyond God the Father*, p. 41.

12. Rich uses the term "inner emigration" which she notes was used by Hannah Arendt to describe the retreat of many Germans during Hitler's rule into "'an interior life, . . . to ignore [the] world in favor of an imaginary world 'as it ought to be' or as it once upon a time had been.' " Adrienne Rich, "Living the Revolution," *The Women's Review of Books*, v. 3, #12, September 1986. In this article, and in her more recent work, Rich has moved away from the cultural feminist views she had propounded in the '70s. See her collected essays, *Blood, Bread, and Poetry* (New York: Norton, 1986).

13. Interview with Meredith Tax. See Appendix D for a discussion of the interviews.

14. Interview with Frances Chapman.

15. Sara Evans, *Personal Politics: The Roots of Women's Liberation in the Civil Rights Movement and the New Left* (New York: Vintage Books, 1979).

16. See, for example, Alison Jaggar, *Feminist Politics and Human Nature* (Totowa, NJ: Rowman & Allanheld, 1983); Judith Clavir Albert and Stewart Albert, eds., *The Sixties Papers* (New York: Praeger, 1984); Jean Bethke Elshtain, *Public Man, Private Woman* (Princeton: Princeton University Press, 1981); Linda Gordon, *Woman's Body, Woman's Right: A Social History of Birth Control in America* (New York: Penguin, 1976), p. 225.

17. Firestone, *The Dialectic of Sex*, p. 38.

18. Marilyn Webb, "We are Victims," *The Voice of the Women's Liberation Movement*, #6, 1969. Kathy McAfee and Myrna Wood, "Bread and Roses," *Leviathan*, #3, June 1969, reprinted in Leslie Tanner, ed., *Voices of Women's Liberation* (New York: New American Library, 1970).

19. Elizabeth Diggs, "What Is the Women's Movement?" *Women: A Journal of Liberation*, v. 2, #4, 1972, pp. 11–12.

20. The Hyde Park chapter of the Chicago Women's Liberation Union, "Socialist Feminism: A Strategy for the Women's Movement," 1972.

21. Brooke Williams, a radical feminist who was associated with the reconstituted Redstockings and was also a writer for the women's liberation newspaper *off our backs*, was the first person I know of to use the term "cultural feminism" to refer to this transmutation of radical feminism. See her essay, "The Retreat to Cultural Feminism," in Redstockings, eds., *Feminist Revolution*. Others, notably Ellen Willis, have also used the term "cultural feminism." See her excellent article, "Radical Feminism and Feminist Radicalism," in Sayres, et al., eds., *The '60's Without Apology*.

22. Harold Cruse, quoted in Clayborne Carson, *In Struggle: SNCC and the Black Awakening of the 1960's* (Cambridge: Harvard University Press, 1981), p. 228.

23. Abe Peck effectively conveys the frustration that led some radicals to drop out or to try, quite literally, to "bring the war home" in his book *Uncovering the Sixties: The Life and Times of the Underground Press* (New York: Pantheon, 1985).

24. According to army intelligence documents obtained by CBS News, approximately one in every six protestors at the August 1968 Democratic Convention in Chicago was an undercover agent. Todd Gitlin, "Seizing History," *Mother Jones*, November 1983, p. 34. Gitlin has since written that the army claim "sounds excessive." But he is quick to point out that even should the figure be inflated by a factor of five or ten, "[t]he number would still be extraordinary and its possible implications sizable, given how few provocateurs it takes to provoke a riot in a delicate situation." *The Sixties: Years of Hope, Days of Rage* (New York: Bantam, 1987), p. 323.

25. The alliance (or merger—it is not clear which it was) between SNCC and the

BPP was uneasy enough without FBI meddling. For more on this see Carson, *In Struggle*, pp. 278–86; and James Forman, *The Making of Black Revolutionaries* (Washington, D.C.: Open Hand Publishing, 1985), pp. 522–43. (Forman's book was originally published in 1972.) The conflict became lethal in early 1969 when US members killed two Panthers on the UCLA campus. (See Carson, p. 283.) Carson also describes in detail the FBI's campaign against radical black groups.

26. For an account of the FBI's surveillance of the movement, see Letty Cottin Pogrebin, "The FBI Was Watching You," *Ms.*, June 1977, p. 42; Frank J. Donner, *The Age of Surveillance: The Aims and Methods of America's Political Intelligence System* (New York: Random House, 1981), pp. 150–55. According to the files, the FBI stopped its surveillance of the women's movement in 1973.

27. The lawyer in question is Leon Friedman. See Leon Friedman, "How to Get Your File," *Ms.*, June 1977, p. 42. The movement was also targeted for surveillance by the CIA's domestic spying project, Operation Chaos. See Donner, *The Age of Surveillance*, pp. 268–75.

28. For a variety of reasons, race did not become a major issue within the women's movement until the mid-'70s. The relationship between black women and feminism is complicated and will be discussed in chapters 1 and 4. Although a 1972 Louis Harris Poll revealed that sixty-seven percent of black women as compared to only thirty-five percent of white women were sympathetic to women's liberation groups, black women initially stayed away from the women's movement. (The figures are from Bell Hooks, *Ain't I a Woman: Black Women and Feminism* [Boston: South End Press, 1981], p. 148.) This was true as well for radical black women who were often dismissive of women's liberation. Black women's indifference to the organized movement had many sources. They might have been more receptive to the movement had white feminists not maintained that male dominance was the primary and original oppression and had they not relied solely on their own experience when theorizing about women's situation. Black women's commitment to achieving racial solidarity and their skepticism about white women's commitment to eradicating racism also had a great deal to do with their decision to devote themselves to the black struggle. And not insignificant was the feeling of some black women that they did not need a women's liberation movement because they were already liberated. For instance, Joyce Ladner, a former SNCC member, argued that women's liberation was superfluous for black women because they were already "liberated from many of the constraints the society has traditionally imposed on women. Although [black women's self-sufficiency] emerged from forced circumstances, it has nevertheless allowed the Black woman the kind of emotional well-being that Women's Liberation groups are calling for." See Ladner, *Tomorrow's Tomorrow: The Black Woman* (Garden City, NY: Doubleday, 1971), p. 46. However, some recent studies have mistakenly attributed this idea that black women were already liberated to white feminists. For instance, Bell Hooks argues that the tendency to "romanticize the black female experience" originated with white feminists. Hooks, *Ain't I a Woman*, p. 6. This mistake is repeated by Sharon Holland in her working paper, " 'Which Me Will Survive?': Audre Lorde and the Development of a Black Feminist Ideology," *Critical Matrix*, Special Issue #1, Spring 1988.

29. Ellen Willis, "Radical Feminism and Feminist Radicalism," in Sayres, et al., eds., *The '60's Without Apology*, p. 91.

30. Ann Rosalind Jones, "Writing the Body: Toward an Understanding of *L'Ecriture Féminine*," *Feminist Studies*, v. 7, #2, Summer 1981, p. 255.

31. Interview with Charlotte Bunch.

32. Jane Alpert, *Growing Up Underground* (New York: William Morrow, 1981), p. 347.

33. Kathy McAfee and Myrna Wood, "Bread and Roses," in Tanner, ed., *Voices from Women's Liberation*, p. 423.

34. Shulamith Firestone, *The Dialectic of Sex*, p. 36.

35. Ibid., p. 12.

36. This point was made by Marlene Dixon, an early women's liberation activist, in her 1975 article "The Rise and Demise of Women's Liberation: A Class Analysis," in Dixon, *Women in Class Struggle* (San Francisco: Synthesis Publications, 1978). Ellen Willis made the same point in her article "Economic Reality and the Limits of Feminism," *Ms.*, June 1973.

37. For a useful history of the woman suffrage movement, see Aileen Kraditor, *The Ideas of the Woman Suffrage Movement* (Garden City, NY: Doubleday, 1971). The phrase, "the second wave of feminism" was coined by Martha Weinman Lear who wrote the first article on the resurgence of feminist activism in the mainstream press. See her article "The Second Feminist Wave," *The New York Times Magazine*, March 10, 1968.

38. Kathie Sarachild and Patricia Mainardi, "*Ms.* Politics and Editing: An Interview," in Redstockings, eds., *Feminist Revolution*, p. 172.

39. Leila Rupp and Verta Taylor, *Survival in the Doldrums: The American Women's Rights Movement, 1945 to the 1960's* (New York: Oxford, 1987), p. 6; John D'Emilio, *Sexual Politics, Sexual Communities: The Making of the Homosexual Minority in the United States, 1940–1970* (Chicago: University of Chicago Press, 1983), p. 240; Aldon Morris, *The Origins of the Civil Rights Movement: Black Communities Organizing for Change* (New York: The Free Press, 1984); Maurice Isserman, *If I Had a Hammer . . . The Death of the Old Left and the Birth of the New Left* (New York: Basic Books, 1987).

40. See Marty Jezer, *The Dark Ages: Life in the United States 1945–1960* (Boston: South End Press, 1982).

41. John D'Emilio acknowledges the "glaring and undeniable" differences between pre- and post-Stonewall gay activists. See D'Emilio, *Sexual Politics, Sexual Communities*, p. 240. Rupp and Taylor admit that "new" feminists developed a far more radical critique of American society than the feminists of the Women's Party, the focus of their study. However, they tend to de-emphasize the extent of the disjuncture between the two waves of feminist activism. For instance, they contend that "it is no coincidence that groups and individuals throughout the movement—from radical to liberal, from moderate to militant—continued to fight for passage of the ERA." (Rupp and Taylor, p. 186.) They fail to mention, however, that many radical and socialist-feminists initially opposed the ERA. See Jane Mansbridge, *Why We Lost the ERA* (Chicago: University of Chicago Press, 1986) pp. 265–66, on the opposition of some women's liberationists to the ERA. Of course, one can make a strong case for continuity between generations of liberal activists. And it is most certainly true that some of the ideas associated with the new left were first articulated by social critics such as C. Wright Mills, Paul Goodman, and Dwight MacDonald. However, I do not agree with Maurice Isserman who has argued that the new left "emerged from the Old Left in ways that made it difficult to perceive exactly where the one ended and the

other began." Although there were exceptions, the non-communist old left of the '50s remained economistic and rigidly anti-communist. Indeed, the fact that the board of the League for Industrial Democracy—the parent organization of SDS—ignored the "values" section of "The Port Huron Statement" suggests the magnitude of the generational divide separating old and new leftists. And although the rift between the old and new left certainly widened considerably during the decade, it is nonetheless true that substantial differences between the two groups arose almost immediately. This is not to say that the old left had no effect on the new. Indeed, Isserman may be right that the generational conflict between new and old leftists set the new left on "a political trajectory leading first toward 'anti-anti-communism' and then onward toward an identification with Third World Communist movements and governments." Isserman, pp. xiii, 210, 209. However, Isserman fails to acknowledge the extent to which anti-communism had become, in Alan Wald's words, "An ideological mask for discrediting movements for radical social change and supporting the status quo. . . . " See Alan M. Wald, *The New York Intellectuals: The Rise and Decline of the Anti-Stalinist Left from the 1930's to the 1980's* (Chapel Hill, NC: University of North Carolina Press, 1987), p. 6.

42. My understanding of '60s radicalism has been very much influenced by the following books and articles: Wini Breines, *Community and Organization in the New Left: 1962–1968* (New York: Praeger, 1982); Carson, *In Struggle*; Aronowitz, "When the New Left was New," in Sayres, et al., eds., *The 60's Without Apology*; James Miller, *Democracy Is in the Streets* (New York: Simon and Schuster, 1987); Richard Flacks, "Making History vs. Making Life: Dilemmas of an American Left," *Working Papers*, v. 2, #2, Summer 1972; Elinor Langer, "Notes for Next Time: A Memoir of the 1960's," *Working Papers*, v. 1, #3, Fall 1973; Carl Oglesby, "Notes for a Decade Ready for the Dustbin," *Liberation*, v. 4, #s 5 & 6, August/September 1969.

43. Interview with Mehrhof.

44. See chapter 3 for more on the protest.

45. The characterization is Ellen Willis's in "Declaration of Independence," *The Voice of the Women's Liberation Movement*, #6, 1969, p. 4.

46. When Mehrhof and Firestone were in Washington for the protest, they stopped by the headquarters of the Women's Party to talk with Paul. At one point Paul looked at them suspiciously and asked them if they were in any way connected with that weekend's protest. Not wanting to spoil the occasion, they denied any connection with it. Interview with Mehrhof.

47. Marilyn Webb, "We Are Victims," *The Voice of the Women's Liberation Movement*, 1969, #6.

48. See Nancy Cott, *The Grounding of Modern Feminism* (New Haven: Yale University Press, 1987), pp. 68–76; Rupp and Taylor, *Survival in the Doldrums: The American Women's Rights Movement, 1945 to the 1960's*, pp. 153–65.

49. For more on nineteenth- and early twentieth-century American feminism, see Aileen Kraditor, *The Ideas of the Woman Suffrage Movement*; Ellen DuBois, *Feminism and Suffrage: The Emergence of an Independent Women's Movement in America, 1848–1869* (Ithaca: Cornell University Press, 1978); Nancy Cott, *The Bonds of Womanhood* (New Haven: Yale University Press, 1977), *The Grounding of Modern Feminism*, and "Feminist Theory and Feminist Movements: The Past Before Us" in Juliet Mitchell and Ann Oakley, eds., *What Is Feminism?* (New York: Pantheon, 1986); William Leach, *True Love and Perfect Union: The Feminist Reform of Sex and Society* (New York: Basic Books, 1980); Carl Degler, *At Odds* (New York: Oxford University

Press, 1980); Judith Schwartz, *The Radical Feminists of Heterodoxy*, (Lebanon, NH: New Victoria Publishers, 1982); William O'Neill, *Everyone Was Brave* (Chicago: University of Chicago Press, 1971). I should point out that I agree with DuBois that woman suffrage was a radical demand in the nineteenth century.

50. Barbara Easton (Epstein) makes this point in her article "Feminism and the Contemporary Family," reprinted in Nancy Cott and Elizabeth Pleck, eds., *A Heritage of Our Own* (New York: Simon and Schuster, 1979).

51. In her study of the woman suffrage movement, Kraditor contended that arguments of "sameness," or what she termed "social justice," prevailed within the movement until the turn of the century when arguments of "difference," or what she called "expediency," supplanted them. However, other historians, notably William Leach in *True Love and Perfect Union*, have challenged this view. Nancy Cott, like Leach, argues that these two approaches were not seen as mutually exclusive during the first wave of feminism. Cott, "Feminist Theory and Feminist Movements: The Past Before Us" in Mitchell and Oakley, eds., *What Is Feminism?*

52. Cott, *The Grounding of Modern Feminism*, p. 42.

53. In particular, see Ellen DuBois and Linda Gordon, "Seeking Ecstasy on the Battlefield: Danger and Pleasure in Nineteenth-century Feminist Thought," in Carole Vance, ed., *Pleasure and Danger: Exploring Female Sexuality* (Boston: Routledge and Kegan Paul, 1984); Judith Walkowitz, "Male Vice and Female Virtue: Feminism and the Politics of Prostitution in Nineteenth-Century Britain," in Ann Snitow, Christine Stansell, and Sharon Thompson, eds., *Powers of Desire* (New York: Monthly Review Press, 1983); Linda Gordon, *Woman's Body, Woman's Right: A Social History of Birth Control in America* (New York: Penguin, 1976); Barbara Epstein, *The Politics of Domesticity: Women, Evangelism, and Temperance in Nineteenth-Century America* (Middletown: Wesleyan University Press, 1981); Carroll Smith-Rosenberg, "The Female World of Love and Ritual: Relations Between Women in Nineteenth-Century America," *Signs*, v. 1, #1, Autumn 1975; Esther Newton, "The Mythic Mannish Lesbian: Radclyffe Hall and the New Woman," *Signs*, v. 9, #4, Summer 1984.

54. Private conversation, Martha Vicinus, June 1988.

55. Nancy Cott, "Passionlessness: An Interpretation of Victorian Sexual Ideology, 1790–1850," *Signs*, v. 4, #2, Winter 1978, p. 233.

56. Nancy Cott, *The Grounding of Modern Feminism*.

57. Ibid., p. 49.

58. Ibid., p. 45.

59. It was Carl Oglesby who distinguished "humanist" from "corporate" liberals in his classic 1965 speech, "Trapped in a System," reprinted in Massimo Teodori, ed., *The New Left: A Documentary History* (Indianapolis: Bobbs Merrill, 1969). See Todd Gitlin's *The Sixties: Years of Hope, Days of Rage* (New York: Bantam, 1987), pp. 127–92, for a useful discussion of the new left's relationship to liberalism. Betty Friedan, *It Changed My Life: Writings on the Women's Movement* (New York: Random House, 1976), p. 153. Friedan was antagonistic to radical feminism from the beginning and rarely missed an opportunity to denounce the man-hating and sex warfare which she claimed it advocated. Her declamations against "sexual politics" began at least as early as January 1969.

60. Aronowitz, "When the New Left was New," in Sayres, et al., eds., *The '60's Without Apology*, p. 32.

61. C. Wright Mills, quoted by James Miller, *Democracy Is in the Streets*, p. 86.

62. The phrase is from SDS's founding statement, "The Port Huron Statement" which is reprinted in full as an appendix to Miller's book *Democracy Is in the Streets*, p. 333. For instance, Irving Howe, an influential member of the old left who attended a couple of SDS meetings, called them "interminable and structureless sessions." Howe, "The Decade That Failed," *The New York Times Magazine*, September 19, 1982, p. 78.

63. The statement appeared in a pamphlet produced by the Economic Research and Action Project of Students for a Democratic Society. Miller quotes it in *Democracy Is in the Streets*, p. 215.

64. See Breines's summary of prefigurative politics in *Community and Organization in the New Left*, pp. 1–8.

65. Chapter 6 contains a fuller discussion of alternative institutions.

66. For more on the prefigurative, personal politics of the '60s see Breines, *Community and Organization in the New Left*; Miller, *Democracy Is in the Streets*; Aronowitz, "When the New Left was New," in Sayres, et al., eds., *The 60's Without Apology*.

67. However, the reclamation of blackness was often articulated in a sexist fashion. For instance, in 1968 Stokely Carmichael declared, "Every Negro is a potential black man." See Stokely Carmichael, "A Declaration of War," in Teodori Massimo, ed., *The New Left: A Documentary History* (Indianapolis: Bobbs Merrill, 1969), p. 277.

68. This criticism came from some who had been involved in '60s movements. See Richard Rothstein, "Representative Democracy in SDS," *Liberation*, February 1972; and Jo Freeman's 1972 article, "The Tyranny of Structurelessness," in Koedt, Levine, and Rapone, eds., *Radical Feminism*. It was also made (although far more categorically) by others, including Irving Howe, who were quite hostile to the new left. Howe argued that participatory democracy as practiced in SDS resulted in "chaos favoring manipulation by tight little sects and grandiose charismatic leaders." Howe, "The Decade That Failed," *The New York Times Magazine*, September 19, 1982, p. 78.

69. For a spirited defense of the new left's anti-organizational impulse, although one that acknowledges its flaws, see Breines, *Community and Organization in the New Left*.

70. See Charlotte Bunch, "The Reform Tool Kit," *Quest*, v. 1, #1, Summer 1974.

71. Richard Flacks, "Some Problems, Issues, Proposals," in Paul Jacobs and Saul Landau, *The New Radicals: A Report with Documents* (New York: Vintage, 1966), p. 168. This was a working paper intended for the June 1965 convention of Students for a Democratic Society.

72. Excerpts from Jerry Rubin's book *Do It* appeared in *Rat*, v. 2, #26, January 26–February 9, 1970.

73. For instance, in her very useful book *Contemporary Feminist Thought* (Boston: G. K. Hall, 1983), Hester Eisenstein focuses primarily upon Firestone, Millett, Adrienne Rich, Nancy Chodorow, and Mary Daly.

74. See Alison Jaggar, *Feminist Politics and Human Nature*. This book has a great deal to recommend it, but it suffers from the failure to situate the women being studied within the movement. As a consequence, Jaggar occasionally misidentifies certain individuals and groups as when she refers to the politico group WITCH as a radical feminist group.

75. Gareth Stedman Jones, "From Historical Sociology to Theoretical History," *British Journal of Sociology* v. 27, #3, September 1976, p. 296.

76. The first women's liberation newsletter, *The Voice of the Women's Liberation Movement*, began publishing in 1968. And there were several journals which began publishing before 1970—New York's annual *Notes*, the Boston-based *No More Fun and Games*, and *Women: A Journal of Liberation* from Baltimore. But only *Women: A Journal of Liberation* devoted any space to movement happenings across the nation.

77. I also interviewed one man, Jesse Lemisch, whose wife, Naomi Weisstein, was too ill to be interviewed.

78. The University of Michigan has a fairly extensive collection of feminist journals and newspapers in its Labadie Collection. I also examined a variety of feminist periodicals at The Women's History Archives at Northwestern University. I have a large collection of these periodicals as well. I examined every available issue of the following newspapers and journals during the period in question: Chicago's *The Voice of the Women's Liberation Movement*; D.C.'s *Quest, off our backs* and *The Furies*; New York's *Majority Report*, the women's *Rat, Woman's World* and *Heresies*; Boston's *No More Fun and Games* and *The Second Wave; Meeting Ground* from New Paltz, New York; the Los Angeles papers *Everywoman* and *Lesbian Tide*, and the journal *Chrysalis*; Iowa City's *Ain't I a Woman*?; Baltimore's *Women: A Journal of Liberation*; Ann Arbor's *her-self*; Denver's *Big Mama Rag*; and *Ms.* magazine. I examined as many issues as I could locate of the following West Coast papers: the Bay Area's *It Ain't Me, Babe*, the spin-off paper, *The Women's Page*, the journal *Tooth and Nail*, and *Plexus; Sister* from Los Angeles; Seattle's *And Ain't I a Woman*. Finally, I looked at a number of leftist periodicals including *New Left Notes*, The *Guardian, WIN* magazine, *Hard Times*, The *Movement, Leviathan, Liberation*, and *Ramparts*. I read less systematically a number of underground papers, including the *Berkeley Barb* and *Tribe, Rat*, and the *Fifth Estate*.

79. There may well have been groups in other parts of the country that developed a body of theoretical writing. It is true that Judith Brown and Carol Giardina of Gainesville (Florida) Women's Liberation, together with Kathie Sarachild and Carol Hanisch of New York, developed an important early strand of radical feminism, the pro-woman line. But this was less a group effort on the part of the Gainesville group than a collaborative effort on the part of women from New York and Gainesville. The one exception I can think of is the 1972 manifesto "Socialist-Feminism: A Strategy for the Women's Movement," which was written by the Hyde Park chapter of the Chicago Women's Liberation Union. However, as a socialist-feminist manifesto it falls outside the purview of this study.

80. Movement veteran Kathie Sarachild made a related point in a 1975 article. Sarachild argued that in naming the journal *Notes from the First Year*, Firestone was "asserting immediate consciousness of present history, daring to take herself seriously and the present generation seriously." Sarachild, "The Power of History," in Redstockings, eds., *Feminist Revolution*, p. 18. However, I think that Firestone's awareness that they were indeed making a movement and her sense of its importance were related to the media attention that New York women's liberationists received.

81. Editorial, *It Ain't Me, Babe*, August 6–20, 1970, v. 1, #11.

CHAPTER 1

1. Robin Morgan, "Introduction: The Women's Revolution," in Robin Morgan, ed., *Sisterhood is Powerful* (New York: Random House, 1970), p. xx.

2. Sara Evans, *Personal Politics: The Roots of Women's Liberation in the Civil Rights Movement and the New Left* (New York: Vintage Books, 1979).

3. Clayborne Carson, *In Struggle: SNCC and the Black Awakening of the 1960's* (Cambridge: Harvard University Press, 1981), p. 2.

4. Stanley Aronowitz, "When the New Left was New," in Sohnya Sayres, Anders Stephanson, Stanley Aronowitz, and Fredric Jameson, eds., *The '60's Without Apology* (Minneapolis: University of Minnesota Press, 1984), p. 21. James Miller insists that participatory democracy was originally seen as a "supplement" to representative democracy, that it was only later that it was seen as supplanting representative democracy. Indeed, Miller contends that participatory democracy was not "widely discussed as an *alternative* to representative institutions" until 1965. See Miller, *Democracy Is in the Streets* (New York: Simon and Schuster, 1987), pp. 142 and 152. However, the SDS inner circle apparently conceived of participatory and representative democracy in oppositional terms at least as early as 1963. For instance, after an explosive October 1963 meeting with several SDS leaders, an exasperated Irving Howe, a prominent old leftist and editor of *Dissent*, complained that the SDS'ers contrasted participatory democracy to representative democracy "as if the two were somehow contraries." Nor does Todd Gitlin, who was among the SDS'ers present that evening, dispute Howe's characterization of their view. Irving Howe, *A Margin of Hope* (New York: Harcourt Brace Jovanovich, 1983), p. 292; Todd Gitlin, *The Sixties: Years of Hope, Days of Rage* (New York: Bantam Books, 1987), p. 172.

5. Maurice Isserman contends that SDS's evolution had a great deal to do with its troubled relationship with the LID. See Isserman, *If I Had a Hammer . . . The Death of the Old Left and the Birth of the New Left* (New York: Basic Books, 1987), pp. 202–19.

6. Ellen Kay Trimberger, "Women in the Old and New Left: The Evolution of a Politics of Personal Life," in *Feminist Studies*, v. 5, #3, Fall 1979, p. 442. See also Aronowitz, "When the New Left was New," and Miller, *Democracy*, p. 177. Early SDS'ers were strongly influenced by the radical sociologist C. Wright Mills who had advised the new left to "kick the labor metaphysic," which recognized only the working class as "*the* historic agency" of change. According to Miller, these SDS'ers were indebted to Mills, not Marx. However, not all SDS'ers agree. In 1972 Richard Rothstein claimed that participatory democracy as it was originally articulated "was largely a generalization adding up to socialism without the word." Rothstein quoted in Wini Breines, *Community and Organization in the New Left: 1962–1968* (New York: Praeger, 1982), p. 57.

7. Greg Calvert, "From Protest to Resistance," *New Left Notes*, January 13, 1967. There were, however, those in SDS who favored greater organizational coherence.

8. Aronowitz, "When the New Left was New," p. 32; Breines, *Community and Organization in the New Left*, pp. 6–7.

9. Carl Davidson quoted by Greg Calvert in "From Protest to Resistance."

10. See Miller, pp. 113–40; Isserman, pp. 202–19.

11. Rennie Davis writing in a 1964 *SDS Bulletin*, quoted in Breines, *Community and Organization in the New Left*, p. 125. For more on ERAP, see Evans, pp. 126–55;

Kirkpatrick Sale, *SDS* (New York: Vintage Books, 1973), pp. 95–150; Aronowitz, "When the New Left was New," pp. 22–24; Miller, pp. 184–217.

12. See, in particular, Carl Oglesby, "Trapped in a System," reprinted in Massimo Teodori, ed., *The New Left: A Documentary History* (New York: Bobbs-Merrill, 1969). SDS president Oglesby delivered this speech at the October 27, 1965 antiwar march in Washington, D.C. SNCC staffers were also growing understandably cynical about liberalism.

13. The figures are from Sale, *SDS*, p. 663. By the end of 1968, the SDS National Office (NO) claimed 80,000 chapter members, while SDS leader Carl Davidson put the membership at 100,000. Sale believed both figures were probably conservative since by the fall of 1968 the NO was so overwhelmed by membership applications that, in the words of one staffer, "we just stopped counting." (Sale, p. 479.)

14. The characterization of SDS as a "wedge into American society" is Greg Calvert's in "From Protest to Resistance." The second quote is from Paul Potter's speech to the April 17, 1965 March on Washington reprinted in Judith Albert and Stewart Albert, eds., *The Sixties Papers* (New York: Praeger, 1984), pp. 223. Here, SDS president Paul Potter was describing the task before the new left.

15. Barbara Epstein, "Women and the Left," *New American Movement*, Summer 1975, p. 15. Barbara Epstein wrote this article when her name was still Easton.

16. Trimberger, "Women in the Old and New Left: The Evolution of a Politics of Personal Life," p. 436.

17. Peggy Dennis, "A Response to Ellen Kay Trimberger's, 'Women in the Old and New Left,' " in *Feminist Studies*, v. 5, #3, Fall 1979, p. 452.

18. Private conversation, Paula Rabinowitz.

19. Wini Breines, "A Review Essay," *Feminist Studies*, v. 5., #3, Fall 1979, p. 504.

20. Evans, *Personal Politics*, p. 172.

21. Quoted in Evans, p. 51.

22. See Evans, pp. 188–89; Marilyn Webb, "Women: We Have a Common Enemy," *New Left Notes*, v. 3, #20, June 10, 1968, p. 15.

23. Evans, p. 140; Breines, *Community and Organization in the New Left*, pp. 123–49; Stanley Aronowitz, "When the New Left was New," p. 22.

24. Evans, p. 150.

25. Evans, p. 164.

26. Evans, p. 149.

27. Evans, p. 140.

28. Evans, p. 149.

29. Quoted in Miller, p. 101.

30. "The Port Huron Statement" is reprinted in its entirety in Miller, *Democracy Is in the Streets*. (See p. 374 for this quote.)

31. Ellen Kay Trimberger makes this point in, "Women in the Old and New Left," pp. 432–50.

32. Evans, p. 221.

33. Evans, pp. 83–101. For another account, see Mary Aickin Rothschild, "White Women Volunteers in the Freedom Summers: Their Life and Work in a Movement for Social Change," in *Feminist Studies*, v. 5, #3, Fall 1979. For a more detailed discussion of Freedom Summer, see Clayborne Carson, *In Struggle: SNCC and the Black Awakening of the 1960's*, pp. 96–129; Mary King, *Freedom Song* (New York: William Morrow, 1987), pp. 367–436.

34. Quoted in Paul Jacobs and Saul Landau, *The New Radicals* (New York: Vintage, 1966), p. 145.

35. Quoted in Evans, p. 80.

36. Quoted in Evans, p. 80.

37. Rothschild, p. 481. Alice Walker writes about interracial sexual relationships during the civil rights movement in *Meridian* (New York: Pocket Books, 1976) and "Advancing Luna and Ida B. Wells," in Mary Helen Washington, ed., *Midnight Birds* (New York: Doubleday, 1980).

38. For details about the paper, see King pp. 443–55.

39. Many feminists have mistakenly attributed the paper to Ruby Doris Smith Robinson, a black woman who was quite prominent in SNCC. For instance, Robin Morgan claimed that "Ruby Doris Smith Robinson, a young black woman who was a founder of SNCC . . . wrote a paper on the position of women in that organization." Morgan, ed., *Sisterhood is Powerful*, p. xxi. Kathie Sarachild made the same error in "The Power of History," in Redstockings, eds., *Feminist Revolution* (New Paltz: The Redstockings, 1975), p. 11. Of course, many feminists found it gratifying to believe that a black woman first raised the issue of sexual discrimination. However, Mary King contends that Robinson was quite hostile to these early feminist stirrings in SNCC. See King, *Freedom Song*, p. 454. Robinson would undoubtedly have set the record straight had she not died of leukemia in 1967 at the age of twenty-five. James Forman has written very movingly about Robinson, who was an important force in SNCC, in *The Making of Black Revolutionaries* (Washington, D.C.: Open Hand, 1985), pp. 474, 480.

40. Not everyone in the meeting was hostile. King recalls that Bob Moses (Parris), Dona Richards, Maria Varela, and Charles Cobb were among those who were supportive. King, p. 450.

41. According to Evans, Carmichael said, "The *only* position for women in SNCC is prone," (my emphasis) p. 87. In a 1977 interview with Clayborne Carson, Carmichael maintained that those staffers who raised the issue of sexual inequality wanted "to stop the movement from going towards nationalism, because they [white women] thought that they were going to be put out of the movement." Carson, p. 325n.

42. Cynthia Washington, "We Started from Different Ends of the Spectrum," *Southern Exposure*, #4, Winter 1977, p. 15.

43. Ibid.

44. Ibid.

45. King objects strongly to Evans's assertion that she and Hayden raised the issue of sex roles because they felt their *status* was deteriorating. To King it was not a matter of status; rather, they felt the organization no longer expressed their values. Perhaps the word "status" sounds too self-interested to King. However, it seems indisputable that SNCC was becoming a less comfortable place for white women by 1965, and that their position paper specifically addressed "the woman problem."

46. The term "freedom high" was pejorative. For more on this debate, see King, pp. 447, 484–505; Carson, pp. 138, 155–57; James Forman, pp. 411–32.

47. King, p. 460.

48. Forman p. 425.

49. Staughton Lynd, "The Movement: A New Beginning," *Liberation*, v. 14, #2, May 1969, p. 19. According to Lynd, the Wobblies argued for building "the new society within the shell of the old."

50. Evans, p. 169.

51. For other discussions of the important rethinking conference of December 1965 see Breines, pp. 83–98; Sale, pp. 248–52; Miller, pp. 255–59.

52. Sale, p. 248.

53. Evans, p. 161.

54. Their paper was subsequently printed in the radical journal *Liberation*, #10, April 1966, pp. 35–36. It is reprinted in Evans, pp. 235–38.

55. Evans, p. 163.

56. Interview with Webb, June 1984.

57. *New Left Notes*, v. 1, #2, January 28, 1966, p. 4.

58. Todd Gitlin, "Notes on the Pathology of the NC," *New Left Notes*, v. 1, #3, February 4, 1966, p. 4.

59. Todd Gitlin, Part Two of "Notes on the Pathology of the NC," *New Left Notes*, v. 1, #4, February 11, 1966, p. 2.

60. "December Conference Impressions," *New Left Notes*, v. 1, #3, January 28, 1966. Reprinted from the San Francisco Regional *Newsletter*.

61. As historian Clayborne Carson has argued, the concept of black power was never precisely defined. Indeed, it derived much of its power from this imprecision. As Robert Allen noted, it was convenient for its major exponent, Stokely Carmichael, to sometimes speak as a "reformer who only wanted to adjust the social system and make it work better," and on other occasions to sound "like a committed revolutionary, who sought to topple the whole system." This ambiguity also enabled moderate blacks to define black power as racial pride and uplift, and made it possible for the Nixon administration to promote black capitalism as a form of black power. See Carson, pp. 215–28; Robert Allen, *Black Awakening in Capitalist America* (New York: Doubleday, 1969), p. 247.

62. Stokely Carmichael, "What We Want," reprinted in Albert and Albert, eds., *The Sixties Papers*, p. 140. It was originally published in *Dissent*, Fall 1966.

63. Malcolm X, "The Ballot or the Bullet," in George Breitman, ed., *Malcolm X Speaks* (New York: Grove Press, 1965), p. 39.

64. Julius Lester, *Look Out, Whitey! Black Power's Gon Get Your Mama!* (New York: Grove Press, 1968), p. 10.

65. By December 1966 black power resulted in the expulsion of whites from SNCC.

66. Carmichael had been pressing for whites to organize in the white community since 1964. In fact, SNCC's first white staffer, Bob Zellner, was originally hired in 1961 to organize whites. See Carson, pp. 52–53.

67. Quoted in Carson, p. 217.

68. Greg Calvert, "A Left Wing Alternative," *Liberation*, v. 14, #2, May 1969, p. 23.

69. While it is true that black power established the right of oppressed groups to organize on their own behalf without interference from others, it is not clear that black radicals promoting black power believed that whites should be counted among the oppressed. The only evidence I have found is in Julius Lester's book *Look Out, Whitey! Black Power's Gon Get Your Mama!* p. 139. "Whites in America are dispossessed also, but the difference is that they will not recognize the fact as yet."

70. Greg Calvert, "In White America: Radical Consciousness and Social Change," in Teodori, ed., *The New Left: A Documentary History*, p. 415. Calvert delivered this speech in February 1967. Calvert was not suggesting that white radicals ignore or

abandon other stuggles. He was careful to point out that "revolutionary consciousness leads to the struggle for one's own freedom *in unity with others* who share the burden of oppression."

71. Staughton Lynd, "The Movement: A New Beginning," *Liberation*, v. 14, #2, May 1969, p. 14.

72. Quoted in Evans, p. 182. Other radical women argued that the anti-draft movement pushed women to the sidelines of radical political activity. See Webb, "Women: We Have a Common Enemy," *New Left Notes*, v. 3, #20, June 10, 1968, p. 15.

73. Evans, p. 179.

74. Staughton Lynd, "The Movement: A New Beginning," *Liberation*, v. 14, #2, May 1969, p. 15.

75. Francine Silbar, "Women and the Draft Movement," *New Left Notes*, v. 2, #12, March 27, 1967, p. 11; Heather Booth, "A Reexamination of the 'We Won't Go' Conference," *New Left Notes*, v. 2, #2, January 13, 1967, p. 3.

76. Quoted in Evans, p. 184.

77. Silbar, "Women and the Draft Movement," *New Left Notes*, v. 2, #12, March 27, 1967, p. 11.

78. New working-class theory did not originate with the American new left, but had been pioneered by French theorists Serge Mallet and André Gorz. It was introduced to the American left by Bob Gottlieb, Gene Tenney, and Dave Gilbert, SDS members and students at the New School for Social Research. Their "Port Authority Statement"—a play on "The Port Huron Statement"—was published in *New Left Notes*, February 13 and May 22, 1967. For other examples of new working-class theory, see Carl Davidson, "The Multiversity: Crucible of the New Working Class," in Immanuel Wallerstein and Paul Starr, eds., *The University Crisis Reader*, v. 2 (New York: Vintage, 1971); Greg Calvert, "In White America," in Teodori; Greg Calvert and Carol Neiman, "Where are We Heading?" *Guardian*, June 15, 1968. For discussions of new working-class theory, see, Breines, pp. 97–115; Sale, pp. 338–40; Gregory Calvert, "Review of Wini Breines' *Community and Organization in the New Left*," *Telos*, Winter 1982–83, p. 197.

79. Portions of "The Port Authority Statement" are quoted in Sale, pp. 338–39.

80. John Veneziale, "Students . . . ," *New Left Notes*, September 25, 1967, v. 2, #33, p. 8.

81. Carl Davidson, "Immunity: Student Organizing," *New Left Notes*, September 25, 1967, p. 1. It is important to note that Davidson's piece was intended as a self-dialogue on the question of student organizing. The statement I have quoted appeared as part of the preface. However, in his "afterthought," Davidson moderated this position somewhat. Later, Davidson would thoroughly repudiate new working-class theory.

82. My description here is drawn from Carl Oglesby's amusing characterization of the anti-student line in "Notes on a Decade Ready for the Dustbin," *Liberation*, v. 14, #'s5–6, August–September, 1969.

83. Calvert, "Review," *Telos*, Winter 1982–83, p. 197.

84. I have taken the language from Breines's description of PL. See Breines, p. 116.

85. Calvert, "Review," p. 197.

86. Carson, p. 197.

87. Carl Davidson,"Institutional Racism," *New Left Notes*, v. 2, #39, November 13, 1967.

88. Tom Hayden, "Rebellion in Newark," excerpted and reprinted in Albert and Albert, eds., *The Sixties Papers*, p. 148. It should be noted that in this 1967 article, Hayden was more cautious than many radicals in his assessment of the riots.

89. Andrew Kopkind, "The New Left: Chicago and After," *The New York Review of Books*, September 1967.

90. Interview with Greg Calvert in *The Movement*, v. 3, #12, p. 6.

91. Staughton Lynd, "The Movement: A New Beginning," *Liberation*, v. 14, #2, May 1969.

92. Sale, pp. 418–20.

93. Quoted in James Miller, p. 205.

94. Greg Calvert, "A Left Wing Alternative," p. 21.

95. Evans, p. 153.

96. Francine Silbar, "Women and the Draft Movement," p. 11.

97. Deirdre English, Gayle Rubin, Amber Hollibaugh, "Talking Sex," *Socialist Review*, #58, July–August 1981, p. 45.

98. Marge Piercy, "The Grand Coolie Damn," in Morgan, ed., *Sisterhood is Powerful*, p. 431.

99. Barbara Epstein, "Family Politics and the New Left: Learning from Our Own Experience," *Socialist Review*, #63–64, May–August 1982, pp. 153–54.

100. Juliet Mitchell, "Women: The Longest Revolution," *New Left Review*, #40, November–December, 1966. Mitchell argues that production, reproduction, sexuality, and the socialization of children constitute the four central structures of women's situation.

101. Sale, p. 362.

102. "Liberation of Women," *New Left Notes*, v. 2, #26, July 10, 1967.

103. Evans, p. 191.

104. Don McKelvey, "Thoughts on the Convention," *New Left Notes*, v. 2, #29, August 21, 1967.

105. Evans, p. 192.

106. Evans, p. 192.

107. Arthur Waskow, *Running Riot* (New York: Herder & Herder, 1970), p. 99.

108. Rennie Davis and Staughton Lynd, "On NCNP," *New Left Notes*, v. 2, #30, September 4, 1967, p. 1.

109. My account of the NCNP conference is culled from: Waskow, pp. 99–105; Carson, p. 270; Evans, pp. 196–99. Alan Jehlen, "The NCNP Convention," *New Left Notes*, v. 2, #35, October 9, 1967; William A. Price, "Behind the NCNP Meeting," *Guardian*, v. 19, #50, September 16, 1967, p. 9; Forman, pp. 497–504.

110. Forman, pp. 501–2.

111. Carson, p. 270.

112. Quoted in Alan Jehlen, "The NCNP Convention." Todd Gitlin agreed with the Black Caucus that "the movement's momentum is mainly black," but he urged black leaders to "lead—and to encourage—white activists to do their work without catcalls." And he cautioned that "Castrated whites won't mobilize a movement worthy of an alliance." See Todd Gitlin's reflections on the NCNP in *Ramparts*, v. 6, #4, November 1967. It is curious that to both Waskow and Gitlin disempowerment suggested castration.

113. Waskow, p. 99.

114. Evans, p. 195.

115. Interview with Freeman, May 1984. While not contesting Freeman's account

of O'Hair's behavior at the NCNP, Ros Baxandall paints a more complex picture of O'Hair. Baxandall contends that O'Hair was "a fifties eccentric" who took progressive stands on race, abortion, birth control, and sexuality. Personal communication, Baxandall, August 1988.

116. Interview with Freeman, May 1984.

117. Price, p. 9.

118. Transcript of the Sandy Springs Conference, August 1968. Evans repeats it on pp.198–99. Freeman is the speaker here. Interview with Freeman.

119. "Chicago Women Form Liberation Group," *New Left Notes*, v. 2. #39, November 13, 1967, p. 2.

CHAPTER 2

1. Kathie Sarachild, "The Men's Page," *Woman's World*, v. 1, #2, July–August, 1971, p. 22.

2. Throughout the book when I am speaking of the nonreformist wing of the women's movement (e.g., both politicos and radical feminists) I will call it the "women's liberation movement" and I will call its participants "women's liberationists." However, when discussing the period between the fall of 1967 and the summer of 1968, when the use of the term "women's liberation" was still debated, I will refer to them also as "radical women" for that is how they often referred to themselves. As one might suspect, the problems of terminology do not end here. Both Marilyn Webb and SDS Inter-Organizational Secretary Bernardine Dohrn called leftist women like themselves "politicos"—Webb in the June 1968 issue of *New Left Notes* and Dohrn in the March 8, 1969 issue of the same paper. However, the term "politico" was not universally embraced by left feminists. Indeed, many politicos were identifying themselves as women's liberationists by 1969. Neither were all "feminists" especially delighted with that label for it failed to distinguish them from the liberal wing of the movement. Despite the fact that "radical feminism" did not enter the vocabulary until the summer of 1968 and remained theoretically inchoate until 1969, I will refer to the "feminists" as "radical feminists," or simply as "feminists."

3. Interview with Ellen Willis.

4. Robin Morgan, *Sisterhood is Powerful* (New York: Random House, 1970), p. xiv. Morgan wrote this after repudiating the politico position. This observation was not limited to die-hard radical feminists. For instance, Marlene Dixon criticized the opportunistic way that politicos regarded women's liberation. Dixon, "On Women's Liberation," *Radical America*, February 1970, p. 28.

5. Interview with Jo Freeman.

6. Marlene Dixon, "On Women's Liberation," p. 28.

7. Private communication, Ellen Willis, 1980.

8. Interview with Jo Freeman.

9. Interview with Jo Freeman.

10. Kathie Sarachild, "Going for What We Really Want," in Redstockings, eds., *Feminist Revolution* (New Paltz: Redstockings, 1975), p. 145.

11. Interview with Amy Kesselman.

12. Interview with Cindy Cisler.

13. This newsletter was published from March 1968 until March 1969. It is re-

quired reading for anyone interested in studying the movement's first year. According to Jo Freeman, the idea of a newsletter was Karen Fuqua's, but it was she who came up with its name. Freeman says that she deliberately named it *The Voice of the Women's Liberation Movement* to pre-empt the whole question of the movement's purpose.

14. Shulamith Firestone, "The Women's Rights Movement in the U.S.: A New View," in Leslie Tanner, ed., *Voices from Women's Liberation* (New York: Signet Books, 1970), p. 433.

15. Interview with Anne Forer.

16. Interview with Amy Kesselman.

17. Although Baxandall notes that as early as 1968 she and several others in the movement read, at Marion Davidson's urging, Gerda Lerner's *The Grimké Sisters* and found their example inspiring. Interview with Baxandall.

18. Firestone, "The Women's Rights Movement in the U.S.: A New View," p. 433.

19. Ibid., p. 434.

20. Marilyn Webb, "Women: We Have a Common Enemy," *New Left Notes*, v. 3, #20, June 10, 1968, p. 15.

21. Atkinson claims to have first used the term "radical feminism" publicly in a press release concerning Valerie Solanas on June 13, 1968. See Atkinson, *Amazon Odyssey* (New York: Links Books, 1974), p. 14. By 1969, most of those radical women who were not politicos defined themselves as radical feminists. Eventually some used feminism and radical feminism interchangeably because they believed that feminism was by definition radical.

22. Interview with Bunch.

23. Webb, "Women: We Have a Common Enemy."

24. Heather Booth, Sue Munaker, and Evelyn Goldfield, "Women in the Radical Movement," mimeo from Tobey Klass's files. The piece was written for *Ramparts* in response to its first article on women's liberation.

25. Ibid.

26. Shulamith Firestone, "The Jeannette Rankin Brigade: Woman Power?" in Firestone, ed., *Notes from the First Year: Women's Liberation* (New York: New York Radical Women, June 1968). Hereafter referred to as *Notes 1*.

27. Passage quoted in Ibid. According to Barbara Leon, Firestone wrote the leaflet from which this is taken. Leon, "Separate to Integrate" in Redstockings, eds., p. 140.

28. Ibid.

29. Quoted in Warren Hinckle and Marianne Hinckle, "A History of the Rise of the Unusual Movement for Women Power in the United States 1961–1968," *Ramparts*, v. 6, #7, February 1968, p. 28. Friedan repeats this in *It Changed My Life* (New York: Norton, 1985), p. 101.

30. Nancy Zaroulis and Gerald Sullivan, *Who Spoke Up? American Protest Against the War in Vietnam 1963–1975* (Garden City, NY: Doubleday, 1984), p. 150; *New York Times*, January 16, 1968, p. 1.

31. Pam Allen, "beyond a . . . feminist stance," *Guardian*, January 27, 1968, p. 2.

32. Ibid.

33. Firestone, "The Jeannette Rankin Brigade: Woman Power?" in *Notes 1*. The whole leaflet is reprinted in Redstockings' *Feminist Revolution*.

34. Quoted in Heather Booth, Sue Munaker, and Evelyn Goldfield, "Women in the Radical Movement," mimeo.

35. Firestone, "The Jeannette Rankin Brigade: Woman Power?"

36. Interview with Baxandall. Recently, a number of feminist scholars have turned their attention to "motherist movements." See, for example, Amy Swerdlow, "Ladies' Day at the Capitol: Women Strike for Peace Versus HUAC," *Feminist Studies*, v. 8, #3, Fall 1982.

37. Interview with Bunch.

38. Judith Hole and Ellen Levine, *Rebirth of Feminism* (New York: Quadrangle Books, 1971), p. 118.

39. Firestone, "The Jeannette Rankin Brigade: Woman Power?"

40. Pam Allen, "beyond a . . . feminist stance," p. 2.

41. It was first published as "Call for a Spring Conference," in the March 1968 issue of *The Voice of the Women's Liberation Movement*, hereafter referred to as *VWLM*. An expanded version of the piece was later printed in the June 10, 1968 issue of *New Left Notes* and was re-titled "Women: We Have a Common Enemy."

42. Webb did not credit Dohrn and Jaffe with this observation. The original quote did not contain the words "for example," thus suggesting that this was the sole strategy. The Dohrn and Jaffe article, "The Look is You" was originally published in the March 18, 1968 issue of *New Left Notes*.

43. Webb, "Call for a Spring Conference."

44. Webb, "Women: We Have a Common Enemy."

45. Webb, "Call for a Spring Conference."

46. Webb, "Women: We Have a Common Enemy."

47. Joreen, "What in the Hell is Women's Liberation Anyway?" *VWLM*, v. 1, #1, March 1968, p. 1.

48. Anne Koedt, "Women and the Radical Movement," *Notes 1*.

49. Evelyn Goldfield, "Towards the Next Step," *VWLM*, August 1968, p. 3.

50. Ibid., p. 5.

51. Shulamith Firestone, *The Dialectic of Sex*, rev. ed. (New York: Bantam, 1970), p. 33.

52. Beverly Jones and Judith Brown, "Toward a Female Liberation Movement," reprinted in Tanner, ed., *Voices from Women's Liberation*. It was subsequently published by Marlene Dixon in the Fall of 1968, then by the New England Free Press, and later by the Southern Student Organizing Committee—an SDS offshoot. Personal communication, Judith Brown, 1988.

53. Ibid., p. 393. The wording here is Brown's, but it describes Jones's contribution as well.

54. Ibid., p. 362.

55. Ibid., p. 397.

56. Ibid., p. 398.

57. Ibid., pp. 414–15.

58. Ibid., p. 411.

59. Ibid., p. 388.

60. Ibid., p. 398.

61. Ibid., p. 405.

62. Ibid., p. 400.

63. Ibid., p. 400.

64. Ibid., pp. 404–5.

65. Personal communication, Judith Brown, October 1987.

66. Ibid., p. 407.

67. Ibid., p. 407.

68. Ibid., p. 411.

69. Ibid., pp. 391, 411.

70. A number, including Firestone, Koedt, Patricia Mainardi, and Irene Peslikis were struggling to be artists.

71. As political scientist Jane Mansbridge points out, women of all classes found themselves, as members of the pink-collar ghetto, "in something like the same boat" before the women's movement. Jane Mansbridge, *Why We Lost the ERA* (Chicago: The University of Chicago Press, 1986), p. 107.

72. Interview with Amy Kesselman.

73. Jones and Brown, "Toward a Female Liberation Movement," p. 398; Interview with Jo Freeman.

74. Interview with Amy Kesselman.

75. Interview with Amy Kesselman.

76. Firestone was also listed as an editor of *Notes from the Third Year*, but as being on leave.

77. Interview with Jo Freeman.

78. Sue Munaker, Evelyn Goldfield, and Naomi Weisstein, "A Woman is a Sometime Thing," in Priscilla Long, ed., *The New Left: A Collection of Essays* (Boston: Porter Sargent, 1969), p. 270.

79. Interview with Jo Freeman.

80. Interview with Amy Kesselman.

81. Interview with Jo Freeman.

82. Interviews with Amy Kesselman and Jo Freeman.

83. Vivian Rothstein, "Women vs. Madison Avenue," *VWLM*, August 1968, p. 7.

84. See ad for the dress in *Everywoman*, v. 1, #5, July 31, 1970.

85. Munaker, et al., p. 270.

86. Interview with Amy Kesselman.

87. Evans, p. 207. The women's caucus of the SDS chapter at the University of Chicago later became the Women's Radical Action Project. WRAP received extensive press coverage for the sit-in they organized to defend sociology professor Marlene Dixon who they believed was fired from UC because of her radical politics and her gender.

88. Interview with Charlotte Bunch.

89. Interviews with Marilyn Webb and Charlotte Bunch.

90. Interview with Charlotte Bunch.

91. Charlotte Bunch, "Ourstory: DC Herstory—a working paper on the DC Women's Liberation Movement 1968–71," compiled for a May 1971 retreat, mimeo, p. 2.

92. Ibid., p. 1.

93. Interview with Marilyn Webb.

94. Bunch, "Ourstory," p. 2.

95. Interview with Frances Chapman.

96. Interview with Ros Baxandall.

97. Interview with Ellen WIllis.

98. Interview with Ros Baxandall.

99. Kathie Sarachild, "The Civil Rights Movement: Lessons for Women's Liberation," 1983 speech at the University of Massachusetts at Amherst, p. 4.

100. Faye Levine, "The Myth of Docility," in Redstockings, eds., p. 59.

101. Shulamith Firestone, *The Dialectic of Sex*, p. 29; interview with Jo Freeman.

102. Interview with Ellen Willis.

103. Interview with Ros Baxandall.

104. Interview with Minda Bikman.

105. Interview with Jo Freeman.

106. Interview with Cindy Cisler.

107. Interview with Carol Hanisch.

108. Interviews with Cindy Cisler and Irene Peslikis.

109. The following women are among those who attended NYRW meetings before July 1968: Pam Allen, Kathie Sarachild, Kathie Barrett, Ros Baxandall, Miriam Boxer, Joan Brown, Sandy Burakoski, Cindy Cisler, Corinne Coleman, Marion Davidson, Peggy Dobbins, Judith Duffett, Pat Fineran, Shulamith Firestone, Florika, Dinky Forman (married to James Forman of SNCC and daughter of Jessica Mitford), Anne Forer, Jennifer Gardner, Beverly Grant, Carol Hanisch, Eve Hinderer, Ruth Hirshberger, Anne Koedt, Lynn Laredo, Liz Levy, Pearl Oil, Alice Robinson, Ellen Shatter, Susan Silverman, Elizabeth Sutherland, and Judy Thibeau (aka Gabree). Between July and that fall they were joined by: Sheila Cronan, Linda Feldman, Elizabeth Fisher, Cynthia Funk, Ruth Glass, Joanne Hoit, Pam Kearon, Helen Kritzler, Joan Lester, Marilyn Lowen, Joyce McDonald, Patricia Mainardi, Barbara Mehrhof, Kate Millett, Robin Morgan, Marge Perry, Irene Peslikis, Margaret Polatnik, Linda Weber Popper, Ingrid Rice, Alix Kates Shulman, and Ellen Willis, among others. A lot of people came very occasionally, including—Susan Brownmiller and the poet Jean Boudin, who is married to leftist lawyer Leonard Boudin and whose daughter, Kathy, joined Weatherman.

110. Interview with Marilyn Webb.

111. Interview with Ros Baxandall.

112. Interview with Ros Baxandall.

113. "Interview with Pam Allen and Julius Lester," May 5, 1968, p. 6. Xerox in file with *Notes 1* at the Women's History Archives at Northwestern University.

114. Ibid., p. 5.

115. Interview with Ellen Willis.

116. Interview with Ellen Willis.

117. Interview with Ellen Willis.

118. Florika, "Towards Strategy," in *VWLM*, v. 1, #3, October 1968, p. 2.

119. Marilyn Lowen, "Women Can Liberate Themselves and Destroy Capitalism Too . . . yup," xerox in Tobey Klass's files of the November 1968 Lake Villa Conference, p. 2.

120. Ibid., pp. 1, 5.

121. Kathie Sarachild, "The Power of History," in Redstockings, eds., p. 17.

122. Ellen Willis, "Sequel: Letter to a Critic," reprinted in Firestone and Koedt, eds., *Notes 2*, p. 57. Willis wrote this letter in response to a woman who had taken exception to her February 15, 1969 *Guardian* article. The *Guardian* did not print Willis's rejoinder.

123. See Bernardine Dohrn, "Toward a Revolutionary Women's Movement," *New Left Notes*, v. 4, #9, March 8, 1969.

124. Interview with Cindy Cisler.

125. Carol Hanisch, " 'Hard Knocks': Working in a Mixed (Male-Female) Movement Group," in Firestone and Koedt, eds., *Notes 2*, pp. 61–62.

126. Willis, "Sequel: Letter to a Critic," p. 57.

127. August 1968 Sandy Springs Conference transcript. The speaker is not noted, but was probably a member of NYRW.

128. Deirdre English discusses this in "The Impasse of Socialist Feminism," *Socialist Review*, #79, January–February 1985, p. 99

129. Firestone, *The Dialectic of Sex*, p. 38.

130. Florika, "Towards Strategy," *VWLM*, v. 1, #3, October 1968, p. 2.

131. As Ellen DuBois has argued, however, it was the antifeminism of the radical Republicans that led woman suffragists to briefly ally themselves with racist Democrats. Ellen DuBois, *Feminism and Suffrage: The Emergence of an Independent Women's Movement in America, 1848–1869* (Ithaca: Cornell University Press, 1978).

132. August 1968 Sandy Springs Conference transcript.

133. Hanisch, p. 62.

134. Kathie Sarachild for NYRW protesting SCEF's advocacy of all-women's groups to work on nonfeminist issues. Originally printed in NY Women's Liberation newsletter, May 1, 1969. Quoted in Redstockings, eds., p. 141.

135. Willis, "Women and the Left," pp. 55, 58.

136. Private communication, Carol Hanisch, 1985.

137. Kathy McAfee and Myrna Wood, "Bread and Roses," reprinted in Tanner, ed., p. 423. It was originally published in June 1969.

138. Interviews with Irene Peslikis and Ros Baxandall.

139. Interview with Ros Baxandall.

140. Interview with Irene Peslikis.

141. Ellen Willis, "Radical Feminism and Feminist Radicalism," in Sayres, et al., eds., p. 94.

142. Ellen Willis, "Sequel: Letter to a Critic," p. 58.

143. Group Interview #1.

144. Firestone, *The Dialectic of Sex*, p. 38.

145. Interview with Ellen Willis. See Carol Hanisch, "The Personal is Political," in *Notes 2*, p. 77.

146. "Interview with Pam Allen and Julius Lester," May 5, 1968, p. 4. Barbara Leon makes a similar point in her article "Separate to Integrate," in Redstockings, eds., p. 140. However, she characterizes Allen's view as "liberal therapeutic."

147. "Interview with Pam Allen and Julius Lester," May 5, 1968, p. 5.

148. Interview with Helen Kritzler.

149. Group Interview I.

150. Interview with Amy Kesselman.

151. Quotations on consciousness-raising taken from the self-description of "The New York Consciousness Awakening Women's Liberation Group," in a handout from the Lake Villa Conference of November 1968 entitled "Who We Are: Descriptions of Women's Liberation Groups." Xerox from Tobey Klass's files.

152. Ibid. See also, Kathie Sarachild, "A Program for Feminist 'Consciousness-Raising,' " in Firestone and Koedt, *Notes 2*, pp. 78–79.

153. Interview with Anne Forer. See Kathie Sarachild, "Consciousness-Raising: A Radical Weapon," in Redstockings, eds., p. 132. Sarachild's version of this meeting differs somewhat from Forer's. In Sarachild's account, Forer already understands some of the ways women are oppressed.

154. Interview with Anne Forer.

155. Sarachild, "Consciousness-Raising: A Radical Weapon," in Redstockings, eds., p. 132.

156. "The New York Consciousness Awakening Women's Liberation Group," in a handout from the Lake Villa Conference of November 1968; Redstockings, eds., p. 184. In the summer of 1968, several months after NYRW had undertaken consciousness-raising, Sarachild read about the Chinese practice of "speaking bitterness" in William Hinton's *Fanshen*. Personal communication, Sarachild, August 1988.

157. Interview with Irene Peslikis.

158. Sarachild, "Consciousness-Raising: A Radical Weapon," in Redstockings, eds., p. 132.

159. Ibid., p. 135.

160. Peggy Dobbins wanted to transform NYRW into a study group that would explore matriarchy and the biological differences between the sexes. When Dobbins was unable to persuade the group to re-orient itself, she and a few others set up a study group outside of NYRW.

161. Marlene Dixon, "On Women's Liberation," *Radical America*, February 1970, p. 28.

162. Group Interview I.

163. Group Interview I.

164. *Chairman Mao Talks to the People*, Stuart Schram, ed. (New York: Pantheon, 1974), pp. 120, 210.

165. Interview with Irene Peslikis. But note that in "Resistances to Consciousness," Peslikis argued, "Even formal education in Marxism-Leninism tends to make people think they know more than they really know. When we think of what it is that politicizes people it is not so much books or ideas but experience." See Tanner, ed., p. 235.

166. Interview with Ros Baxandall.

167. Interview with Pam Kearon.

168. Private communication, Jean Tepperman.

169. Kathie Sarachild, "Consciousness-Raising: A Radical Weapon," in Redstockings, eds., p. 136.

170. Carol Hanisch, "The Personal is Political," in Firestone and Koedt, *Notes 2*, p. 76.

171. Napalm is a petroleum jelly product which sticks to everything it touchs, including human flesh. It burns at a temperature of 1000 F, and the Vietnamese unlucky enough to encounter it were horribly scarred and crippled.

172. Sarachild, quoted in Barbara Leon, "Separate to Integrate," in Redstockings, eds., p. 141.

173. Interview with Ros Baxandall.

174. Friedan, *It Changed My Life*, p. 163. See also, Gail Paradise Kelly, "Women's Liberation and Cultural Revolution," *Radical America*, February 1970; McAfee and Wood, "Bread and Roses," Tanner, ed.

175. See Hanisch, "The Personal is Political"; and Irene Peslikis, "Resistances to Consciousness," in Firestone and Koedt, eds., *Notes 2*, p. 76.

176. Sarachild, "Consciousness-Raising: A Radical Weapon," in Redstockings, p. 135.

177. Group Interview II.

178. Group Interview II.

179. Hanisch, "The Personal is Political," in *Notes 2*, p. 76.

180. Interviews with Carol Hanisch and Ros Baxandall.

181. Pamela Allen, "Free Space," in Anne Koedt and Shulamith Firestone, *Notes*

from the Third Year: Women's Liberation, (New York: New York Radical Feminists, 1971).

182. Ibid.

183. Sarachild, "Consciousness-Raising: A Radical Weapon," in Redstockings, eds., p. 135.

184. Interview with Ros Baxandall.

185. Interview with Ellen Willis.

186. Firestone, p. 39.

187. Group Interview I.

188. Sarachild, "A Program for Feminist 'Consciousness-Raising,' " p. 80. Some effort apparently was made to discuss class and race in NYRW. Baxandall, personal communication, August 1988.

189. Sarachild, "Consciousness-Raising: A Radical Weapon," in Redstockings, eds., p. 134.

190. Interview with Carol Hanisch.

191. Interview with Ann Snitow.

192. Interview with Ann Snitow. While with NYRF Snitow helped a number of groups get started, thus the reference to visiting groups.

193. Ellen Willis, "Sisters Under the Skin? Confronting Race and Sex," *Village Voice Literary Supplement*," #8, June 1982, p. 11.

194. Interview with Ann Snitow.

195. Willis, "Sisters Under the Skin?"

196. Interview with Ann Snitow.

197. Interview with Pam Kearon.

198. Carol Hanisch, "The Personal is Political," in Firestone and Koedt eds., *Notes 2*, p. 76.

199. Ibid.

200. Ellen Willis, "Up from Radicalism: A Feminist Journal," *US* Magazine, 1969.

201. Interview with Pat Mainardi.

202. Personal communication, Ellen Willis.

203. Carol Hanisch, "A Critique of the Miss America Protest," in Firestone and Koedt eds., *Notes 2*, p. 86.

204. Charlotte Curtis, "Miss America Pagaent is Picketed by 100 Women," *New York Times*, September 8, 1968.

205. Ibid.

206. Ibid.

207. Judith Duffett, "Atlantic City Is a Town with Class—They Raise Your Morals While They Judge Your Ass," *VWLM*, v. 1, #3, October 1968.

208. Ibid.

209. Friedan, *It Changed My Life*, p. 108.

210. Group Interview I; Curtis.

211. Curtis.

212. Group Interview I.

213. For instance, Robin Morgan correctly labeled the bra-burning a media fiction. Yet she did not explain to her readers that they had indeed planned to burn a bra.

214. Duffett, "Atlantic City"; for more on NBC's blackout see Jack Gould, *New York Times*, September 9, 1968.

215. Dobbins was held on $1,000 bail, and faced a two-to-three year sentence for her protest before the charges were dropped.

216. Hanisch, "A Critique of the Miss America Protest," in Firestone and Koedt, eds., *Notes 2*, p. 87.

217. Interview with Baxandall (Group I).

218. Group Interview I.

219. Hanisch, "A Critique," p. 87.

220. Duffett, "Atlantic City."

221. "No More Miss America: Ten Points of Protest," in Robin Morgan, ed., *Sisterhood is Powerful*, p. 522.

222. Hanisch, "A Critique," p. 87.

223. Ibid., p. 87.

224. Duffett, "Atlantic City."

225. Duffett, "Atlantic City."

226. Interview with Ros Baxandall.

227. Interview with Carol Hanisch.

228. Robin Morgan, *Going Too Far* (New York: Random House, 1978), p. 72.

229. "Who We Are: Descriptions of Women's Liberation Groups," handout from the Lake Villa Conference, November 1968.

230. WITCH statement in the 1969 "Female Liberation Newsletter" out of Boston.

231. Robin Morgan, *Going Too Far*, p. 72. Indeed, in the aforementioned 1969 statement, WITCH took credit for a number of "invisible actions" including the "snuffing out of Lurleen Wallace," wife of Alabama Governor George Wallace who had recently died of breast cancer.

232. Interview with Ellen Willis.

233. Ibid., p. 74.

234. Interview with Cindy Cisler.

235. Interview with Carol Hanisch.

236. Robin Morgan, *Going Too Far*, p. 74.

237. Ibid., p. 74.

238. Interview with Baxandall.

239. The term is Corinne Coleman's. However, Coleman maintains that the problem was not so much group size, but the sectarian left women. Morgan disagrees. *Going Too Far*, p. 71.

240. Interview with Pat Mainardi.

241. Interview with Pat Mainardi.

242. Carol Hanisch, "The Liberal Takeover of Women's Liberation," in Redstockings, eds., p. 128.

243. Group Interview II.

244. Interview with Pat Mainardi.

245. Group Interview II, specifically, Irene Peslikis, Anne Forer, and Corinne Coleman.

246. Carol Hanisch, "The Liberal Takeover of Women's Liberation," in Redstockings, eds., p. 128.

247. Group Interview.

248. Interview with Pat Mainardi.

249. Group Interview.

250. Interview with Barbara Mehrhof.

251. Interview with Pat Mainardi.

CHAPTER 3

1. Marilyn Salzman Webb, "Call for a Spring Conference," *Voice of the Women's Liberation Movement*, v. 1, #1, March 1968, p. 4. (Hereafter referred to as *VWLM*.)

2. Florika, "Towards Strategy," *VWLM*, v. 1, #3, October 1968, p. 2. According to Brown, she and Beverly Jones were involved in the initial organizing for the Sandy Springs meeting. They met in the Baltimore-D.C. area with Marilyn Webb of D.C. and Dee Ann Pappas of Baltimore in late June/early July. Brown and Pappas had been high-school friends in Gainesville. Personal communication, Judith Brown, 1987.

3. Interview with Hanisch.

4. Transcript of Sandy Springs meeting.

5. Transcript of Sandy Springs meeting, pp. 25–27.

6. Transcript of Sandy Springs meeting, p. 16.

7. Transcript of Sandy Springs meeting, p. 16.

8. Interview with Charlotte Bunch, June 1984. Bunch didn't attend the conference, but a number of her friends did go to Sandy Springs.

9. Valerie Solanas, *SCUM Manifesto* (New York: Olympia Press, 1968). Excerpts from *SCUM* are reprinted in Robin Morgan, ed., *Sisterhood is Powerful* (New York: Random House, 1970).

10. Very little has been written on Solanas. See Vivian Gornick's "Introduction" to the Olympia Press edition of *SCUM*; Andy Warhol and Pat Hackett, *POPism* (New York: Harcourt Brace Jovanovich, 1980), pp. 271–79.

11. Interview with Ros Baxandall.

12. Interview with Marilyn Webb.

13. Transcript of Sandy Springs meeting, p. 34.

14. Transcript of Sandy Springs meeting, p. 37.

15. Transcript of Sandy Springs meeting, p. 34.

16. Hanisch maintains that the pro-woman faction favored contacting black women. Interview with Carol Hanisch. Ros Baxandall corroborates this. Personal communication, Baxandall, August 1988.

17. Transcript of Sandy Springs meeting, p. 36.

18. I say "apparently" because the transcript ends at about the point that this suggestion was made. Transcript of Sandy Springs meeting, p. 38.

19. The following are recent works that grapple with the issue of black women's relationship to feminism: Bell Hooks, *Ain't I a Woman: Black Women and Feminism* (Boston: South End, 1981); *Conditions: Five, The Black Women's Issue*, 1979; Gloria Joseph and Jill Lewis, *Common Differences: Conflicts in Black and White Feminist Perspectives* (New York: Doubleday/Anchor, 1981); Paula Giddings, *When and Where I Enter: The Impact of Black Women on Race and Sex in America* (New York: Bantam Books, 1985); Ellen Willis, "Sisters Under the Skin? Confronting Race and Sex," *Village Voice Literary Supplement*, #8, June 1982; Diane Lewis, "A Response to Inequality: Black Women, Racism and Sexism," *Signs* v. 3, #2, 1977, pp. 339–61; Cherrie Moraga and Gloria Anzaldua, eds., *This Bridge Called My Back: Writings by Radical Women of Color* (Watertown, MA: Persephone Press, 1981); Barbara Smith, ed., *Home Girls: A Black Feminist Anthology* (New York: Kitchen Table Press, 1983); Alice Walker, *In Search of Our Mothers' Gardens* (New York: Harcourt Brace Jovanovich, 1983); Angela Davis, *Women, Race and Class* (New York: Random House, 1981).

20. SNCC, "Black Women's Liberation," *Women: A Journal of Liberation*, v. 1,

#2, Winter 1970. Authorship of this article is attributed to SNCC, but it is clearly an early draft of SNCC staffer Frances Beale's, "Double Jeopardy: To Be Black and Female," which was published in Morgan's, *Sisterhood is Powerful*, pp. 340–53. According to historian Clayborne Carson, Beale directed the Third World Women's Alliance, the only successful SNCC project in the early '70s. See Carson, *In Struggle: SNCC and the Black Awakening of the 1960's* (Cambridge: Harvard University Press, 1981), p. 296. For other early expressions of black feminism, see "Birth Control Pills and Black Children: The Sisters Reply," and Patricia Robinson, "Poor Black Women," both of which are reprinted in Judith Clavir Albert and Stewart Albert, eds., *The Sixties Papers* (New York: Praeger, 1984), pp. 478–83; Gloria Martin, "Women, Organize Your Own Fighting Forces!" *The Movement*, November 1967 (excerpted in Redstockings, eds., *Feminist Revolution* (New Paltz: The Redstockings, 1975), p. 11; Toni Cade, ed., *The Black Woman: An Anthology* (New York: New American Library, 1970); Joyce Ladner, *Tomorrow's Tomorrow* (New York: Anchor Books, 1972). Michele Wallace's, *Black Macho and the Myth of the Superwoman* (New York: Warner Books, 1978) is also essential reading.

21. Davis is quoted in Giddings, *When and Where I Enter*, p. 316.

22. Julia Herve, "*Black Scholar* Interviews Kathleen Cleaver," *Black Scholar*, December, 1971, p. 56. Herve is Richard Wright's daughter.

23. Frances Beale, "Double Jeopardy: To Be Black and Female," in Morgan, ed., *Sisterhood is Powerful*, p. 343.

24. Ellen Willis, "Sisters Under the Skin? Confronting Race and Sex," *Village Voice Literary Supplement*, #8, June 1982, p.11.

25. Transcript of Sandy Springs meeting, p. 38. I say "regrettably" because given the context, it strikes me that the word, "muddied," reflects an unconscious racism on the part of the speaker.

26. Interview with Helen Kritzler.

27. Interview with Helen Kritzler.

28. Interview with Bunch.

29. Conference Summary, from Tobey Klass's files. See also, Judith Hole and Ellen Levine, *The Rebirth of Feminism* (New York: Quadrangle, 1971), p. 130.

30. One of the women involved contends that it was a good thing the media were excluded because this allowed some California women whose boyfriends were in jail as a result of their activities in the Resistance to admit that their imprisonment actually gave them the space to be themselves. Of course, they would never have discussed this had they thought it would be reported. Bunch mentioned the issue of surveillance as a factor. Interview with Bunch.

31. Conference Summary.

32. Warren and Marianne Hinckle, "A History of the Rise of the Unusual Movement for Women Power in the United States 1961–1968," *Ramparts*, v. 6, #7, February 1968. Shortly thereafter the following article appeared in the mainstream press: Martha Weinman Lear, "The Second Feminist Wave," *New York Times Magazine*, March 10, 1968, pp. 24ff.

33. Maurine Ness, letter to the editor, *Ramparts*, v. 6, #9 & 10, May 1968, p. 4.

34. Ibid., p. 31.

35. Evelyn Goldfield (with Sue Munaker and Heather Booth), "Women in the Radical Movement," written for *Ramparts* in response to their issue on the women's movement. *Ramparts* declined to print their letter, but it did print several critical letters, including those from Jo Freeman, Abby Rockefeller, and historian William

O'Neill. Interestingly, Jeannette Rankin wrote a letter praising the article. Many women's liberationists were particularly angry with Marilyn Webb who was listed as a reporter for the story. A comparison of this article with Webb's February 1968 *New Left Notes* piece reveals some similarities, especially regarding radical women's preference for "colorful dress." Webb says she had no idea the article would be so denigrating. But her association with the piece no doubt reinforced New York radical feminists' opinion of her as an "arch politico."

36. Marlene Dixon, "On Women's Liberation," *Radical America*, February 1970, pp. 26–29.

37. Interview with Bunch.

38. Interview with Irene Peslikis.

39. Interview with Ros Baxandall.

40. Dixon, pp. 26–29.

41. Interview with Heather Booth.

42. Interview with Baxandall.

43. The earliest version of Koedt's article appeared in *Notes from the First Year: Women's Liberation* (New York: New York Radical Women, 1968). An expanded version appeared in Shulamith Firestone, and Anne Koedt, eds., *Notes from the Second Year: Women's Liberation* (New York: Radical Feminists, 1970). Hereafter referred to as *Notes 2*.

44. Interview with Amy Kesselman.

45. Baxandall's memory of the incident matches Coleman's account. Personal communication, Baxandall, August 1988.

46. Interview with Corinne Coleman. Firestone called pregnancy "barbaric" in her book *The Dialectic of Sex*, p.198.

47. My account of these workshops is based on the conference summary unless otherwise indicated.

48. Jo Freeman (also known as Joreen) wrote about the syndicate in "Violating the Reality Structure," *VWLM*, v. 1, #7, pp. 19–20.

49. There were other workshops as well. The "radical feminist consciousness-raising" workshop ran continuously throughout the conference. They described the workshop as one that would appeal to "those of us here who are feeling more and more that women are about the grooviest people around, at this stage of time, anyway, and that the seeds of a new and beautiful world society lie buried in the consciousness of this very class." Finally, there was the "Human Expression" workshop where women "expressed [themselves] through sound and movement," and the "Caste and Class" workshop which combined the proposed workshops on working-class women and professional women. The women in this workshop agreed that "women are a caste, with common problems that cross class lines," but they failed to "clarify whether those lines were generally stronger than class lines dividing women."

50. Dolores Bargowski, "Letter," *VWLM*, v. 1, #5, January 1969, p. 11.

51. Interview with Baxandall.

52. Interview with Mehrhof.

53. Ellen Willis, "Women and the Left," *Guardian*, February 15, 1969. It was reprinted in the *VWLM* and in Firestone and Koedt, eds., *Notes 2*.

54. Webb, "We are Victims," *VWLM*, v. 1, #6, p. 1.

55. Willis, "Women and the Left."

56. Ellen Willis, Barbara Mehrhof, Sheila Cronan, and Linda Feldman, "New York Women Reply," *VWLM*, v. 1, #7, p. 2.

57. Willis, "Women and the Left."

58. Interview with Webb. However, in her *Voice of the Women's Liberation Movement* article, "We are Victims," Webb's statement was highly ambiguous. She characterized voting as "a mockery of democracy and power." She then wrote that the protest was intended as a "symbolic statement of the past cooptation [sic] and the beginning of a new revolutionary struggle for liberation." She failed to mention whose co-optation and whose struggle. People's? Women's?

59. Interviews with Forer, Mehrhof, and Kritzler.

60. Willis, Mehrhof, Cronan, and Feldman, "New York Women Reply," p. 2.

61. Interview with Baxandall.

62. Webb, "We are Victims," *VWLM*, v. 1, #6,, p. 1.

63. Shulamith Firestone, "Shulie's Reply," *VWLM*, v. 1, #7, p. 1.

64. Even a number of New Yorkers wanted Firestone to tone down her speech, but she refused. Interview with Baxandall.

65. Both Webb's and Firestone's speeches were reprinted in the *VWLM*, v. 1, #6.

66. Robin Morgan, "WITCH at the Counter-Inaugural" originally appeared in *Rat* and was reprinted in Robin Morgan, *Going Too Far* (New York: Random House, 1978), p. 78.

67. Interviews with Anne Forer and Barbara Mehrhof; Jane Addams, "Factionalism Lives," in the *VWLM*, v. 1, #6, p. 10, alludes to the conflict.

68. Interview with Helen Kritzler.

69. Jane Addams, "Factionalism Lives," p. 10.

70. Shulamith Firestone, "Letter," *Guardian*, February 1, 1969, p. 12.

71. Willis, "Women and the Left."

72. Interview with Webb.

73. Willis, "Women and the Left."

74. Interview with Webb.

75. Ellen Willis, "Up from Radicalism: A Feminist Journal," mimeo in author's collection. It originally appeared in *US* magazine, 1969.

76. Interview with Webb. Baxandall, however, claims that she saw no evidence of male support for their action. Personal communication, Baxandall, August 1988.

77. Addams claimed that neither speech really addressed the action. However, Firestone's speech did refer to the destruction of voter registration cards.

78. Jane Addams, "Factionalism Lives," p. 10.

79. Webb, "We are Victims," p. 1.

80. Willis, Mehrhof, Cronan, and Feldman, "New York Women Reply," p. 3.

81. Firestone, "Shulie's Reply," p. 1.

82. Willis, Mehrhof, Cronan, and Feldman, "New York Women Reply," p. 3.

83. Firestone, "Letter." It is interesting to note that Firestone defines herself here as a member of the "New Feminists."

84. WITCH, "WITCHes Reply," *Guardian*, February 15, 1969, p. 12.

85. Willis, "Up from Radicalism: A Feminist Journal."

86. Interview with Webb.

87. Ibid.

88. Ellen Willis, "Radical Feminism and Feminist Radicalism," in Sohnya Sayres, Anders Stephanson, Stanley Aronowitz, Fredric Jameson, eds., *The '60's Without Apology* (Minneapolis: University of Minnesota Press, 1984), p. 94.

89. Quoted in Marlene Dixon, "Why Women's Liberation?" *Ramparts*, v. 8, #6, December 1969, p. 60.

90. Quoted in Sale, *SDS*, p. 526.

91. Julius Lester, "From the Other Side of the Tracks," *Guardian*, January 4, 1969, p. 13.

92. Eileen Klehr, "SDS Recognizes XX," *VWLM*, v. 1, #5, January 1969.

93. See, for example, the Weatherman position paper "You Don't Need a Weatherman to Know Which Way the Wind Blows"; Cathy Wilkerson, "Toward a Revolutionary Women's Militia"; and "Honky Tonk Woman," reprinted in Harold Jacobs, ed., *Weatherman* (New York: Ramparts, 1970).

94. Bernardine Dohrn, "Toward a Revolutionary Women's Movement," *New Left Notes*, v. 4, #9, March 8, 1969.

95. For the text of the resolution, see, "Women's Liberation," in *New Left Notes*, v. 3, #1, January 8, 1968.

96. Noel Ignatin,"Revolutionary Struggle for Women's Liberation," *New Left Notes*, v. 3, #39, December 23, 1968, p. 2. Ignatin's resolution was amended by the women's caucus. For the final text, see "Advance of Women's Struggle," *New Left Notes*, v. 4, #1, January 8, 1969, p. 8.

97. Sale, pp. 508–9; Eileen Klehr, "SDS Recognizes XX," *VWLM*, v. 1, #5, January 1969.

98. Sale, pp. 563–79; Margie Stamberg, "SDS Deals with the Woman Question," *Guardian*, June 28, 1969, p. 7; Andrew Kopkind,"The Real SDS Stands Up," *Hard Times*, #38, June 30–July 7, 1969.

99. Quoted in Sale, p. 567.

100. The RYM factions were careful to expel PL for its anti-communism so that it would not appear that communism was the issue. Kopkind, "The Real SDS Stands Up."

101. Ibid.

102. Ibid.

103. Margie Stamberg, "SDS Deals with the Woman Question."

104. Stamberg, "SDS Deals with the Woman Question," p. 10.

105. Kopkind,"The Real SDS Stands Up," *Hard Times*, #38, June 30–July 7, 1969.

106. Stamberg, "SDS Deals with the Woman Question," p. 7.

107. Richard Flacks, "Making History vs. Making Life: Dilemmas of an American Left," *Working Papers*, v. 2, #2, Summer 1972, p. 68.

108. Kathy Boudin, Bernardine Dohrn, and Terry Robbins, "Bringing the War Home: Less Talk, More National Action," originally printed in *New Left Notes*, v. 4, #28, August 23, 1969, excerpted and reprinted in Jacobs, ed., *Weatherman*, p. 176.

109. Carl Oglesby, "Notes on a Decade Ready for the Dustbin," *Liberation*, v. 4, #s 5 & 6, August/September 1969, p. 17.

110. The reference to "part-time radicalism" was made by "a daughter of the American Revolution," in "It's Just a Shot Away" [a line from the Rolling Stone's "Gimme Shelter"] *Rat*, v. 3, #4, April 17, 1970.

111. Cathy Wilkerson, Les Coleman, and Mike Spiegel, "The False Privilege," *New Left Notes*, v. 3, #31, October 7, 1968, p. 8.

112. Sale, p. 560.

113. Jacobs, ed., *Weatherman*, p. 58.

114. Shin'ya Ono, "You Do Need a Weatherman," originally published in *Levia-*

than, December 1969, excerpts reprinted in Albert and Albert, eds., *The Sixties Papers*, p. 255.

115. Staughton Lynd, "A Good Society," *Guardian*, May 18, 1968, p. 8.

116. Sources on the Black Panthers include: Clayborne Carson, *In Struggle*, pp. 278–86; Andrew Kopkind, "To Off a Panther," *Hard Times*, #60, January 12–19, 1970; Sol Stern, "The New Guerrillas: America's Black Guerrillas," *Ramparts*, v. 6, #2, September 1967. Newton and Seale were inspired by the SNCC-sponsored Lowndes County Freedom Organization in Alabama which had taken as its symbol the black panther.

117. See Sol Stern, "America's Guerrillas."

118. Bobby Seale quoted in Stern, "The New Guerrillas."

119. A number of prominent white liberals held fund-raising parties for the Black Panthers, which were satirized by Tom Wolfe in his article "Radical Chic," reprinted in *Radical Chic and Mau-Mauing the Flak Catchers* (New York: Bantam Books, 1971).

120. Kopkind, "To Off a Panther."

121. Bobby Seale interview with Robert Allen, "Panthers Sound Off: Freedom and Power Now," *Guardian*, June 1, 1968, p. 7.

122. John Jacobs, Weather leader and an author of "You Don't Need a Weatherman to Know Which Way the Wind Blows," quoted in Peter Collier and David Horowitz, "Doing It: The Inside Story of the Rise and Fall of the Weather Underground," *Rolling Stone*, September 30, 1982.

123. Andrew Kopkind, "To Off a Panther," p. 3.

124. This was the infamous gun battle that resulted in Panther Bobby Hutton's death. See Todd Gitlin, *The Sixties: Years of Hope, Days of Rage* (New York: Bantam Books, 1970), p. 350.

125. The figure is Kopkind's. The Party claimed that twenty-eight members had been killed by police or police agents between 1968 and 1969. Gitlin notes that Edward Jay Epstein disputes their claims. See Gitlin, *The Sixties: Years of Hope, Days of Rage*, p. 350.

126. Jon Grell, "Panther Conference," *Rat*, v. 2, #16, August 12–26, 1969, p. 30.

127. Bo Burlingham, "huey newton's revival meeting in oakland," *Ramparts*, v. 11, #3, September 1972.

128. Quoted in Sale, p. 590.

129. Sale, p. 591. As Sale points out, Weatherman was eventually persuaded of this.

130. Haber quoted in Perri Knize, "Anatomy of a Visionary," *Ann Arbor Observer*, March 1987.

131. Margie Stamberg, "Women at UFAF and After," *Guardian*, August 2, 1969, p. 5.

132. Haber quoted in Perri Knize, "Anatomy of a Visionary."

133. Ibid. Just before the UFAF, Eldridge Cleaver issued a statement admitting that the BPP had been guilty of male chauvinism, but pledging the Party's commitment to "purging" it from its ranks. But to Cleaver, women's liberation seemed to mean that women should be equal participants in the black struggle. And his language—references to "our women"—suggested a less than progressive view of women. See "Eldridge Cleaver on Women's Liberation," *Guardian*, August 2, 1969, p. 5.

134. "The Impasse of Socialist Feminism: A Conversation with Deirdre English, Barbara Epstein, Barbara Haber, Judy MacLean," *Socialist Review*, January–February 1985, p. 94.

135. Commenting on SDS's ultrademocratic structure, Rudd said, "I hate SDS, this weird liberal mass of nothingness." Rudd quoted in Sale, p. 599.

136. Interview with Meredith Tax.

137. Roughly 200 were injured as well. Sale, p. 613.

138. Dave Dellinger, *More Power Than We Know* (New York: Doubleday, 1975), p. 307.

139. Marge Piercy, "The Grand Coolie Damn," in Robin Morgan, ed., *Sisterhood is Powerful*, p. 426.

140. Todd Gitlin, *The Whole World is Watching* (Berkeley: University of California Press, 1980), p. 195.

141. A daughter of the American Revolution, "It's Just a Shot Away," *Rat*, v. 3, #4, April 17, 1970. Jane Alpert, who was charged with several NYC bombings, was among the *Rat* staffers.

142. For instance, Jerry Rubin argued that a "movement cannot grow without repression." *Rat*, v. 2, #26, January 26–February 9, 1970.

143. "one white woman," untitled, *Rat*, v. 3, #2, March 20–April 4, 1970.

144. Jacobs, ed., *Weatherman*, p. 143.

145. The term is Richard Flacks's in "Making History vs. Making Life," *Working Papers*, v. 2, #2, Summer 1974, p. 68.

146. Huey Newton, "Revolutionary Suicide," reprinted in Albert and Albert, eds., *The Sixties Papers*; "David Hughey Speaks," *Rat*, v. 2, #23, December 3–16, 1969.

147. Quoted in Alexander Cockburn and James Ridgeway, "Hayden: From Chicago Back to the Mainstream," *Village Voice*, June 17–23, 1981, p. 97. Hayden never went so far as to join Weatherman, but he readily conceded that he was far from immune to the sort of politic that was founded on "hate" and "mistrust." For Hayden's less than enthusiastic reaction to the Days of Rage, see Hayden, "Justice in the Streets," reprinted in Jacobs, ed., *Weatherman*.

148. Quoted in Margie Stamberg, "The New Feminism," p. 10.

149. Interview with Kesselman.

150. Richard Flacks, *Youth and Social Change* (Chicago: Markham Publishing, 1971), p. 118.

151. Barry Bluestone, letter to the editor, *New Left Notes*, v. 2, #15, April 17, 1967, p. 4.

152. Sale, p. 601.

153. Quoted in Meredith Tax and Cynthia Michel,"An Open Letter to the Boston Movement," Summer 1969, mimeo from Tax's files.

154. Interview with Meredith Tax.

155. "Honky Tonk Women," 1969 article reprinted in Jacobs, ed., *Weatherman*, p. 319.

156. Bread and Roses Collective, "Weatherman Politics and the Women's Movement," originally published in Winter 1970, reprinted in Jacobs, ed., *Weatherman*, p. 334.

157. A Weatherwoman, "War Report," *Rat*, v. 2, #28, February 23–March 7, 1970, p. 7.

158. Sale, pp. 3–5; Paul Berman, "A Change in the Weather," *Village Voice*, October 28–November 3, 1981; Collier and Horowitz, "Doing It: The Inside Story of the Rise and Fall of the Weather Underground," *Rolling Stone*, September 30, 1982.

159. Weatherman's "New Morning" statement appeared in a number of periodi-

cals, including the women's liberation newspaper *off our backs*, v. 1, #18, February 26, 1971, pp. 6–7.

160. Sale, p. 600. Immediately following the Days of Rage, Yippie leader Stew Albert declared that he would not follow the Weatherline because he was "not organizing a movement around suffering." Albert quoted in "Chicago: Weathereport," *Rat*, October 29–November 12, p. 16.

161. Sale, p. 615.

162. Carl Oglesby, "Notes on a Decade Ready for the Dustbin," p. 5.

163. Perri Knize, "Anatomy of a Visionary," *Ann Arbor Observer*, March 1987. Robert Scheer, former editor of *Ramparts*, maintains that agents played a large role in the Movement's demise. "At any one of those attempts to bring cohesion to the left, there would be the introduction of sudden madness. Some lunatic would get up and say, "Well, we shouldn't be hammering out this program, we should be blowing up the building." "America After Bob Scheer," *Berkeley Barb*, #495, February 7–13, 1975.

164. Elinor Langer discusses this in her provocative essay "Notes for Next Time: A Memoir of the 1960's," *Working Papers*, v. 1, #3, Fall 1973.

165. Piercy, "The Grand Coolie Damn," in Morgan, ed., p. 422.

166. Ibid; Robin Morgan, "Goodbye to All That," *Rat*, v. 2, #27, January 6–23, 1970.

167. Interview with Ann Snitow.

168. "The Impasse of Socialist Feminism: A Conversation with Deirdre English, Barbara Epstein, Barbara Haber, and Judy MacLean," p. 94.

169. "The Impasse of Socialist Feminism," p. 98.

170. Interview with Heather Booth.

171. Barbara Ehrenreich, "Life Without Father: Reconsidering Socialist-Feminist Theory," *Socialist Review*, #73, January–February 1984, p. 56.

172. The CWLU had a paid membership of 500 at its peak. Interview with Heather Booth. CWLU was the first of the women's unions, but Bread and Roses was the first "socialist women's liberation organization" that I know of. The Boston-based group was formed sometime in the summer of 1969.

173. Lecture by Bonnie Kay, former CWLU member, on the women's health movement, The University of Michigan, 1986; Rosalind Petchesky, *Abortion and Woman's Choice: The State, Sexuality and Reproductive Freedom* (New York: Longman Press, 1984), p. 128. According to Kay, the clinic was closed down only after a relative of one of their patients filed a complaint with the police. The police had known all along about the clinic, but chose not to bust it because the clinic was, in the words of one staffer, "providing a necessary service for policemen's wives, mistresses and daughters and for all policewomen." Quoted in Petchesky. The case against the Jane staffers was dismissed after the 1973 Supreme Court decision, *Roe v. Wade*. According to Petchesky, the one written source on Jane is Pauline Bart's unpublished manuscript, "Seizing the Means of Reproduction: An Illegal Feminist Abortion Collective, How and Why It Worked."

174. Barbara Ehrenreich, "Life Without Father," p. 49.

175. I do not mean to suggest that the demise of organized socialist-feminism was entirely the result of left obstructionism. As Barbara Haber and Barbara Epstein point out, socialist-feminism became embedded in the academy in large part because many of the women developing it were intellectuals who had graduate degrees and could re-enter academia. See "The Impasse of Socialist-Feminism," pp. 102–3.

Chapter 4

1. However, the term "gender" did not enter the movement's lexicon until quite a bit later.

2. Cell 16 is somewhat anomalous in this respect. The group was formed in the summer of 1968, well before any of the other groups examined in this chapter. Probably as a consequence, Cell 16 initially straddled the politico-feminist fracture.

3. Interview with Willis.

4. Interview with Willis.

5. December 1973 Redstockings' flyer announcing the group's reconstitution. Reprinted in their May 9, 1975 press release on Gloria Steinem and the CIA. The group's name prompted the politicos of WITCH, thinking they were " 'more together' than Redstockings," to joke about changing their name to "The Pantyhose." Robin Morgan, *Going Too Far* (New York: Random House, 1978), p. 73.

6. Interview with Willis. It should be noted that some members of Redstockings saw themselves as founders of the group with Willis and Firestone. However, Hole and Levine's account corroborates Willis's version of events.

7. Private communication, Sarachild, August 1988.

8. Interviews with Mehrhof, Kearon, Peslikis, Willis, and Hanisch.

9. Rosalind Petchesky, *Abortion and Woman's Choice: The State, Sexuality and Reproductive Freedom* (New York: Longman Press, 1984), p. 127.

10. Lucinda Cisler, "Unfinished Business: Birth Control and Women's Liberation," in Robin Morgan, ed., *Sisterhood is Powerful* (New York: Random House, 1970), p. 276.

11. Ellen Willis, *Village Voice*, March 3, 1980, p. 8. Other useful sources on the feminist reproductive rights struggle include: Lucinda Cisler, "Abortion Law Repeal (sort of): a Warning to Women," in Anne Koedt, Ellen Levine, and Anita Rapone, eds., *Radical Feminism* (New York: Quadrangle, 1973); Hole and Levine, *Rebirth of Feminism*, pp. 278–302; Adele Clark and Alice Wolfson, "Socialist-Feminism and Reproductive Rights: Movement Work and Its Contradictions," in *Socialist Review*, no. 78; and Lucinda Cisler's very instructive essay "Abortion: The 'Right' That Dare Not Speak Its Name," unpublished, 1984.

12. Ellen Willis, "Up from Radicalism: A Feminist Journal," *US* magazine, October 1969, p. 4. I believe that the seven women were Alix Kates Shulman, Ellen Willis, Anne Forer, Helen Kritzler, Ros Baxandall, Kathie Sarachild, and Shulamith Firestone. The fact that several of these women were not Redstockings' members caused me to question whether this was indeed a Redstockings action. However, in the leaflet that they passed out that day, the group identified itself as Redstockings. I imagine that in the initial stage of its formation, the group's membership was somewhat fluid.

13. Sarachild quoted in Edith Evans Asbury, "Women Break Up Abortion Hearing," *New York Times*, February 14, 1969, p. 42. Sarachild identified herself to the press later, but used the name Amatniek. Sarachild was chosen by lot to lead off the protest. Private communication, Sarachild, August 1988.

14. Willis, "Up from Radicalism," p. 4.

15. Quoted in Margie Stamberg, "The New Feminism/3," *Guardian*, April 19, 1969, p. 11.

16. Interview with Peslikis.

17. Willis, "Up from Radicalism," p. 5.

18. Claude Servan-Schreiber, "What French Women Are Up To," *Ms.*, November 1972, pp. 30–31.

19. Interviews with Mehrhof and Kearon.

20. Interview with Willis.

21. Interview with Willis.

22. Interview with Mehrhof. Mehrhof's notes of the meeting would seem to confirm this. But Sarachild does not recall making this proclamation and further notes that Mehrhof's notes were unofficial and never approved by the group. Private communication, Sarachild, August 1988. However, Baxandall's recollection of Sarachild's stance toward the group matches Mehrhof's account. Private communication, Baxandall, August 1988.

23. Interview with Baxandall.

24. For instance, Redstockings helped organize abortion marches, both Congresses to Unite Women, and the *Ladies Home Journal* sit-in. Private communication, Sarachild, August 1988. Some members also took part in the women's takeover of the underground paper *Rat*. Robin Morgan, *Going Too Far*, p. 116.

25. Interviews with Peslikis, Mehrhof, Kearon.

26. Shulamith Firestone, *The Dialectic of Sex*, rev. ed. (New York: Bantam, 1970), p. 2.

27. Ellen Willis, "Radical Feminism and Feminist Radicalism," in *The 60's Without Apology*, Sohnya Sayres, Anders Stephanson, Stanley Aronowitz, Fredric Jameson, eds. (Minneapolis: University of Minnesota Press, 1984), p. 96.

28. Redstockings Manifesto, in Shulamith Firestone and Anne Koedt, eds., *Notes from the Second Year: Women's Liberation* (New York: Radical Feminists, 1970), p. 113. (Hereafter referred to as *Notes 2*.)

29. Jennifer Gardner, "False Consciousness," in Firestone and Koedt, eds., *Notes 2*, p. 82.

30. Interview with Willis.

31. Interview with Willis.

32. Barbara Leon, "Brainwashing and Women," *It Ain't Me, Babe*, v. 1, #11, August 6–20, 1970, p. 17.

33. Redstockings Manifesto, in Firestone and Koedt, p. 113.

34. Patricia Mainardi, "The Marriage Question," in Redstockings, eds., *Feminist Revolution* (New Paltz, 1975), p. 105.

35. Ibid., p. 107.

36. Kathie Sarachild, "Going For What We Really Want," in Redstockings, eds., *Feminist Revolution*, p. 147. Sarachild delivered this speech at the second Women's Strike for Equality March on August 26, 1971.

37. Leon, "Brainwashing and Women," p. 14.

38. Group Interview 1.

39. Willis, "Radical Feminism and Feminist Radicalism," in Sayres et al., eds., p. 94.

40. Group Interview 1. Sarachild quoted in Sheila Cronan, "Marriage," in Anne Koedt, Anita Rapone and Ellen Levine, eds., *Notes from the Third Year: Women's Liberation*, (New York: Radical Feminists, 1971), p. 62. (Hereafter referred to as *Notes 3*,) Sarachild's article was originally published in May 1969.

41. Although Sarachild likes this statement, she does not remember having ut-

tered it. Baxandall, however, does remember her having said it. Private communication, Sarachild and Baxandall, August 1988.

42. Interview with Willis.

43. Willis, "Radical Feminism and Feminist Radicalism," in Sayres, et al. eds., pp. 103–4.

44. Interview with Willis.

45. This passage is taken from Sarachild's introduction to the consciousness-raising program she wrote for the Lake Villa Conference. Tobey Klass's files.

46. William Hinton, *Fanshen: A Documentary of Revolution in a Chinese Village* (New York: Vintage Books, 1966).

47. Willis, "Radical Feminism and Feminist Radicalism," p. 100. Willis points out that *Fanshen* was Redstockings' model.

48. Willis, "Radical Feminism and Feminist Radicalism," p. 104.

49. Redstockings Manifesto, in Firestone and Koedt, eds., *Notes 2*, p. 113.

50. Willis, "Radical Feminism and Feminist Radicalism," p. 97.

51. Patricia Mainardi, letter, *Majority Report*, v. 2, #7, November 1972, p. 2.

52. Firestone, *The Dialectic of Sex*; Ellen Willis, "Sequel: Letter to a Critic," in Firestone and Koedt, eds., *Notes 2*, pp. 57–58.

53. Firestone, *The Dialectic of Sex*, p. 12.

54. Interview with Mehrhof and Kearon.

55. Mehrhof, unpublished paper of 1969.

56. Pamela Kearon, "The Dangers of the Pro-Woman Line," pp. 5–6. Mimeo from Minda Bikman's files. The paper is signed by a "Jeanne Arrow," a name Kearon sometimes used.

57. Kearon, "The Dangers of the Pro-Woman Line," p. 2.

58. Interview with Willis.

59. Kearon, "The Dangers of the Pro-Woman Line," p. 2.

60. The three-part series ran from March to April 1969 in the *Guardian*. In her interview Peslikis remembered that they had been interviewed and that it had caused problems, but could not remember the paper in question.

61. Mehrhof's meeting notes.

62. Of course, the lot system was used earlier during the reorganization of NYRW. However, I am not sure if it was used as it was in The Feminists to ensure that everyone would share both clerical and creative work.

63. Willis's father was a New York City policeman.

64. Willis, "Radical Feminism and Feminist Radicalism," p. 110.

65. Interview with Willis.

66. Mehrhof's meeting notes.

67. Quoted in Margie Stamberg, "The New Feminism," *Guardian*, March 22, 1969, p. 11.

68. Firestone, *The Dialectic of Sex*, p. 39.

69. Interview with Willis.

70. Cellestine Ware, *Woman Power* (New York: Tower Publications, 1970), p. 44. Ware was one of the few black women involved in New York women's liberation. She was a founding member of New York Radical Feminists.

71. Interview with Baxandall (2).

72. According to Karla Jay, who was among the newcomers, the group's founders were also worried that expansion might facilitate government infiltration and subversion. Interview with Karla Jay. However, both Sarachild and Bax-

andall maintain that although they joked about the possibility of government infiltration, they did not take it seriously. In fact, some of the group's activities were reported to the FBI. See Letty Cottin Pogrebin, "The FBI Was Watching You," *Ms.*, June 1977.

73. Interview with Peslikis.

74. It should be noted that although the founders resisted any revision, the atmosphere in which the manifesto was originally written was open. Interview with Peslikis. Private communication, Baxandall, August 1988.

75. Interview with Karla Jay.

76. Interview with Peslikis.

77. Interview with Willis.

78. Mehrhof's notes. In a 1972 article, Firestone mentioned that at the time she edited *Notes from the Second Year* (early 1970) she disagreed with aspects of the pro-woman line. "Why I Support This Action," *Woman's World*, July–September 1972.

79. They were later joined by Hanisch.

80. Hole and Levine, pp. 140–42.

81. Interview with Peslikis.

82. Hanisch, "The Liberal Takeover of Women's Liberation," in Redstockings, eds., p. 128; Barbara Leon, cited in Nancy Borman, "Redstockings Are Back On Their Feet," reprinted in *Lesbian Tide*, v. 3, #8, April 1974, p. 12.

83. Kathie Sarachild, "Consciousness-Raising: A Radical Weapon," in Redstockings eds., p. 134.

84. Kathie Sarachild and Patricia Mainardi, "Ms. Politics and Editing: An Interview," in Redstockings, eds., p. 172.

85. Willis, "Radical Feminism and Feminist Radicalism," p. 100.

86. Redstockings Manifesto, in Firestone and Koedt, eds., *Notes 2*, p. 113. And if other women were always one's allies, one's sisters, how should one proceed when other feminists advanced ideas at odds with one's own analysis? One Bay Area feminist, Lynn O'Connor, who had initially embraced the pro-woman line, argued that it encouraged the suppression of conflict within the movement. "Many of us adopted this line, and when we later found ourselves driven out of our small groups and the women's movement, we were unable to clearly understand what had happened. According to our 'line' women were our sisters and men were our enemies. But in fact, it was women (and not under the direction of men) who had betrayed, subverted, and attempted to destroy us. To declare these women our enemies was a sacrilidge [*sic*], 'anti-woman' as they called it, against the 'line.' " Lynn O'Connor, "Instructions from the Women's Page on Method, Organization, Program," *The Women's Page*, #5, April–May 1971, p. 4. Interestingly, Judith Brown and Carol Giardina—two of the pro-woman line's earliest advocates—are listed on that issue's masthead. *The Women's Page* began as a supplement to the Bay Area women's paper *It Ain't Me, Babe*. However, the content of the supplement—especially the frequent attacks on other feminists—estranged the staff of the paper. When the paper's staff refused to print one of the group's supplements, they formed their own paper of the same title. Eventually, they disavowed the women's movement and changed the paper's name to *The Second Page* in an effort to disassociate the paper from the "bourgeois" women's movement.

87. This passage is taken from the Redstockings' Manifesto. The Carmichael

quote can be found in his speech, "A Declaration of War," reprinted in Teodori Massimo, ed., *The New Left: A Documentary History* (Indianapolis: Bobbs-Merrill, 1969), p. 281. Carmichael delivered this speech at a February 1968 Panther-organized rally on the occasion of Huey Newton's birthday. Over 5,000 people attended the Oakland, California rally to demand Newton's release from prison.

88. Kathie Sarachild, "The Men's Page," *Woman's World*, v. 1, #2, July–August, 1971, p. 8. By contrast, Firestone called NOW members "conservative feminists" and charged that they focused on "the more superficial symptoms of sexism." Firestone, *The Dialectic of Sex*, p. 32. Atkinson was the harshest toward NOW. See her "Resignation from N.O.W.," "The Equality Issue," "Movement Politics and Other Sleights of Hand," in *Amazon Odyssey* (New York: Links Books, 1974).

89. Kathie Sarachild, "A Review of Ms. Magazine," *Woman's World*, v. 1, #4, March–May 1972, p. 22.

90. Ibid., p. 24.

91. Sarachild and Mainardi, "Ms. Politics and Editing: An Interview," in Redstockings, eds., pp. 171–72.

92. According to Sarachild, the original incorporators were Leon, Mainardi, and Amatniek. Private communication, Sarachild, August 1988. Mainardi was not a member at the time of the group's attack on Steinem.

93. This was the title of the book's section on Steinem and *Ms.* magazine.

94. Jennifer Gardner, "The Small Group: Prison Guards at Work," *The Women's Page*," #4, February 18, 1971, p. 7.

95. Kathie Sarachild and Barbara Leon, "Founding Statement," *Woman's World*, v. 1, #2, July–August 1971.

96. Redstockings, "The Pseudo-Left/Lesbian Alliance," in Redstockings, eds.

97. Patricia Mainardi, "The Marriage Question," in Redstockings, eds. Although Mainardi contributed to this book, she was not a member of the re-formed Redstockings.

98. Interview with Willis.

99. Judith Brown, editorial, *Radical Therapist*, Special Issue on Women, v. 1, #3, August–September, 1970, p. 2.

100. Interview with Mainardi. According to Sarachild, she and others of the pro-woman persuasion have also been developing a critique of the the pro-woman line. Private communication, Sarachild, August 1988.

101. Interview with Willis.

102. Hole and Levine, p. 142.

103. Anselma dell'Olio, "Movement Farewell," *Everywoman*, January 1, 1971. Dell'Olio delivered the speech at the second Congress to Unite Women in May 1970. The title of her speech was "Divisiveness and Self-Destruction in the Women's Movement: A Letter of Resignation." See, Hole and Levine, p. 162.

104. See Kathie Sarachild, "A Review of Ms. Magazine," *Woman's World*, v. 1, #4, March–May 1972.

105. Interview with Brownmiller.

106. Sara Evans, *Personal Politics* (New York: Vintage Books, 1979), p. 209.

107. Cell 16 mimeo on the SWP's efforts to infiltrate the group. Quoted in Hole and Levine, p. 164.

108. Roxanne Dunbar, "What Is To Be Done?" *No More Fun and Games*," #1, October 1968, unpaginated. I will hereafter refer to the journal as *NMF&G*.

109. Dunbar, "Female Liberation as the Basis for Social Revolution," *NMF&G*, #2, February 1969, p. 10. Note that this early version is very different from the later version which was published in both *Sisterhood is Powerful* and in *Notes from the Second Year*.

110. Interview with Tax.

111. Dunbar, "Female Liberation as the Basis For Social Revolution," p. 9.

112. See especially the revised version of "Female Liberation as the Basis For Social Revolution," in Morgan, ed., *Sisterhood is Powerful*.

113. Ibid., p. 9.

114. See, editorial, "What Do Women Want?" *NMF&G*, #2, February 1969.

115. Lisa Leghorn, "The Dialectics of Oppression," *NMF&G*, #3, November 1969, unpaginated.

116. Dana Densmore, "Who Is Saying Men Are the Enemy?" *NMF&G*, #4, April 1970. Reprinted in Sookie Stambler, ed., *Women's Liberation: Blueprint for the Future* (New York: Ace, 1970), p. 51.

117. Ibid., p. 48.

118. Densmore, "On Female Enslavement . . . and Men's Stake in It," *NMF&G*, #1, October 1968.

119. Dunbar, "What Is To Be Done?"

120. Dunbar, "Female Liberation as the Basis For Social Revolution," p. 8; "What Do Women Want?" p. 9.

121. Dunbar, "Female Liberation as the Basis For Social Revolution," p. 12.

122. See Firestone, *The Dialectic of Sex*; Ti-Grace Atkinson, "The Institution of Sexual Intercourse," in *Amazon Odyssey* (New York: Links Books, 1974).

123. Ibid., p. 8.

124. Dunbar, "Who Is the Enemy?" p. 7.

125. Most women's liberationists were still wearing their hair very long in 1969.

126. Interview with Brownmiller. For an account of the action, see Hole and Levine, p. 151.

127. Betsy Warrior, "Man As an Obsolete Life Form," *NMF&G*, #2, February 1969.

128. Dunbar, "Asexuality," *NMF&G*, #1, October 1968.

129. Densmore, "Sexuality," *NMF&G*, #1, October 1968.

130. Densmore, "Without You and within You," *NMF&G*, #4, April 1970, p. 52. The article was apparently written in June 1969.

131. Ibid., p. 54.

132. Abby Rockefeller, "Sex: The Basis of Sexism," *NMF&G*, #6, May 1973, p. 25.

133. Ibid., p. 33.

134. Donna Allen, "The Women's Revolution: The Political Significance of the Genetic Differences between Men and Women," *NMF&G*, #5, July 1971, p. 105. Although the article appeared in 1971, it was written in 1970.

135. Firestone, *The Dialectic of Sex*, p. 11.

136. Kate Millett, "Sexual Politics: A Manifesto for Revolution," in Firestone and Koedt eds., *Notes 2*.

137. Densmore, "Sexuality."

138. Densmore, "On Celibacy," *NMF&G*, #1, October 1968.

139. Dunbar, "Sexual Liberation: More of the Same Thing," *NMF&G*, #3, November 1969.

140. Dunbar, Asexuality."

141. Warrior, "All or Nothing," *NMF&G*, #3, November 1969. See, also, Warrior, "Battle Lines," same issue.

142. Densmore, "Without You and within You," p. 55.

143. Densmore, "Sexuality."

144. Dunbar and Leghorn, "The Man's Problem," *NMF&G*, #3, November 1969, p. 315.

145. Quoted in Rita Mae Brown, *A Plain Brown Rapper* (Baltimore: Diana Press, 1976), p. 50.

146. Dunbar, "Sexual Liberation: More of the Same Thing."

147. Leghorn, "Feminism Undermines," *NMF&G*, #4, April 1970, p. 61.

148. Densmore, "On Unity," *NMF&G*, #5, July 1971. This speech was originally given in October 1970.

149. See Hole and Levine, pp. 164–65.

150. Former members of the Southern Female Rights Union, "Spies in Women's Liberation," *Everywoman*, July 31, 1970, p. 16. Dunbar is not listed as the author of the statement, but she was the leader of the group.

151. Quoted in *It Ain't Me, Babe*, v. 1, 38, June 11–July 1, 1970, p. 5.

152. She has more recently been involved in organizing Indians in Nicaragua.

153. Helen Dudar, "Four of a Kind—Yet Different," *Newsweek*, March 23, 1970, p. 72.

154. Atkinson, letter, *oob*, v. 10, #5, May 1980, p. 19.

155. For instance, Roxanne Dunbar of Cell 16 cited *The Second Sex* as the book that "changed our lives." See Dunbar, "Sources of Information," *No More Fun and Games*, #2, February 1969. Shulamith Firestone dedicated her book *The Dialectic of Sex* to de Beauvoir. And Kathie Sarachild called the book "crucial to the development of the WLM." See Sarachild, "The Power of History," in Redstockings, eds., p. 18. Shortly after her death Redstockings organized a memorial service for de Beauvoir.

156. Betty Friedan, *It Changed My Life* (New York: Norton, 1985), p. 109.

157. Atkinson, "Resignation from N.O.W.," reprinted in Atkinson, *Amazon Odyssey* (New York: Links Books, 1974), pp. 9–11. Most of the writings in Atkinson's book are speeches she delivered on the lecture circuit.

158. Atkinson, letter, *oob*, v. 10, #5, May 1980, p. 19.

159. Ibid.

160. Cisler, "Abortion: The 'Right' That Dare Not Speak Its Name," unpublished essay.

161. Atkinson, "Resignation from N.O.W.," p. 9.

162. See Hole and Levine, p. 91.

163. Friedan, *It Changed My Life*, p. 109. Warhol was shot by Solanas in the abdomen, not the genitals.

164. Martha Weinman Lear, "The Second Feminist Wave," *New York Times Magazine*, March 10, 1968.

165. Atkinson, "Resignation from N.O.W.," p. 10.

166. Ibid., p. 10.

167. Atkinson, "Betty Friedan, the C.I.A. and Me," in *Majority Report*, v. 2, #12, April 1973, p. 1.

168. Atkinson, "Movement Politics and Other Sleights of Hand," March 4, 1970, in *Amazon Odyssey*, p. 98.

169. Atkinson,"Self-Deception," August, 6, 1971, in *Amazon Odyssey*, p. 213.

170. Interviews with Mehrhof, Kearon, Rainone.

171. The Feminists always capitalized the group's name, so it appeared THE FEMINISTS.

172. Hole and Levine, p. 143.

173. Ibid., pp. 144–45; The Feminists describe this action in their biography of the group which was published in Susan Rennie and Kirsten Grimstad, *The New Woman's Survival Catalogue* (New York: Coward, McCann and Geoghegan, 1973), p. 209.

174. Jane Alpert, "Women Bolt the Bridal Path," *Rat*, v. 2, #20, October 8–21, 1969, p. 10.

175. Ibid.

176. Pam Kearon, "The Dangers of the Pro-Woman Line," mimeo. Atkinson also saw consciousness-raising as a retreat from action. See Atkinson, p. 145.

177. Willis makes this point in "Radical Feminism and Feminist Radicalism," in Sayres, et al., eds., *The '60s Without Apology* (Minneapolis: University of Minnesota Press, 1984), p. 102.

178. "The Feminists: A Political Organization to Annihilate Sex Roles," in Firestone and Koedt, eds., *Notes 2*, pp. 114–18.

179. "The Feminists: A Political Organization to Annihilate Sex Roles," p. 114.

180. Ibid., p. 43.

181. Atkinson, "Declaration of War," April 1969, *Amazon Odyssey*, p. 49.

182. Ibid., p. 103.

183. Kearon, "The Dangers of the Pro-Woman Line," p. 1.

184. The Feminists, "Feminist Resolutions," *Rat*, v. 3, #8, June 5–19, 1970, p. 9.

185. "The Feminists: A Political Organization to Annihilate Sex Roles," p. 114.

186. Atkinson, "Declaration of War," p. 55.

187. "The Feminists: A Political Organization to Annihilate Sex Roles," p. 118.

188. Atkinson,"Movement Politics and Other Sleights of Hand," pp. 103–4.

189. Barbara Mehrhof and Pamela Kearon, "Rape: An Act of Terror," in Koedt, Rapone, and Levine, eds., *Notes 3*, p. 80.

190. "The Feminists: A Political Organization to Annihilate Sex Roles," p. 117.

191. Atkinson, "The Institution of Sexual Intercourse," November 1968, *Amazon Odyssey*, p. 21.

192. Atkinson, "Lesbianism and Feminism," February 1970, in *Amazon Odyssey*, p. 85.

193. Ibid., p. 86.

194. Interview with Peslikis.

195. "The Feminists: A Political Organization to Annihilate Sex Roles," p. 118.

196. Willis, "Radical Feminism and Feminist Radicalism," p. 103.

197. Atkinson, "Movement Politics and Other Sleights of Hand," p. 107.

198. Valerie Solanas, *SCUM Manifesto* (New York: Olympia Press, 1968), p. 30.

199. Firestone, *The Dialectic of Sex*, p. 209.

200. Karen Lindsey, "Thoughts on Promiscuity," *The Second Wave*, v. 1, #3, 1971, p. 3.

201. Millett contended that "sexual freedom has been partially attained, but it is now being subverted beyond freedom into exploitative license for patriarchal and reactionary ends." Millett, "Sexual Politics: A Manifesto for Revolution," in Koedt, Levine, and Rapone, eds., p. 366.

202. Each section of the manifesto was drafted at different points throughout the summer—from June 13 to August 26. It is conceivable that Koedt and Karp attended the meeting where the group's "conceptual analysis" was voted on.

203. Ibid., p. 115.

204. Hole and Levine, p. 146.

205. "The Feminists: A Political Organization to Annihilate Sex Roles," pp. 116–17. The Feminists called this the "consistency issue."

206. Interviews with Mehrhof and Kearon.

207. Interview with Rainone.

208. Interview with Kearon.

209. Interview with Mehrhof.

210. Kearon, "The Dangers of the Pro-Woman Line," pp. 3–4n.

211. Ibid., p. 5.

212. Interview with Peslikis.

213. Interview with Peslikis.

214. Atkinson, "The Political Woman," February 1970, in *Amazon Odyssey*, p. 90. Atkinson on married women as "hostages," quoted in Kearon, "The Dangers of the Pro-Woman Line."

215. Atkinson, "Radical Feminism and Love," April 1969, in *Amazon Odyssey*, p. 44.

216. Atkinson, "The Political Woman," p. 90.

217. Quoted in Dudar, "Four of a Kind—Yet Different," p. 73.

218. Atkinson, "The Political Woman," p. 91.

219. Quoted in Dudar, "Four of a Kind—Yet Different," p. 73.

220. Atkinson, "Radical Feminism and Love," p. 41.

221. Atkinson, "The Equality Issue," February 1970, in *Amazon Odyssey*, p. 69.

222. Atkinson, "Movement Politics and Other Sleights of Hand," p. 99.

223. Interviews with Mehrhof and Kearon.

224. Atkinson, "Untitled: Some Notes Toward a Theory of Identity," in *Amazon Odyssey*, p. 114n.

225. Atkinson, "The Equality Issue," p. 73. According to Barbara Mehrhof, Marcia Winslow was the only black member who was ever in the group.

226. Ibid., p. 71.

227. Barbara Mehrhof, "On Class Structure within the Women's Movement," in Firestone and Koedt, eds., *Notes 2*, p. 104.

228. Ibid., p. 107.

229. Atkinson, "The Equality Issue," p. 71. In contrast to Mehrhof, Atkinson believed the problem was one of power, not of "male-identification."

230. Interview with Mehrhof.

231. The Feminists, "Feminist Resolutions," *Rat*, v. 3, #8, June 5–19, 1970, p. 9.

232. Ibid.

233. Interviews with Mehrhof and Kearon.

234. Interview with Kearon.

235. The Feminists, "Feminist Resolutions," p. 9.

236. Interviews with Mehrhof and Kearon.

237. Rennie and Grimstad, *The New Woman's Survival Catalogue*, p. 209.

238. Interview with Kearon.

239. Mehrhof and Kearon, "Rape: An Act of Terror," in Koedt, Rapone, and Levine, eds., *Notes 3*, p. 79.

240. Interview with Kearon.
241. The Feminists, letter, *Majority Report*, v. 2, #10, February 1973, p. 2.
242. Interview with Kearon.
243. Interview with Kearon.
244. Interviews with Kearon and Mehrhof.
245. Rennie and Grimstad, p. 209.
246. See Atkinson, "Resignation from N.O.W.," p. 10.
247. Quoted in "The Women's Page," *It Ain't Me, Babe*, July 23–August 5, 1970, p. 15.
248. Atkinson, letter, *Majority Report*, v. 4, #2, October 3, 1974, p. 2.
249. For Atkinson's account, see "Self-Deception" in *Amazon Odyssey*, pp. 199–221.
250. Ibid., pp. 211 and 204.
251. Atkinson, p. 221.
252. Kate Millett wrote about the event in her autobiographical novel *Flying*, pp. 502–14.
253. Atkinson, "Strategy and Tactics: A Presentation of Political Lesbianism," in *Amazon Odyssey*, p. 136. She gave the talk at the dedication of Daughters of Bilitis' New York Lesbian Center on January 4, 1971.
254. Interview with Minda Bikman.
255. Firestone, "Organizing Principles of the New York Radical Feminists" in Firestone and Koedt, eds., *Notes 2*, p. 119.
256. Interview with Ann Snitow.
257. Hole and Levine, p. 153.
258. Interview with Snitow.
259. Interview with Bikman.
260. Hole and Levine, p. 152.
261. Vivian Gornick, "The Next Great Moment in History is Theirs," *Village Voice*, November 1969. Reprinted in Gornick, *Essays in Feminism* (New York: Harper and Row, 1978).
262. Koedt, "Politics of the Ego: A Manifesto for N.Y. Radical Feminists," in Firestone and Koedt, eds., *Notes 2*, p. 124.
263. Ibid., p. 124.
264. Willis, "Radical Feminism and Feminist Radicalism," p. 105.
265. Interview with Snitow.
266. Willis, "Radical Feminism and Feminist Radicalism," p. 105.
267. Koedt, "Politics of the Ego: A Manifesto for N.Y. Radical Feminists," p. 125.
268. This quote is from the slightly modified version of the manifesto which was reprinted in *Radical Feminism*, p. 382.
269. Willis, "Radical Feminism and Feminist Radicalism," p. 105.
270. Koedt, "Politics of the Ego: A Manifesto for N.Y. Radical Feminists," p. 126.
271. Firestone, "Organizing Principles of the New York Radical Feminists," p. 119.
272. Ibid., p. 120.
273. Ibid., p. 120.
274. Ibid., p. 121.
275. Ware, *Woman Power*, p. 61.
276. Interview with Brownmiller.

277. Interview with Snitow.
278. Interview with Snitow.
279. Interview with Brownmiller.
280. Interview with Snitow.
281. Private communication, Susan Brownmiller, 1985.
282. Interviews with Bikman and Brownmiller.
283. Interview with Snitow.
284. Interview with Snitow.
285. Interview with Brownmiller.
286. Firestone, *The Dialectic of Sex*, pp. 37–38.
287. Ibid., p. 207.
288. Willis, "Radical Feminism and Feminist Radicalism," p. 107.
289. Hole and Levine, p. 156.
290. Susan Brownmiller, *Against Our Will: Men, Women and Rape* (New York: Simon and Schuster, 1975).
291. Ibid., p. 157.
292. Interview with Brownmiller; Kate Millett, *The Prostitution Papers* (New York: Ballantine Books, 1973), p. 38.
293. Interview with Alix Kates Shulman; Kathie Sarachild, "Notes on the Prostitution Conference," *Woman's World*, v. 1, #4, March–May 1972, p. 12.
294. Interview with Snitow.
295. Sarachild, "Notes on the Prostitution Conference," p. 15. See also "Prostitution Conference: Aftermath," *Majority Report*, v. 1, #9, January 1972, p. 11; and The *Village Voice*, December 1971.
296. Private communication, Susan Brownmiller, 1985.
297. Verna Tomasson, "Ladies Home Journal 2," *Rat*, v. 3, #3, April 4–18, 1970, p. 5. This is most likely a pseudonym.
298. One of the protestors, Karla Jay, believing that Firestone was going to lunge at Carter, grabbed Firestone from behind. Jay wanted to prevent her from harming Carter and landing herself in jail. However, Baxandall maintains that Firestone had no intention of attacking Carter. Interviews with Karla Jay and Ros Baxandall.
299. Karla Jay, "Ladies Home Journal 1," *Rat*, v. 3, #3, April 4–18, 1970, p. 22.
300. Tomasson, "Ladies Home Journal 2," p. 5.
301. Ibid., p. 5.
302. Ibid., p. 5.
303. Interview with Baxandall.
304. Baxandall, letter, *Women: A Journal of Liberation*, Summer 1970, p. 58.
305. Tomasson, "Ladies Home Journal 2."
306. Karla Jay, "Ladies Home Journal 1," p. 22.
307. Interview with Baxandall.
308. Interview with Baxandall.
309. Interview with Bikman.
310. Interview with Alix Kates Shulman.
311. For an account of the strike, see Hole and Levine, *The Rebirth of Feminism*, pp. 92–93.
312. Sarachild and Leon, "Founding Statement," *Woman's World*, v. 1, #2, July–August 1971.
313. Hole and Levine, p. 161.

314. Nora Ephron, *Crazy Salad: Some Things about Women* (New York: Bantam, 1976), p. 19. This essay was written in August 1972.

315. Redstockings' statement reported in Nancy Borman, "Redstockings Back on Their Feet," *Lesbian Tide*, v. 3, #8, April 1974.

316. Ellen Willis, "Economic Reality and the Limits of Feminism," *Ms.*, June 1973, p. 111.

317. For an incisive critique of *Ms.* politics, see Ellen Willis's letter of resignation from *Ms.* in *oob*, v. 5 #8, September–October 1975, p. 7. See also Willis, "Radical Feminism and Feminist Radicalism," for her discussion of liberal feminism's evolution.

318. Friedan quoted in Zillah Eisenstein, *The Radical Future of Liberal Feminism* (New York: Longman, 1981), p. 182. In fact, not only did Friedan deny that men were the enemy, she suggested that women with their capacity for self-deprecation were their own worst enemies. See Betty Friedan, *It Changed My Life* (New York: Norton, 1983), p. 152.

319. Nor would men "have to spend a lifetime living with inferiors; with housekeepers, or dependent creatures who are still children." Gloria Steinem, "What It Would Be Like If Women Win," *Time*, August 31, 1970, p. 22.

320. Sherna Gluck notes that in the early days of the movement feminists were better able to accept women who dressed traditionally because many of them had until recently done so as well. "Sisterhood Revival Collective," *Sister*, v. 7, #2, December–January 1976.

321. Quoted in Jane Mansbridge, *Why We Lost the ERA* (Chicago: University of Chicago Press, 1986), p. 266. The Feminists were not alone in their opposition to the ERA. Many women's liberationists, especially politicos, attacked it. The Seattle-based women's liberation newspaper "And Ain't I A Woman," advocated the extension of protective legislation to men and argued that the ERA would result in greater exploitation. Bread and Roses issued a statement contending that employers favored passage of the ERA because they believed the amendment would weaken the position of workers. See *Women: A Journal of Liberation*, v. 2, #1, Fall 1970, p. 59. Opposition of this sort dissipated when it became clear that both the federal courts and the Equal Employment Opportunity Commission were interpreting Title VII as invalidating protective legislation and were extending most traditional protections to men rather than removing them.

322. "Women's Liberation Testimony," *oob*, v. 1, #5, May 1970, p. 7.

323. Firestone, *The Dialectic of Sex*, p. 206. Although many radical feminists disagreed with Firestone, the fear of being co-opted seems to have discouraged radical feminists from doing more to mobilize women around the issue of child care. Child-care centers required either governmental or corporate funding, and many women feared that such funding would have a corrupting influence. See Ros Baxandall, "City Money for Nursery," *Woman's World*, v. 1, #1, April 15, 1971; Hole and Levine, *The Rebirth of Feminism*, p. 312.

324. Interview with Ann Snitow. NYRF held its first speak-out on rape in January 1971. The earliest radical feminist articles on rape—by California feminist Susan Griffin and Kearon and Mehrhof of The Feminists—appeared in 1971.

325. The Redstockings Manifesto did note that women's "prescribed behavior is enforced by the threat of physical violence." *Notes 2*, p. 112. But violence against women was not initially a central focus of feminist analysis. For instance, the issues deemed especially important at the first Congress to Unite Women in

November 1969—a conference that brought together both women's liberationists and NOW feminists—were child care, abortion, sex roles, and discrimination in education and employment. "What Do Women Want?" *Notes 2*, p. 96–97.

326. Alison Jaggar, *Feminist Politics and Human Nature* (Totawa, NJ: Rowman and Allanheld, 1983), pp. 93–94.

Chapter 5

1. Interview with Ann Snitow.

2. Robin Morgan, "The Proper Study of Womankind," in *Going Too Far* (New York: Random House, 1978). She gave the talk before the schismatic Western Women's Studies Conference in the Summer of 1973. Kathy Barry, "West Coast Conference: Not Purely Academic," *oob*, v. 3, #10, September 1973, p. 25.

3. Kathy Barry, "West Coast Conference: Not Purely Academic," p. 25.

4. Redstockings,"The Pseudo-Left/Lesbian Alliance," in Redstockings, eds., *Feminist Revolution* (New Paltz: Redstockings, 1975), p. 191.

5. See Marge Piercy, "The Grand Coolie Damn," in Robin Morgan ed., *Sisterhood is Powerful* (New York: Random House, 1970).

6. Interview with Meredith Tax.

7. For the best critique from within the women's movement, see Joreen (Jo Freeman), "The Tyranny of Structurelessness," in Anne Koedt, Ellen Levine, and Anita Rapone, eds., *Radical Feminism* (New York: Quadrangle, 1973).

8. Interview with Meredith Tax. See also Carol McEldowney and Rosemary Poole, "A Working Paper on the Media," v. 1, #3, *Women: A Journal of Liberation*, Spring 1970. McEldowney and Poole were Bread and Roses members.

9. Interview with Marilyn Webb.

10. According to *oob* co-founder, Marilyn Wickes, the newspaper's name "reflected three things. We wanted to be off our backs in terms of being fucked. We wanted to be off our backs in terms of being the backbone of America or every society and culture with no power. And we wanted the flack we would get from everyone about being strong to roll off our backs." Interview with Marlene Wickes, *oob*, v. 10, #2, February 1980, p. 4. Webb, who at the time of her ouster was a correspondent for the leftist newspaper the *Guardian*, was in large part inspired to start a feminist newspaper because the *Guardian* had a "consistent blackout on feminist news." *oob*, v. 10, #2, February 1980, p. 5.

11. Interview with Willis.

12. Interview with Kritzler.

13. Ellen Willis, Group Interview I. Of course, as Baxandall points out, many within the movement welcomed the publication of Firestone's book.

14. Interview with Alix Kates Shulman.

15. Interviews with Mehrhof and Kearon.

16. Interview with Kearon.

17. "What Can We Do about the Media," Spring 1970, leaflet in Irene Peslikis's files.

18. Interview with Brownmiller.

19. Interview with Kearon.

20. This shift might be related to changes in the group's composition. All three members of the Class Workshop whom I interviewed—Kearon, Mehrhof, and

Peslikis—claimed they were no longer involved in the group at the time of the second Congress. However, the Class Workshop's demands at the Congress did not differ substantially from what Kearon and Mehrhof were advocating in The Feminists.

21. Judy White, "Women Divided," *oob*, v. 1, #5, May 16, 1970, p. 5.

22. "What Can We Do about the Media."

23. Interview with Susan Brownmiller.

24. "What Can We Do about the Media."

25. Interview with Ann Snitow.

26. Susan Brownmiller, "Sisterhood is Powerful," *The New York Times Magazine*, March 15, 1970.

27. Elinor Langer, "Notes for Next Time: A Memoir of the 1960's" *Working Papers*, v. 1, #3, Fall 1973, pp. 79–80.

28. Lemisch contends that "similar problems brought about the destruction of her band, the Chicago Women's Liberation Rock Band, where again a difference in skills led to unresolvable conflicts." Interview with Jesse Lemisch.

29. Interview with Frances Chapman. Chapman's definition of a leader is "purely functional—a leader is not someone with special skills, but rather someone who performs a time-limited role, ideally using persuasion, not coercion."

30. Joreen, "The Tyranny of Structurelessness," in Koedt, Levine, and Rapone, eds., *Radical Feminism*, p. 286.

31. Interview with Patricia Mainardi.

32. Rita Mae Brown, "Leadership vs. Stardom," reprinted in Rita Mae Brown, *A Plain Brown Rapper* (Baltimore: Diana Press, 1976), p. 143. The article originally appeared in *The Furies*, February 1972.

33. For example, see Ti-Grace Atkinson's February 1970 speech, "Lesbianism and Feminism," reprinted in *Amazon Odyssey* (New York: Links Books, 1974), p. 83. The exception here is Judith Brown's portion of the "Florida Paper," or, "Toward a Female Liberation Movement," in Leslie Tanner, ed., *Voices from Women's Liberation* (New York: New American Library, 1970).

34. Kate Millett, "Sexual Politics: A Manifesto for Revolution," in Firestone and Koedt, eds., *Notes from the Second Year: Women's Liberation* (New York: New York Radical Feminists, April 1970), p. 112. Millett wrote this article in 1968. The printing of *Notes 2*, as it will be referred to hereafter, was subsidized by *The New York Review of Books*. See Vivian Gornick, *Essays in Feminism* (New York: Harper and Row, 1978), p. 24.

35. Shulamith Firestone, *The Dialectic of Sex: The Case for Feminist Revolution*, rev. ed. (New York: Bantam, 1970), p. 209.

36. Anne Koedt, "The Myth of the Vaginal Orgasm," in Firestone and Koedt, eds., *Notes 2*, p. 41.

37. Abby Rockefeller, "Sex: The Basis of Sexism," *No More Fun and Games*, #6, May 1973, p. 31.

38. Ti-Grace Atkinson, "Lesbianism and Feminism," in *Amazon Odyssey*, p. 86. As I mention at the conclusion of this chapter, Atkinson changed her position on lesbianism.

39. Reported in Sidney Abbott and Barbara Love, *Sappho was a Right-On Woman* (New York: Stein and Day, 1973), p. 117.

40. Interview with Marilyn Webb.

41. Interview with Ros Baxandall.

42. Interview with Irene Peslikis.

43. Judith Brown and Beverly Jones, "Toward a Female Liberation Movement," in Tanner, ed., *Voices from Women's Liberation*, p. 407. It is important to note that Brown, in contrast to lesbian-feminists, did not see women turning away from men permanently.

44. Friedan quoted in Susan Brownmiller, "Sisterhood Is Powerful," *New York Times Magazine*, March 15, 1970, p. 140. Brownmiller wrote, "The supersensitivity of the movement to the lesbian issue, and the existence of a few militant lesbians within the movement once prompted Friedan herself to grouse about 'the lavender menace' that was threatening to warp the image of women's rights." By contrast, Brownmiller argued that militant lesbians were "a lavender *herring* perhaps, but surely no clear and present danger."

45. DOB may very well have been deliberately omitted, but is important to point out that the leaflet also failed to mention NY-NOW as a participating group. Abbott and Love, p. 111.

46. Quoted in Toby Marotta, *The Politics of Homosexuality* (Boston: Houghton Mifflin, 1981), p. 235.

47. Rita Mae Brown, "Take a Lesbian to Lunch," reprinted in *Plain Brown Rapper*, p. 91. It was first published in the lesbian journal *The Ladder* (April–May 1970). My account of this period is drawn from Marotta, pp. 230–55; Abbott and Love, pp. 113–15; and interviews.

48. March Hoffman later changed her name to Artemis March.

49. Interview with Jennifer Woodul.

50. Interview with Coletta Reid.

51. At Yale they confronted Naomi Weisstein, who, unlike Dunbar or Dixon, was very willing to acknowledge the relevance of lesbianism to feminism. Rita Mae Brown, "Yale Break," reprinted in *A Plain Brown Rapper*, pp. 37–40. It was first published in *Rat*, February 1970.

52. Dixon was obviously so taken aback that she was unable to see that she was using this much parodied line in the same way that white liberals did when accused of racial prejudice.

53. Rita Mae Brown, "Say It Isn't So," *A Plain Brown Rapper*, p. 50.

54. Marotta, p. 240.

55. "Women's Liberation is a Lesbian Plot," *Rat*, v. 3, #6, May 8–21, p. 12.

56. Interview with Woodul.

57. Marotta, p. 244.

58. Radicalesbians, "The Woman-Identified Woman," in Anne Koedt, Anita Rapone, and Ellen Levine, eds., *Notes from the Third Year: Women's Liberation*, (New York: New York Radical Feminists, 1971).

59. Interview with Jennifer Woodul.

60. Brown's early '70's pieces are available in *A Plain Brown Rapper*; Shelley's "Step N'Fetchit Woman" was reprinted as "Notes of a Radical Lesbian" in Morgan, ed., *Sisterhood is Powerful*.

61. Private communication, Ellen DuBois. DuBois reconsidered her initial response and was among the first heterosexual feminists to challenge sexual conservatism, and specifically homophobia, within the movement.

62. Sue Katz, "The Sensuous Woman," in *Rat*, v. 3, #18, January 12–January 29, 1971. Katz wrote a letter protesting the article's retitling and the accompanying graphic of pre-Raphaelite women frolicking in a stream. See also Sue Negrin,

"A Weekend in Lesbian Nation," *It Ain't Me, Babe*, v. 2, #1, April 1971, p. 11. Negrin wrote, "Gay feminism is the only space in which to develop nonsexual *sensuality*."

63. Unsigned, "Thoughts to Keep in Mind As We Find Out More About Ourselves," *It Ain't Me, Babe*, v. 1, #15, April 30, 1971. Reprinted from Ann Arbor's lesbian paper, the *Spectre*.

64. Rita Mae Brown, "Coitus Interruptus," *A Plain Brown Rapper*, p. 29. It was originally printed in *Rat*, v. 2, #27, February 6–23, 1970.

65. Unsigned, "Lesbians as Bogeywomen," *It Ain't Me, Babe*, v. 1, #8, June 11–July 1, 1970, p. 15. See also, a Redstockings sister, "A Mother and a Lesbian," in *Rat*, v. 3, #12, August 9–23, 1970, pp. 13–14.

66. Susan Helenius, "Returning the Dyke to the Dutchess," *Everywoman*, v. 2, #10, July 9, 1971.

67. Sharon Deevey, a founding member of the lesbian-feminist Furies collective, went so far as to argue that "*every* fuck is a rape even if it feels nice because every man has power and privilege over women whether he uses it blatantly or subtly. Sharon Deevey, "Such a Nice Girl," in Nancy Myron and Charlotte Bunch, eds., *Lesbianism and the Women's Movement* (Baltimore: Diana Press, 1975), p. 21.

68. Interview with Pam Kearon.

69. Interviews with Ros Baxandall and Ann Snitow.

70. "Women's Lib: A Second Look," *Time*, December 14, 1970, p. 50. The *Time* writer gloated that the "disclosure is bound to discredit her as a spokeswoman for her cause, cast further doubt on her theories and reinforce the views of those skeptics who routinely dismiss all liberationists as lesbians."

71. Abbott and Love, p. 124.

72. Abbott and Love, p. 126; Marotta, p. 259n.

73. In January 1971, Ti-Grace Atkinson declared that lesbians were "the greatest counterrevolutionary force *within* the early women's movement." Atkinson was, of course, a leader within NOW in the early days of the movement. Atkinson, "Lesbianism and Feminism: Justice for Women as 'Unnatural,' " *Amazon Odyssey*, p. 145. And interview with Cindy Cisler.

74. Abbott and Love, p. 134.

75. Garman had been involved in SNCC earlier.

76. Charlotte Bunch, "Ourstory: DC Herstory," May 21, 1971, p. 9. Bunch is listed as the person who did the most work on the paper.

77. Interview with Joan Biren. They also "plastered" all over D.C. "An Open Letter to Martha Mitchell" in 1970. Martha Mitchell, who was married to Attorney General John Mitchell, had publicly declared her intention to join the women's movement. The letter informed Mitchell that she was welcome to join the women's movement, but she would have to repudiate her "upper-class economic and white-skin privileges" and her "empty identity." See Bunch, "Ourstory: DC Herstory," May 21, 1971, p. 7; Letty Pogrebin, "The FBI Was Watching You," *Ms.*, June 1977, p. 39.

78. Interview with Marilyn Webb. Both Davis and Dellinger were Chicago Seven defendants.

79. Interview with Charlotte Bunch.

80. Interview with Marilyn Webb; Marilyn Webb, untitled, *oob*, v. x, #2, February 1980, p. 5.

81. Interview with Charlotte Bunch (LV).

82. Interview with Marilyn Webb.

83. Marilyn Webb and several others decided against participating when the anti-imperialist women invited an acquaintance from Chicago to join the commune. Webb and others suspected the woman of being an agent. They conducted an investigation into her background, but nothing was confirmed. Some women's liberation activists believe that agents were responsible for some of the havoc wreaked upon the movement in this period. Webb, who has seen some FBI files on the DCWLM, is convinced that someone within *oob* was informing and manipulating the issues of elitism and lesbianism to debilitate the movement. No doubt agents did aggravate frictions within the movement, but the frictions were not simply the work of agents.

84. Interview with Marilyn Webb; Webb, *oob*, v. x, #2, p. 5. The commune included Marlene Wickes, Coletta Reid, Susan Gregory, Susan Hathaway, Marilyn Webb, Tasha Peterson, Betty Garman, Charlotte Bunch, and Judy Spellman.

85. The Women's Commune, "Mind Bogglers," *oob*, v. 1, #'s 9–10, July 31, 1973, p. 13.

86. Interview with Coletta Reid.

87. Private communication, Jean Tepperman.

88. Haber quoted in Perri Knize, "Anatomy of a Visionary," *Ann Arbor Observer*, March 1987, p. 31.

89. See, for example, A Weatherwoman, "Inside the Weather Machine," *Rat*, v. 2, #27, February 9–23, 1970. "Sex becomes entirely different without jealousy. Women who never saw themselves making it with other women begin digging each other sexually. People who live together and fight together, fuck together."

90. Interviews with Coletta Reid and Joan Biren.

91. Nancy Ferro, Coletta Reid Nolcomb, and Marilyn Webb, in *Woman: A Journal of Liberation*, v. 1., #4, Summer 1970, p. 58.

92. Unsigned, "Philly Convention," *Rat*, v. 3, #13, September 11–25, 1970, p. 17. Undoubtedly, the convention's major attraction was Huey Newton, who had recently been released from jail.

93. Anonymous, "The Days Belonged to the Panthers," and "lesbian testimony," *oob*, v. 1, #11, September 30, 1970, pp. 4–5. See also, Martha Shelley, "subversion in the women's movement: what is to be done," *oob*, v. 1, #13, November 8, 1970, pp. 5–7.

94. Interview with Coletta Reid.

95. Interview with Joan Biren.

96. Marotta, pp. 249–55.

97. Deevey became involved with a longtime veteran of DCWL and Bunch with one of the lesbian-feminists from New York. Deevey's involvement, in particular, sent shockwaves through the community because it was the first such "conversion." See Sharon Deevey, "Such a Nice Girl,"in Myron and Bunch, eds., *Lesbianism and the Women's Movement*. Webb corroborated this in her interview.

98. Interview with Coletta Reid.

99. Interview with Joan Biren.

100. Interview with Joan Biren.

101. Interview with Ginny Berson.

102. Rather, they seem to have been deliberately excluded. Bunch and Brown were reportedly excluded for largely personal reasons—Brown because of per-

sonal antagonisms with some of the members of Amazing Grace, and Bunch primarily because of her marriage to Jim Weeks. Interview with Charlotte Bunch.

103. Interview with Ginny Berson.

104. Helaine Harris notes that there was much intermingling of these three groups, so it is possible that the composition changed somewhat. Private communication, Helaine Harris, 1986.

105. Charlotte Bunch, "Ourstory: DC Herstory," compiled for a women's retreat on May 21, 1971. In Bunch's files; interview with Coletta Reid.

106. Bobbie Goldstone, *oob*, v. 1, #20, April 1971.

107. "Joanne," "Goodbye Ruby Tuesday," *oob*, v. 1, #21, May 6, 1971, p.18.

108. Coletta Reid, "Coming Out in the Women's Movement," in *Lesbianism and the Women's Movement* (Baltimore: Diana Press, 1975), Charlotte Bunch and Nancy Myron, eds., p. 95.

109. Signed by "Those Women," "Lesbians and Day-Care," *Rat*, v. 3, #23, June 14–July 10, 1971, p. 13.

110. Interview with Charlotte Bunch. (LV)

111. Webb alleges that they found identification papers on this woman which linked her to the Chicago police. Interview with Webb. This is the same woman referred to in fn. 76.

112. Interview with Helaine Harris. According to Harris, Berson, Hathaway, Peterson, and she were particularly involved in this case.

113. Interview with Bunch (LV).

114. "Security Is," *Rat*, v. 3, #23, June 14–July 10, 1971, p. 22.

115. Interview with Helaine Harris.

116. Interview with Joan Biren.

117. Although some groups that followed were only more so, most notably the anonymous women who wrote the "C.L.I.T. [collective lesbian international terrors] Papers" which *oob* published in v. 4, #s 6 and 8.

118. There were other lesbian-feminist papers in the early seventies, including: LA's *Lesbian Tide*, Chicago's *Lavender Woman*, Ann Arbor's *Spectre*, and Iowa City's *Ain't I A Woman* which was run by a lesbian collective for a while.

119. Interview with Charlotte Bunch.

120. Interview with Helaine Harris.

121. Interview with Charlotte Bunch. (LV)

122. Interview with Jennifer Woodul.

123. Interview with Charlotte Bunch. (LV)

124. Private communication, Helaine Harris, 1986.

125. Interview with Ginny Berson.

126. Interview with Jennifer Woodul.

127. Interview with Coletta Reid.

128. Interview with Charlotte Bunch. (LV)

129. Interview with Coletta Reid.

130. Private conversation, Bev Manick (Fisher).

131. Interview with Helaine Harris.

132. Brown, "Introduction," *A Plain Brown Rapper*, p. 15. The term was more commonly socialist-feminism, although one occasionally finds the term feminist-socialist in the literature of the day.

133. Brown, "Roxanne Dunbar," reprinted in *A Plain Brown Rapper*, p. 121.

134. Berson, "The Furies," in Bunch and Myron, eds., p. 18.

135. Bunch, "Lesbians in Revolt," in Bunch and Myron, eds., p. 33.

136. Brown, "The Shape of Things to Come," in Ibid., p. 74.

137. Interview with Charlotte Bunch.

138. Interview with Helaine Harris.

139. Interview with Charlotte Bunch. And in March 1971, Rita Mae Brown argued that confronting the issue of lesbianism might ease the movement into exploring the issues of class and race. Brown reasoned that women would be better able to deal with lesbianism because heterosexuality, unlike race or class, could be "transcended." In other words, "every woman . . . has the potential to be a Lesbian." "Hanoi to Hoboken: A Round Trip Ticket," in *A Plain Brown Rapper*, p. 69.

140. Interview with Joan Biren.

141. Interview with Helaine Harris.

142. Interview with Helaine Harris.

143. Interview with Charlotte Bunch.

144. Interview with Alexi Freeman.

145. Interview with Bev Manick.

146. Interview with Charlotte Bunch. (LV)

147. Brown, "Introduction," *A Plain Brown Rapper*, pp. 13–14. I am not sure why the communal clothing was such a divisive issue in Amazing Grace and not in The Furies.

148. Brown, "Introduction," *A Plain Brown Rapper*, p. 17.

149. Interview with Helaine Harris.

150. Interview with Helaine Harris. However, Bunch, who dates the Furies' formation later than Harris, remembers this woman resigning from the lesbian C-R group. Personal communication, Bunch, July 1989.

151. Interview with Marilyn Webb.

152. Interview with Charlotte Bunch.(LV)

153. See the collection of The Furies writings on class, *Class and Feminism* (Baltimore: Diana Press, 1974), Bunch and Myron, eds. Barbara Ehrenreich uses this term in "Life Without Father," *Socialist Review*, #73, January–February 1984, p. 49.

154. Ibid., p. 20.

155. Brown, *A Plain Brown Rapper*, p. 16.

156. Interview with Helaine Harris.

157. Bunch and Myron, p. 10.

158. Interview with Helaine Harris.

159. Interview with Charlotte Bunch.

160. Interview with Helaine Harris.

161. Interview with Charlotte Bunch.

162. Brown, *A Plain Brown Rapper*, p. 18.

163. Interview with Charlotte Bunch.

164. Quoted in Abbot and Love, p. 117; Cited by Anne Koedt, "Lesbianism and Feminism," in Koedt, Levine, and Rapone, p. 246.

165. Interview with Frances Chapman.

166. Deirdre English, Amber Hollibaugh, Gayle Rubin, "Talking Sex: A Conversation on Sexuality and Feminism," *Socialist Review*, #58, July–August 1981, p. 44.

167. Interview with Atkinson, *oob*, December 1979, p. 23.

168. Interview with Helaine Harris.

169. Interview with Marilyn Webb.

170. Private communication, Jean Tepperman.

171. Interview with Patricia Mainardi.

172. Interviews with Charlotte Bunch, Bev Manick, and Alexi Freeman.

173. Interview with Susan Brownmiller.

174. For instance, The Furies were annoyed with the New Haven Women's Liberation Rock Band for delivering a political lecture about abortion to women at a D.C. dance. The Furies felt that abortion was a "straight women's issue."

175. Julia Penelope Stanley, "Notes on the Edge," *Win*, June 26, 1975, p. 9. For an earlier, more tentative version of this stance, see an untitled, unnamed article in the Iowa City feminist paper *Ain't I A Woman*, v. 1, #6, June 4, 1971. The writer proclaims that "as a result of living in a female [lesbian] subculture for a year now, I find that it's very hard for me to relate to many of the problems that the other women see as important, i.e. their husbands."

176. Sharon Deevey, "Such a Nice Girl," in Myron and Bunch, eds., p. 23. Of course, many lesbians remained involved in the reproductive rights struggle.

Chapter 6

1. Ann Fury, "Ideological Myths in Women's Liberation," *Everywoman*, December 11, 1970.

2. Rosalind Delmar and Juliet Mitchell, "Women's Liberation in Britain," *Leviathan*, v. 2, #1, May 1970, p. 38. This issue of the leftist newspaper was devoted to the women's liberation movement.

3. "Woman . . . Towards a New Culture," *It Ain't Me, Babe*, v. 1, #5, p. 2.

4. Robin Morgan, "Rights of Passage," *Ms.*, September 1975, p. 99.

5. Ibid., p. 77.

6. Ibid., p. 99.

7. Barbara Burris, "The Fourth World Manifesto," in Anne Koedt, Ellen Levine, and Anita Rapone, eds., *Radical Feminism* (New York: Quadrangle, 1973). Although Burris was assigned authorship of the article, five other Detroit women—Kathy Barry, Joanne Parrent, Terry Moore, Joanne DeLor, and Cate Stadelman—were listed as "in agreement" with the article. And the article—with the exception of the author's 1973 postscript—reads like a collective effort, with constant references to "we," not "I."

8. Although the conference was originally proposed by Women Strike for Peace, anti-imperialist feminists, like those in D.C., quickly became involved, reportedly out of a desire to "work against the war with a women's liberation consciousness." See D.C. Conference Committee, "Our Vision and How It Failed," *Women: a Journal of Liberation*, v. 2, #4, 1972.

9. A number of D.C.'s anti-imperialist women were involved in planning this conference. However, all the women who were to be Furies members—with the exception of Charlotte Bunch—withdrew from the conference coordinating committee before the conference occurred.

10. Although Lisa Leghorn of Cell 16 did just that in an April 1970 article, "Feminism Undermines," in *No More Fun and Games*, #4, April 1970.

11. Ibid., p. 331.

12. Ibid., p. 332. The "Manifesto's" stance on class and race bears a resemblance to what Dana Densmore of Cell 16 had said a mere six months earlier at a Washington, D.C. conference. To those who argued that the women's movement was divided, Densmore defensively maintained the "unity of women already exists" because "we suffer exactly the same oppression as women." Densmore concluded her speech by declaring that "[t]here are no classes among women."

13. Ibid., p. 355.

14. "Reflections," *Rat*. v. 3, #23, June 14–July 10, 1971, p. 7.

15. Burris, "Fourth World Manifesto," pp. 355–57.

16. Jane Alpert, "Mother Right: A New Feminist Theory," *Ms.*, August 1973. This article appeared in a number of feminist periodicals, including *off our backs* (*oob*) and *Big Mama Rag*.

17. My account of the bombings and the trial is taken from Alpert's autobiography, *Growing Up Underground* (New York: William Morrow, 1981) and the following issues of *Rat*: v. 2, #23, December 3–16, 1970, p. 3; v. 2, no. 26, January 26–February 9, 1970, p. 3; v. 3, #6, May 8–21, 1970, p. 7.

18. Ibid., p. 250.

19. Interview with Alpert.

20. Robin Morgan, "Letter to a Sister Underground," in Robin Morgan, ed., *Sisterhood is Powerful* (New York: Random House, 1970), p. xxxix.

21. Alpert, *Growing Up Underground*, p. 369.

22. The rebellion was motivated by inhumane prison conditions. According to other sources thirty, not forty-two, prisoners and nine prison guard-hostages were killed when 1,700 police and National Guard stormed the prison. A New York State Appeals Court later determined that the government had "intentionally used excessive force" in quelling the rebellion. Abe Peck, *Uncovering the Sixties* (New York: Pantheon, 1985), p. 273.

23. Alpert, "Mother Right," p. 88.

24. Jane Alpert, "Inside the House of D," *Rat*, v. 2, #23, December 3–16, 1969, p. 8.

25. Alpert, "Mother Right," p. 88.

26. Ibid., pp. 90–91.

27. Ibid., p. 92.

28. Ibid., p. 93.

29. Ibid., p. 94.

30. Robin Morgan, "The Rights of Passage," *Ms.*, September 1975, p. 77.

31. Jane Alpert, "Letter from the Underground," *oob*, v. 3, #8, May 1973, p. 27. This letter accompanied "Mother Right," but *Ms.* did not print it.

32. Alpert, "Mother Right," p. 94.

33. Interview with Jane Alpert.

34. See Morgan's influential "Goodbye to All That," which originally appeared in the February 6–23, 1970 issue of *Rat*, v. 2, #27, and was widely reprinted. It appears in Morgan's collected essays, *Going Too Far* (New York: Random House, 1978). Also see her introduction to *Sisterhood is Powerful*.

35. Robin Morgan, "Goodbye to All That," in *Going Too Far*, pp. 126, 129.

36. Alpert, *Growing Up Underground*, 346.

37. Elizabeth Gould Davis, *The First Sex* (Baltimore: Penguin Books, 1973).

38. Alpert described Davis's book as "among the more visionary and lyrically persuasive (if somewhat factually problematic) studies" of ancient matriarchies. "Mother Right," p. 91. Davis's book soon became a cultural feminist classic.

39. Daly, "The Spiritual Dimension of Women's Liberation," in Anne Koedt, Ellen Levine, and Anita Rapone, eds., *Notes from the Third Year: Women's Liberation* (New York: New York Radical Feminists, 1971), pp. 263, 260.

40. Mary Daly, *Beyond God the Father: Toward a Philosophy of Women's Liberation* (Boston: Beacon, 1973), especially pp. 32–33.

41. Kenneth Pitchford, "Sexual Liberation to Revolutionary Effeminism," *Double F*, #1, Summer 1972, p. 6. Pitchford emphasized that Cell 16 influenced his thinking about feminism. In the same article he also proposed the establishment of a "faggot laboratory where faggot scientists could search out the implications of such things as the disastrously high levels of testosterone currently found in straight men." He asked, "would the cruelty exhibited by straight men be reduced if these levels were artificially lowered?" p. 10.

42. Alpert, *Growing Up Underground*, p. 346.

43. Barbara Deming, "To Those Who Would Start a People's Party," *Liberation*, v. 18, #4, December 1973, p. 24.

44. The Feminists, *oob*, v. 3, #9, July–August 1973, p. 26.

45. Betsy Warrior, *oob*, v. 3, #9, July–August 1973, p. 25.

46. Alpert, *Growing Up Underground*, p. 347.

47. Wittig quoted in Hester Eisenstein, *Contemporary Feminist Thought* (Boston: G. K. Hall, 1983), p. xviii.

48. Morgan, "The Proper Study of Womankind," reprinted in *Going Too Far*, p. 197.

49. Kathleen Barry, "West Coast Conference: Not Purely Academic," in *oob*, v. 3, #10, September 1973, p. 25.

50. Barbara McLean, "Diary of a Mad Organizer," *Lesbian Tide*, v. 2, #s10–11, May–June 1973, p. 38.

51. Morgan, "Lesbianism and Feminism," reprinted in *Going Too Far*, p. 176.

52. Quoted in Fran Pollner, "Robin: Harbinger of a New Season," *oob*, v. 2, #17, March 1972, p. 23.

53. Morgan, "Lesbianism and Feminism," in *Going Too Far*, p. 183.

54. Ibid., p. 171.

55. Ibid., p. 181.

56. Ibid., p. 187.

57. In fact, Alpert asserts that in the summer of 1972 both she and Morgan faithfully watched the BBC series on Elizabeth I's life. Alpert claims that Morgan was so impressed by the queen's "unbridled power" that she "invented a new slogan, a half-joking paraphrase" of the radical slogan, "Ho Chi Minh, Live Like Him"—'Elizabeth R, Live Like Her'—"and began to cautiously repeat it around the women's movement." To Alpert, this half-joke revealed that Morgan was rejecting the left for its radicalism. Alpert, *Growing Up Underground*, pp. 333–34.

58. Ann Froines, *oob*, v. 3, #11, October 1973, p. 19.

59. Quoted in *oob*, v. 4, #12, December 1974, p. 5.

60. Madeleine Janover, "Up From Under," *oob*, December 1974, p. 5.

61. Quoted in the petition, "Loyalties in Face of the State," *Majority Report*, v. 4, #22, March 8, 1975.

62. Ibid.

63. Ti-Grace Atkinson, Florynce Kennedy, Susan Sherman, and Joan Hamilton, "The Crisis in Feminism," *Majority Report*, v. 4, #22, March 8, 1975. The newspaper mistakenly labeled their letter, "Petition #2." Atkinson's allegiance to Swinton is somewhat ironic given Swinton's unapologetic heterosexuality. In an interview shortly after her arrest Swinton said that when she first became involved in the women's movement she was "appalled" by some feminists' thinking on sexuality. She declared that, in contrast to some feminists, she "just love[d] to screw." Grace Shinell, "Pat Swinton: Jane Taught Me Feminism," *Majority Report*, v. 4, #25, April 19, 1975, p. 4. Swinton later complained of distortions in this article. Letter to the editor, *Majority Report*, v. 4, #26, May 17, 1975.

64. "Vindication of the Rights of Feminists," in *Majority Report*.

65. Apparently not everyone whose name was listed was consulted. Some women, like Ros Baxandall, report that their names appeared without their consent. Interview with Ros Baxandall.

66. Some contend that the pro-Alpert forces tried to pressure women to sign the petition. Interviews with Alix Kates Shulman and Susan Sherman.

67. Rennie and Grimstad, "Jane Alpert Talks about Feminism and the Left," *Big Mama Rag*, v. 3-A, #2, p. 8.

68. Both Alpert and Morgan are quoted in Jeanne Cordova and Ann Doczi, "Power or Paralysis," *Lesbian Tide*, May–June 1975, p. 34.

69. Interview with Jane Alpert.

70. Alpert, *Growing Up Underground*, p. 362.

71. Interview with Jane Alpert.

72. *Plexus*, August 1975, p. 5.

73. *Newsweek*, March 24, 1975.

74. Swinton, letter to the editor, *Majority Report*, v. 4, #26, May 17, 1975.

75. Bob Gibbs, letter, *Win*, v. 11, #30, September 18, 1975. Gibbs wrote to correct the misimpression that the newsletter was an organ of the National Laywers Guild.

76. Ruth Shearer and Jeanne Cordova, "Underground Activist Acquitted," *Lesbian Tide*, November–December 1975, p.10.

77. The organizers believed that this had been the case.

78. Alpert, *Growing Up Underground*, p. 366. According to Alpert, Morgan formed the group. However, Morgan's name is not listed in a letter announcing the formation of the Circle of Support. See *her-self*, November 1975, p. 2. Susan Brownmiller and Leah Fritz, a frequent contributor to *Win*, also joined the group. See Louise Thompson, "Circle Continues Support for Alpert," *Majority Report*, v. 6, #3, June 12–25, 1976, p. 4.

79. Quoted in Claudia Morrow, "Robin Morgan," *her-self*, June 1975, p. 1.

80. Quoted in Mikki Jackson, "Stalking Steinem," *Sister*, v. 6, #21, June 1975, p. 5.

81. "Anna Ruth," letter, *oob*, v. 5, #7, August 1975, p. 27.

82. Regarding Swinton's defense committee, see Pat Swinton, Ti-Grace Atkinson, Sharon Krebs, and Margo Jefferson, "What You Do Matters," *oob*, v. 5, #6, July 1975, p. 2; Shereff and Cordova, *Lesbian Tide*, p. 11.

83. *Plexus*, v. 2, #6, August 1975.

84. Susan Saxe, "Statement-March 27," *oob*, v. 5, #5, July 1975, p. 6.

85. Reported in Susan Stein, "Salt: One View (New York)," *oob*, v. 6, #2, April 1976, p. 21.

86. The government initiated grand juries in Lexington, Kentucky and in New Haven, Connecticut—two cities where Saxe and Kathleen Powers, her friend and co-conspirator, were known to have been. Several people who refused to cooperate with the grand jury were incarcerated for several months.

87. Jill Johnston, "Lesbian Feminism Isn't a White Male Trip," reprinted in the *Berkeley Barb*, #508, May 9–15, 1975, p. 5.

88. Virginia Blaisdell, "Correct Line-ism and the Grand Jury Sausage-Meat Machine," *Sister: The Monthly Newsletter of New Haven Women's Liberation*, v. 4, #s 5–7, July 1975, p. 5; Johnston, "Lesbian Feminism Isn't a White Male Trip."

89. Morgan, "Rights of Passage," *Ms.*, September 1975, p. 75.

90. However, Morgan attributed women's violence to their maternalism. "Women have been violent when protecting their young, and have killed for this reason." Morgan quoted in Constantina Velma-Daughter, "Blood Thirst among the Vegetarians," *Majority Report*, v. 4, #8, August 8, 1974. And in the spring of 1971, Morgan proposed the establishment of "Women's Skill Summer Sessions" where women would learn such things as self-defense, the use of firearms, basic emergency medical techniques, plumbing, carpentry and electrical skills, and "basic tactical chemistry." "On Violence and Feminism," in *Going Too Far*, pp. 137–38.

91. Stein, "Salt: One View (New York)."

92. Editorial, *Second Wave*, v. 4, #1, Spring 1975, p. 3.

93. Interview with Swinton, Atkinson, Krebs, and Jefferson in *oob*, v. 5, #6, July 1975.

94. They timed its release during the MORE Convention. MORE was an organization of liberal and radical journalists.

95. Sol Stern, "NSA/CIA," *Ramparts*, v. 5, #9, March 1967. Steinem's former connection with the CIA was also mentioned in a *Newsweek* feature article on her. Elizabeth Peer, Ann R. Martin, Lisa Whitman, and Richard Boeth, "Gloria Steinem: The New Woman," *Newsweek*, August 16, 1971, p. 53.

96. Steinem may have remained involved in the IRS past 1962. According to Allard Lowenstein's biographer, Richard Cummings, Steinem recruited Eugene Theroux to work for the IRS in 1965. Theroux was to be part of an American delegation to the 1965 Festival in Algiers. However, the ousting of Algerian ruler Ben Bella forced the cancellation of the Festival. Richard Cummings, *The Pied Piper: Allard K. Lowenstein and the Liberal Dream* (New York: Grove Press, 1985), pp. 186–87.

97. "CIA Subsidized Festival Trips," *New York Times*, February 21, 1967. When questioned later that year by a *Washington Post* reporter about her involvement with the CIA, she "flatly says she would again accept its funds to support her ideas." She further said that "[i]n my experience the Agency was completely different from its image; it was liberal, non-violent, and honorable." Nancy L. Ross, "Writer's Life Can Be Glorious and Beautiful," The *Washington Post*, December 3, 1967, pp K6–7.

98. The two groups did have one meeting at Steinem's house. Brownmiller recalls that Steinem asked what they might put in a feminist magazine. When someone suggested that they could print feminist reviews of books and movies, Steinem reportedly replied, "I never thought of that." Although Steinem at that point in time lacked Brownmiller et al.'s vision, Steinem received seed money

from Clay Felker, publisher of *New York* magazine. Interview with Susan Brownmiller.

99. Barbara Leon, "Gloria Steinem & the CIA," in Redstockings, eds., *Feminist Revolution*, (New Paltz: Redstockings, 1975), p. 161.

100. Ibid., p. 152.

101. *Lesbian Tide*, v. 4, #7, July–August 1975, p. 39. Of course, some feminists came to Steinem's defense. For letters that support Steinem, see *Hera*, September 1975, p. 18. Friedan's collection of essays, *It Changed My Life* (New York: Norton, 1985) contains several references to Steinem which are clearly intended to be unflattering. See pp. 244–45, 259, 343. While Friedan did not accuse Steinem of having had CIA associations, she did nothing to silence those charges. Explaining her silence a year later, she said, "if the charges [about Steinem's past CIA involvement] were true, no appeal to 'sisterhood' could gloss over the implications and dangers to the movement, and I would not be intimidated into silencing those questions." (*It Changed My Life*, p. 343.)

102. Ellen Willis, "Statement," *oob*, v. 5, #8, September–October 1975, p. 7. The article in question—Robin Morgan, "The Rights of Passage," *Ms.*, September 1975.

103. For instance, *Newsweek* reported on the group's efforts to "pack the 400-man [American] delegation with 'as many mature, informed people as possible,' " and to brief them on "effective ways of attacking Communist propaganda." See "Our 400 and the Reds," *Newsweek*, July 6, 1959, p. 78. Theroux served as the chairman of the Metropolitan New York region of NSA. For more on the festivals, see Cummings, *The Pied Piper: Allard K. Lowenstein and the Liberal Dream*, pp. 61–64, 186–87.

104. See Cummings, *The Pied Piper: Allard K. Lowenstein and the Liberal Dream*. In fact, Cummings contends that Lowenstein was a CIA agent from 1962–1967. Both Cumming's scholarship and perceptiveness have been questioned by some reviewers, including Hendrik Hertzberg, "The Second Assassination of Al Lowenstein," *The New York Review of Books*, October 10, 1985, pp. 34–41. *The Pied Piper* would undoubtedly have been a better book had Cummings been more interested in analyzing Lowenstein's liberal anti-communism and less anxious to prove that he was a CIA operative.

105. This account is drawn from Janis Kelly and Fran Moira, "Sagaris: A Case of Mistaken Identity," *oob*, v. 5, #9, November 1975, pp. 14–15; *Hera*, September 1975.

106. The controversy around Steinem and her past association with a CIA front raged again briefly when an expurgated version of Redstockings' *Feminist Revolution* was published by Random House in 1979. Random House excised the chapter on Steinem after she threatened to sue the publisher for libel. Nancy Borman wrote an article detailing the publishing history of the book in the May 21, 1979 issue of the *Village Voice*. The Borman account, which was very sympathetic to Redstockings, prompted a number of angry letters.

107. See Redstockings, "The Pseudo-Left Lesbian Alliance," and Patricia Mainardi, "The Marriage Question" in *Feminist Revolution*. Carol Hanisch's stance toward lesbians and gay men grew increasingly antagonistic. (She contends that her growing contentiousness on the issue was in response to the pervasive conflation of lesbianism and feminism. Private communication, Carol Hanisch, August 1988.) In her article, "Homosexuality: Toward a Radical Feminist Analy-

sis,'' Hanisch likened lesbianism to mutual masturbation and asked if there "is something intrinsically valuable in lesbianism that demands its continued existence?'' Hanisch thought not, arguing that lesbianism would wither away with the elimination of male supremacy. By contrast, "[t]he obvious intrinsic value in heterosexuality,'' Hanisch claimed, "is the continuation of the human race.'' *Meeting Ground*, #4, March 1978. According to Brooke Williams, who was acquainted with the reorganized Redstockings, some Redstockings members "expressed harsher views [on lesbianism] even than their published articles.'' Brooke, letter to the editor, *oob*, v. 10, #7, July 1980.

108. I am thinking in particular of Rita Mae Brown and the Furies members who formed Olivia Records and *Quest*. The term is Robin Morgan's. See *The New Woman's Survival Sourcebook* (New York: Knopf, 1975), p. 109.

109. Wini Breines, *Community and Organization in the New Left: 1962–1968* (New York: Praeger, 1982), p. 95.

110. Clayborne Carson, *In Struggle* (Cambridge: Harvard University Press, 1981), p. 128. Moses also proposed that blacks of Nashoba County recognize only the authority of their own "Freedom Sheriff.'' (Carson, p. 178.)

111. See James Miller, *Democracy Is in the Streets* (New York: Simon & Schuster, 1987), pp. 234, 239.

112. The Atlanta Project's position paper is reprinted with the somewhat misleading title, "SNCC Speaks for Itself,'' in Judith Clavir Albert and Stewart Albert, eds., *The Sixties Papers*, p. 122. The title the anthologizers have given it is a misnomer because in the spring of 1966 when it was written it did not reflect majority opinion in SNCC.

113. Amiri Imanu Baraka, "A Black Value System,'' *The Black Scholar*, November 1969.

114. Tom Hayden, "Democracy Is . . . in the Streets,'' *Rat*, v. 1, #15, August 23–September 5, 1968, p. 5.

115. "Rape: An Act of Terror,'' in Koedt, Levine, and Hole, *Notes from the Third Year*, p. 81.

116. Kathy Barry, "West Coast Conference: Not Purely Academic,'' p. 25.

117. Pride quoted in Gayle Kimball, ed., *Women's Culture: The Women's Renaissance of the Seventies* (Metuchen, NJ: The Scarecrow Press, 1981), p. 2. Pride was the editor of KNOW Press.

118. Mary Daly, *Beyond God the Father*, p. 41.

119. Ibid., p. 156.

120. Susan Rennie and Kirsten Grimstad, eds., *The New Woman's Survival Sourcebook* (New York: Alfred Knopf, 1975), p. 236.

121. Ibid., p. 106. Included in the *Sourcebook* is a long interview with Robin Morgan and Adrienne Rich.

122. "Put a Women's Revolution First,'' *Lesbian Tide*, v. 2, #9, April 1973. This article is an edited transcript of a talk Brown gave in L.A. on April 13, 1973.

123. Helaine Harris and Lee Schwing, "Building Feminist Institutions,'' *The Furies*, v. 2, #3, May–June 1973.

124. Interestingly, the name Diana Press "was agreed upon as a compromise between those who wanted to commemorate Weatherwoman Diana Oughton and others who saw Diana as a symbol of ancient women's culture.'' Rennie and Grimstad, *The New Woman's Survival Catalogue* (New York: Coward, McCann and Geoghegan, 1973), p. 9.

125. Coletta Reid, "Taking Care of Business," *Quest*, v. 1, #2, Fall 1974, p. 8.

126. Robin Morgan, "The Rights of Passage," *Going Too Far*, p. 78.

127. According to Morgan, the Sisterhood is Powerful fund had channeled $27,000 to feminist groups by mid-1973. However, the fund's continued existence was jeopardized in 1973 when feminist abortion-rights activist Lucinda Cisler sued Robin Morgan on the grounds that she had plagiarized Cisler's widely read bibliography, *Women: a Bibliography* (*W:aB*) in her anthology. Cisler contended that sales of her bibliography—which she claimed subsidized her pro-abortion activism—plummeted after publication of *Sisterhood is Powerful*. Morgan denied having plagiarized her bibliography. However, at the preliminary injunction hearing the presiding judge told Random House lawyers, "obviously you can use [*W:aB*] as a source. But it seems to me that mathematically I have got to come to the conclusion that it was an editing job of [Cisler's] bibliography." Shortly after it appeared that Random House might settle with Cisler out of court, a group of feminists circulated "An Open Letter to the Women's Movement," which valorized Morgan and vilified Cisler. (See *Big Mama Rag*, v. 3, #2, August 1974.) The signers—Mary Daly, Kathleen Barry, Adrienne Rich, and Joan Hoff Wilson—attacked Cisler for endangering the fledgling female culture which the SIP fund was helping to subsidize. Despite considerable pressure to drop her suit, Cisler persisted and won a $10,000 settlement from Random House. To avoid imperiling the SIP fund, Cisler's lawyer requested that the publisher be reimbursed from the royalties of books that Morgan had written. However, the Random House lawyers insisted on compensation from *Sisterhood is Powerful* royalties. Although Morgan had her supporters, many feminists, including Anne Koedt, Ellen Levine, and Naomi Weisstein defended Cisler. Ellen Levine compared the Morgan-Cisler affair to a rape trial "in which the victim has become the offender, and the offender, somehow, the victim." She contended, "that Cisler's work was stolen is obvious when one looks at the evidence; that some women in the movement are ignoring the injustice and talking only about the 'rape' of the Sisterhood Fund is outrageous. . . . Rape in the name of sisterhood, is indeed powerful." Her letter appeared in *oob*, v. 5, #1, January 1975, p. 25. For an account of the controversy, see, *oob*, v. 4, #10, October 1974; and the letters section of December 1974 *oob*, v. 4, #12.

128. Rennie and Grimstad, eds., *The New Woman's Survival Sourcebook*, p. 29.

129. Mary Daly, Kathleen Barry, Adrienne Rich, and Joan Hoff Wilson, "An Open Letter to the Women's Movement," *Big Mama Rag*, v. 3, #2, August 1974. See footnote 127 for background on the letter.

130. Kathy Barry, et al., "F.E.N.," *oob*, v. 6, #10, January 1977, p. 16.

131. Ibid.

132. Morgan, "Rights of Passage," *Ms.*, September 1975, p. 99.

133. Rita Mae Brown, "The Lady's Not for Burning," in Brown, *A Plain Brown Rapper* (Baltimore: Diana Press, 1976), p. 209.

134. For a critique of feminist businesses, see Brooke Williams and Hannah Darby, "god, mom & apple pie: 'feminist' businesses as an extension of the american dream," *oob*, v. 5, #11, January–February 1976.

135. "the muses of olivia: our own economy, our own song," *oob*, v. 4, #9, August/September 1974, p. 3.

136. Editors' introduction to "An Interview on Women's Health Politics," with Frances Hornstein of the FWHC. *Quest*, v. 1, #1 (Summer 1974), p. 27. For more

on the FWHC's philosophy, see FWHC co-founder Carol Downer's "What Makes the Feminist Women's Health Center 'feminist'?" *oob*, v. 4, #7, June 1974. For instance, Downer proclaimed that whether a woman worked as a "volunteer, or for low pay, or for high wages" she "will never be exploited" for "when a woman works for the FWHC, she knows that her labor is contributing solely to the achievement of the betterment of her sex."

137. For one account of working conditions at the Orange County FWHC, see "What is 'Feminist' Health?" *oob*, v. 4, #7, June 1974. On the credit union's expansionist designs, see Belita Cowan and Cheryl Peck, "The Controversy at FEN," *her-self*, May 1976.

138. The speaker here is Joanne Parrent of the DFFCU, quoted in Martha Shelley, "What is FEN?" self-published.

139. My account of FEN is drawn largely from the following sources: Cowan and Peck, "The Controversy at FEN," *her-self*, May 1976; Shelley, "What is FEN?"; Jackie St. Joan, "Feminist Economic Seeds Split," *Big Mama Rag* v. 4, #1; Janis Kelly, et al., *oob*, v. 6, #1, March 1976.

140. Quoted in Cowan and Peck.

141. Kathy Barry, et al., "F.E.N.," p. 16.

142. Private conversation, Bev Manick, 1981.

143. Eight individual women applied for $31,250 each in loans from the DFFCU to circumvent the National Credit Union Administration's regulation forbidding federal credit unions from granting loans to businesses. When the women received their loans they bought the City Club and assigned their interest in the Club to the FEN Corporation. In return they received a promissory note from FEN. Cowan and Peck, "The Controversy at FEN," *her-self*, May 1976, p. 10.

144. Kathy Barry, et al., "F.E.N.," p. 16. Barry presented herself as the sole author of this article. However, the feminist newspaper *Plexus*—to whom Barry had first submitted the article—discovered that Barry had written it collaboratively with several of the women who founded FEN. *Plexus* refused to publish the article because of the apparent subterfuge. See Martha Shelley, "What is FEN?" self-published, p. 18.

145. Private conversation, Bev Manick, 1981.

146. Kathy Barry, et al., "F.E.N.," p. 16.

147. Quoted in Cowan and Peck, p. 10.

148. Quoted in Shelley, p. 19.

149. Kathy Barry, et al., "F.E.N.," p. 16.

150. Quoted in Cowan and Peck.

151. Quoted in Jackie St. Joan, "Feminist Economic Seeds Split."

152. Barbara Leon in Redstockings, p. 160. For instance, in 1977 Rita Mae Brown argued that the movement had not achieved more because many feminists feared success. "If we wanted to succeed, by god, we would. We have the woman power, we have the brains, and we have the money. . . . But the point is we don't want to succeed or we would." *Longest Revolution*, v. 1, #4, April 1977.

153. Robin Morgan, "The Rights of Passage," p. 99.

154. Ibid., p. 99.

155. Quoted in Cowan and Peck, p. 10.

156. Naomi Weisstein and Heather Booth, "Will the Women's Movement Survive?" reprint from *Sister: The Monthly Newsletter of New Haven Women's Liberation*, v. 4, #12, 1976.

157. For example, in the late '70s Olivia Records cut its staff from fourteen to eight and eliminated its collective structure in order to survive. Michelle Kort, "Sisterhood is Profitable," *Mother Jones*, July 1983, p. 44.

158. Kort, "Sisterhood is Profitable," p. 44.

159. Ehrenreich quoted in Carol Ann Douglas, "Second Sex 30 Years Later," *oob*, v. 9, #11, December 1979, p. 26.

160. Adrienne Rich, "Living the Revolution," *The Women's Review of Books*, v. 3, #12, September 1986.

161. Reported by Alison Colbert, letter, *oob*, v. 5, #9, November, 1975, p. 20.

162. Rennie and Grimstad, eds., *The New Woman's Survival Sourcebook*, p. 139. Of course, the irony is that *oob* actually represented the politico position when it was formed in 1970, and its shift to radical feminism was gradual.

163. Kathy Barry, et al., "F.E.N.," p. 17.

164. Robin Morgan, "The Rights of Passage," p. 99.

165. Ellen Willis, "Statement," *oob*, v. 5, #8, September–October 1975, p. 7.

166. Atkinson and Sarachild quoted in *Majority Report*, v. 6, #2, May 29–June 12, 1976, p. 3.

167. Atkinson quoted in Judy Antonelli, "Atkinson Re-evaluates Feminism," *oob*, v. 5, #5, May–June 1975, p. 19.

168. Weisstein and Booth, "Will the Women's Movement Survive?" p. 5.

169. Brooke, "The Retreat to Cultural Feminism," in Redstockings, eds., *Feminist Revolution*, p. 68.

170. Kimball, *Women's Culture*, p. 22.

171. Friedan, *It Changed My Life*, p. 258.

172. See Adrienne Rich, *Of Woman Born* (New York: Norton, 1976), pp. 39–40, 283–85; Janice Raymond, *The Transsexual Empire* (Boston: Beacon Press, 1979), pp. 107, 114; Susan Griffin, *Woman and Nature: The Roaring Inside Her* (New York: Harper & Row, 1978); Mary Daly, *Gyn-Ecology* (Boston: Beacon Press, 1978). As one might expect, cultural feminists were not especially fond of androgyny. In renouncing androgyny, cultural feminists were not only repudiating liberal social scientists' formulation of androgyny, which had too often assumed an uncritical stance toward masculinity, they were also rejecting radical feminism's vision of deconstructing gender. I agree, however, that androgyny is in some respects a problematic concept. As Catharine Stimpson has observed, proponents of androgyny often retained the categories of masculinity and femininity rather than "conceptualiz[ing] the world in a new way that leaves 'feminine' and 'masculine' behind." Stimpson, "The Androgyne and the Homosexual," *Women's Studies* #2, 1974, pp. 237–38.

173. By contrast, when spirituality was first advanced, the feminist press responded skeptically. For instance, *oob* published a piece that criticized a 1976 women's spirituality conference in Boston for encouraging a retreat into goddess worship. See Hope Landrine and Joan Regensburger, "through the looking glass: a conference of myopics," *oob*, v. 6, #4 June 1976, p. 12. In large part because of the furor caused by the negativity of that article, *oob* sent two regular staffers to cover a New York women's spirituality conference only a few months later. Interestingly, one reporter filed an almost wholly negative report, the other a considerably more generous and optimistic one. See Janis Kelly and Fran Moira, "New York Spirituality Conference," *oob*, v.6, #9, December 1976.

174. Brooke, "The Chador of Women's Liberation: Cultural Feminism and the

Movement Press," *Heresies*, v. 3, #1, 1980. Note that the use of the singular "woman's" in *Chrysalis's* self-description implies that there is a universality to women's experiences.

175. The phrase is Firestone's. She is quoted in Margie Stamberg, "The New Feminism," *Guardian*, March 22, 1969, p. 11.

176. According to Zillah Eisenstein, the Houston report specifically demanded: an end to violence against women and the establishment of shelters for battered women; a solution to child abuse; federally funded nonsexist child care; a policy of full employment so that all women who wish to and are able to may work; the protection of homemakers; reproductive freedom for women and an end to involuntary sterilization; the elimination of sexism in the media; a remedy for the double discrimination experienced by women of color; a revision of criminal codes dealing with rape; an end to discrimination on the basis of sexual preference; the establishment of nonsexist education; an analysis of all welfare reform proposals for their impact on women. Eisenstein, *The Radical Future of Liberal Feminism* (New York: Longman, 1981), p. 232.

177. See Brett Harvey, "Give 'Em Ellie," *Village Voice*, February 11, 1986; Ellen Willis, "Betty Friedan's 'Second Stage': A Step Backwards," *The Nation*, November 14, 1981.

178. I do not mean to suggest that socialist-feminists and liberal feminists had no important part in bringing about many of these changes. However, with the exception of women's health care, which initially attracted many left feminists as well, radical feminists provided the initial spark and analysis.

Epilogue

1. However, anti-pornography feminists are often quite antagonistic to the left. Andrea Dworkin demonizes the left in "Why So-Called Radical Men Love and Need Pornography," in Laura Lederer, ed., *Take Back the Night* (New York: William Morrow, 1980). In the spring of 1987, anti-pornography feminists organized a conference, "Sexual Liberals and the Attack on Feminism," in which leftists and liberals who had criticized the anti-pornography movement were accused of attacking feminism. Feminism's relationship to the gay movement was a divisive issue in the pre-AIDS period. Cultural feminists repudiated gay men's promotion of casual sex. For a discussion of this, see Alice Echols, "The Taming of the Id," in Carole Vance, ed., *Pleasure and Danger* (New York: Routledge & Kegan Paul, 1984).

2. Betty Friedan, *The Second Stage* (New York: Summit Books, 1981). Elshtain has written widely, and the following list is very partial: Elshtain, *Public Man, Private Woman: Women in Social and Political Thought* (Princeton: Princeton University Press, 1981); "Against Androgyny," *Telos*, #42, Spring 1981; "Feminism, Family and Community," *Dissent*, Fall 1982. Although both Friedan and Elshtain revalue femaleness, their repudiation of sexual politics and their promotion of the nuclear family put them at odds with cultural feminists. Judith Stacey has termed both Friedan and Elshtain "new conservative feminists." See her essay "The New Conservative Feminism," *Feminist Studies*, v. 9, #3, Fall 1983. And for a critique of Friedan's *Second Stage*, see Ellen Willis, "Betty Friedan's 'Second Stage': A Step Backward," *The Nation*, November 14, 1981.

3. As Judith Stacey points out, this new conservative feminism was foreshadowed by Alice Rossi's article "A Biosocial Perspective on Parenting," *Daedalus*, #106, Spring 1977.

4. There is in Gilligan's work, as the historian Joan Scott has pointed out, a slippage in the attribution of causality as the argument moves away from an emphasis on women's experiences as formative (i.e., social constructionist) to the standard precultural explanation—"women think and choose this way because they are women." Gender differences become reified and assume a kind of inevitability. Moreover, in all of this work there is an unwillingness to confront the possibility that female values are implicated in women's subordination. Joan Scott, "Gender: A Useful Category of Historical Analysis," *American Historical Review*, #91, December 1986. For a critique of Gilligan's work, see Judy Auerbach, Linda Blum, Vicki Smith, and Christine Williams, "Commentary: On Gilligan's *In a Different Voice*," *Feminist Studies*, v. 11, #4, Spring 1985.

5. Deborah Rhode, "Feminist Perspectives on Legal Ideology," in Juliet Mitchell and Anne Oakley, eds., *What is Feminism: A Re-examination* (New York: Pantheon, 1986), p. 157. For instance, according to one study, gender-neutral, no-fault divorce laws have contributed to female impoverishment. Lenore Weitzman, *The Divorce Revolution: The Unexpected Social and Economic Consequences for Women and Children in America* (New York: Free Press, 1985). However, some critics of gender-neutral laws do seem to be essentialists. For example, Dorothy Wickenden assails "equal rights' feminism" for assuming that "social, legal, and economic equality must be pursued in defiance of gender differences." See Wickenden, "What NOW?" *The New Republic*, May 5, 1986.

6. For examples of eco-feminism and feminist pacifism, see *Heresies*, Feminism and Ecology Issue, #13, 1981; a number of the essays in Pam McAllister, ed., *Reweaving the Web of Life: Feminism and Nonviolence* (Philadelphia: New Society Publishers, 1982). Not all feminists who argue for feminist mobilizations against militarization are cultural feminists or essentialists. For example, both Sara Ruddick and Jean Bethke Elshtain attribute women's greater pacifism to their responsibility for child-rearing rather than biology. See Ruddick, "Preservative Love and Military Destruction: Some Reflections on Mothering and Peace," in Joyce Trebilcot, ed., *Mothering: Essays in Feminist Theory* (Totowa, NJ: 1984); Elshtain, "Women, War and Feminism," *The Nation*, June 14, 1980. For critiques of feminist pacifism, see: Ellen Willis's June 23, 1980 column in the *Village Voice*; Micaela Di Leonardo, "Morals, Mother, and Militarism: Antimilitarism and Feminist Theory," *Feminist Studies*, v. 11, #3, Fall 1985; and much of the coverage of the 1980 Women's Pentagon Action in the January 1981 issue of *oob*.

7. Two of the earliest feminist critiques of pornography were: Roxanne Dunbar, " 'Sexual Liberation': More of the Same Thing," *No More Fun and Games*, #3, November 1969; Ti-Grace Atkinson, "Individual Responsibility and Human Oppression," a May 1970 speech that appears in *Amazon Odyssey* (New York: Links Books, 1974). But Robin Morgan's 1974 article, "Theory and Practice: Pornography and Rape," was the most influential. It is reprinted in *Going Too Far* (New York: Random House, 1978). Perhaps the earliest feminist action against pornography was in September of 1969 when Bay Area Women's Liberation protested a local underground paper's decision to publish a pornographic magazine to support the paper (reported in *Tooth n' Nail*, October 1969). Again in the spring of 1970 Bay Area women's liberationists protested another underground paper's

"degrading use of [women's] bodies" (reported in *It Ain't Me, Babe*, August 6–20, 1970). The issue of pornography was also one of the factors in the women's takeover of *RAT* in January 1970. It's probably not coincidental that these protests began occurring in 1969 and 1970, for in the spring of 1969 record companies began pulling ads from underground papers, thus depriving these papers of much of their revenue and indirectly encouraging many of them to publish pornography to sustain themselves. There is considerable evidence that record company executives were persuaded to withdraw their ads by the FBI. But the founding of *Rolling Stone*, the aboveground rock n'roll magazine which continued to get ad revenue from record companies, was certainly a contributing factor. Of course, the use of sexist pornography was often not seen as contradicting countercultural values because the counterculture was itself deeply sexist. See Abe Peck, *Uncovering the Sixties* (New York: Pantheon, 1985), pp. 169–77; Geoffrey Rips, *The Campaign Against the Underground Press* (San Francisco: City Lights Books, 1981). One of the most publicized protests against pornography occurred in the spring of 1970 when a group of feminists, including Robin Morgan, led demonstrations against Grove Press and a boycott against its books. The protest originated with the firings of several Grove Press employees who had been trying to organize a union at the Press. See Robin Morgan, *Going Too Far*, pp. 132–33.

8. Major anti-pornography texts include: Laura Lederer, ed., *Take Back the Night*; Susan Griffin, *Pornography and Silence* (New York: Harper and Row, 1981); Andrea Dworkin, *Pornography: Men Possessing Women* (New York: Perigee, 1981). The following books contain sections on pornography: Kathleen Barry, *Female Sexual Slavery* (Englewood Cliffs, NJ: Prentice-Hall, 1979); Andrea Dworkin, *Right-Wing Women* (New York: Perigree, 1983); Catherine MacKinnon, *Feminism Unmodified: Discourses on Life and Law* (Cambridge: Harvard University Press, 1987).

9. For instance, Bobbie Goldstone in *oob* declared "it's no secret that pornography degrades women. But so in all fairness to pornographers, do Doris Day movies." Goldstone, "The Politics of Pornography: The Pornography of Politics," *oob*, v. 1, #14, December 14, 1970, p. 10.

10. Like many women's liberationists, *oob* writer Bobbie Goldstone opposed censorship, arguing, "[W]hen Public Decency comes charging through, it gets the good, the bad and the ugly." Ibid.

11. For instance, one of the major figures in the anti-pornography movement, Andrea Dworkin, has declared that "the heart of sex oppression [is] the use of women as pornography, pornography as what women *are*." Dworkin, *Right-Wing Women*, p. 237.

12. Women's sexuality is characterized as more spiritual than sexual. For example, see Robin Morgan, "Lesbianism and Feminism," *Going Too Far*, p. 181; Adrienne Rich, "Compulsory Heterosexuality and Lesbian Existence," in Catharine Stimpson and Ethel Spector Person, eds., *Women: Sex and Sexuality* (Chicago: University of Chicago Press, 1980), p. 81. And all too often male sexuality is treated as though it were intrinsically uncontrollable and violent. See Andrea Dworkin, "Why So-Called Radical Men Love and Need Pornography," in Laura Lederer, ed., *Take Back the Night*.

13. This is not to say that all anti-pornography feminists are essentialists. For example, both Andrea Dworkin and Catherine MacKinnon have repudiated essentialism. See Dworkin, "Biological Superiority: The World's Most Dangerous

Weapon," *Heresies*, #6, Summer 1978; Catharine MacKinnon, "Desire and Power," *Feminism Unmodified*. However, their view of male dominance as eternal and unchanging makes social constructionism, in their hands, virtually indistinguishable from essentialism. Gender might be socially constructed rather than biologically determined, but if the social structure is as impervious to change as they suggest, it might as well be biologically fixed. I am indebted to Ann Snitow for helping me to understand this. For a discussion of feminism and difference which touches on this, see Janice Doane and Devon Hodges, *Nostalgia and Sexual Difference* (New York: Methuen, 1987).

14. Ann Snitow, "Retrenchment vs. Transformation: The Politics of the Anti-Pornography Movement," in *Caught Looking: Feminism, Pornography and Censorship* (New York: Caught Looking Inc., 1986), pp. 11–12.

15. For example, see Judith Bat-Ada, "Playboy Isn't Playing Anymore," in Laura Lederer, ed., *Take Back the Night*.

16. Many criticisms have been made of the anti-pornography movement. Perhaps the most commonly voiced concern was that anti-pornography ordinances, such as those proposed in Minneapolis and Indianapolis and endorsed by the feminist group Women Against Pornography, would seriously erode free speech. Many feminists also objected to the movement's exaggeration of difference, and to its depiction of difference as timeless and perhaps permanent. They pointed out that the movement's depiction of men's and women's sexuality reflected and reinforced dominant cultural assumptions. Feminist critics contended that the anti-pornography movement reduced women to helpless victims, without any agency whatsoever. And they argued that the movement's definition of pornography as male propaganda that could only disgust women could unwittingly reinforce women's sexual guilt and fortify the pernicious "good girl-bad girl" distinction.

Feminist critiques of the anti-pornography movement can be found in the following books and journals: Ann Snitow, Christine Stansell, and Sharon Thompson, eds., *Powers of Desire* (New York: Monthly Review Press, 1983); Carole Vance, ed., *Pleasure and Danger*; F.A.C.T. Book Committee, *Caught Looking*; *Heresies 12: The Sex Issue* (New York: Heresies Collective, 1981). Articles that do not appear in these collections include: Deirdre English, "The Politics of Porn: Can Feminists Walk the Line?" *Mother Jones*, April 1980; Deirdre English, Amber Hollibaugh, and Gayle Rubin, "Talking Sex: A Conversation on Sexuality and Feminism," *Socialist Review*, #58, July/August 1981; Dorothy Allison, "Lesbian Politics in the '80's: Erotic Blasphemy," *New York Native*, December 7–20, 1981.

17. For a discussion of first-wave feminist thinking on sexuality, see Ellen DuBois and Linda Gordon, "Seeking Ecstasy on the Battlefield: Danger and Pleasure in Nineteenth Century Feminist Thought," Vance, ed., *Pleasure and Danger*.

18. There is, for example, a striking similarity between MacKinnon's ideas on sexuality and those expressed by The Feminists fifteen years earlier. For example, MacKinnon argues that "sexual desire in women is socially constructed as that by which we come to want our own self-annihilation." MacKinnon, "Desire and Power," *Feminism Unmodified*, p. 54.

19. The term "compulsory heterosexuality" was coined by Adrienne Rich in her widely anthologized article, "Compulsory Heterosexuality and Lesbian Existence," in Stimpson and Person, eds., *Women: Sex and Sexuality*. It was subsequently reprinted in *Powers of Desire*. The editors of this anthology engaged Rich in a dialogue about the piece, and parts of their correspondence appear as an after-

word to the original essay in Rich, *Blood, Bread and Poetry, Selected Prose, 1979–1985* (New York: Norton, 1986).

20. For instance, Catharine MacKinnon suggests that "sexual intercourse under conditions of gender inequality . . . [is] an issue of forced sex." "The Male Ideology: A Feminist Perspective on the Right to Abortion," *Radical America*, v. 17, #4, July/August 1983. See Rosalind Petchesky's response, "Abortion as 'Violence Against Women': A Feminist Critique," *Radical America* v. 18, #s2–3, March/June 1984.

21. Samois, *Coming to Power: Writings and Graphics on Lesbian S/M* (Berkeley, CA: Samois, 1981; Pat Califia, "Feminism and Sadomasochism," *Heresies 12: The Sex Issue*; Amber Hollibaugh and Cherrie Moraga, "What We're Rolling Around in Bed With: Sexual Silences in Feminism," in Snitow, Stansell, and Thompson, eds., *Powers of Desire*; Paula Webster, "The Forbidden: Eroticism and Taboo," Joan Nestle, "The Fem Question," Muriel Dimen, "Politically Correct? Politically Incorrect?" Dorothy Allison, "Public Silence, Private Terror," all in Vance, ed., *Pleasure and Danger*.

22. It is important to point out that I have not been a disinterested observer throughout the recent sex debate. For my critique of the anti-pornography movement, see "The Taming of the Id: Feminist Sexual Politics, 1968–83," in Vance, ed., *Pleasure and Danger*; "The New Feminism of Yin and Yang," in Snitow, Stansell, and Thompson, eds., *Powers of Desire*.

23. For the initial announcement of the NBFO's founding see *oob*, v. 3, #10, September 1973, p. 9. For further coverage of the NBFO in *oob*, see v. 4, #2, pp. 1–2; v. 4, #3, p. 2.

24. E. Francis White, "Listening to the Voices of Black Feminism," *Radical America*, v. 18, #s2–3, March–June 1984, p. 9.

25. Diane Lewis, "A Response to Inequality: Black Women, Racism and Sexism," *Signs*, v. 3, #2, 1977, pp. 339–61.

26. *Conditions 5: The Black Women's Issue*, Autumn 1979; Gloria Josephs and Jill Lewis, *Common Differences* (Garden City, NY: Doubleday, 1981); Combahee River Collective, "A Black Feminist Statement," in Zillah Eisenstein, ed., *Capitalist Patriarchy and the Case for Socialist Feminism* (New York: Monthly Review Press, 1979); Bell Hooks, *Ain't I A Woman: Black Women and Feminism* (Boston: South End Press, 1981); Cherríe Moraga and Gloria Anzaldúa, eds., *This Bridge Called My Back: Writings by Radical Women of Color* (Watertown, MA: Persephone Press, 1981); Gloria Hull, Patricia Scott, and Barbara Smith, eds., *But Some of Us Are Brave* (New York: Feminist Press, 1982); Barbara Smith, ed., *Home Girls: A Black Feminist Anthology* (New York: Kitchen Table Press, 1985); Alice Walker, *In Search of Our Mothers' Gardens* (New York: Harcourt Brace Jovanovich, 1983); Audre Lorde's collection of essays, *Sister Outsider* (Trumansberg, NY: The Crossing Press, 1984); Hazel Carby, "White Woman Listen! Black Feminism and the Boundaries of Sisterhood," in *The Empire Strikes Back: Race and Racism in '70's Britain* (London: Hutchinson and Co., 1982); Barrie Thornton Dill, "Race, Class and Gender: Prospects for an All-inclusive Sisterhood," *Feminist Studies*, v. 9, #1, Spring 1983; Paula Giddings, *When and Where I Enter: The Impact of Black Women on Race and Sex in America* (New York: Bantam Books, 1985).

27. Hortense Spillers, "Interstices: A Small Drama of Words," Carole Vance, ed., *Pleasure and Danger*, p. 78. Spillers points out that "when we say 'feminism'

without an adjective in front of it, we mean, of course, white women, who, as a category of social and cultural agents fully occupy the territory of feminism." But when we speak of "other communities of women," we inevitably use "some qualifying term." Thus, people will often speak of "liberal feminism," "radical feminism," "socialist-feminism," and "black feminism," a formulation which suggests that "black feminism" stands completely outside of these other strands of feminism. In *Common Differences* (Garden City, NY: Doubleday, 1981) Gloria Josephs and Jill Lewis have tried to break out of this locution by using the terms "Black feminism" and "White feminism." However, Ellen Willis notes that the term "White feminism" is "as self-contradictory as, say, 'male socialism'; while one can speak of a feminism limited and flawed by white racist bias, it is *feminism* only to the extent that it challenges the subjection of women as a group." Willis, "Sisters Under the Skin? Confronting Race and Sex," *Village Voice Literary Supplement*, #8, June 1982, p. 12.

28. Lorraine Bethel, "What Chou Mean *We*, White Girl?" *Conditions 5: The Black Women's Issue*, Autumn 1979.

29. Hooks, *Ain't I a Woman*, pp. 150–51; 195.

30. Combahee River Collective, "A Black Feminist Statement," in Eisenstein, ed., *Capitalist Patriarchy and the Case for Socialist Feminism*, p. 362.

31. The Combahee River Collective wrote of experiencing different oppressions "simultaneously." I believe that the phrase "simultaneity of oppresssions" is Adrienne Rich's. See her 1984 essay, "A Politics of Location," in *Blood, Bread and Poetry*, p. 218.

32. E. Frances White, "Listening to the Voices of Black Feminism," *Radical America*, pp. 17–21; Hazel Carby, "White Women, Listen! Black Women and the Boundaries of Sisterhood," in *The Empire Strikes Back: Race and Racism in '70's Britain*. This issue was raised in the mid-'70s by anthropologist Mina Davis Caulfield in relation to colonized cultures. Caulfield, "Imperialism, the Family and Cultures of Resistance," in Alison Jaggar and Paula Rothenberg, eds., *Feminist Frameworks* (New York: McGraw-Hill, 1978).

33. Rayna Rapp and Ellen Ross, "The Twenties Backlash: Compulsory Heterosexuality, the Consumer Family and the Waning of Feminism," in Amy Swerdlow and Hannah Lessinger, eds., *Race, Class and Sex, the Dynamics of Control* (Boston: G. K. Hall, 1983); Nancy Cott, *The Grounding of Modern Feminism* (New Haven, CT: Yale University Press, 1987).

34. Susan Bolotin, "Voices from the Postfeminist Generation," *The New York Times Magazine*, October 17, 1982. In a recent article on postfeminism, Deborah Rosenfelt and Judith Stacey argue against any simple conflation of postfeminism with antifeminism. They contend that "postfeminism demarcates an emerging culture and ideology that simultaneously incorporates, revises, and depoliticizes many of the fundamental issues advanced by Second Wave feminism." Rosenfelt and Stacey, "Second Thoughts on the Second Wave," *Feminist Studies*, v. 13, #2, Summer 1987, p. 341.

35. This attitude is by no means characteristic of all postfeminists. In fact, most articulate postfeminist critics of feminism take a far less sanguine view of women's situation. These writers blame the women's movement for a variety of social problems, from the "male shortage" facing college-educated women born in the mid-'50s to the persistent income gap between men and women. For an analysis of

several postfeminist texts, see Rosenfelt and Stacey, "Second Thoughts on the Second Wave."

36. I do not mean to suggest that the struggle for the ERA was a wasted effort. The campaign for equal rights did succeed in raising consciousness and did keep feminism in the public eye. However, political scientist Jane Manbridge argues that the "ERA would have had much less substantive effect than either proponents or opponents claimed." Mansbridge points out that the amendment applied only to the government and not to private businesses, and thus would have done little or nothing to diminish the gap between men's and women's wages. Moreover, by the 1970s the Supreme Court started using the Fourteenth Amendment "to declare unconstitutional almost all laws and practices Congress had intended to make unconstitutional when it passed the ERA in 1972." Mansbridge, *Why We Lost the ERA* (Chicago: University of Chicago Press, 1986), p. 2.

37. Rosenfelt and Stacey, "Second Thoughts on the Second Wave," p. 353.

38. Audre Lorde, "The Master's Tools Will Never Dismantle the Master's House," *Sister Outsider*, p. 112.

Appendixes

APPENDIX A
Discussion at Sandy Springs Conference, August 1968

(The following discussion on black women and women's liberation occurred at the August 1968 Sandy Springs Conference, and is taken directly from the transcript of that conference. Unfortunately, the transcript does not denote speakers.)

Discussion on involving black radical women's groups: (It was already agreed that the conference would only involve our groups, and the people close to us).

This was not taped from the beginning. I believe that before this discussion, someone suggested that we contact the Black Panthers that they had a women's group. It was proposed that Liz Sutherland contact Kathleen Cleever [*sic*]. Then the question was raised as to whether it would be good to invite blacks to our first meeting.

. . . they have the right to say no. Like women have the right to exclude men, but men do not have the right to exclude us. Blacks have the right to exclude whites but whites don't have the right to exclude blacks.

No one wants to exclude blacks; we've had black women in our groups; her concern is different; we began with the whole idea of how the black movement is different. They do have different problems than we do. There's a lot of difference. . . . Black women I talk to say they are not concerned with the women's thing. But do [*sic*] go out and beg them to come to our group is a different thing.

In the Black Panthers the male leaders have expressed such a fantastically chauvinistic . . .

I know that but I still think we should give women the option to.

I think that the reason we don't want to do this is that we are afraid to deal with black women.

I really think that statement is unfair and baiting.

No, I'm saying that of myself.

The reason she said you're opening a can of worms is that they are going to want to discuss different things, have different concerns. We're going to get so involved with them that we are not going to talk about female liberation.

I have problems dealing with black people; I'm sure that everyone does.

ok . . . I have problems dealing with black people; I think everyone in this room does, with men or women. I think if we are really honest about it we don't want to work with black women because we are not sure what our relationship is.

That's another problem.

That's not another problem if we are talking about building a women's liberation movement in this country. It's very much our problem and it's our problem because we are racists.

I've talked at length with some black militant friends for the last year about women's liberation and they think it's a pile of shit. They think that women's liberation means that women should be able to have babies and that whites would tell them that they shouldn't; they disagree with the women consciousness thing; they can't relate to it in any way similarly to what we've been doing. On my trip to ______ there was a black and Puerto Rican woman on the trip and there were men who were closer in their understanding about what the problems were which faced women [than] those women were and were prepared to deal with it. If we made a decision to involve those women who are already involved in groups and are close to us, then if you call Kathleen Cleever [*sic*] and she had a group and it is close then I say yes and bring her, but if she has a group . . . of black women who is giving support to the men and saying yes we should go back into the home and give support to them because they've never had that kind of support before, then I don't think they ought to be invited. I think that it's only a distinction of [whether] they [are] close to us?

That's all I'm saying. I also understand there's a black group in Brooklyn; maybe I'm all wrong. Maybe these are all groups which say they are ready to support men. But I have a feeling that there are a few black women who are thinking along the lines we are and I think we ought to make an effort to dig them out.

We have one such woman in our group; she is very militant on both the women thing and the black power thing.

It's up to us to make that effort. If they say no, my feelings won't be hurt a bit.

One of the problems is that you said, they define what women's liberation is. Now if *they* define women's liberation as having babies, I . . .

I meant how they deal with that.

Deal with that is alright. As long as we understand that they define it the way we do.

I explore and see what happens.

I don't think we should make it a big thing; to make sure that they come if they are not into what we are. The priorities of this conference are to see where all of our groups are and to share and not to deal with how we deal with other groups. But generally to talk about what we think women's liberation is. Anything that gets us fucked up into anything should not be brought to this conference.

If the thing is that black women can come to the conference if they are interested, then that's not sufficient because we've excluded them in the planning session. If you know of black women who are feminists, our problem is really getting black women on the planning session. Then why don't we put that woman who we already know is a feminist on the planning session. That takes care of the problem.

The problem with that is tokenism. It is worse to do that than not do anything.

It's true that represents an opinion; but what do we want, someone who represents a group.

I think the Panther women, whatever they thought would be antagonistic to that situation. To the situation of the one black woman from their group sitting on the board because that doesn't allow them the kind of freedom . . .

If there is a black woman's movement or momentum or dynamic or anything going, we should have those people involved in that and if we are going to have a black woman who is involved in the planning, she ought to be somebody who's involved in that, not someone from a white group. It would seem that that woman would be closer to talking about black women's liberation, and to talk with other black women in the country; I would see that as being her function: to bring other black women to the conference and to do whatever special things have to be done with black women at such a conference.

There are people in the country such as Flo Kennedy who probably would not want to be included in a thing like that but who would be good for leads.

Really upset with the direction of the discussion. Yesterday we talked about not talk[ing] about black oppression and woman oppression because we are not as oppressed as the blacks. The oppression is different. We don't really understand our racism at all, our own oppression or our relationship to ourselves, let alone blacks. If we are going to be faithful, really, to figuring out how to fight that oppression whether it is black, white, whatever, we're going to have to find out where that oppression lies for each of us and how best to fight it. Each group gets that oppression in different ways. My understanding from talking with a woman from Black Student Union [is] that their women's liberation groups are into very different things. That's good because they are defining it in terms of their own oppression. From my discussion with her it was my feeling of what she felt we had to do was to work out the ways in which our oppression was hitting us in the same ways that they were doing it. At this point there were very different kinds of concerns. I suspect that if we say if you define women's liberation in the same way we define it, that's a very white racist thing to do. That's not where we should be at. At this point we should be defining what we think about our racism and our oppression and . . . we should not pass judgement on their liberation movement at all. The priorities we should be placing at this meeting are in fact where is it that our oppression lay, to see if there is a common bond of where we should build and only after we work that out, and we know where we're at can we begin to build coalitions.

Just realized what is causing part of this confusion; we're seeing that next meeting as a planning conference for a national meeting. That's not right. That meeting is a chance for us to get together in a meeting again with all of our people. Now if that group decides that it wants to have a planning conference, then what will happen there clearly is that we will elect representatives to plan it. That's the beginning of a group that seeks to make a coalition.

Either way it matters. This question of how we work out how we are oppressed I don't think we are going to be able to work that out without the experience of black women in the room. If we are going to find out what is common in our oppression vs what's different in our oppression, we can't do that with just a white women's group. It's absolutely essential for our ideology that we have militant black power women in on the formation of our ideology. It's for our own good that we need it.

Would like to hear black women speak and hear what they have to say; that has nothing to do with coalition.

Question is do we have to do it at this meeting or . . .

I don't understand why we don't have the WSFP [*sic*], the Now [*sic*], VietNamese [*sic*], Cubans, I think that . . . what you're talking about is very important, but I don't understand how what you're talking about is important to this white group here. For the most part black women don't come to our meetings. Black militant women are into very different things. I don't understand how if you're women and your concentration is on women, why you are just picking black, militant women as opposed to all of the other kinds of women with different ideologies.

Again we have to stop thinking in terms of representation. It's a thing where all of us from different groups can get together to talk about issues. What is more important in terms of identification, race or sex. You have that question in a workshop and if you have black women who are concerned about talking about that and really interacting [*sic*] with the women go to that workshop.

If you get black women there, who have by and large worked a hell of a lot harder, and been oppressed a hell of a lot more and here we or at least I have been talking about the oppression of the middle class wealthy housewife, I think what you get are snickers and sneers. In great measure we are talking about the shitty jobs you can get . . . only $70.00/week. Well, for some of those women that's damn good. Do you think it would interrupt real interchange among white women?

Why is there such a great problem? We're talking about a national meeing of groups which exist. There are lots of groups of women that exist. If there are black groups which exist, maybe they should be represented. On the other hand NOW firmly believes they are a women's liberation group, regardless of what we think of the goals they put forth. If we're having a national meeting or conference or whatever you want to call it of groups which exist, that have been working with what they feel is women's liberation, I don't see where there is any problem. If the black women are made aware of this national meeting and they choose to attend, no one is going to exclude them. If NOW wants to come, I don't know what we would do.

Black people may not know that white women don't want them there.

There's going to be a selective process in the kinds of black women who come. And we're going to get the worst kind. Because they are into women's liberation instead of black liberation.

If they are really groovy women and they come into a white thing, they are going to have to do one of two things: they are either going to have to caucus, and they are going to take up a lot of our time because that's going to be a political event, and there is also going to be a one-upmanship kind of radicalism where they say we aren't militant enough and we start thinking about problems that are certainly not our problems. We have to understand those problems but they are not the gut kinds of things that they are going to put over on us. We're going to buy it too a lot of us. At least while we're there, we're going to buy it. Talk about consciousness, it is so low even with many of us here.

We have to face it. I heard about a conference in Boston where there was a welfare mother sit in. And their militancy started the big Boston riot. Descriptions of those meetings [showed] they talked as much about their problems with men as their problems with welfare.

But I'm saying that when you get Black and white together, all kinds of other sparks fly. We don't really need that right now. It will reemphasize all kinds of hang-ups. Don't you believe they would caucus. Wouldn't you?

I think they would caucus. But I think they need that perspective as well.

Having experience with a black welfare group that had white women in it, I know that the black militant women rule the day. They set the tone and they managed to completely cow the white women in welfare organizations. I've seen it time and time again. I understand the problem. But they hold the cards on oppression, they hold the cards on being shot down in every single way and they let white women know that. I don't want to go to a conference to hear a black militant women tell me she is more oppressed and what am I going to do about it.

That's true but she is not only going to talk about her oppression on the race thing, but she is also going to come on with her oppression on the woman thing in a way which will shock us.

If we ever schedule a national conference, do we invite black women?

Of course, and NOW and WISP [*sic*] and all the rest of them.

Caucus or no caucus, right.

But what I think that . . . everybody should be aware of is that maybe non-white women, middle class or poor may not be involved at all in what we are involved in so that this group would expand and expand and expand and may be essentially all white. Now that's a really real possibility.

That's what we are saying. If that happens, our ideology will be wrong.

I agree with that but something different is being said. In our group there is a Mexican woman. She was part of a community organization in a Mexican community. Some of those women have had discussions on women's liberation. But they don't meet the way we do. When there is a problem, they handle it. For example, there was one man who was particularly brutal to his wife. The whole community organization discussed it and decided it was a community problem and they kicked him out until he could shape up. This woman is in our group as well and we learn from her what these experiences are. That is where this should happen on the local level. Those of us who have relationships with black women we can talk to should begin to build . . . discussions of what are the similarities and the differences? We've been talking for two days and I still don't understand your position completely and I would like to talk with you for two more days. If I have to talk with black women about their oppression at the same time that I [am] trying to understand what your group is talking about, how are we ever going to build an understanding of where we (meaning whites) are.

I think the presence of black women in a meeting will strengthen my position.

If your group feels that way it ought to work from now to November to recruit black women to bring them there, and the other groups work the way they have. I agree that I still don't understand your position and want to understand it. That if your group came half black, half white and they shared your position I'd be glad to hear it.

They won't share our position.

They'd be Toms.

We all agree that the women in Algeria, Viet Nam and Cuba, the consciousness of them affects the consciousness we have. But I would be more comfortable discussing this with men whom I know than with black women at this point. It's entirely a question of tactics.

We should talk specifically about how our presence can become known to women's groups in the black movement or black women's groups. Maybe we can clarify it, we can talk about who we talk to.

That when we have a planning group, after each group has made a decision on its position on its oppression and after each group has a position solidified, we have a meeting with women who represent what in fact the black women's liberation movement is. Ask Liz [Sutherland] and Kathleen [Cleaver] if they would be interested in having that meeting sometime in the future and at that time we work out those issues on which we have common oppression.

So you see what you are doing? You are going to pick out who the women liberationists are in the black movement. I am telling you that there are women liberationists in my state who wouldn't think of coming here . . . it's not fair to say they are Toms, but by your talking to those women . . .

You misunderstood me. . . . The question of bringing black women to the conference now, muddies up the issue. That what we have to do is have our own meeting and if we are really concerned with black women's liberation and how it relates to us, we have to wait to some future time to set that meeting up. But right now we have to concentrate on our own oppression. What we have to do is begin to make inquiries with [*sic*] women who we know and also have them talk to people they know to find out what black women are doing. Then hold a conference specifically to deal with that issue.

They won't come. There are some kinds of female consciousness groups which don't speak to whites on policy. They negotiate with whites on [*sic*] very strategic situations. It is very indirect. They would be killed if they came to this conference.

Their [*sic*] in a funny position. They'd be accused of disloyalty, but they may not be disloyal, you see. They'd be accused by their men of disloyalty, but in fact they might not be.

I can't impose that on them. I can't understand why you want to self select who comes. You'll only get toms. You won't get some of the best.

Why do you assume they'll be toms?

(Note: the rest of discussion was not transcribed)

APPENDIX B
Brief Biographies of Women's Liberation Activists

(Note that these biographies do not cover the activities of individuals after 1975.)

Allen, Pam (now known as Chude)—SNCC; co-founder of New York Radical Women; the San Francisco women's liberation group, Sudsofloppen. Allen authored the pamphlet *Free Space*, a guideline to small group consciousness-raising.

Alpert, Jane—involved in several bombings of military and war-related corporate buildings in New York City in late 1969. Alpert went underground from 1970 to 1974 and in 1973 wrote the cultural feminist classic "Mother Right," which was published in *Ms.* magazine. Her surrender and reported cooperation with federal authorities convulsed the movement in 1975. While in prison for the bombings she wrote her autobiography, *Growing Up Underground*.

Atkinson, Ti-Grace—founding member of the New York chapter of NOW; founder of The October 17th Movement, later renamed The Feminists. Atkinson left The Feminists in 1970 after the group passed a resolution barring individual members from talking to the press. *Amazon Odyssey*, her collected essays, was published in 1974.

Barry, Kathleen—leading proponent of cultural feminism; listed as "in agreement with" the 1971 article "The Fourth World Manifesto"; supporter of FEN.

Baxandall, Ros—Mobilization for Youth (welfare rights); SDS; antiwar movement; New York Radical Women; Redstockings. Baxandall was instrumental in establishing city-financed child-care facilities in New York City.

Berson, Ginny—anti-war movement; writer for the leftist newspaper *Hard Times*; The Furies and Olivia Records.

Bikman, Minda—Redstockings; Stanton-Anthony Brigade of New York Radical Feminists.

Biren, Joan E. (aka JEB)—anti-war; founding member of Amazing Grace and The Furies.

Booth, Heather—SDS; civil-rights movement; the Westside group; co-founder of the socialist-feminist organization The Chicago Women's Liberation Union; founder of the Midwest Academy, a training institute for community and "citizens action" organizers.

Borman, Nancy—new left; NOW; Women's Strike for Equality; editor of New York feminist newspaper *Majority Report*.

Brown, Judith—CORE; SDS; co-author of the "Florida Paper"; co-founder of the first women's liberation group in the South, Gainesville Women's Liberation.

Brown, Rita Mae—NY-NOW; The Furies; important architect of lesbian-feminism in the '70s. She has written a number of novels, including the classic *Rubyfruit Jungle*. Her political essays are available in *A Plain Brown Rapper*.

Brownmiller, Susan—Reform Democratic politics in New York City in the early '60s; civil-rights movement. Brownmiller was a leading member of New York Radical Feminists. She is the author of the groundbreaking study of rape, *Against Our Will* (1975), and numerous articles on feminism.

Bunch, Charlotte—University Christian Movement; civil rights; DC women's liberation; The Furies. Later she edited the feminist journal *Quest*. Bunch is the author of many articles on feminism and was a major force in the articulation of lesbian-feminism.

Burris, Barbara—author of "the Fourth World Manifesto"; member of women's liberation in Detroit.

Chapman, Frances—civil rights; DC women's liberation and writer for *off our backs* from 1970 until late 1975.

Cisler, Lucinda (Cindy)—New York Radical Women; NOW; national chairperson of NOW's Task Force on Abortion; founder of New Yorkers for Abortion Law Repeal; secretary of NARAL; author of *Women: a Bibliography* and the prescient "Abortion Law Repeal (sort of): a Warning to Women" (1970).

Coleman, Corinne—New York Radical Women; Redstockings; editor of short-lived women's liberation magazine *Feelings*.

Cronan, Sheila—Redstockings; The Feminists; author of the 1970 article "Marriage."

Daly, Mary—author of *The Church and the Second Sex* (1968), *Beyond God the Father* (1973) and professor of theology at Boston College.

Deevey, Sharon—new left; DC women's liberation; The Furies.

Densmore, Dana—Cell 16; author of numerous articles on sexuality, karate, and women's liberation.

Dixon, Marlene—Chicago women's liberation. Dixon's firing from the sociology faculty at the University of Chicago prompted a sit-in by women's liberationists. She is the author of numerous articles on women.

Dobbins, Peggy—Southern Student Organizing Committee; SDS; New York Radical Women and WITCH.

DuBois, Ellen—SDS; Chicago Women's Liberation Union.

Duffett, Judith—New York Radical Women; WITCH; author of "The Secretarial Proletariat."

Dunbar, Roxanne—new left; founder of Cell 16; organizer of the Southern Female Rights Union in New Orleans.

Ehrenreich, Barbara—new left; major socialist-feminist thinker and writer.

English, Deirdre—Like her frequent collaborator, Barbara Ehrenreich, English has been involved in the new left and the socialist-feminist wing of the women's movement.

Epstein, Barbara (formerly Easton)—Communist Party; SDS; Bay Area women's liberation.

Feldman, Linda—Redstockings; The Feminists.

Firestone, Shulamith—co-founder of New York Radical Women, Redstockings and New York Radical Feminists; important radical feminist thinker; author of *The Dialectic of Sex*.

Florika—new left; New York Radical Women; WITCH.

Forer, Anne—new left; member of New York Radical Women who participated in Redstockings' abortion speak-out.

Freeman, Jo (aka Joreen)—Southern Christian Leadership Conference; Chicago's Westside group. Freeman is the author of "The Tyranny of Structurelessness," "The Bitch Manifesto," "Trashing," and the 1975 book *The Politics of Women's Liberation*.

Gardner, Jennifer—New York Radical Women; Bay Area women's liberation. She also worked on the Bay Area women's liberation newspaper *The Women's Page*.

Garman, Betty—SDS; SNCC; IPS fellow; DC women's liberation.

Giardina, Carol—civil rights movement; co-founder of Gainesville women's liberation; advocate of consciousness-raising and pro-woman line.

Goldfield, Evelyn—SDS; Chicago's Westside group.

Gordon, Linda—new left; Bread and Roses; important socialist-feminist activist and theoretician.

Hanisch, Carol—civil-rights worker in Mississippi 1964–65; Southern Conference Educational Fund; New York Radical Women; Gainesville women's liberation; reconstituted Redstockings. Hanisch is the author of several important early radical feminist articles, including "The Personal is Political" and "Hard Knocks."

Harris, Helaine—fundraiser for the Venceremos brigade; co-founder of the Southwest Female Rights Union; The Furies; early member of Olivia Records collective; co-founder of Women in Distribution, a distributor for small women's presses.

Hathaway, Susan—defense committee for Chicago 7; The Furies.

Jay, Karla—Redstockings; Media Women; writer for *Rat*.

Johnston, Jill—*Village Voice* columnist and author of *Lesbian Nation*.

Jones, Beverly—Gainesville SDS and CORE; co-author of the "Florida Paper."

Kearon, Pam—New York Radical Women; Redstockings; The Feminists; the Class Workshop; The Circle of Support for Jane Alpert. Kearon wrote several articles, including, "Man-Hating," and co-authored "Prostitution" and "Rape: An Act of Terror," with Barbara Mehrhof.

Kennedy, Florynce—New York NOW; civil rights lawyer; Kennedy co-wrote the 1971 book *Abortion Rap*, with Diane Shulder. Kennedy was one of the few black women involved in the early women's liberation movement.

Kesselman, Amy—civil rights; president of the City College Independent Committee to End the War in Vietnam; Citizens for Independent Political Action; Westside group; Chicago Women's Liberation Union.

Koedt, Anne—SDS; New York Radical Women, The Feminists and co-founder of New York Radical Feminists. Koedt was the author of several important articles, including "The Myth of the Vaginal Orgasm," and "Lesbianism and Feminism." She also co-edited *Notes 2* and *Notes 3*.

Kritzler, Helen—anti-war movement; New York Radical Women.

Leghorn, Lisa—Cell 16; frequent contributor to *No More Fun and Games*; exponent of wages for housework.

Mainardi, Patricia—New York Radical Women; Redstockings; author of widely reprinted "The Politics of Housework"; editor of the journal, "Woman and Art."

Manick, Bev (formerly Fisher)—DC women's liberation; editor of the feminist journal *Quest*.

Mehrhof, Barbara—New York Radical Women; Redstockings; The Feminists; the Class Workshop; The Circle of Support for Jane Alpert; co-author with Pam Kearon of "Prostitution" and "Rape: An Act of Terror."

Millett, Kate—New York NOW; New York Radical Women; author of the best-selling book *Sexual Politics*. Millett also wrote *Flying* and *The Prostitution Papers*.

Morgan, Robin—anti-war movement; Yippies; New York Radical Women; WITCH; editor of the popular 1970 anthology *Sisterhood is Powerful*; contributing editor of *Ms.* Her collected essays, including her influential "Goodbye to All That," were published as *Going Too Far* in 1978.

Peslikis, Irene—New York Radical Women; Redstockings; very briefly, The Feminists; author of "Resistances to Consciousness-Raising"; major proponent of c-r and the pro-woman line; editor of the journal "Woman and Art."

Piercy, Marge—SDS; staff member of *Leviathan*; poet, novelist, and author of the widely read 1969 article "The Grand Coolie Damn."

Rainone, Nanette—The Feminists, New York Radical Feminists; director of WBAI's program "Womankind."

Reid, Coletta—anti-war movement; DC women's liberation; The Furies; Diana Press; FEN.

Rich, Adrienne—anti-war movement; poet and important cultural feminist thinker in the '70s.

Rockefeller, Abby—Cell 16.

Rothstein, Vivian—SNCC; Council of Federated Organizations; Free Speech Movement; JOIN; Westside group; Chicago Women's Liberation Union.

Sarachild (aka Amatniek), Kathie—the Harvard peace group TOCSIN; Harvard *Crimson* editor; organizer for Summer Voter Registration Project in Mississippi from 1964 to 1965; New York Radical Women, Redstockings, and the reconstituted Redstockings. Sarachild was the major architect of consciousness-raising and one of the most vocal proponents of the pro-woman line. She co-founded the New York feminist newspaper *Woman's World.*

Shelley, Martha—Gay Liberation Front; Radicalesbians; author of articles on feminism and lesbianism and "What is FEN?"

Shulman, Alix Kates—New York Radical Women, Redstockings, New York Radical Feminists; writer whose novel *Burning Questions* is about the women's liberation movement.

Snitow, Ann—anti-war; Stanton-Anthony Brigade of New York Radical Feminists; contributer to WBAI's "Womankind" program.

Solanas, Valerie—author of the 1967 *SCUM Manifesto*; shot Pop artist Andy Warhol in June 1968.

Tax, Meredith—anti-war movement; Bread and Roses; October League.

Tepperman, Jean—ERAP; Bread and Roses; poet and writer.

Thibeau (formerly Gabree), Judy—New York Radical Women, Class Workshop.

Ware, Cellestine—Stanton-Anthony Brigade of New York Radical Feminists. Ware was among the very few black women who were active in women's liberation; author of *Woman Power* (1970).

Warrior, Betsy—Cell 16; frequent writer for *No More Fun and Games*; advocate of wages for housework.

Webb, Marilyn—SDS; Vietnam Summer; DC women's liberation; instructor at Sagaris.

Weisstein, Naomi—SDS, CORE, Westside group; Chicago Women's Liberation Union; author of " 'Kinde, Kuche, Kirche' As Scientific Law: Psychology Constructs the Female."

Willis, Ellen—New York Radical Women, co-founder of Redstockings; rock critic and writer for *The New Yorker, Rolling Stone, Ms.*, and the *Village Voice*. Her important early articles include "Women and The Left" and " 'Consumerism' and Women."

Woodul, Jennifer—The Furies; Olivia Records.

APPENDIX C
A Guide to Women's Liberation Groups

Bread and Roses—(Boston) was founded by Meredith Tax and Linda Gordon in the summer of 1969. The group was politico in orientation and included Jean Tepperman, Fran Ansley, Judy Ullman, and Trude Bennett. Their largest meetings drew approximately 200 women. The organization lasted at least until 1973.

Cell 16—(Boston) was formed by Roxanne Dunbar in the summer of 1968. Cell 16 was a small cadre-like group and among the first radical feminist groups in the country. Its members included Dana Densmore, Abby Rockefeller, Lisa Leghorn, and Betsy Warrior. The group was targeted for take-over by the Socialist Workers Party in 1970. It disbanded in 1973.

Chicago Women's Liberation Union—socialist-feminist organization which was founded in 1969 by a number of women, including Heather Booth, Amy Kesselman, and Vivian Rothstein. At its largest the group had 500 dues-paying members. It dissolved around 1977.

The Class Workshop—(New York) was formed by Barbara Mehrhof and Pam Kearon in the winter of 1970. The group grew out of The Feminists and was composed of women from both The Feminists and Redstockings. It dissolved within a year of its formation.

DC Women's Liberation—politico group formed in the winter of 1968. Marilyn Webb, Charlotte Bunch, Alice Wolfson, Norma Lesser, Judy Coburn, and Barbara Haber were among the first members. This loosely organized group functioned at least until 1971.

Feminist Economic Network (FEN)—an explicitly capitalist venture that was started in November 1975 by women from Oakland Feminist Women's Health Center, the Detroit Feminist Federal Credit Union, and Diana Press. During its 10-month existence it was based in Detroit.

The Feminists—(New York) originally known as the October 17th Movement, it was a splinter group from NOW which Ti-Grace Atkinson formed in October 1968. One of the earliest radical feminist groups, its members included Barbara Mehrhof, Pam Kearon, Sheila Cronan, and Linda Feldman. Anne Koedt, Lila Karp, Nanette Rainone, and Anne Calderman were also members; however, they dropped out after the group passed a series of restrictive rules. The group dissolved in 1973.

The Furies—(Washington, D.C.) lesbian feminist collective formed in May 1971. The group consisted of: Rita Mae Brown, Charlotte Bunch, Coletta Reid, Helaine Harris, Ginny Berson, Joan Biren, Sharon Deevey, Tasha Peterson, Susan Hathaway, Nancy Myron, Jennifer Woodul, and Lee Schwing. It disbanded in April 1972.

New York Radical Feminists—was founded by Shulamith Firestone and Anne Koedt in the fall of 1969. Other members of the founding Stanton-Anthony Brigade were: Diane Crothers, Minda Bikman, Ann Snitow, Cellestine Ware, and Marsha Gershin. The group's structure was voted down in the summer of 1970 and, as a result, the Stanton-Anthony Brigade folded. The organization continued to function until 1972.

New York Radical Women—was the first women's liberation group in New York City. It was formed by Shulamith Firestone and Pam Allen in the fall of 1967. Kathie Sarachild, Carol Hanisch, Irene Peslikis, Ros Baxandall, Ellen Willis, Robin Morgan, and Patricia Mainardi were among its members. It dissolved in the winter of 1969.

Redstockings—(New York) was founded by Shulamith Firestone and Ellen Willis in February 1969. The group became closely associated with consciousness-raising and the pro-woman line. Kathie Sarachild, Irene Peslikis, Ellen Willis, Patricia Mainardi, Barbara Mehrhof, and Pam Kearon belonged to the group. It functioned until the fall of 1970.

Westside group—(Chicago) the earliest women's liberation group in the country. It was formed in the fall of 1967 and included Heather Booth, Amy Kesselman, Vivian Rothstein, Naomi Weisstein, Jo Freeman, Evelyn Goldfield, and Sue Munaker.

WITCH—(New York) was an early politico group founded by Robin Morgan, Florika, Peggy Dobbins, Judy Duffett, Cynthia Funk, and Naomi Jaffe on Halloween in 1968. The group specialized in zap actions until the winter of 1969 when it shifted its focus to consciousness-raising.

APPENDIX D
A Note on the Oral Interviews

When I began the dissertation out of which this book emerged, I intended to interview fifteen to twenty women's liberation activists. The first women I contacted were those whose names I had encountered in the literature—Ros Baxandall, Susan Brownmiller, Shulamith Firestone, Kathie Sarachild, Ann Snitow, and Ellen Willis. Those who responded often suggested names of others who were active at the time but were less well known. When I began interviewing I started to accumulate even more names. Indeed, in the end, I interviewed forty-two people. I could have interviewed many more, but I decided to concentrate on interviewing women who were active in the period before 1972 when the movement's written record was far from complete. Limited funding prevented me from doing much interviewing outside three cities—New York, Washington, D.C., and Chicago.

When possible, I contacted people by letter six to eight weeks before I planned to conduct the interview. In the letter I briefly explained my dissertation topic and the interview process. I made it clear that the interview would be taped, but I also emphasized that I would refrain from using any quote unless I had the person's permission to do so. I established the same ground rules over the phone with those people who were recommended to me after I had begun interviewing.

Of the women I contacted the vast majority not only agreed to be interviewed, but were interested in talking about their experiences in the movement. There were important exceptions, however. I wrote to Shulamith Firestone several times, but received no response. Anne Koedt declined to be interviewed when I contacted her. Kathie Sarachild also declined to be interviewed, but on the grounds that the written record of the movement was sufficient. However, we did meet and had a long conversation about the movement. And she did read and comment on the manuscript. In other cases, there were logistical problems. Florynce Kennedy answered my letter long after I had stopped interviewing. Kate Millett and I tried to coordinate an interview, but were unable to do so. The publication of *Sisterhood is Global* prevented Robin Morgan from doing an interview. Finally, Naomi Weisstein was too ill to be interviewed so, at her suggestion, I interviewed her husband, Jesse Lemisch, in her stead.

With the exception of Heather Booth, who was interviewed in Chicago, all the interviewing was done on the East Coast in the spring and summer of 1984. In the case of Jean Tepperman of Boston, the interview was done by letter. When the interviewee requested the questions in advance, I mailed them out a few days before the interview. In several cases I sent follow-up questions to people I had interviewed. The interviews lasted anywhere from one to six hours, with the average interview running about two to three hours. Every interview was taped. I generally interviewed people individually; however, I conducted two group interviews in New York. The first group interview was arranged by Anne Forer and included Anne, Ros Baxandall, Cindy Cisler, Corinne Coleman, Helen Kritzler, Irene Peslikis, Alix Kates Shulman, and Ellen Willis. The second group interview included Cisler, Coleman, Forer, Kritzler, and Peslikis. Although the group interviews were spirited, and perhaps too unstructured, wonderful material emerged from them. Moreover, the energy and contentiousness of these sessions gave me an idea of what those early New York Radical Women meetings must have been like. With the exception of Forer and Kritzler, I interviewed each of the participants individually as well. (When the quotation is from a group interview, I have designated this in the notes.) I also conducted two joint interviews—one with Barbara Mehrhof and Pam Kearon in New York, the other with Alexi Freeman and Bev Manick in Washington, D.C.

Most of the women I interviewed were quite forthcoming, perhaps in part because my initial letter had assured them that I would be clearing any direct quotations with them. The only question I asked every woman was whether she had been politically active before joining the women's liberation movement and, if so, in what groups. Beyond that, the questions were not uniform, but depended upon the nature of each woman's involvement in the movement. For each interviewee I devised a list of questions based largely upon which group or groups she had participated in. Women who were part of the same group were asked essentially the same set of questions about that group.

Lucia Valeska was kind enough to let me copy the transcripts of her 1978 interviews with former Furies members, many of whom were living in California. I have quoted from these interviews, especially in chapter 6. In the case of Charlotte Bunch who was interviewed by both Valeska and myself I have identified in the notes when Valeska was the interviewer by placing (LV) next to Bunch's name.

After I had written the next-to-last draft of the dissertation I sent each woman whose interview I quoted from (including those interviewed by Valeska) a list of the quotes I wanted to use. With the exception of one person, everyone gave me permission to use these quotes, some with absolutely no changes, and many with minor changes, usually for the sake of clarification. In only a few instances did people ask that I refrain from using a particular quote. And, I obliged.

Below the reader will find a list of the people I interviewed, and the date and place of the interview. Not everyone that I interviewed is quoted in the book. This is particularly true of women who entered the movement in the post-'72 period, or whose involvement occurred in places other than Chicago, New York, D.C., or Boston.

Allison, Dorothy. Brooklyn, New York. May 6, 1984.
Alpert, Jane. New York, New York. May 29, 1984.
Atkinson, Ti-Grace. New York, New York. June 6, 1984.
Baxandall, Ros. New York, New York. June 23, 1984.
Bikman, Minda. New York, New York. May 2, 1984.
Booth, Heather. Chicago, Illinois. March 17, 1984.
Borman, Nancy. New York, New York. May 4, 1984.
Brownmiller, Susan. New York, New York. April 30, 1984.
Bunch, Charlotte. Brooklyn, New York. June 3, 1984.
Chapman, Frances. New York, New York. May 30, 1984.
Cisler, Cindy. New York, New York. August 15, 1984.
Coleman, Corinne. New York, New York. August 16, 1984.
Cowan, Belita. Washington, D.C. May 21, 1984.
Cronan, Sheila. Rosslyn, Virginia. August 20, 1984.
Ellis, Kate. New York, New York. May 7 and 10, 1984.

Freeman, Alexi. Washington, D.C. May 20, 1984.
Freeman, Jo. Washington, D.C. May 18, 1984.
Gair, Cynthia. Washington, D.C. May 19, 1984.
Hanisch, Carol. New Paltz, New York. June 2, 1984.
Harris, Helaine. Washington, D.C. August 22, 1984.
Jay, Karla. New York, New York. May 31, 1984.
Kearon, Pam. New York, New York. May 13, 1984.
Kesselman, Amy. New York, New York. May 2, 1984.
Klass, Tobey. New York, New York. August 16, 1984.
Lemisch, Jesse. New York, New York. May 29, 1984.
Mainardi, Patricia. New York, New York. May 9, 1984.
Manich, Bev. Washington, D.C. May 20, 1984.
Mehrhof, Barbara, New York, New York. May 13, 1984.
Morley, Evan. New York, New York. August 16, 1984.
Peslikis, Irene. New York, New York. May 27, 1984.
Rainone, Nanette. Brooklyn, New York. August 17, 1984.
Rapp, Rayna. New York, New York. May 30, 1984.
Rush, Florence. New York, New York. June 6, 1984.
Sherman, Susan. New York, New York. June 6, 1984.
Shulman, Alix Kates. New York, New York. May 26, 1984.
Snitow, Ann. New York, New York. June 14, 1984.
Tax, Meredith. New York, New York. June 4, 1984.
Tepperman, Jean. By mail. Summer 1984.
Webb, Marilyn. New York, New York. June 5, 1984.
Willis, Ellen. New York, New York. May 1, 1984.

The first group interview occurred May 14, 1984 in New York City and included:

Ros Baxandall
Cindy Cisler
Corinne Coleman
Anne Forer
Helen Kritzler
Irene Peslikis
Alix Kates Shulman
Ellen Willis

The second group interview occurred May 24, 1984 in New York City and included:

Cindy Cisler
Corinne Coleman
Anne Forer

Helen Kritzler
Irene Peslikis

Lucia Valeska's interviews were as follows:

Berson, Ginny. West Coast, 1978.
Biren, Joan. Washington, D.C. December, 1978.
Bunch, Charlotte. Brooklyn, New York. September 14, 1978.
Myron, Nancy. Brooklyn, New York. September 14, 1978.
Reid, Coletta. West Coast, 1978.
Woodul, Jennifer. West Coast, 1978.

Index

Index

Index

Index

Index

Index

Alice Echols is a visiting assistant professor at the University of Arizona at Tucson. She received her M.A. and Ph.D. from the University of Michigan in U.S. history, specializing in women's history and social history. Echols has received several awards and grants, including the University of Michigan's Horace H. Rackham Distinguished Dissertation Award in 1987. Her articles have appeared in the books *Pleasure and Danger: Exploring Female Sexuality* (edited by Carole Vance, 1984), and *Powers of Desire: The Politics of Sexuality* (edited by Ann Snitow, Christine Stansell, and Sharon Thompson, 1983), and in *The Women's Review of Books* and *Social Text*.